Preservation of Paper and Textiles of Historic and Artistic Value

Preservation of Paper and Textiles of Historic and Artistic Value

John C. Williams, EDITOR

Library of Congress

A symposium sponsored by the

Cellulose, Paper and Textile

Division at the 172nd

Meeting of the American Chemical

Society, San Francisco, Calif.,

Aug. 30–31, 1976.

ADVANCES IN CHEMISTRY SERIES **164**

AMERICAN CHEMICAL SOCIETY

WASHINGTON, D. C.   1977

Library of Congress CIP Data

Preservation of paper and textiles of historic and artistic value.
(Advances in chemistry series; 164 ISSN 0065-2393)

Includes bibliographical references and index.

1. Books—Conservation and restoration—Congresses.
2. Paper—Preservation—Congresses. 3. Textile fabrics—Preservation—Congresses.
I. Williams, John Covington, 1911–   . II. American Chemical Society. Cellulose, Paper, and Textile Division.
III. Series: Advances in chemistry series; 164.

QD1.A355 no. 164   [Z701]   025.8'4   77-13137
ISBN 0-8412-0360-1   ADCSAJ 164 1-403 (1977)

Advances in Chemistry Series

Robert F. Gould, *Editor*

FOREWORD

ADVANCES IN CHEMISTRY SERIES was founded in 1949 by the American Chemical Society as an outlet for symposia and collections of data in special areas of topical interest that could not be accommodated in the Society's journals. It provides a medium for symposia that would otherwise be fragmented, their papers distributed among several journals or not published at all. Papers are refereed critically according to ACS editorial standards and receive the careful attention and processing characteristic of ACS publications. Papers published in ADVANCES IN CHEMISTRY SERIES are original contributions not published elsewhere in whole or major part and include reports of research as well as reviews since symposia may embrace both types of presentation.

CONTENTS

ESTIMATION OF PERMANENCE

PREFACE

The manufacture of paper and textiles has undergone extensive development in the past 200 years. Production rates have risen astronomically. Unfortunately, the permanence of the goods has not improved or even stayed the same. Rather it has gone down.

Paper in particular is a problem today; much of it is still being made on the acid side from the use of alum rosin sizes, and this limits its life. There are 150 years of similar bad paper on the shelves. Librarians are the custodians of millions of books which are too brittle to use. Often there is nothing to be done but to cut the books apart, microfilm the information, and discard them. Textiles too have been subjected to the exigencies of rapid machine production and mishandled so that their permanence has dropped. The artifacts of our present civilization are fragile, and much of our cultural heritage is slipping silently away.

The restorers, who are at work on the monumental tasks of preserving the remnants, need the advice of restoration scientists. How does one select the treatments which will make books and textiles last longer? A great many of the answers come from the extensive studies of cellulose fibers made over the past 100 years. Other information has been gained from accelerated-aging procedures. Materials and methods can be evaluated by subjecting an expendable article to high temperatures and monitoring the increased rate of degradation. If the logarithms of the rate of change of a selected property plotted against the reciprocal of the absolute temperatures give a straight line, the line may be extrapolated to find the rate of change at room temperature, and the permanence of the material may be calculated. This is the Arrhenius relation.

The determination of a complete Arrhenius relation is a long procedure. Even for quite unstable materials, degradation rates are low as room temperatures are approached, yet room temperature must be approached to minimize the errors of extrapolation. Once the slope of the line is established for a given material, the regression data from one oven-aging experiment can be translated to life at room temperature for other samples. Unfortunately, much of the Arrhenius data at hand for paper does not separate hydrolytic from oxidative degradation. The method will make more reliable predictions when such a separation is made.

For both paper and textiles made from cellulose fiber, permanence can be improved by bringing the pH to 7 or slightly higher. An alkaline earth carbonate such as calcium carbonate or magnesium carbonate is deposited to protect the material against acid atmospheres or the acid generated in situ from oxidation. Strong bleaches or treatments that leave oxidizing residues are to be avoided. In this field there is a major place for the expertise and judgment of the conservator in the repair and display of books, documents, and textiles.

The papers contributed to the symposium and this book are divided into sections on paper and on textiles. There are discussions on how to care for each; treatments which slow degradation are described; and finally, there are a number of papers concerned with the prediction of permanence.

The symposium was suggested by Tyrone Vigo, who also is a contributor. It received the backing of Robert Read, Program Chairman of the Cellulose, Paper, and Textile Division of the American Chemical Society, as well as of Robert Gould, editor of the *Advances in Chemistry Series*.

I have been encouraged and advised by Frazer Poole, Assistant Director for Preservation at the Library of Congress, and Peter Waters, Restoration Officer. I also have been greatly helped by the staff of the Preservation Office. To all these, my grateful thanks.

Washington, D.C.   JOHN C. WILLIAMS
November 1976

Care and Preservation
of Books and
Manuscripts

Book Preservation for the Librarian

BERNARD C. MIDDLETON

3 Gauden Road, Clapham, London SW4 6LR England

Vast numbers of books need to be restored, and they increase yearly, but there is no prospect that more than a small percentage can be treated professionally and competently. Limited funds and labor need to be incorporated effectively by using sound, economical binding structures and restoration techniques, by utilizing only chemically and mechanically good materials, and by making containers for fragile items. The provision of near-ideal environmental conditions will significantly slow down future deterioration and effect immense savings. Old books should perhaps be furbished and be given very minor restorative treatment by responsible amateur-binder volunteers under supervision and by library technicians with limited duties. Both categories would also serve a vital conservation function in making protective boxes and folders.

The thought has occurred to most people at some time or other that certain industrial executives have heavy responsibility in the form of a complex and immensely expensive plant and that a wrong decision can be disastrous. Few, I suspect, give thought to the immensity of the burden carried by hundreds of librarians. The librarian of even a relatively obscure institution may well be responsible for a collection which in monetary terms is worth 10–20 million dollars and in cultural terms is of incalculable value. During a term of office of, say, 15 years, the librarian of a learned society containing 100,000 antiquarian books could cause the ruination of hundreds of fine volumes and, in the long term, place the rest in jeopardy.

The case must not be overstated, but the responsibility *is* considerable and the associated difficulties *are* immense. Unfortunately, few librarians have anything but the haziest notions of what is involved in a sound conservation program, a shortcoming they share, one fears, with many trade binders and restorers. Antiquarian booksellers, too, have a heavy responsibility because many of them during a lifetime of dealing handle as many books as stock a substantial library, but that is another story and, in the main, a sad one.

In Britain, most libraries have no conservation program and no early prospect of one. For example, in London the libraries of the oldest learned societies have no air conditioning, expenditure is restricted to binding periodicals, and the restoration of old books is not contemplated, except on special occasions, because of the cost and the difficulty of finding skilled restorers to whom the work can be entrusted. One of the oldest learned societies in London, with one of the largest and finest libraries of its kind in the world, spends less than £1000 per annum on its maintenance. Every year of neglect involves increased costs in real terms, and each year creates extra demands for higher degrees of skill because of the poorer condition of the books. Such skill is not available and is not likely to be in the foreseeable future.

If the outlook in Britain is gloomy, it is no less so in the United States because although funds are more abundant, the number of books requiring attention is equally astronomical, and the extremes of climate to which most of the volumes have been subject over a fairly long period has rendered them in far worse condition than is usual in Britain.

In some ways it may be fortunate that the establishment of conservation departments and centers has been slow because much irreversible damage would otherwise have been done and much money would have been wasted through the use of chemically unsound materials and faulty structural techniques. Also, public sympathy would have been alienated. Clearly, much remains to be learned, but perhaps enough progress has been made to enable us to embark on conservation programs with a reasonable degree of confidence in the efficacy of our techniques until better ones have been developed. What a tragedy it is, though, that when first-rate craftsmen were abundant, materials were poor, and only a few thought intelligently about structure; science has now advanced excitingly, but craftsmanship has in general suffered a serious decline.

If the hard-pressed librarian is faced with the choice of establishing a conservation department or installing air conditioning with a humidity control and acid filtration, it is arguable that the latter should take precedence, though one would hope also for at least a small conservation unit which could be gradually built up. Dare one piously hope that both air conditioning and a conservation department would take precedence over nonessential acquisition of books, however prestigious?

The purpose of this paper is not to castigate library personnel, who have a difficult job and tend to be overworked, but to offer a few helpful hints which can extend the life of books and bindings and save money in the long term. The following are generally accepted to be desirable environmental conditions for the storage of books and related material.

Air Conditioning

This is of paramount importance, and in conservation terms there can be no better investment. An air-conditioning unit should be installed which will provide book-stack temperatures of 60°–65°F with a relative humidity of 45–60%. Below this range, embrittlement of materials will occur, and covers may warp; above it, the growth of mold is encouraged. Deterioration of book materials is minimized when the temperature and the relative humidity are constant. The system should water-wash air free of sulfur dioxide, which is the most effective purifying method available, and it should eliminate ozone (*1*).

Lighting

Ultraviolet light causes serious chemical deterioration of organic materials and should therefore be eliminated or at least reduced. The simplest procedure is to curtain windows, but if this creates difficulties, plastic sheeting can be used. If walls and ceilings are painted white, nearly all the damaging radiation is removed from the reflected light. Ultraviolet ray-absorbent plastic sleeves should be fitted to fluorescent tubes. The sleeves are inexpensive, they filter out nearly all uv rays, and only slightly reduce lighting efficiency (*2*).

Pest Control

Insects of many kinds can do much damage in little-used sections of libraries, so the need for good housekeeping and frequent inspection is clear. Insects feed on dirt, and mold breaks down book materials thus providing more food as encouragement for their proliferation. It is possible to arrange monthly pest-control spray contracts relatively inexpensively, a valuable service in bad areas.

Affected books should be treated immediately, and of course newly acquired books which exhibit signs of infestation should be treated before being placed on the shelves or anywhere near other books. The number of volumes to be treated at one time is not likely to be great so a small fumigation chamber will suffice, and almost anything will do (even a large plastic bag) if it is air-tight. The books are put in together with a tray of *p*-dichlorobenzene crystals at a rate of 1 kg/m^3 of air space at a minimum temperature of 68°F. Insects die quickly, but exposure to the vapor should last at least three weeks to cover the incubation period of the eggs. A watch should be kept on the books for some months to ensure that the eggs have not matured into larvae after fumigation. The fumes irritate the eyes, so if a large chamber which lacks an extractor fan is opened, the windows of the room should be open and a fan set going to clear the atmosphere quickly.

Mold Control

If incoming books are found to be infected, they should be brushed clean in the open air. As soon as possible they should be sterilized, and this is vital if the temperature and the relative humidity in the library are usually high—i.e., in excess of 65°F and 60%, respectively.

Sterilization is easily accomplished by placing the books in an airtight container and supporting them in such a way that the leaves are fanned out—this is important because penetration between the leaves is essential. A tray of thymol crystals (50 g/m^3) is placed close to a 40-watt electric lamp, the heat from which is sufficient to vaporize the crystals. The lamp is switched on for about two hours daily for a week. The chamber should have a glass front so that the position of the books and the vaporization of the thymol can be checked. All materials are safe under this treatment with the exception of oil paints and varnishes and silk-screen printing inks, which are softened.

Alternatively, books can be sprayed with a 10% solution of thymol in industrial methylated spirit, but this process involves more labor and would not normally be used. It might, however, be necessary in an emergency when fumigating capacity is inadequate.

Maintenance

In many libraries, if deterioration of the collections is to be minimized, a certain amount of work must be done on them by specially recruited library technicians or even by assistant librarians, all of whom would be trained to carry out a few essential tasks. The reasons for this are: (a) it is inconvenient to have books away from the library, possibly for weeks or months, when all they need is minor attention; (b) the work costs more when sent out than when it is done on the premises, even allowing for the slowness of semiskilled staff; and (c) many librarians are not in touch with trustworthy binders to whom the work can be sent. If they do know a good binder or restorer, he is almost certainly already overburdened with work.

In addition to using suitable members of the staff on strictly limited maintenance work, it should be possible in some areas to enlist the services of one or two amateur binders who have retired from their professions and would enjoy working one or two days a week in the library, with or without remuneration, or possibly for a good lunch. Most amateur binders reach only a modest level of attainment (as indeed do many professionals), and their experience in handling early books is likely to be minimal, so their activities would have to be very severely restricted and supervised. Herein lies a difficulty, for many amateurs will have ambitions beyond their ability. However, if the people concerned are carefully selected and can be trusted, their help could be extremely valuable; of course, it is essential that they be competently supervised.

Assuming that the foregoing policy is adopted and that some skilled and sympathetic labor is available, the following are some of the questions which need to be answered:

• Which books should be replaced rather than restored for economic reasons?

• Which, because of lack of use or importance, can safely be neglected in favor of more urgent items?

• Which should be given priority treatment to prevent extra damage, which in bindings tends to be at a compound rate?

• Which little-used books of special importance need to be boxed rather than restored because, for example, structural work would cover features which must be accessible—or which need to be boxed as a stop-gap measure until skilled treatment can be undertaken?

• Which books must be sent out to skilled binders or restorers?

• Which can be safely entrusted to the ministrations of library assistants?

Ideally, a conservator would be commissioned to go through the library and prescribe treatment for each book, but there are too many libraries and too few experienced conservators for this to be a feasible proposition, so the following observations may be of interest:

(1) The restoration of leather bindings calls for much skill, experience, and a feeling for the past—without this last attribute the skill is largely wasted. Bad work often permanently ruins bindings and at best is likely to be costly to rectify; so no structural restoration of important books should be attempted by untrained assistants or by professional restorers whose work is not known to be satisfactory.

(2) Many 19th century cloth bindings are as difficult, and in some cases more difficult, to restore as leather bindings because of the scarcity of matching repair materials and the fact that the grained cloths, patterned papers, and colored "surface" papers are easily stained by accident during the course of restoration. Generally speaking, the preservation of cloth bindings of this period is desirable, so here again unskilled labor should not be used except possibly for the reattachment of sound cases when, as often happens, the book has fallen out (*see* p. 12).

(3) The full-scale furbishing of a leather binding by an experienced restorer involves thorough washing of all parts of the binding, cleaning of the book edges, consolidation of battered board corners, recoloring of rubbed areas of leather, restoration of missing gold tooling and onlays, fastening down of rucked up leather on the sides or board edges, reattachment of loose flyleaves, the mending of inner joints with matching

paper, and final application of a dressing. Much of this is beyond the capabilities of the library assistant, but useful work can be done (*see* p. 15).

(4) Vellum bindings can be furbished, but apart from the aesthetic gain there is little point in it, and the time can be better spent on other things. However, some advice is given below (*see* p. 18). Structural restoration of vellum bindings is very much a matter for the experienced restorer, but it should be possible for those who have some experience of the craft to fasten books back into their vellum cases (*see* p. 12).

(5) Boxes for books and folders for loose papers are of great importance to their conservation. Slip-cases are of little value apart from their usefulness in holding together books which have a tendency to sag and flop. Often, much damage is caused by abrasion and by the clumsy who jab the book with the edges of the case when they miss the opening. Perfectly fitting slip-cases are not easily made, so many are too tight, and it is difficult to extricate the contents.

Pull-off boxes (often erroneously known as solander cases in the United States) should not be specified because besides being extremely expensive to produce, very few craftsmen remain who can make them properly. Certainly, a well-made pull-off box does provide good protection against the elements and, it is said, fire, but damage can be caused when the books are inserted and removed.

Buckram drop-back boxes (which are an elementary form of the solander case) provide the best form of economical protection because no abrasion is involved in the insertion of the book, ultraviolet light is excluded, extremes of temperature and humidity are reduced, and the restricted circulation of air minimizes the absorption of sulfur dioxide. Box-making materials, especially the inner linings, should be nonacidic to prevent the migration of acid to the contents.

Boxes are such good conservation devices that it is to be hoped that librarians will consider sending one of two members of their staff to a competent binder for training. In the long term, the outlay would be fully justified. It is possible that in one month, a person with aptitude could acquire sufficient skill to be useful, though for some time the boxes would inevitably lack "finish." Spine labels would have to be typed or produced by some means other than by traditional binders' methods.

The "phase box" developed by the Conservation Department in the Library of Congress is more easily learned and made but has the disadvantage for many libraries that it is less effective than the drop-back box in excluding polluted atmospheres and climatic extremes.

The alternative is to send the books away for box making, which is inconvenient and costly if special insurance cover has to be given. It is not advisable to send measurements instead, unless they are taken by an experienced person, because the irregular shape of many early books makes it unlikely that a good fit will be achieved, and a very slight error can prevent the book's going into the box at all. If boxes have to be made by professionals, it may be possible to save financially by grouping the books roughly by size, have all the boxes made to common dimensions for each group, and then ask the library's voluntary helpers to fit inner linings so that the contents are snugly accommodated.

Boxes with leather spines look attractive on the shelves, but full buckram ones will prove to be more durable, and, of course, they are much less expensive. Ready-made, acid-free boxes are available from TALAS (104 Fifth Ave., New York, N.Y. 10011), but most would need alteration with acid-free materials to make them effective fits.

Prevention of Damage

Contrary to widespread belief, books are very delicate objects and are easily damaged, but the rate of deterioration can be drastically reduced by intelligent shelving and careful handling. Unfortunately, a sizeable percentage of people who handle books, and not excluding those who constantly handle fine volumes, are clumsy to an alarming degree. I have noticed that even some of the greatest collectors have no idea how to hold and look at their treasured possessions.

(1) Books with metal fittings should be kept in boxes so that adjacent volumes are not damaged. If this cannot be done, a board should be slipped in between the volumes on either side to prevent contact.

(2) Books should be packed tightly enough on the shelves to provide some support but not to the extent that they can be removed only with difficulty. Books should not be allowed to lean at an angle because this subjects the binding structure to unnecessary strain.

(3) Very fat books should be laid on their sides; otherwise, the text-block will almost inevitably sag and cause the binding eventually to disintegrate.

(4) When books are removed from the shelves, one should not pull on the headcaps. The best method is to push the books on either side forward so that the sides of the required volume can be gripped. Damage to the top of the spine of fine leather-bound books can cost $30 or more and much inconvenience to rectify, and carelessness of this kind can spoil the quality of a collection in a very short time.

(5) It is not an uncommon practice for disintegrating books to be held together with rubber bands. As their removal often causes much damage to powdering leather spines, it is clearly a costly and unwise practice.

(6) Books often have notes, tickets, and much other extraneous matter inserted between the leaves or inside the front cover. This throws undue strain on the joints, so, ideally, all such matter should be removed and kept in an acid-free envelope along-side the book. Apart from causing mechanical damage, such material is often acid, and this may result in acid migration and the staining and embrittlement of adjacent leaves.

(7) Shelves should be regularly cleaned so that detached fragments from old bindings will not chafe edge-gilding and board edges. Apart from these hazards, dirt harbors pests. Shelves and fittings should occasionally be sterilized, and of course this must be done immediately if there is evidence of mold or of pest activity. This can be done by brushing on a solution of Dowicide-1 (Topane) prepared at the rate of 10 g/L of white spirit.

Work Area

Some work can be done close to the book stacks, and this has advantages when the space is available and the lighting is good; much time can be saved when books do not have to be moved and their positions do not have to be recorded. Inevitably, though, much work will need to be done away from the shelves, and this can be more conveniently carried on in a separate room reserved for the purpose rather than in a corner of the storage area. In most libraries, furbishing has to be done over a long period, but if it is to be a big, short-term effort, good organization is essential to avoid confusion and time-wasting. In these cases Carolyn Horton's recommendations (3) should be considered.

The room needs to be dry, well ventilated, and lighted, have running water nearby, and have generous table or bench surfaces. Ideally, it should be equipped with a fumigating chamber, which can easily be made locally. A fume extractor for the chamber is not vital provided that the fumes can be cleared from the room quickly when the chamber is opened. This is necessary when *p*-dichlorobenzene crystals are used for pest control (*see* p. 5). A small office letterpress or binder's nipping press is an asset. It is also useful to have at least one really solid bench with a thick lithographic stone or piece of marble lying on one corner over a leg of the bench so that the corners of boards can be tapped with a minimum of noise—tapping in the middle of flimsy tables creates intolerable discomfort.

Minor Structural Restoration

Leather Bindings. Some 19th century and later bindings have their boards laced on with only three thin cords, and they were often unnecessarily provided with a hollow back, the result being that the book has in many instances fallen out. If the text paper is thin and the back margins are wide, it may well be that the book can be reinserted with a tight back and no loss of function and possibly lessening of strain on weak but unbroken sewing. The fastening in is best done with PVA (polyvinyl acetate, a white creamy substance with low water content and strong rubbery adhesive qualities when dry), adhesive (Jade No. 403, obtainable from TALAS), which can be applied with the fingers—not liberally because when the book is recased and the boards are closed, the adhesive may squeeze out of the end of the spine and along the inner joints. The book should be laid on its side and not touched until the following day so that the adhesive can set. It may be necessary to finger the book into a more rounded shape so that it will fit right back into the spine of the binding for maximum contact and adhesion, in which case it is a good plan to put a weight on the side of the book after adjustment to prevent loss of shape. Mending the inner joints with paper is a risky procedure because the extra bulk can split the outer joints when the repair paper is dry and the boards are closed—the inexperienced should not attempt it.

Books which will not function properly if fastened in with a tight back will need to be treated differently. This is best done with cloth joints which are sewn to the shoulders of the book and then pasted down under the endpapers (4), but the more delicate bindings such as those bound in calf are a risk, so this technique should not be attempted by the inexperienced. A safer but less secure method is to attach a new hollow back and then insert the book, but if the hollow is too bulky, it is quite likely that the book will not fit in comfortably, and the joints will be strained. The following is the procedure for making a thin hollow back. Place the book with the spine uppermost in a finishing press or if this is not available, horizontally in a nipping press with the spine protruding two or three inches for accessibility. Remove loose lining materials. Strictly speaking, all of it should be removed because the paper used in most hollow-backed books is of inferior quality and very acid, but in difficult cases damage may be done to the sewing in the process. Cut a piece of jaconet (white cotton cloth with a glaze which remains stable for a short period after the application of adhesive) slightly more than twice the width of the spine and a little longer than the book. If the warp runs parallel with the spine, the strength of the folds can be increased if the material is folded obliquely; a tube is formed the width of the spine with the edges of the jaconet just overlapping. Rub PVA adhesive onto the spine with the fingers, then lay down the jaconet hollow with the joint attached to the spine. The overlap prevents seepage of the adhesive into the interior of the tube. Rub it down to ensure adhesion and leave overnight to set. When dry, trim the ends level with the headbands, apply a moderate amount of PVA to the jaconet, and insert the book into its cover.

If only the front of the book has come away, it can be secured by the insertion of a strip of jaconet the length of the book and an inch or so wide and folded down the middle, the fold being placed close to the joint. This will withstand normal occasional use but cannot be expected to stand up to heavy everyday wear and tear on the reference shelves.

Vellum Bindings. Most early vellum bindings are sound apart from the fact that they have come away from the book because the narrow vellum strips by which they were attached have snapped. The sewing of nearly all the books is intact, and there is little point in resewing them just for the sake of reattaching the covers in the original manner, especially since the reattachment can be affected more strongly and cheaply with overcast cloth joints without alteration of the appearance of the binding. It is not suitable for the comparatively small number of large books sewn on heavy raised bands and covered with thin vellum because the binding does not come away like a case although the cloth joints can be used as part of the rebacking process.

Cloth Bindings. Many Victorian books in publisher's cloth are falling out of their cases or are very shakily attached because the lining material which is stuck to the spine and extends across the joints and under the pastedowns is usually flimsy and the paper of most endpapers is thin and weak. Very often, too, the sewing is weak and loose, if not actually broken, because the paper and sections are too thick and the book has been sewn two-on—i.e., one length of thread secures two sections.

The sewing can be considerably tightened and the case can be reattached by means of a hollow back, preferably made of jaconet rather than the usual paper.

The back should be cleared of loose, flakey linings, then manipulated with the fingers until it has a good, regular shape, and any sections which have "started" should be pushed back. If they will not retreat under ordinary finger pressure, which is usually the case, a thin card or tin should be placed in the middle of each one, the spine should be placed on the table, and each card in turn should be pressed down to force the back of the section into the spine.

The next operation is to apply a hollow back and insert the book into its case as described above (p. 11). This procedure strengthens the sewing to a remarkable degree and provides moderately strong attachment for the case, but the mending of the inner joints is important as a stabilizer as well as being an improvement aesthetically. Mending the inner joints of cloth-cased books does not strain the outer ones as it does those of leather-bound books; there is more looseness in the joints, and it is this source of weakness, to which a contributory factor is the softness of cloth, which needs to be stabilized and therefore strengthened.

Even professional restorers with large collections of old paper often experience difficulty in matching the endpapers, and the search can be very time-absorbing; however, if the paper is somewhat similar and the work is well done, the results need not be offensive. The repair paper should be cut to provide two strips the length of the book, the width being the distance from the top edge of the board to the bottom of the shoulder, which in most cloth-cased octavos is little more than 1/4 in. PVA is applied to each strip, preferably with the fingers, and then each is rubbed and embedded into the inner joints, also with the fingers, with the boards fully thrown back. They can be closed after about 30 minutes. The repair shows less if the flyleaf is detached before the new joint is stuck down and is then edged back on top of the new paper with PVA. Some restorers make the strip wider so that one side can be stuck down under the pastedown. This would be done if a cloth reinforcement were sewn on, but I see no point in doing this with paper which, if it is not too thick and is well stuck down with strong adhesive, holds well.

PVA adhesive is much more effective than other types because it has quick "tack," has a remarkably good hold, and also somewhat strengthens paper to which it has been applied. An additional advantage is that it remains flexible. Spots of PVA inadvertently dabbed on to the wrong places should be wiped off immediately with a damp cloth because they are not readily soluble when dry.

The machine direction of the paper should run along the length of the strips because although the paper is stronger initially across the grain, continual bending of the fibers causes weakness. In any case, the paper is more easily stuck down and molded in if the grain is parallel with the joints rather than at right angles to them.

Very often the boards are still held by the tapes on which the book was sewn, but the folds of the endpapers are broken with resultant looseness in the joints and a tendency for the book to sag between the boards. In this case, all one needs to do is mend the inner joints as described above.

Some cloth-cased books are loose even though none of the materials are broken. This shakiness may well be a result of inadequate pasting of the endpapers near the joints and/or too little pressing immediately afterwards. Horton has described (5) how this defect can be rectified with the aid of PVA, a knitting needle, pressing boards, and a press. Briefly, this involves placing the needle into a tall bottle of PVA and then sliding the coated needle under the loose endpaper from one end of the book, distributing the adhesive as much as possible, and then nipping the book.

Caoutchouc Bindings. The process of binding with single leaves stuck in with liquid rubber instead of the traditional sewn sections was patented in Great Britain in 1836 and was commercially exploited three years later. Most volumes so bound have disintegrated and need to be reconstituted with PVA adhesive in place of the short-lived rubber. Some of the smaller ones, particularly those with card-like leaves, are easily done, but some of the larger tomes, especially those which have been printed on thin paper, need a great deal of knocking up if the realignment of the leaves is to be satisfactory. There can be difficulties with the reinsertion of the text-block into its cover, so inexperienced workers would be well advised not to attempt the task.

Paper Mending. In all libraries, much damage is done to book paper, some of which could be tolerably well rectified by inexperienced assistants, particularly in the field of semirare books. There is the argument that this year's semirare book may be next year's rare one, but there is no end to this line of thinking, and often something must be done on the principle that "a stitch in time . . ."

Perhaps the most common damage encountered in books is in the large maps or plates which fold in at the head or tail and are set too far into the spine so that the folding in or out has to be done on the curve of the text-block, resulting in a tear near the spine. Damage also frequently occurs at the right angle folds. Mending can be done with paste, but there is a great danger that the unskilled will inadvertently smear it in the wrong places so that when the volume is closed for drying, the adjacent leaves will stick to the map or to the blotting paper used for drying, a misadventure which can happen to anybody from time to time. A safer and easier method is to cover the tear with a narrow strip of acrylic-impregnated nylon web which can be fused into the paper with a hot spatula. No moisture or pressing of the volume is involved. The basics of this and of the preparation of the nylon could be learned sufficiently well for the purpose under discussion in three days from a professional restorer.

A simpler but less sightly method is to use Dennison's Transparent Mending Tape, a glassine paper with a water-soluble backing. Carolyn Horton reports (6) that although the tape eventually turns yellow, she has never heard of it staining the page on which it has been used.

Another difficulty with large plates, especially those on thin paper, is that they are frequently folded in the wrong places, with the result that they become crumpled. Not only does this spoil the plate, but the extra bulk can damage the binding, so it is important that the paper be flattened and reset in its correct folds. This can be done with a hot iron, but there is a danger that the inexperienced will scorch the paper. In any case, moisture and pressure are more effective.

Ideally, the plate is removed from the book and is then moistened and pressed between blotting papers for about an hour, subsequently being refolded and tipped back into the book. In some cases it may be feasible to flatten the plate while it is in situ in the book and folded, but a disadvantage is that unless blotting paper can be strategically positioned, the folds of the plate may be creased too sharply and to their detriment.

The dry cleaning of grubby paper should be tackled before any moistening for flattening is done; otherwise, the dirt may be fixed. Some dirt can be removed with wallpaper cleaner. Absorbene, a proprietary brand, has been tested and found harmless. Opaline, a cloth bag containing absorbent powder, among other constitutents, can be used on fragile paper, and more stubborn marks can be worked on with Pink Pearl and Magic-Rub, which are abrasive and must be used with care over printed areas and on some coated papers. Horton has discussed the use of these materials (7). The bleaching of paper and the removal of stains by means of solvents should not be attempted by untrained personnel because catastrophic damage is more than likely to result.

Furbishing

Leather Bindings. · The purpose of furbishing is to extend the life of the binding by nonstructural means and to improve its appearance. When only basic resources and limited skills are available, even this has to be restricted to washing and dressing.

Bindings covered with vegetable-tanned leather are washed with pure toilet soap, saddle soap, or mild, high quality surgical toilet soap and a 7–10% solution of potassium lactate. 0.25% of p-nitrophenol can be added as a fungicide, but this is not necessary if the temperature and relative humidity are constantly satisfactory (*see* p. 5). The lactate, when applied to new vegetable-tanned leather, is thought to protect the leather from the deleterious action of sulfuric acid which usually forms in leather when sulfur dioxide is absorbed. It is probable that it has little efficacy once chemical deterioration has started, and for some years doubt has been cast on its effectiveness, even on new leather, despite favorable results in laboratory tests. However, it is used, and its use is advocated just in case it is beneficial.

Cotton wool or a sponge should be used, and the lactate content should be minimal, the duration of washing should be as short as possible, and the pressure exerted should be no greater than is absolutely necessary so that the gold tooling and the surface of the leather will not be disturbed. Alum-tawed leather (most often found on German bindings and somewhat similar in appearance to vellum) is not affected by absorbed sulfur dioxide and need not be treated with potassium lactate, but its appearance is often much improved if it is washed fairly dryly with soap and water. In all cases, the soap should be rinsed off with clear solution; otherwise, it may appear as a white bloom when dry. It is important to work as dryly as is compatible with good results because, apart from the points already mentioned, the danger of the solution running out of control and possibly seeping into the edges of the book is minimized. The edges of the boards can be cleaned, but inexperienced workers should perhaps leave the turn-ins. The joints, otherwise, may be broken or severed, and the pastedowns may be stained.

Calf bindings which have started to powder should not be washed because the worse affected areas, almost invariably the spine and covers near the edges of the boards, are likely to become severely darkened and even take on a charred appearance. Lettering labels are usually of goatskin and can be washed with safety. Most goat bindings of all periods are safe, but some produced in the second half of the 19th century and the early years of this one suffer from red rot and can be seriously affected by aqueous treatment.

Suede bindings—i.e., those covered with the flesh side of the skin outermost—are better not touched with potassium lactate or water. Horton has found that spraying them with Krylon No. 1301 consolidates powdering effectively.

When rinsed, the books should be stood on end or on their fore-edge, depending on their nature, and the next day they can be examined for defects. Loose flyleaves can be tipped in with an edging of PVA adhesive which should be applied to the paper by the method I have illustrated (8). Snags of leather and rubbed areas should be stuck down and consolidated with paste. Worn corners of boards should be opened up a little and thick paste forced in, afterwards being lightly tapped with a hammer. The paste thus squeezed out is wiped away with the fingers, which are also used to shape the corners. The book should now be laid on its side to dry overnight or possibly for two days if the boards are thick and have absorbed much paste.

Most pre-18th century leather is brown, and rubbed areas do not need to be recolored partly because the color (which results from the tannage) is much the same throughout the thickness of the skin. In the 18th century, colored skins became much more popular, and they involve more work in the furbishing because they were mostly surface stained over a creamy color (characteristic of sumach tanning which in England in the 16th century followed oak bark tanning), so rubbed areas are more evident and need attention. This is best done before the application of dressing, especially if the coloring is to be done with water colors. Sometimes, if the areas concerned are not large—e.g., along the joints and edges of boards—poster color is useful because it is opaque. When dry, it rather alarmingly turns much lighter than is required, but it usually reverts to its wet color when leather dressing is applied. Aniline water stains and artists' water colors can be used; also, Martin's Synchromatic Transparent Water Colors are known to be safe (9). Spirit stains can be used very effectively on certain occasions, but they should not be used by the inexperienced because much damage can be caused by penetration of the stain through cracked joints and thin leather into the paper of the book. Neither should faded tooled spines be recolored by the novice as it is difficult to avoid staining the gold.

The gold tooling and blocking on many early bindings has been lost or has become "thin" for one reason or another, usually in small areas. One effective method of restoration is to paint the lacunae with shell gold using a fine brush. Since the medium is water, this is best done before the application of leather dressing and after the coloring of adjacent leather. Shell gold is powdered gold leaf held together by gum, so it has a granular appearance which suits much early gilding which has deteriorated, but by the same token it is not successful as a means of restoring brilliant tooling of the 19th century and later.

Leather lettering pieces on the spines of leather-bound books are usually very thin and were attached with little paste. For this reason and because of chemical decay, many labels have either disappeared or can be levered off without difficulty. Reattachment with wheat paste can be hazardous for the novice because of the immediate weakening effect of the adhesive on the extremely thin and weak leather, which may also be darkened in the process. PVA is to be preferred because it has low water content. However, this may militate against its sticking to powdering leather, so it may be a good plan to paste the foundation of the panel and let it dry before reattaching the label with PVA.

The leather dressing, much favored in the United States, is a mixture of 60% neat's foot oil and 40% anhydrous lanolin. A quantity is put into a saucer so that a wad of cotton can be moderately charged. During the time the dressing is being applied, some workers keep one hand clean and hold the text-block under partly opened boards. Others prefer to have the book lying on its side while the dressing is applied, a method which perhaps allows more control and imposes less strain on the joints. When the charged cotton wool is applied, it should be used sparingly and be moved in a rapid circular motion at the start to prevent too much oil penetrating certain places and causing unsightly staining. This having been done, one can go back over the cover more thoroughly and with more oil without the risk of uneven staining. Dressing can be applied to the paper and cloth sides of most old half-bindings with improvement to their appearance, but some, especially of the late 19th century onward, may be disfigured.

Books which have been treated with dressing containing a spirit such as hexane need to be set out to allow evaporation, but those given the recommended neat's foot oil and lanolin can be piled with paper between them to prevent sticking. The dressing should have been absorbed after two days, usually less. A fairly soft cloth should be used to polish the leather and remove oil residue, especially from the less absorbent covers such as the highly polished and varnished goat and calf bindings of the 19th century. Accidental seepage of the oil on to the paper of the book can be removed with toluene, hexane, or another spirit on cotton wool.

Leather dressing serves a number of important purposes. It can sometimes soften hard leather and help to prevent pieces breaking off, it consolidates powdering, and to some extent prevents absorption of sulfur dioxide. The last factor is an important one in the case of new leathers which have not started to rot.

Vellum Bindings. Most vellum bindings are no dirtier than leather ones, but of course the grime shows more. In most cases it is satisfyingly easy to remove by aqueous means, but over-enthusiastic ablutions must be discouraged because much damage can be done—gold tooling is easily washed away from the firm surface and inscribed lettering is readily lost or dimmed.

Completely plain bindings can be washed with water (there is no advantage in using potassium lactate) and saddle soap or with milk alone, the fat content of which imparts a pleasant finish. As the dirt is usually easily removed, there is no point in using a lot of moisture, and in any case it is not essential to remove every vestige of grime. As already indicated, the stricture regarding moisture applies particularly to gold-tooled and inscribed volumes. In these cases it may be advisable for the very inexperienced to limit themselves to dry cleaning with Pink Pearl or Magic-Rub erasers or, if necessary, following this with a brief wipe-over with a slightly damp cloth and scarcely touching the lettering area. The application of leather dressing provides a pleasant surface, but it does no more than this so the amount should be minimal.

Cloth Bindings. Many cloth covers need to be cleaned and have rubbed areas improved. Horton has said (*10*) that the marketed cloth cleaners are not very effective, and this has been the present writer's experience. Soap and water certainly remove dirt without difficulty, but it also removes the color from many bookcloths of the Victorian period and later, and it affects colored printing and blocking on most bindings of that period. A certain amount of dirt can be removed by dry cleaning with Pink Pearl and Magic-Rub erasers. Afterwards, plain bindings can be freshened if they are gone over with cotton wool slightly moistened with water; this will remove some dirt and help to even out signs of wear. Rubbed areas can be touched up with the water colors already mentioned and board corners can be consolidated with thick paste as described above (p. 16). When dry, the surface is much improved if it is rubbed with slightly greased cotton wool or with a little leather dressing.

Caution: bottles and other containers are very easily knocked over when many books are being handled, so it is safer to stand them below one's working level, and one needs to ensure that the books cannot fall down onto the bottles and saucers containing liquids.

Storage of Prints

Most libraries have considerable holdings of maps, prints, broadsides, and ephemera of many varieties, many of which are vulnerable to damage, especially those which are acid and brittle or unmanageably large.

Much of this material should be deacidified, but only the experienced can decide whether aqueous or nonaqueous methods should be used, and only they are likely to have the manual dexterity and knowledge of handling techniques which in many instances are essential if damage is to be avoided. The method of deacidification depends on the nature of the paper and inks and pigments. Sometimes the paper cannot be treated at all because the colors of the image would be changed.

However, much can be done to minimize damage caused on the shelves or by library users if the material is stored in acid-free folders. They are easily fabricated and many types suitable for archive use are available commercially. It is essential that clearly acid papers be stored separately from nonacid ones in order to prevent migration of the acid. Some conservators place a sheet of buffered paper in the folder to absorb free acid from the print.

In some cases a transparent holder is needed. The most inert of the transparent flexible materials is Mylar (polyester), which is used extensively for storage purposes. If only one side of the document needs to be seen, acid-free board can be cut to size, then a strip of Mylar is cut the width of the board but slightly longer. The overlapping ends are creased around the ends of the board and secured with tape. This arrangement enables the document to be seen and handled with safety, and air can circulate. Alternatively, if the document is to be seen on both sides, two sheets of Mylar can be secured around the four edges with double-sided, pressure-sensitive tape (3M Tape No. 415, which is safe for archival use) but leaving a short length unsecured so that air can circulate. These methods can be quickly mastered and the benefits to the library in the long run must surely be immense.

Elimination of Waste

It is a sad fact of life that the world's financial resources and available skilled manpower are hopelessly inadequate to deal with the restoration and conservation of all the books and related materials which are deemed worthy of preservation. Indeed, there is no prospect that skilled craftsmen ever will be available to do all that is required, even in the unlikely event that natural disasters never again cause havoc in public and private libraries, so a sizeable percentage will seriously deteriorate or be butchered by hacks. As it is, shocking damage is being done every day by semiskilled binders who have no interest in or feeling for the books they handle. This being so, it is clearly vital that maximum use should be made of such resources as do exist. At present, there is waste in both the short and the long term. The following are a few of the many factors which should be considered by librarians and collectors.

Resewing and Its Alternatives. It is often assumed that when old books are rebound or restored, they should also be resewn, but in many cases this is not essential, and in some it may be inadvisable. Even books which seem to have weak sewing when the covering leather has deteriorated or the linings have come away become strong and functional again when the new spine has been attached. Unnecessary resewing can waste an immense amount of time, and it also often destroys the original "feel" of the book. Apart from this, some of the folds of the sections are quite likely to be broken and may need to be mended, which means more wasted time and possible technical problems with excessive swelling.

If the book is not resewn, there are various methods of reinforcing the attachment of the boards involving the passing of threads through the sections and/or around the original raised thongs or cords. An easier and stronger method is to stick a strip of jaconet or thin linen to each joint and then sew through it (11). After the book has been rebacked or covered, the strip is stuck down under the pastedown on the board or inserted into a split board if the book is large and heavy. This method has the additional merit of strengthening the attachment of the end leaves of text which are frequently loose.

It is of the greatest importance that this or some other sound method of reinforcement be specified, otherwise an immense amount of money is going to be wasted, and the binding and book will deteriorate during the repeated process of restoration. The problem of the unreinforced rebacking is not so much that the rebacking will be pulled away from the spine, but that when the leather eventually rots, the strain on it will be unnecessarily great, and the boards will just fall away instead of being secured on the inside.

Oversewing. Some old books have to be resewn, so the most effective and economical method must be considered, and this one has much to commend it, certainly for books of lesser value.

The sewing is achieved by stabbing the leaves about 1/8 in. from the back at about 3/4-in. intervals and doing it so that as each group of leaves is attached; the needle and thread pass through the previous group. It is a quickly executed method and one most effectively used on books with thin paper and reasonably wide back margins although if the book is suitable and is properly bound, it will open as well as if it were sewn all along.

There is much prejudice against oversewing because it and similar methods have been grossly misapplied to books printed on thick paper and thus prevented their being opened without damage and also because it has been done in a manner which perforated and weakened the leaves. On the right book, an immense amount of time can be saved because the making up of single leaves into sections which can be sewn through the folds is dispensed with and the sewing operation is quicker and easier. Again, on the right book, this method is so strong that it is unlikely to need resewing in the future, and broken bindings can be removed and renewed or restored with strong reinforcement of the attachment and no adverse effect on the text-block. If the physical nature of the book is suitable for oversewing, it is probably suitable to have a tight back— i.e., the adhesion of the covering leather straight on to the backs of the sections, with or without intermediate linings—and this in combination with overcast cloth joints provides great strength at comparatively little cost.

Rebacking "Boarded" Books. These paper-covered retail bindings of the end of the 18th century and early decades of the 19th usually need to be rebacked. This can be done very convincingly and sympathetically with old paper or old-looking new paper, but the repair will be short-lived if the paper is not lined on the underside with jaconet, fine lawn, or other material depending on the size of the volume. The reinforcement makes the spine covering stronger than it was originally, and the extra cost is negligible.

Rebacking Cloth Books. It is difficult and often impossible to reback 19th century cloth-cased books with strong modern cloth which will harmonize with the original material in color and calendered grain, so very often it is necessary to use cloth of the period taken from the sides of folio half-bindings. As most of the cloth is and probably always has been quite weak, it should be lined with fine material to increase its strength. The edges of the reinforcement should be short of the edges of the old rebacking cloth so that the ridge on the sides is minimized.

Other Reinforcements. Much-used books being rebound with leather spines should be given small vellum corners or tips on the boards instead of leather ones. This involves no extra expense and the gain in durability is indisputable. Books being rebound in buckram or cloth should have string inserted in the turn-in at the ends of the spine as a strengthener. Large and heavy volumes, especially much-used ones, bound in these materials should have the English tight joint because although the french groove in newly bound books is stable, the material softens in time, the boards spread outward, and the book falls between them setting up strains which eventually cause the breakdown of the structure.

Materials

The correct choice of materials is a vital factor in the long-term economy of a library because the wrong choice can bring forward by several decades the time when work needs to be redone.

Leather. Calfskin is most used in the restoration of bindings. Its quality varies greatly, and some clearly will not last long. The calf supplied by Franz Hoffmann of Stuttgart appears to be more mature than most English-tanned calf, having good substance and flexibility. The calf supplied by the Harrold Leather Manufacturing Co., Ltd. of Bedford, England is partly chrome-tanned but has no working disadvantages apart from the fact that blind tooling does not darken satisfactorily for restoration purposes. Most owners of rare books wish to have them restored as inconspicuously as possible, but when this factor is of secondary importance, the use of smooth-grained goatskin may be preferred for the restoration of calf bindings.

There are occasions when, if the volume is not small and the raised bands on the spine are not very prominent, suspect new leather, if it must be used at all, can be reinforced on the underside with soft, stretchy cloth. How much the cloth is likely to be affected by migration of acid from rotting leather is a matter for conjecture.

Sheepskin has a bad reputation because it has often been split to the thinness of paper, has been crushed and grained with heated plates, and generally been maltreated in the course of manufacture. It is true that its surface can in some cases be easily abraded, but the leather has good fiber and, depending on whether the animal was bred in the mountains or on the plains, it can be a durable leather for volumes which are being restored or rebound in period style, provided they are not subject to rough daily use. Most, if not all, sheepskin is supplied unprotected, so it needs to be treated by the binder with potassium lactate, and this should be specified by the librarian.

Valuable early books look well bound in tawed pigskin, which is certain to be durable. It is not a cheap leather, but the skins are very large, so covers can be cut out very economically.

Vellum. There is a great deal to be said for this material which has proved durability and is certain to last much longer than any present-day vegetable-tanned leather. Difficulties can arise with full-vellum bindings because in dry conditions the covers tend to warp outward unless special precautions have been taken in the process of binding, but there need be no such hazards with half-vellum bindings with paper or cloth sides.

Limp or semi-limp vellum bindings are suitable for the smaller books. Experience has shown that they are durable, difficulties with warping are minimal, and they can be produced economically.

Buckram and Cloth. For box-making and the rebinding of books larger than octavo, linen or cloth buckram should be used in preference to cloth because much of the latter is little stronger than good paper, and although the best buckram may be three or four times the cost of poor cloth, the difference per volume is not great. Also, the eventual savings in rebinding costs, damage to the volume, and inconvenienec will be considerable.

Literature Cited

1. Wessel, C. J., "Environmental Factors Affecting the Permanence of Library Materials," *Deterior. Preserv. Libr. Mater., Annu. Conf. Grad. Libr. Sch., (Pap), 34th, 1969,* Chicago, 1970, 39–84.
2. "Control of Light," *Library and Archives Conservation,* The Library of the Boston Athenaeum, 1972, 73–78.
3. Horton, Carolyn, "Cleaning and Preserving Bindings and Related Materials," 2nd Ed., American Library Association, 1972, 1–20.
4. Middleton, B. C., "The Restoration of Leather Bindings," American Library Association, 1972, 82–85.
5. Horton, "Cleaning and Preserving Bindings and Related Materials," 29–32.
6. Ibid., 27–28.
7. Ibid., 32–33.
8. Middleton, "Restoration of Leather Bindings," 89.
9. Horton, "Cleaning and Preserving Bindings and Related Materials," 36–37.
10. Ibid., 34–35.
11. Middleton, "Restoration of Leather Bindings," 81–83.

RECEIVED February 18, 1977.

2

The Development of Permanent Paper

RICHARD A. STUHRKE

Process Chemicals Division, Hercules, Inc., Wilmington, Del. 19899

Permanency of paper was not questioned seriously until only recently when modern paper showed signs of excessive deterioration. In a relatively short time the technology was developed and standards were set for modern paper with specific, predictable permanency properties. Today, "permanent" paper is readily available and is competitively priced. Moreover, the alkaline papermaking process that is required for the manufacture of permanent paper is proving to some manufacturers to be more efficient in terms of costs, corrosion of equipment, and pollution control.

The thoughts, ideas, and discoveries of great men, the eyewitness accounts of great events, and the prose and poetry of civilzations are priceless treasures that must be passed on from generation to generation, yet it is to something as fragile as a piece of paper that this awesome responsibility is most often entrusted. Paper is composed primarily of cellulose fibers, organic substances which degrade and disintegrate with time.

Today, three general methods are used to ensure preservation of the written or printed word. Perhaps the most common method involves preservation of the information itself—microfilming, electrostatic reproduction, and short-run reprints. The second method aims at preserving the paper after the information has been printed on it. This could include plastic lamination, cold storage, and specific chemical treatments. The third method involves the use of permanent paper. The technology has been developed and standards have been set for paper with specific, predictable permanency properties.

None of the procedures listed in the first two methods is entirely satisfactory because of cost. Estimates can run up to several hundred dollars for a 500-page book, depending upon the procedure used. When cost is a factor, one must be selective. No one today can predict what will be important to historians and others 400 years from now. Present researchers are using literature several hundred years old which was originally intended to serve no lasting purpose. The use of permanent paper in books and documents of lasting importance and value is easily the most practical method that can be used to ensure preservation of the printed word. Today, permanent paper is readily available and is competitively priced compared with nonpermanent printing papers. Moreover, the alkaline papermaking process, which is required in the manufacture of permanent paper, can be beneficial to the papermaking process in terms of costs, corrosion to equipment, and pollution control.

Definition

Paper permanence is not an absolute property. The stresses and treatments applied during printing, converting, handling, and storage as well as the process by which the paper is made all affect the useful life of paper. No one can anticipate the conditions to which paper will be exposed or the use to which it will be put. It is only known for certain that a paper will last 300 years, in a book for example, when that book is 300 years old and is still usable. However, experiments begun several years ago by the National Bureau of Standards and verified in recent years have shown that if paper is heated at 100°C for 72 hr, it is artificially aged to a condition comparable with that of about 25 years under normal storage. It is now generally accepted that extending artificial aging to 48 days equals 400 years natural aging (1).

Most modern papers have a reasonable life expectancy of about 50 years. Permanent paper is paper that can have a reasonable life expectancy exceeding 200 years. The important phrase in this definition is "reasonable life expectancy." Permanent paper is still a fragile commodity, and the papermaker has no control over paper processors and ultimate users or abusers.

Background

The durability or permanence of paper was not seriously questioned until perhaps the early 1950s when libraries throughout the country and the Library of Congress began to complain about the quality of the paper in their so-called permanent books. The extent of the problem was illuminated in a study conducted in 1955 which showed that many books published in the first half of the 20th century would not last until the year 2000. The report further stated that more than 75% of books published before 1940 would be unusable in less than 25 years (2). Obviously, the life of a book is important to libraries; some spend up to half as much money on preserving books as on buying new ones. The New York

Public Library between 1955 and 1965 spent more than $1,000,000 on microfilming to preserve information contained in books, journals, and newspapers which had begun to disintegrate.

As the parts of problem began to come into sharper focus, five significant facts come to light:

1. Most books that were only 20–50 years old were already starting to deteriorate, whereas books over 100 years old were still in good condition. Two books, a 1908 economics text and a 1681 edition of *Constantia and Philetus* published in England, provided examples for some early research. The economics text had already decayed to the point where pages would break down when folded. The 17th-century English book was still usable (3).

2. Before 1870, almost all high-grade paper was made from cellulose fibers derived largely from linen and cotton rags. In recent years, to meet the huge increase in demand for papermaking fibers, this relatively pure form of cellulose largely gave way to less expensive wood fibers. Rag pulp fibers are generally stronger and more resistant to attack by chemicals in the atmosphere than bleached wood fibers. Naturally, book publishers often choose the less expensive grades of paper to keep costs down.

3. Old manuscripts printed on high grade paper with acid inks, in particular the iron inks commonly used in the Middle Ages, showed significantly greater deterioration than manuscripts printed with neutral or alkaline inks (2).

4. The most commonly used sizing agent for paper has been rosin size. Rosin size requires alum and an acidic environment in the papermaking process. This results in acidity in the paper itself.

5. Analysis of healthy and mature paper samples dating back to the 17th century showed them to contain relatively large amounts of calcium and magnesium salts. Extract pH determinations confirmed the presence of alkalinity and the absence of acidity (2). (Extract pH is the solution pH of ground samples of the paper slurried in distilled water.)

Subsequent studies of these and other facts spawned several research projects in the latter part of the 1950s aimed at identifying causes and developing remedies. Perhaps the most definitive of these studies was conducted by W. J. Barrow under a grant from the Ford Foundation. In 1959 and 1960 the Virginia State Library published two reports on Barrow's work (1). Using the accelerated-aging technique prescribed by the National Bureau of Standards (72 hr @ 100°C = 25 yr), Barrow correlated the degradation of book papers with acidity of the paper. He concluded that book paper produced under controlled alkaline conditions meeting a specific initial strength of fold and tear would have a reasonable life expectancy exceeding 200 years (1). Shortly after publication of this excellent work on factors affecting the longevity of book papers, several manufacturers started producing writing and printing papers formed under alkaline conditions from 100% wood fiber. With the aging test techniques used in the Barrow study, these manufacturers claimed that their papers had a life expectancy that exceeded that of rag papers produced under acid conditions. These claims inspired somewhat of a controversy with the rag paper manufacturers. Subsequent test data showed that neither all-rag nor part-rag content alone necessarily ensures permanence in book papers. Acidity and fiber length (strength) affect the permanence and durability of paper regardless of fiber type. The controversy resolved itself when it was learned that the same techniques used to make wood fiber paper permanent could be used to improve both the durability and quality of rag content papers.

Interest in permanent paper remains strong among publishers and printers. Many paper mills now produce permanent paper under alkaline conditions on a regular basis. The standards set forth by the work of W. J. Barrow, for the most part, remain the industry guidelines by which permanent paper is produced both in terms of papermaking additives and test specifications. Mills are finding that the alkaline papermaking process can be a more desirable as well as a more economical way of making paper. A current trend indicates that more and more alkaline paper will be produced. As this occurs, we can expect that printing and writing paper as well as other grades will become inherently stronger and more durable, approaching the quality and longevity of "permanent" paper. Perhaps the most important factor in this trend has been the development of suitable substitutes for rosin size. Since 1960, significant advances have been made in this area of papermaking technology. Today, there is an "alkaline size" that can be substituted for rosin size in most any grade of paper and paperboard that is produced.

Factors Affecting the "Reasonable Life Expectancy" of Paper

Acidity. For many years the pH of the paper has been considered an important characteristic affecting peramnence. Permanency specifications exist which call for paper with a pH of 6.5 or higher. Other specifications say that the pH should not be lower than 5.5. There is no disagreement, however, about the poor permanency of paper when it is under pH 5.5 (4). In this context, paper pH is determined by the extraction procedure already described. The acidity that is present in the paper will promote acid hydrolysis of the glucosidic bonds of cellulose. To prevent this type of degradation and to produce paper with a high extract pH, the paper machine process water system must be controlled at a neutral to alkaline pH with a minimum of total acidity, preferably with an excess of alkalinity. The term total acidity is used to describe the concentration of all dissolved ions and particles in the process water that contribute to acidity in the system and a low extract pH in the paper. For example, papermaker's alum dissociates to aluminum and sulfate ions in water. The aluminum ions further react with water to form: Al^{3+}; $Al(OH)^{3+}$; $Al(OH)_2^+$; and $Al(OH)_3^+$. With the exception of $Al(OH)_3$, the first three ionic forms will effect an acidic environment. The pH of the papermaking process water, at best, is only an indirect measure of all the acidity present in the system. Total acidity is determined by titrating a sample of water with standard sodium hydroxide to a phenolphthalein end point. It is usually expressed as ppm $CaCO_3$ and sometimes as ppm H_2SO_4 or alum.

The neutral or alkaline pH of the paper machine system necessary for a high extract pH in the paper is not compatible with the rosin size–alum sizing system. To set rosin size properly on fiber, alum is required. Since total acidity is an approximate measure of the amount of alum in solution, it is often used as a control in connection with rosin sizing. The most effective size–alum precipitate forms at a papermaking pH between 4.2 and 4.8 and a total acidity between 90 and 150 ppm. The low pH of the process water, high total acidity, excess alum, and the size–alum precipitate all place a severe limit on the permanency properties of paper.

Sizing. The basic sizing unit of rosin size is a discrete particle consisting of rosin soaps and free resin acids. The size–alum precipitate becomes electrostatically attached to the fiber surface, and as the sheet passes through the dryer section of the paper machine, heat causes the particle to melt and to flow out over the fiber surface. These mechanisms of adhesion and extended surface coverage are vital to the sizing function with rosin size. The basic sizing unit of most alkaline sizing agents is a single molecule consisting of a hydrophobic group and a hydroxyl reactive group. The function of the reactive group is to seek out an available hydroxyl group along the fiber surface and react with it chemically. A covalent bond results which permanently links the hydrophobic portion of the molecule to the surface of fiber. Alkaline sizes are sometimes referred to as cellulose reactive sizing agents. With rosin size, the bond between hydrophobic material and fiber is a combination of an electrostatic attraction, van der Waals forces, and hydrogen bonding. These are relatively weak, destructible bonds. On the other hand, the covalent bond of an alkaline size is not easily destroyed nor can it be removed with solvent extraction.

One of the first commercially successful alkaline sizing agents was developed by Hercules, Inc. of Wilmington, Del. and is sold under the trademark Aquapel. Aquapel is cellulose reactive. The hydrophobic group is a long-chain, linear saturated hydrocarbon. The hydroxyl reactive group is a lactone ring. A common hydroxyl reactive group found in other commercially available cellulose reactive sizes is the acid anhydride group. Both the lactone ring and the acid anhydride group provide efficient sizing. The sizing reaction does not take place until after the sheet is formed, most of the water is removed, and heat is applied as the sheet passes through the dryer section of the paper machine. Alkaline sizing agents, using the acid anhydride group, develop sizing at a somewhat faster rate than Aquapel. This is an advantage in some papermaking systems and a disadvantage in others. In the early work in which the tests and specifications for permanent book paper were developed, Aquapel sizing agents were used. Synthetic sizing technology has now advanced to the point where practically any grade of paper or paperboard produced today can be sized economically with a commercially available synthetic size.

Fillers. The buffering action of an alkaline filler is necessary to ensure permanence in filled paper. Retained alkalinity in the paper as it ages would resist any drop in pH that might result from absorption of either carbon dioxide or sulfur dioxide from the air. Acidic fillers, such as certain types of clay, accelerate the aging process. Calcium carbonate is an ideal filling material for permanent paper as well as for some grades not requiring permanency. In fact, the work of Barrow made the use of calcium carbonate a requirement in the manufacture of permanent book papers (1).

Alkaline Papermaking. An alkaline papermaking system can offer potential benefits to the papermaker beyond the durability and permanence of the product he produces. There are six areas where improvements to the entire papermaking process have been realized from alkaline papermaking and the use of an alkaline or cellulose reactive size (5). It must be understood, however, that these six benefit areas do not all become automatically available to every mill that makes the transition from an acid to an alkaline system. In practice, only one or two of the six benefit areas prove important enough for a given mill to justify changing systems. The specific value of alkaline papermaking can only be determined at the mill site individually. This section reviews the six major benefits so that each mill can better assess the potential of an alkaline system for its particular situation. These are summarized as follows:

SHEET ECONOMICS. Forming the sheet at high pH and removing rosin size and alum increases the potential to develop greater sheet strength. In filled paper, the stronger alkaline sheet has allowed incremental increases in filler loading as a direct substitute for fiber. The cost of fiber is considerably more than the cost of primary filling materials such as clay and calcium carbonate. A direct exchange of 1% is a savings of $2–3/ton. A limiting factor in fiber substitution, however, is maintaining caliper and surface smoothness in high-finish grades. The added filler does not have the necessary bulk in some cases to allow proper calendering techniques. The higher strength of an alkaline sheet has allowed direct substitution of weaker, lower cost fibers and in some cases complete elimination of $1/ton or more worth of dry strength resins.

Alum, in addition to being an essential part of the size–alum precipitate, can also provide other benefits to the papermaking process such as drainage, drying, dye retention, pitch control, and water treatment. The extent to which alum makes a contribution in any or all of these auxillary benefits depends on the mill; specific papermaking equipment used; grades of paper produced; influence of other additives already in furnish; and water conditions. Maintaining sheet quality or production rates under alkaline conditions may require further adjustments in the additive furnish to make up for the removal of alum from the system. In a few cases, it was found that small amounts of alum in the presence of excess alkalinity at a neutral to alkaline pH provided a drainage and drying effect. The added costs that otherwise may be necessary to compensate for the removal of most or all of the alum must be included when analyzing the economics of an alkaline sheet.

CALCIUM CARBONATE. Calcium carbonate, in addition to providing a natural buffer to inhibit the aging process, has four important properties which contribute to its value as an internal filler for paper: (1) in solution it provides ideal pH and alkalinity control for the papermaking process; (2) its surface area is similar to fines, making it a suitable substitute for fiber and relatively easy to size; (3) as a pigment it has high brightness properties; and (4) the calcium ion adds positive charges to help balance the electrophoretic mobility of the papermaking process water system. Calcium carbonate is already widely used as a pigment in paper coatings. Some mills acid-treat recycled coated paper to remove any traces of carbonate before reintroducing it into the papermaking process. This is costly, wastes a valuable pigment, and places an added burden on effluent treatment facilities.

Calcium carbonate cannot be used in the same low pH papermaking process that contains alum and rosin size. The presence of carbonate in an acid papermaking process causes severe problems such as foam, excess alum demand, inefficient sizing conditions with rosin size, and troublesome deposits. The alkaline system, therefore, enables the papermaker to use calcium carbonate as a primary filler as well as to use more recycled paper.

POLLUTION. The flow of water required to form a sheet of paper in the papermaking process is quite large. Average water flow at the point of sheet formation is 40,000–60,000 gal water/ton paper produced. Of course, a high percentage of this process water is recycled within the machine system. Depending on the percent recycle, the volume of effluent discharge can be as high as 20,000 gal/ton. The paper industry is being required to reduce effluent discharge and reuse ever increasing percentages of its own process water. Across the paper machine, this is known as closing up the white water system.

Papermaker's alum dissociates in water to form alumina and sulfate ion. Sulfate ion and some forms of alumina are highly corrosive, form scale and deposits, and create inefficient sizing conditions. These soluble salts have no particular affinity for cellulose and do not retain well in the paper during sheet formation (6). Consequently, a buildup occurs in the paper machine process water. The more the system is closed, the greater the buildup. Although there is nothing wrong with alumina—since most of it is purged from the system in the wet web—nor with acid per se, the high input of soluble salts associated with the use of alum and an acid system does in fact impose more of a limit on process water reuse than an alkaline system. Several mills have been able to close up their white water system since converting to an alkaline process. One cylinder-based mill in the midwest reported reducing their effluent discharge from 14,000 gal/ton to less than 5000 gal/ton.

ENERGY. Papermaking has a high energy requirement; costs can run as high as $60/ton. The three major areas of energy consumption are drying, refining, and in some cases, process water temperature control. The impact of alkaline papermaking on each of these areas of energy usage must be determined at the mill.

Water removal during sheet formation and wet pressing is critical to drying. Refining, alum, ionic polymers, water hardness, stock temperature, and other stock conditions all affect water removal before drying. The change that the alkaline system brings to these factors, in turn, will affect water removal properties either positively or negatively. However, once the sheet is in the drying section, the removal of rosin size, a relatively bulky, movable hydrophobic mass, allows easier water vapor release. On balance, the alkaline system may require further adjustments in wet end conditions to minimize any increase in drying requirements. However, some mills have realized a decrease in drying requirements.

An improvement in strength can allow a potential reduction in refining. Usually, any strength increase in an alkaline sheet is taken not as a reduction in refining but rather as a quality improvement or offset in some other area such as increased use of filler or cheaper fiber.

Some mills maintain high stock temperatures for drainage, water marking, or slime control. Fresh water added to the system is water that consumes energy usually in the form of steam added directly to the stock system. As an example, raising the temperature of 1000 gal of water 30°F requires 252,000 Btu or 252 lb steam. At today's energy costs, this is approximately $0.75 worth of steam. If the alkaline system allows further reductions in fresh water usage by increasing the level of process water reuse and steam is used to heat the stock, then significant reductions in steam usage can be achieved. In the case cited earlier where the midwestern cylinder board mill reduced effluent discharge 9000 gal/ton, steam is used to maintain stock temperatures at 150°F. The steam savings was calculated to be in excess of $10/ton.

PRODUCTIVITY. A single paper machine requires a capital investment upwards of $50 million. In addition, replacement parts, general maintenance, and routine upkeep of a paper machine are a significant part of the papermaking cost. The return on this huge investment is measured in number of tons produced per unit of time—i.e., productivity.

An acid papermaking environment is corrosive. In the same manner that acidity can affect the reasonable life expectancy of paper by breaking down the amorphous structure of cellulose, acidity can affect the reasonable life expectancy of the working parts of a paper machine by corroding the exposed metal surfaces. An alkaline papermaking environment is noncorrosive, extends life, and reduces maintenance costs. Paper machine systems get dirty, and dirt affects the quality of the paper.

Paper machines must be shut down, flushed out, and cleaned routinely to continue to operate efficiently. An alkaline papermaking system is cleaner than an acid system so downtime for wash-ups are less.

A few of the alkaline sizes that are available today are supplied as prepared emulsions. Large investments in handling systems become unnecessary. With no alum required and given a fairly wide papermaking pH range within which they function, maintaining proper sizing conditions can be simpler for an alkaline size than for rosin size. An alkaline system requires fewer additives and is less complex.

These factors mean that an alkaline papermaking process contributes to smoother running conditions. The result can be a significant increase in paper machine productivity and paper mill profitability.

PAPER QUALITY. An alkaline sheet of paper, as discussed earlier, can be stronger than an acid sheet and is permanent with respect to aging characteristics of its important structural properties. In addition some alkaline sizing agents can impart extremely high levels of sizing against both acid and alkaline penetrants. These features have gained premiums in some markets and expanded the utility of paper into new markets.

In conclusion to this section specifically devoted to alkaline papermaking, the statement must be reiterated that it is very unlikely that any single paper mill will realize all six benefits. The value of an alkaline system vs. an acid system depends on the particular set of papermaking conditions, grade structure, and market requirements which exist for each mill.

Strength. Strength makes a definite contribution to permanence. A strong sheet can lose a portion of its strength under poor storage conditions and still be serviceable. A sheet that is not strong to begin with is not permanent in the real sense of the word. The rate of deterioration of paper strength is not constant but decreases with time. The older the paper, whether naturally or artificially aged, the more slowly it loses strength. The loss in tear and fold appears to follow first-order kinetics. The relationship between initial fold and tear can provide a clue as to the rate of strength deterioration for papers made of wood fiber. In work done by Barrow, the researchers, by knowing the rates of loss in both tear and fold, were able to state the initial tear resistance which paper of a given basis weight should have to hold both kinds of strength evenly throughout life. As a result of this work, specific initial strength standards for both fold and tear at different basis weight are considered necessary for permanent book paper. Permanent paper, to meet these specifications, usually contains a high percentage of long and stable fibers.

Pulps. The type of pulp from which the paper is made affects its permanency properties as well as its ability to withstand different conditions of use and abuse over time. Rag fiber is inherently stronger and more resistant to chemical attack than wood fiber and therefore better able to withstand the uncontrollable aspects of end use. Carefully made, all-rag papers have excellent permanency properties; of this there can be no doubt because old specimens are still in existence. However, there is evidence that rag paper can have just as short a life as most modern wood fiber papers if made with acidic chemicals instead of the alkaline chemicals in use 100 years ago. There is no such thing as a very old and carefully made wood pulp paper because the industry is too young. The paper industry still disagrees as to the permanency properties of 100% rag paper vs. alkaline wood pulp paper. However, the need for permanent paper, particularly in the book markets, may be greater than the production capacity of the rag paper manufacturers. Therefore, any claims made for permanent paper composed of wood fiber and calcium carbonate pose no real threat to the rag paper industry.

Experiments with wood fiber pulps by the National Bureau of Standards have shown that the purer the pulp (higher the α-cellulose content) the more permanent it is. Moreover, as the α-cellulose content in these pulps approaches that of the α-cellulose content of rag fibers, the permanence of these fibers likewise approaches that of rag fiber. Therefore, paper made from sulfite pulps which have a high α-cellulose content would have better permanency properties than sulfate pulps provided that they are carefully made.

Unbleached pulps and groundwood pulps have poor permanency properties. Both pulps retain a high percentage of natural wood resin residuals independent of cellulose which readily decompose in the sheet. This affects color, strength, and sizing. It is generally specified that permanent paper must not contain either unbleached or groundwood fibers.

Oxidation and Bleaching. Cellulose itself is not particularly prone to free radical chain oxidation, but it is attacked by free radicals generated when other substances are oxidized in its presence. The manner by which these oxidation reactions contribute to paper deterioration is not well understood. The presence of certain metallic ions promotes oxidation, and particularly harmful are manganese, copper, and cobalt. Copper sulfate is sometimes used in paper mills as a slimicide and should not be used in the manufacture of permanent paper. With respect to bleaching agents, chlorite and chlorine dioxide are less prone to oxidative degradation than are hypochlorite and chlorine. Hypochlorite and chlorine bleaches leave reactive carbonyl groups in the cellulose chains and allow them to degrade progressively until the chain is destroyed by initiating oxidative degradation. Therefore, if in producing permanent paper the papermaker has a choice, pulp that has been subjected to final bleaching with either chlorite or chlorine dioxide would be preferred.

Heat. Heat accelerates the aging process in paper. Studies by the National Bureau of Standards led to the generally accepted principle that paper held for 72 hr at 100°C will undergo aging equivalent to 25 years at ambient temperatures. The heat aging vs. natural aging curve is considered linear. Consequently, 48 days at 100°C is equivalent to 400 years of natural aging. This is a fundamental relationship upon which most of the work that led to the development of permanent papers is based.

The moisture content of paper subjected to elevated temperatures for extended periods, however, will be abnormally low. Moisture content can also affect deterioration (12). Therefore, the more convenient "dry" aging technique may not be entirely accurate. Many researchers have suggested that moisture be held constant at normal levels during heat aging (10, 11). This has been done by supplying the heat chamber with air containing the proper moisture content and also by aging the samples conditioned to the desired moisture content in sealed tubes. "Moist" aging at high temperature should be more accurate than dry aging since conditions more closely resemble reality. However, this has yet to be well demonstrated (12).

Conversely, a preservation method often suggested is cold storage. Studies have shown that the reasonable life expectancy of paper can be increased by a factor of 10 if the paper is stored at a temperature 25°C lower than normal and by 10 times again if the storage temperature is lowered by still another 25°C. If permanent paper has a reasonable life expectancy of 400 years, then cold storage at −15°F would increase its life to 40,000 years. Archaeologists digging in high dry places have found specimens of old paper, and there, findings have confirmed this sort of figuring (3).

Ultraviolet Light. At least one other source of cellulose degradation should be mentioned: the destruction of cellulose by ultraviolet light absorption. Under certain conditions, it might be worthwhile to consider incorporating into the manufacture of permanent paper an ultraviolet light absorber. Most papers will not be subjected to intense uv light, however, and this should not be a problem.

Manufacture of Permanent Paper

The previous section was devoted to separate discussions of the various factors which affect the permanency and durability of paper. These include the ingredients of the paper, the process by which the paper is produced, and external conditions to which the paper is exposed. Each plays an important role in the process of evaluating and defining a criterion for the manufacture and testing of permanent paper. Summing up, the pH of paper is the most important characteristic contributing to permanence, but it must never be considered alone. Alkalinity to buffer a pH change, initial sheet strength, and the type pulp and sizing agent all must be considered if permanency is to be ensured. There are two unique aspects to permanent paper that deserve mention. First, the work which led to the development of permanent paper not only enhanced the value and utility of paper but has also helped lead the paper industry into a better way of making paper. Second, the development of permanent paper is a case in which the key to the solution of a modern problem was obtained from written records of the past. However, the clues were found not in the words that were written but in the paper on which the words were written.

Preservation of Old Paper

The procedures and practices that have been devised for restoring old paper involve the same principles used in the manufacture of new permanent paper. Embrittlement and discoloration of documents in storage are aging phenomena caused primarily by acids present in the paper or formed in the paper during storage. Consequently, any method designed to preserve paper has to begin with a neutralization treatment without making the paper too strongly alkaline at any time. Subsequent treatments of protein gels and gums to restore strength, alkaline sizing agents to restore sizing, wet strength resins, and other specific additives are sometimes used, depending upon the particular properties that are needed to complete the restoration.

In work done at Washington State University in Pullman, experiments were conducted with polymeric types of buffering agents such as alkali salts of organic polyacids. This type buffering agent has a two-fold function: (1) neutralization of the acidity in the paper and (2) strengthening of the paper structure by its film-forming properties. The agent chosen by the researchers was CMC, the sodium salt of carboxymethylcellulose. Treatments with the product proved that it is possible not only to terminate the aging process and restore most of the original strength in some papers but to impart permanency properties to the paper and make its reasonable life expectancy superior to that of the original untreated, unaged paper (7). Individual preservation is expensive and depending upon the condition of the document to be restored, must be done with extreme care, usually by hand. Consequently, only those documents of significant historic or artistic value can justify the expense and effort that is required.

Conclusion

Once the problem of premature aging of modern paper was identified and defined, cooperative efforts from independent research foundations, universities, and private industry were required to find answers and create solutions. The job was done and done well in a relatively short time. Thanks to the efforts of the W. J. Barrow Research Laboratory; the S. D. Warren Co., Westbrook, Maine; Standard Paper Manufacturing Co., Richmond, Va.; Hercules, Inc., Wilmington, Del.; Washington State University; and many others, the technology of producing permanent paper is now well understood and universally practiced in mills throughout the free world. The decision to preserve the printed word need no longer be controlled by cost or left to the unknown ravages of time.

Literature Cited

1. "The Manufacture and Testing of Durable Book Papers;" "Deterioration of Book Stock, Causes and Remedies;" (two studies on the permanence of book paper conducted by W. J. Barrow); Randolph W. Church, Ed., Virginia State Library, Richmond, 1959 and 1960.
2. Church, R. W., "Is There a Doctor in the House?" *Publisher's Weekly*, **175**, No. 1, January 5, 1959.
3. Arthur D. Little, Inc., "Aged in Wood," Bulletin No. 831, December, 1960.
4. Evanoff, P. C., Kruser, H. W., "Paper Permanence as Viewed by the Papermaker," Customer Services Department, Mead Co.
5. Stuhrke, R. A., "Alkaline Papermaking Pros & Cons," Hercules, Inc., presented at Pima Conference, March 31, 1976.
6. Alexander, S. D., Dobbins, R. J., Roscoe, R. W., "The Influence of Dissolved Electrolytes in a Closed Paper Mill System," St. Regis Paper Co.
7. Rudolf, A. V. R., Herrick, I. W., Adams, M. F., "Archives Document Preservation," *Northwest Sci.* (1966) **40**, No. 1.
8. Conference on a Permanent/Durable Book Paper (summary of discussion), William S. Dix, Chairman, Virginia State Library, Richmond, September 16, 1960.
9. Booth, *Tappi* (1967) **50** (11) 74.
10. Luner, P., *Tappi* (1969) **52** (5) 796.
11. Cardwell, R. D., "The Thermal Stability of Papermaking Pulps," Ph.D. thesis, Syracuse University, 1972.
12. Roberson, D. D., "The Evaluation of Paper Permanence and Durability," *Tappi* (1976) **59** (12).

RECEIVED February 21, 1977.

Metallic Catalysts in the Oxidative Degradation of Paper

J. C. WILLIAMS, C. S. FOWLER, M. S. LYON, and T. L. MERRILL

Preservation Research and Testing Office, Library of Congress, Washington, D.C. 20540

Impermanent acid papers can ordinarily be stabilized using alkaline earth carbonates. However, paper which contains transition metal catalysts, compounds of copper, cobalt, or iron can still fail by oxidative degradation. Paper was treated with copper acetate at various pH levels, given accelerated aging, and the degradation was followed by the change in folding endurance. There was more drop in folding endurance in the humid than in the dry oven. Dry-oven aging has little predictive value for oxidative degradation.

Paper, which was invented in China around the beginning of the Christian era, lasts well when properly made and properly stored.

A specimen of what once was considered the oldest paper in the world was found in 1942 in the ruins of a watchtower in Tsakhortei, south of the Bayan Bogdo mountains in the modern Ninghsia area. This fragment, discovered by Professors Lao Kan and Shih Chang-ju of the Academia Sinica, is a crumpled ball of coarse, heavy paper on which are written about two dozen decipherable characters. The fragment is believed to have been buried accidentally around A.D. 109 when the military post was abandoned during an attack by the western Hsi-ch'iang tribe. In Professor Lao's opinion, the paper, made of vegetable fibers, was produced about the time of Ts'ai Lun (1).

A more recent discovery at a tomb at Pa-ch'iao in Sian, a modern city in Shensi province, yielded paper specimens that may be older than those found at Tsakhortei. Scraps of thin, yellowish paper found there in May 1957 are believed to belong to the western Han dynasty, 202 B.C–A.D. 9 (1).

In the early papermaking process, a wet mass of short cellulose fiber was pounded and worked until, on stirring into water, the fibers gave a smooth dispersion. The sheet was formed by filtration on a flat screen. On drying, the fibers bonded together as a result of the beating. Simple as papermaking thus appears, the invention seems to have been made only once, in China, and all papermakers derive their art from the orient.

The Chinese managed to keep papermaking a secret for several centuries. However, the knowledge was finally spread by the fortunes of war. Papermaking was introduced to the city of Samarkand in A.D. 751.

According to an old Arabic manuscript, "Routes of Travel and Kingdoms," two papermakers were among the prisoners taken by the governor of Samarkand on a raid of Chinese territory. The two captives offered to exchange the knowledge of their craft for their freedom. Samarkand, with its abundant stock of flax and hemp and a ready supply of water from irrigation canals, was naturally suited to papermaking. The craft developed quickly and "Paper of Samarkand" soon became an important article of commerce. A second factory was started in Baghdad in A.D. 795 when Harun al-Rashid brought Chinese papermakers to the capital city (2).

More than a thousand years passed between the invention of paper and its introduction into Spain by the Moors. After learning the trade at Samarkand, the Arabs monopolized papermaking in the West for five centuries. Not until Spain was captured by the Moors did papermaking spread to Europe.

The Arab conquerors of the Iberian peninsula wasted no time in establishing local mills for the production of paper and by the middle of the twelfth century, papermaking was an industry in the Spanish cities of Xativa (or Jativa) and Toledo. An early reference to papermills in Spain is found in the writings of traveler Abu 'Abdallah Muhammad al-Idrisi. Describing Xativa in A.D. 1150, he wrote: "Schatiba is a charming town with castles whose beauty and strength have become proverbial. Paper is there prepared as nowhere else in the civilized universe and is sent both East and West (3).

The papermaking process which the Europeans learned from the Arabs made excellent, long-lasting paper. Here are directions written in A.D. 1025:

According to ibn Badis, the flax is soaked in quicklime, rubbed with the hands, and spread out in the sun to dry. It is then returned to fresh quicklime. This is repeated a number of times. Then it is washed free of the quicklime many times, pounded in a mortar, washed, and introduced into molds of the proper measure. Care is exerted so that the thickness of the paper is regular. It is then left to dry. It is treated with rice water or bran water. Starch is also used for this purpose. It also helps to glaze the surface of the paper (4).

While the papermakers stayed with these fundamentals, they made excellent paper. The old books in the libraries of Europe are still, generally, in good condition. However, as the demand for paper grew, changes were made in the process, which, while they increased production, proved unfortunate from the standpoint of the permanence of the paper and of the records kept thereon.

"Improvements" in the Papermaking Process

The Chinese and Arabs worked the cellulose fibers by beating the moist fibrous mass or pounding it in a mortar and pestle. The resulting "fibrillation" gave the necessary fiber-to-fiber bond in the sheet. Europeans exchanged the mortar and pestle for iron shod stampers driven by water power. In 1700, the Hollander beater came into use. The "Hollander" moved the stock in a circular path with a wheel on which iron bars were set. These bars worked the fibers against a stationary, iron-bed plate. The fibers were fibrillated as desired. They were also bruised, fractured, and disintegrated. The iron beating tackle wore away, introducing iron into the paper where, functioning as an oxidation catalyst, it caused yellowing and foxing.

Scheele's discovery of chlorine in 1774 led to its use to bleach stock. This often brought the degree of oxidation of the stock too high with disastrous consequences to the life of the paper. As demand for paper continued to increase, the supply of rags could not meet the requirements. The papermaker was forced to turn to wood for the necessary fiber. Chemical methods for separating cellulose from the lignin in wood were developed. These rather severe treatments often brought the degree of polymerization of the cellulose too low for permanence.

The paper machine came into use around 1830. Before, paper had been sized in a separate operation with gelatine or glue. Now a new size was introduced, rosin and alum, which could be added to the beaten stock. The paper then came from the machine in the sized condition. The amount of alum required for sizing left the paper acid. This was the final blow to permanence. Acid paper does not last well; it quickly turns brown and brittle. The life of paper which under good conditions could be 2000 years now was reduced to around 75 years.

Consumer Reaction

The new, poor-quality papers brought forth many well-deserved adverse comments. These continue to the present day. Murray (5) wrote in 1824, "I have in my possession a large copy of the Bible, printed at Oxford, 1816, (never used) crumbling literally into dust." In 1825 Thomas Hansard (6) spoke of "whole piles of quired stock, meaning books unbound . . . crumbling to dust in the warehouses of booksellers." In 1856 Herring (7) noted, ". . . It was not at all an uncommon occurrence for a parcel of paper to become so completely perished from the circumstances of its not having been thoroughly washed after bleaching that an entire ream, composed of 480 sheets, might be as readily snapped asunder as a piece of rotten wood."

There were many people who believed that the problems arose from abandoning rag as the source of the fiber. In 1891 Johnson (8) wrote: "Centuries hence, some bibliographer will construct an ingenious theory to explain why no books were printed between 1870 and 19—, the date at which we accomplish the destruction of the forests and begin again on cotton."

Kingery (9) spoke for all librarians in 1960 when he stated that half of the books in the N.Y. Public Library needed repair. "A casual examination of the current intake indicates that about 25% of it will require attention with nine years. Ten percent should have immediate attention . . . we are well along towards spending half as much each year on keeping our collection as we are in adding to it . . . disregarding what we spend on binding."

Suggestions began to be made on methods of holding brittle paper and its message together. Martens (10) in 1911 advocated treating decayed papers and parchments with a cellulose acetate solution. Lydenberg (11) in 1915 described a method of protecting paper with rice paste and Japanese tissue. He calculated that to bind an ordinary daily paper in this way would cost $420 a year. By now a multitude of methods of preserving information are available—lamination of paper or encapsulation, microforms, magnetic tape, etc. Each new method brings in new unknowns in regard to its own permanence, and many would not be necessary or desirable if paper were made correctly.

Finding the Trouble

Scientific investigations were launched to discover what had gone wrong with paper. In 1912 Hjelmsatter (12) exposed a number of papers to sunlight from June to August and measured the loss in properties. In all the papers, including some tub-sized, hand-made papers, the exposure to light produced a profound deterioration in the resistance to folding. The size disappeared in all cases, and the rosin-sized samples were badly discolored. From tests in which papers were steeped in solutions of aluminum sulfate, potassium sulfate, and aluminum acetate and then exposed to light, Hjelmsatter concluded that the deterioration was brought about by the presence of aluminum sulfate.

Kohler and Hall (13) reached a similar conclusion in 1925 that the acidity produced by the use of aluminum sulfate was the root of the problem. Their research brought together techniques which have become standard. Chemical degradation of paper is speeded by raising the temperature; Kohler and Hall accelerated the aging of paper by exposing

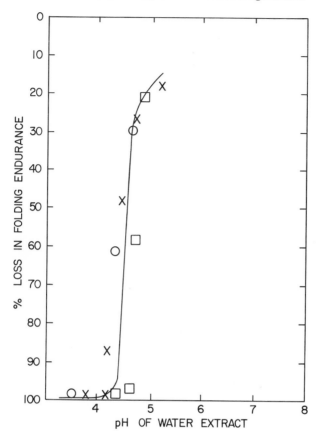

Figure 1. Waterleaf sheet aged 3 days at 100°C (12).
$\times$, $Al_2(SO_4)$; $\bigcirc$, H_2SO_4; $\square$, HCl.

it to 100°C in the dry oven. They thus brought laboratory investigations into a reasonable time frame. Folding endurance was selected as the most sensitive indicator of physical degradation. In this period, paper scientists came to realize that it was the concentration of hydrogen ions in the water content of the paper that governed acid hydrolysis rather than the total acidity. Measurement of the pH of extracts from the paper or of the paper slurry itself came into use. The effect of low pH, whether produced by aluminum sulfate, sulfuric acid, or hydrochloric acid on a water leaf rag sheet, is shown in Figure 1, adapted from data by Jarrell, Hankins, and Veitch (*14*).

Solutions

Since low pH makes paper age rapidly, neutralizing and even alkalizing it should improve permanence. This has proved to be the case.

There is a striking difference, however, in the action of various alkaline materials. Neutralizing acid paper with sodium carbonate, as is shown later, prolongs its life. Alkalizing paper to pH 10 with sodium carbonate causes paper to darken, to oxidize, and to degrade. The effects are most pronounced in humid-oven accelerated aging, less so in the dry-oven aging.

Neutralizing or alkalizing with the alkaline earth hydroxides or carbonates produces the good effects without the bad ones. Schierholz (15) recognized the superior protective power of the divalent alkalis and added them to acid paper in the form of the bicarbonates. His first claim reads, "Process of stabilizing paper and rendering it non-tarnishing which comprises impregnating the paper with an alkaline earth metal bicarbonate in aqueous solution."

Barrow, who was developing cellulose acetate lamination as a method of preserving documents, took the step of applying the bicarbonate solutions to the preservation of acid papers, both those still with adequate strength and those weak and requiring lamination. According to Clapp (16): "He perceived the need of neutralizing this acid condition if the documents which he was laminating were not to continue to deteriorate, and, in addition, to contaminate the cellulosic material which he was using to protect them." Barrow used both calcium and magnesium bicarbonates to protect paper. The effect of magnesium carbonate in prolonging the life of an acid paper is shown in Figure 2 and Table I.

Other evidence that calcium carbonate stabilizes paper accumulated. Sutermeister (17) had set aside six papers made between 1896 and 1901.

Table I. Foldur Kraft—No Treatment

Fold (1/2 kg)

Days in Oven	Dry oven (100°C)	Humid oven (90°C, 50% r.h.)	Brightness		pH		meq/kg	
			D.O.	H.O.	D.O.	H.O.	D.O.	H.O.
0	1367 ± 220		74.5		4.8		20	
7	117 ± 31	78 ± 40	70.8	69.0	4.9	4.8	—	—
12	9 ± 4	4 ± 1	70.0	66.2	4.8	4.7	36	38
25	0	0	65.6	61.0	4.7	4.7	40	40
36	0	0	59.8	53.3	4.7	4.6	42	52

Foldur Kraft—Barrow Magnesium Bicarbonate Treatment[a]

0	1966 ± 264		72.3		9.4		428	
12	1090 ± 56	1328 ± 125	66.1	67.3	9.7	9.5	262	262
24	769 ± 99	1218 ± 120	64.3	66.4	9.3	9.5	357	238
42	360 ± 37	1018 ± 112	62.1	63.4	9.3	9.3	285	214
60	157 ± 44	1035 ± 133	62.5	60.6	9.4	9.2	167	167

[a] Data from Tang of the Library of Congress Preservation Office Laboratory.

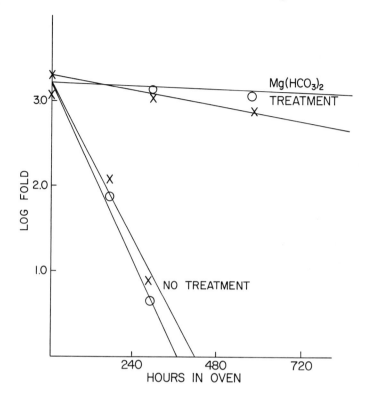

Figure 2. Paper treated with Mg(HCO₃) at pH 9.4. The paper control is at pH 4.8. ○, humid oven; ×, dry oven.

Five were clay filled and one had "lime mud" (calcium carbonate) as filler. The fiber furnish varied from all rag to mixtures of rag and sulfite wood pulp, to all wood fibers. . . . The sixth sample which had the lime mud was 75% sulfite and 25% soda wood fibers: it had a pH of 8.9, while the other five samples had pH values varying from 3.6 to 4.3. When Edwin Sutermeister examined the samples in 1929 and retested them, his report said, "all of the acid samples were badly discolored and were absolutely without strength, while the lime mud sample was much whiter and seemed as strong as ever."

Hanson (*18*) examined a book from the year 1576 in which some sheets were in good condition while others were brown and weak. The strong white sheets contained 2.5% calcium carbonate. Their pH was 7.5. The weak brown sheets contained no carbonate and had a pH of 4.9.

The culmination of Barrow's important investigations was the production in 1959 of an alkaline engine-sized paper loaded with calcium carbonate (*19*). The sizing was accomplished using new materials from Hercules, Inc., Kymene and Aquapel. This paper, made from 50% Swedish sulfate and 50% soda pulp, met Barrow's stringent requirement for retention of physical properties on dry-oven accelerated aging. Barrow thus solved the problem of the rapid degradation of acid paper which had plagued the world for over 100 years. Unfortunately, paper-makers have not generally followed Barrow's lead. They still make acidic paper, thus jeopardizing the life of important books and documents, reducing the value of recycled paper, and wasting forest resources and energy.

While Barrow solved the main problem, there are other modes of degradation which must be considered. As an organic material, cellulose and paper can be easily oxidized. Very small amounts of the transition metals, compounds of iron, copper, and cobalt, under humid conditions can accelerate oxidation and embrittlement of paper. This type of degradation, as is shown later, does not show up in the dry-oven accelerated aging which Barrow used. Thus his alkaline papers, if they contained the oxidation catalysts, may not always have been permanent.

The present report is concerned with explorative investigations undertaken in the Preservation Office Laboratory of the Library of Congress on the role of the transition metal catalysts in the oxidative degradation of paper.

Theoretical Considerations

Cellulose fibers have complex structures which are characteristic of the source of the fiber. Cowling (20) gives a number of schematic representations. The fiber is composed of fibrils, the fibrils of microfibrils, and all are based on the high-molecular-weight cellulose polymer.

Working a wet mass of fibers, as is done to prepare them for paper-making, produces a microfibril fuzzy structure at the surface of the fibers (which can be seen only at high magnifications). As fibers are brought together in sheet formation, the microfibrils intertwine. During drying, surface-tension forces clamp the microfibrils together, and as the sheet dries they adhere by hydrogen bond formation. When this process does not occur, the sheet is weak. Short synthetic fibers can be beaten, slurried in water, and formed into a sheet which is cohesive when wet. After the sheet is dried, a vigorous shaking will cause it to fly apart. The same effect is produced if the freshly formed sheet of cellulose fibers is frozen and then freeze dried, thus eliminating the action of surface tension.

Fiber-to-fiber bonds and the fibers themselves behave differently as paper degrades. In new paper, where the fiber is strong, tearing the paper produces an edge with a great deal of fiber-show. In degraded paper, the tear is sharp with practically no fiber-show. This indicates that fiber rather than fiber-to-fiber bonds degrades as paper ages. Tests of the paper indicate that tensile strength remains fairly constant during long periods. However, folding endurance determinations show that the fiber and the paper become brittle as degradation occurs.

Cellulose is a linear polymer of anhydroglucopyranose units linked by β-1-4-glucosidic bonds. The number of the units per molecule, the degree of polymerization, can range from 400 in a cellulose xanthate which is to be spun into rayon to 10,000 in a cotton. The glucosidic bond is stable under neutral and alkaline conditions but is hydrolyzed in acid. The rate of hydrolysis increases in proportion to the hydrogen ion concentration.

The cellulose polymer chains are considered to run in the direction of the fibrils and are largely in crystalline form. The molecules, however, periodically get out of the ordered relation. The fibril at this point becomes amorphous and of lower density. This region being more open absorbs moisture, which acts to plasticize the fiber. The amorphous region is also the point at which acid or enzyme can penetrate to cut the molecule.

Acid Hydrolysis

The degree of crystallinity of the fibers and the structure of the approximately 80% crystallinity, kraft with 60%, and regenerated cellulose fiber with around 50% show differing degrees of accessibility. A cotton-based paper does have longer life, under adverse conditions, than one made from rayon. However, given acid conditions, all the cellulose fibers finally do degrade and become brittle.

The work of Battista (*21*) is interesting in this connection. The brittle character of the acid-attacked cellulose was put to use:

In natural cellulose, the microcrystals are packed tightly in the fiber direction in a compact structure resembling bundles of wooden match sticks placed side by side. Unhinging the interconnecting chains by acid treatment does not destroy this structure. However, the unhinged crystals are now free to be dispersed by mechanical disintegration. . . . We immediately set out to explore this new avenue, developing uses for colloidal dispersions of microcrystalline celluloses, known commercially as Avicel.

Evidence has accumulated that the molecules in the amorphous region crystallize after being cut once the constraint is gone. Possibly the crystallization does not happen at once; it can progressively increase as paper is exposed to cycles of humidity. Recrystallization accounts for the fact that tensile remains high in degraded paper. It also explains drop-in-moisture regain. The fiber without amorphous regions and the plasticizing effect of absorbed water becomes brittle.

Alkaline Paper and Alkaline Degradation

As mentioned, conservators halt acid degradation by spraying or immersing paper to raise the pH. Barrow used a lime solution, followed by a calcium bicarbonate solution. He also sprayed with magnesium bicarbonate solution. These treatments leave the paper with a pH (by extraction) as high as 9.8. The Chicago Process invented by Smith uses magnesium methoxide in organic solvent which may leave the pH at 10.5. The increased rate of oxidation of alkaline cellulose is well known. Cellulose also degrades by alkaline hydrolysis. The data in the literature, however, are largely devoted to high pH produced by sodium compounds, while conservators use the alkaline earth compounds.

Golova and Nosova (22) have reviewed the alkaline degradation of cellulose and of oxidized celluloses:

The main processes occuring in the alkaline degradation of cellulose are the so called degradation of cellulose from the reducing end of the molecule and the alkaline hydrolysis of glycosidic bonds. The former process is observed almost exclusively at temperatures up to 150°C.

. . . Davidson suggested that degradation consists in the successive detachment of units, from the end of a molecular chain, possessing reducing properties. . . . The alkaline degradation of cellulose never goes to completion, and the final polysaccharide becomes stable towards alkali. This stability is due to conversion of the usual terminal glucose units into nonreducing units containing carboxyl groups. The main product was identified as D-metasaccharinic acid. . . . Alkaline earth metal ions—calcium, strontium and barium—are evidently more effective than sodium ions in catalyzing the conversion of reducing terminal units in cellulose into metasaccharinic acid residues.

. . . Investigators came to link the degradation of oxidized cellulose, by the action of alkalis, with the formation of carbonyl groups, which facilitate the rupture of glycosidic bonds. . . . Kaverzneva and Kist showed that the presence of a considerable quantity of ketonic groups in cellulose oxidized with nitrogen dioxide is the main reason for its degradation in alkaline media.

The dominant effect of carbonyl groups on the degradation of oxidized cellulose in an alkaline medium is evident also from the conversion of alkali-unstable oxidized celluloses into stable materials by reduction with sodium tetrahydroborate in a weakly alkaline medium, i.e., under conditions such that aldehyde groups are converted into alcoholic groups. The stability of oxidized celluloses is considerably enhanced also when carbonyl groups are oxidized to carboxy groups.

Machell and Richards and Colbran and Davidson . . . assumed that degradation ceased not only when the reducing terminal unit of cellulose was converted into a metasaccharinic acid residue but also when the reactant end of the molecule reached inaccessible (crystalline) regions of the cellulose fiber. . . . The available data indicate that the less ordered portions of cellulose are the more reactive. Thus the rate of oxidation of alkaline cellulose is considerably increased if the cellulose has first been swollen in alkali.

While some of the above can occur with cellulose treated with the alkaline earth hydroxides or carbonates, their tendency to insolubilize compounds with carboxyl groups will work against swelling and the increase in accessibility. For example, cellulose oxidized with N_2O_4 swells and dissolves in sodium hydroxide but is not soluble in lime solution.

Oxidation of Alkaline Cellulose

There have been many investigations on the oxidation of sodium hydroxide-alkalized cellulose for the preparation of rayon and lacquers, for the oxygen bleaching of fiber, and for the oxygen pulping of wood chips.

For rayon production, a controlled cleavage of the cellulose molecule is required to reduce the viscosity of the cellulose xanthate so that it can be forced through fine spinnerets. A similar reduction of viscosity is required for cellulose which will be sprayed as a lacquer. This cleavage is brought about by the air oxidation of alkali cellulose, and the process is speeded by the addition of a few parts per million of a transition metal compound which functions as an oxidation catalyst.

The pulping of alkaline wood chips with gaseous oxygen has received a great deal of attention in the past 10 years. Fiber yields are high, and the production of environmental pollutants is low. In the process, lignin is oxidized and then solubilized so that it can be washed away from the fiber. Cleavage of the cellulose molecule is not desired because it weakens the fiber; however, since a great deal does occur, research has been directed towards minimizing it. Ericsson, Lindgren, and Theander (23) state:

Some observations indicate that the non-reducing (cellulose) units are not, or only to a minor extent, attacked directly by molecular oxygen. It was observed by Samuelson and Stolpe that the oxygen oxidation of cellobiitol, a model compound for the non-reducing glucose units in cellulose, is initiated by addition of glucose or sulphate lignin. Furthermore, a cellulose sample containing a large number of carbonyl groups is attacked more rapidly than cellulose virtually free from carbonyl groups. It was therefore concluded that the cellulose chains are split by attack of peroxides which are formed from oxidation of oxidizable groups in lignin and of reducing end groups in the carbohydrates.

The least active of the oxidizing agents present during bleaching is oxygen. The most active ones are the radicals $HO_2 \cdot RO_2 \cdot$, $OH \cdot$, and $RO \cdot$, which are known as very strong oxidizing agents. Thus the active oxidizing agents obtained by O_2 oxidation of a compound A can oxidize a compound B which does not react with O_2. Compound A thus induces the oxidation of compound B (23).

The detrimental effect could also be explained by the fact that hydrogen peroxide and hydroperoxides are produced by the oxidation of phenols, lignin and xylan. These peroxides easily decompose in the presence of metals like cobalt and iron, producing radicals like OH· and HO$_2$· which are certainly very reactive (23).

Kleinert and Marraccini (24) state:

Aging of bleached pulps in presence of high humidity results in higher values of peroxide formed than aging at low humidity. The total amount of peroxide increases linearly with the time of aging. . . . Moisture was found to promote not only peroxide formation but, to some extent, also, brightness reversion, particularly in absence of air. Aldehyde groups formed by hydrolysis were found to be involved in peroxide formation.

Since the transition metal catalysis—compounds of iron, copper, and cobalt—are found in most woods, the oxygen/alkali, wood bleaching/ pulping process did not appear feasible until Robert, Traynard, and Martin-Borret (25) showed that magnesium carbonate in the slurry would stabilize the cellulose. In one of their patent examples, 1% magnesium carbonate, based on the fiber, held the folding endurance to 1850, while the unprotected control gave a sheet with a folding endurance of only 50. Thus, the same alkaline salt which Barrow used to protect paper against acid degradation was shown to function as an excellent cellulose stabilizer during pulping. According to Noreus and Samuelson (26), however, Barrow's other alkaline salt, calcium carbonate, is relatively ineffective in protecting cellulose in oxygen pulping.

Minor and Sanyer (27) found that potassium iodide harmlessly decomposes hydrogen peroxide and thus protects cellulose during pulping. It is interesting that peroxides have been found in paper and paperboard and that iodides have been used to decompose them. According to McCamy and Pope (28), blemishes in stored microfilm have been traced to peroxides formed in paper leaders and to the cardboard boxes used for storage. Henn and Mack (29) reported that the blemishes can be prevented by the addition of 0.2 g/L potassium iodide to the film-fixing bath. This addition has become a standard practice in photography to solve the problem of blemishes.

Since paper forms peroxides on aging and since wood fiber contains trace oxidation catalysts, free radicals will be generated in paper; these then can rapidly lower the degree of polymerization of the cellulose. In this connection note that in paper processing more of the catalysts accumulate. Borchardt and Butler (30) state that copper is picked up during cooking fiber and beating and as the sheet is formed on a metal Fourdrinier wire. As a result "paper and paperboard may contain upwards of 20 ppm of copper." Praskievicz and Subt (31) found new papers showing an average of 4 ppm copper. Papers from recycled fiber averaged 12 ppm. One paper contained 77 ppm copper. Paper generally also contains relatively large amounts of iron from processing machinery and the water used in its manufacture.

Gilbert, Pavlovova, and Rapson (*32*) studied the protective action of magnesium compounds. They note:

Especially important are the radical-redox reactions by which transition metals promote free radical generation by catalyzing the decomposition of the peroxides formed during bleaching. This faster free radical generation results in higher oxidation rates and a more extensive depolymerization of the cellulose.

Transition metals such as cobalt, copper, iron, and manganese catalyze free-radical oxidation of cellulose pulps when present in low concentrations. Nickel is harmless.

Magnesium compounds retard cellulose depolymerization by deactivating the transition metal catalysts. In alkaline media where hydroxyacids or products of polysaccharide degradation are present, magnesium forms stable complexes with transition metals. The formation of iron–magnesium complexes in particular is supported by interactions approximating the coordination number of iron (6) and one half the coordination number (3).

Removal of the deleterious metal ions with complexing agents stabilizes the cellulose molecular weight, but this is only as effective as the purification is complete. Work done by Ericsson et al. and also here has shown in-situ complexing by common agents to be unsatisfactory because EDTA, phenols, and hydroxy acids actually accelerate metal-catalyzed degradation. Presumably, the higher oxidation rate results because the complexing agents permit easier diffusion of the metals to the peroxide sites. It may well be that degradation catalysis would be impossible in an alkaline medium were it not for the homogenizing influence of complexing by-products of lignin and cellulose degradation.

However, given the presence of these complexing agents in oxygen bleaching, what is required to prevent catalyzed oxidation is a stronger, stable complex that will not permit participation of the transition metals in the radical-redox reactions. This appears to be the most plausible role to ascribe to magnesium.

Manoucheri and Samuelson (*33*) found magnesium compounds to inactivate iron catalysts but stated that a higher molar ratio of magnesium to iron was required than that recommended by Gilbert et al.

Aims of the Research

The present research therefore has two aims, the first to show that paper alkalized with a sodium compound—sodium carbonate—behaves in the presence of a transition metal catalyst in the manner indicated by the literature. The second aim is to learn to what extent the behavior of paper alkalized with the alkaline earth compounds differs from this.

From the previous discussion, when paper is alkalized to pH 10 with sodium carbonate, it should show an increase in the rate of degradation under humid conditions, especially if the cellulose has been oxidized. The presence of the transition metal catalysts will further speed the action. The addition of magnesium hydroxide or carbonate should retard the degradation.

The condition of the cellulose fiber in a pulping operation is often followed by measuring the viscosity—degree of polymerization (DP) of the cellulose. In the present work, an increase in brittleness of the paper is the property of interest, and this will be followed by the change in folding endurance. Oxidation of the cellulose will show up by the increase in the carboxyl group. This will be estimated by the pH and titration values of the slurried fiber.

Experimental

The work was done with paper from one roll of Champion Foldur Kraft, the properties of which are given in Table II. To alkalize the paper, the sheets were soaked in sodium carbonate solution, laid on porous Cerex plastic, and air dried overnight. When the transition metal catalyst was to be added, the air-dried alkalized paper was weighed, placed on a plastic pan on a top-loading balance, and sprayed with copper acetate in 50:50 water:ethanol to give 50 ppm copper. The sheet was turned at half weight. The series was run twice although only the second is reported here. In the first trial, the paper was immersed in

Table II. Foldur Kraft

Basis weight (25 × 38 − 500)		70 lb
Thickness		0.006 in.
Tensile, 15-mm strip	MD	10.2 kg
	CD	5.3 kg
Elongation at break	MD	1.73%
	CD	3.21%
Elmendorf tear (Single sheet)	MD	127 g
	CD	120 g
Brightness		75.2
pH (cold)		4.8
Titration		24 meq/kg
Fiber		Softwood-bleached kraft
Filler		8%

Atomic Absorption Analyses

Magnesium	9 ppm
Copper	3 ppm
Iron	123 ppm
Cobalt	1 ppm

dilute copper acetate solution, air dried on Cerex, and then immersed in the sodium carbonate solution. Copper pick-up was hard to control in this method. The copper, however, was evidently in better contact with the cellulose. Degradation was more pronounced, but trends were the same in both series.

Accelerated Aging. Humid aging was carried out at 90°C and 50% relative humidity in the circulating-air oven, Blue M model AC-7502 HA-1. Dry-oven aging was done at 100°C in the circulating-air oven, Blue M model POM-203A-1. The rack carrying papers for humid aging was given 20 min in the 100°C dry oven before being placed in the humid oven so that the papers came from the dry side. Papers coming from humid aging were given 3 hr at 39°C before being conditioned 12 hr at 23°C and 50% relative humidity for test.

Test Methods. Folding endurance was run for each sample on 12 strips, machine direction, at 0.5 kg load using the MIT test unit. The pH of the paper was taken by dispersing 2.5 g in 250 mL of cold distilled water in the Waring Blendor and reading with the slurry stirred with a magnetic stirrer. The acid slurry was then titrated with 0.1N alkali to pH 7. For alkaline samples, the pH of the slurry was brought to 2.8 with 0.1N acid, the slurry was boiled 2 min, cooled, and back-titrated to pH 7. Values are calculated in milliequivalents per kilogram. Brightness readings were taken using a Photovolt meter No. 670. Six readings were taken from each side of the paper and averaged.

Table III. Foldur Kraft—No Treatment

Hours in Oven	Fold Dry oven (100°C)	Fold Humid oven (90°C, 50% r.h.)	Brightness D.O.	Brightness H.O.	pH D.O.	pH H.O.	meq/kg D.O.	meq/kg H.O.
0	1470 ± 153		75		4.7		26	
69	—	428 ± 115	—	71	—	4.7	—	24
78	617 ± 144	—	73	—	4.8	—	24	—
120	—	213 ± 55	—	68	—	4.6	—	26
221	56 ± 22	—	71	—	4.8	—	22	—
221	—	12 ± 9	—	65	—	4.6	—	28
380	—	2 ± 1	—	61	—	4.4	—	30
645	—	0.5 ± 1	—	57	—	4.4	—	38
645	1 ± 0	—	67	—	4.6	—	32	—

Foldur Kraft—50 ppm Copper

Hours in Oven	Fold Dry oven (100°C)	Fold Humid oven (90°C, 50% r.h.)	Brightness D.O.	Brightness H.O.	pH D.O.	pH H.O.	meq/kg D.O.	meq/kg H.O.
0	2010 ± 346		74		4.8	—	20	
24	—	865 ± 170	—	70	—	4.7	—	24
74	—	299 ± 107	—	67	—	4.6	—	44
84	843 ± 171	—	72	—	4.8	—	28	—
176	214 ± 61	—	70	—	4.8	—	26	—
176	—	6 ± 5	—	61	—	4.6	—	36
336	—	0.8 ± 0.7	—	51	—	4.3	—	44
600	—	0.5 ± 0.5	—	45	—	4.3	—	48
600	2 ± 0.5	—	67	—	4.8	—	32	—

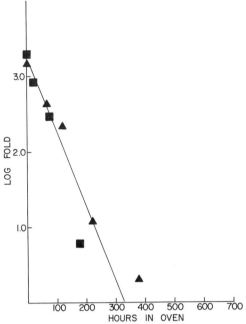

Figure 3. For test in humid oven at 90°C and 50% r.h. ▲, *control;* ■, *50 ppm copper.*

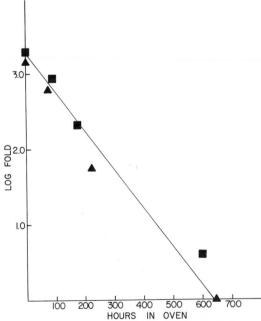

Figure 3A. For test in dry oven at 100°C. ▲, *control;* ■, *50 ppm copper.*

Results

The results of the work are shown in the tables and curves. As shown in Figures 3 and 3A and Table III (paper at pH 4.8), there was an increase in folding endurance from 1470 to 2010 on spraying the sheet with 0.0314% Cu $[(CH_3 COO)_2 \cdot H_2O]$. Such an increase is usual when a calendered sheet is wetted and relaxed. The expected rapid loss of folding endurance for a sheet of this pH showed up in both dry and humid ovens.

Figures 4 and 4A and Table IV show the results when the paper was neutralized by immersion in 0.1% sodium carbonate. The aging results are now surprisingly good, almost equal to those obtained with magnesium as given in Figure 2 and Table I. The paper, however, does not have an alkaline reserve and will not be stable in an acid atmosphere. Furthermore, as the next experiment shows, an alkaline reserve cannot be established using sodium carbonate.

Figures 5 and 5A and Table V show the results when the paper at pH 9.9 was alkalized with sodium carbonate. It maintained reasonable folding strength in the dry oven, and not much acid was produced by the

Table IV.   Foldur Kraft—0.1% Na_2CO_3

Hours in Oven	Fold Dry oven (100°C)	Fold Humid oven (90°C, 50% r.h.)	Brightness D.O.	Brightness H.O.	pH D.O.	pH H.O.	meq/kg D.O.	meq/kg H.O.
0	1942 ± 277		74		8.4		28	
69	—	1369 ± 224	—	67	—	7.0	—	0
78	1634 ± 255	—	69	—	6.5	—	4	—
120	—	1623 ± 421	—	66	—	6.8	—	0
221	1356 ± 295	—	68	—	6.5	—	6	—
221	—	1018 ± 136	—	64	—	6.4	—	8
380	—	1006 ± 164	—	62	—	6.7	—	4
645	—	599 ± 118	—	58	—	6.3	—	10
645	922 ± 213	—	65	—	6.7	—	4	—

Foldur Kraft—0.1% Na_2CO_3, 50 ppm Copper

Hours in Oven	Fold Dry oven (100°C)	Fold Humid oven (90°C, 50% r.h.)	Brightness D.O.	Brightness H.O.	pH D.O.	pH H.O.	meq/kg D.O.	meq/kg H.O.
0	2193 ± 488		73		7.3		14	
24	—	1405 ± 233	—	68	—	7.0	—	0
74	—	1672 ± 315	—	67	—	6.6	—	4
84	1884 ± 284	—	70	—	6.8	—	2	—
176	—	1053 ± 292	—	62	—	6.2	—	10
176	1487 ± 212	—	68	—	7.0	—	0	—
336	—	908 ± 229	—	55	—	6.2	—	8
600	—	360 ± 188	—	55	—	6.0	—	18
600	1125 ± 175	—	65	—	6.3	—	8	—

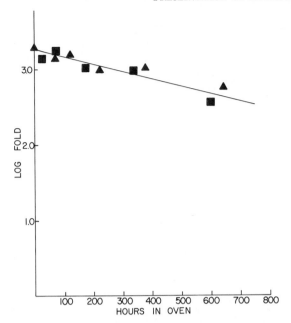

Figure 4.   For test in humid over at 90°C and 50% r.h. ▲, *control;* ■, *50 ppm copper and 0.1% Na_2CO_3.*

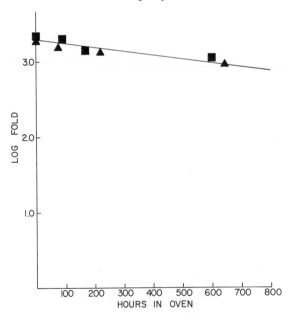

Figure 4A.   For test in dry oven at 100°C. ▲, *control;* ■, *50 ppm copper and 0.1% Na_2CO_3.*

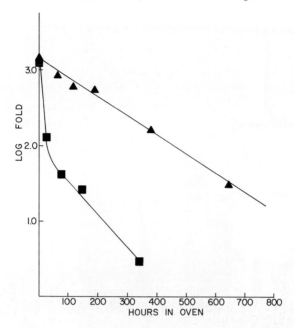

Figure 5.   For test in humid oven at 90°C and 50% r.h. ▲, *control;* ■, *50 ppm copper and 1.0% Na₂CO₃.*

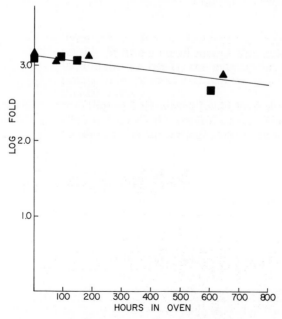

Figure 5A.   For test in dry oven at 100°C. ▲, *control;* ■, *50 ppm copper and 1.0% Na₂CO₃.*

Table V.   Foldur Kraft—1% Na$_2$CO$_3$

Hours in Oven	Fold Dry oven (100°C)	Fold Humid oven (90°C, 50% r.h.)	Brightness D.O.	Brightness H.O.	pH D.O.	pH H.O.	meq/kg D.O.	meq/kg H.O.
0	1444 ± 166		72		9.9		273	
69	—	900 ± 189	—	48	—	7.3	—	32
78	1147 ± 142	—	42	—	9.4	—	152	—
120	—	613 ± 160	—	48	—	7.0	—	0
189	—	551 ± 241	—	48	—	6.9	—	0
189	1369 ± 349	—	41	—	8.6	—	128	—
380	—	158 ± 42	—	43	—	6.8	—	4.0
645	—	31 ± 16	—	38	—	7.1	—	0
645	752 ± 136	—	43	—	7.8	—	84	—

Foldur Kraft—1% Na$_2$CO$_3$, 50 ppm Copper

Hours in Oven	Dry oven (100°C)	Humid oven (90°C, 50% r.h.)	Brightness D.O.	Brightness H.O.	pH D.O.	pH H.O.	meq/kg D.O.	meq/kg H.O.
0	1317		71		9.8		273	
24	—	143 ± 63	—	37	—	7.6	—	34
74	—	41 ± 24	—	36	—	7.0	—	0
84	1215 ± 283	—	38	—	9.1	—	146	—
144	—	25 ± 26	—	30	—	6.6	—	8
144	1164 ± 149	—	38	—	9.3	—	108	—
336	—	3 ± 3	—	23	—	6.7	—	4
600	—	0.6 ± 0.5	—	19	—	6.6	—	10
600	474 ± 63	—	40	—	7.6	—	40	—

slow oxidation taking place. Brightness has been lost. In the humid oven, more acid was produced and the pH dropped sharply. The copper-containing sample fell off badly in folding endurance as well as in brightness. This appears to be the free radical effect. The experiment illustrates that the dry oven gives much less information than the humid oven.

In the experiment (Figures 6 and 6A and Table VI) the copper catalyst was added to the paper before the alkaline salt. Paper was sprayed on both sides with dilute copper acetate solution until the wet weight indicated 50 ppm copper and then it was air dried. One set of paper dipped in magnesium bicarbonate solution (9 g/L magnesium carbonate). One set was given the Barrow two-step treatment—immersion in lime followed by immersion in calcium bicarbonate. Accelerated aging was carried out in the dry and humid ovens. In the humid oven, the copper–magnesium treated-paper regression line is close to that of the paper alkalized with magnesium carbonate. The calcium carbonate-treated paper is not so well protected. This bears out the findings from the oxygen–alkaline pulping process that magnesium is a more effective

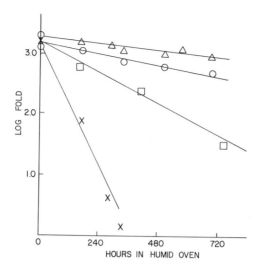

Figure 6. Calcium and magnesium carbonates compared as stabilizers in copper-treated paper. ○, 50 ppm copper–magnesium carbonate; □, 50 ppm copper–2-step calcium carbonate; △, control–magnesium carbonate; ✕, control at pH 4.8.

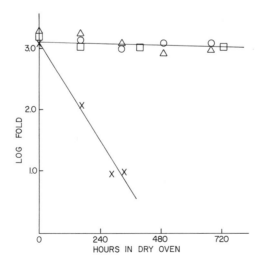

Figure 6A. Oxidative degradation effects shown in the humid oven (see Figure 6) disappear in the dry oven. ○, 50 ppm copper–magnesium carbonate; □, 50 ppm copper–2-step calcium carbonate; △, control–magnesium carbonate; ✕, control at pH 4.9.

Table VI. Foldur Kraft—50 ppm Copper, Magnesium Bicarbonate

Hours in Oven	Fold (½ kg)		Brightness		pH		meq/kg	
	Dry oven (100°C)	Humid oven (90°C, 50% r.h.)	D.O.	H.O.	D.O.	H.O.	D.O.	H.O.
0	1668 ± 334		72.8		8.7		140	
168	1394 ± 186	1176 ± 187	68.8	63.5	8.9	9.0	142	116
336	1024 ± 254	775 ± 129	67.3	59.5	8.5	8.5	110	96
504	1221 ± 288	634 ± 187	67.4	57.4	8.6	8.3	82	—
696	1077 ± 177	479 ± 125	66.8	57.7	8.8	8.3	100	100

Foldur Kraft—50 ppm Copper, Barrow Two-Step Calcium Treatment

Hours in Oven	Dry oven	Humid oven	D.O.	H.O.	D.O.	H.O.	D.O.	H.O.
0	1665 ± 229		73.5		8.5		366	
168	1229 ± 168	664 ± 144	70.4	62.8	8.8	8.6	388	378
408	1145 ± 198	240 ± 135	69.6	59.3	8.8	8.8	384	342
744	1061 ± 150	34 ± 24	68.6	55.5	9.3	8.2	382	347

stabilizer than calcium carbonate. Note that all points fall on the same line in the dry-oven aging as shown in Figure 6A.

The effect of KI is shown in Fiugre 7 and Table VII. A commercial paper bulked with plastic microspheres was analyzed using atomic

Table VII. Paper Bulked with Plastic Microspheres

Hours in Oven	Fold (½ kg)		Brightness		pH		meq/kg	
	Dry oven (100°C)	Humid oven (90°C, 50% r.h.)	D.O.	H.O.	D.O.	H.O.	D.O.	H.O.
0	1602		76.0		8.7		408	
144	1535	1012	69.6	66.0	8.6	9.0	496	474
312	929	652	64.8	60.4	8.5	8.5	494	454
888	137	11	50.7	48.7	8.2	8.3	462	304

Paper Dipped in 1% KI

Hours in Oven	Dry oven	Humid oven	D.O.	H.O.	D.O.	H.O.	D.O.	H.O.
0	1836		68.8		8.8		478	
72	1642	—	65.7	—	9.7	—	328	—
96	—	1189	—	64.8	—	8.7	—	448
144	1434	1607	60.4	63.6	8.5	8.8	474	472
288	981	1537	57.9	60.5	8.6	8.9	452	296
864	430	1270	43.4	53.2	8.4	8.7	330	264
1440	87	906	39.8	47.2	8.3	8.7	460	260

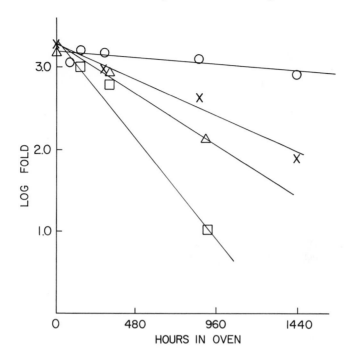

Figure 7. Potassium iodide represses humid oven oxidation in microsphere bulked paper. ○, *KI–humid;* □, *control–humid;* ×, *KI–dry;* △, *control–dry.*

absorption by L. Tang of this laboratory and found to contain 16 ppm copper, 341 ppm iron, and 0.7 ppm cobalt. The paper was given accelerated aging in the dry and humid ovens as received and after being immersed in 1% KI. The results are shown in the graph and tables. The bulked paper, as shown in the figure, gave a highly improved regression line for humid-oven aging after the iodide treatment.

Trier (*34*) described one bulked paper as being loaded with microspheres of a copolymer of vinylidene chloride and acrylonitrile. Such polymers are known to split off hydrochloric acid. While this may have occurred in oven aging, the pH of the sample did not drop below 7 so acid degradation does not seem to have been involved. On the other hand, the paper did degrade rapidly in the humid oven, and this was very well corrected by the KI treatment. From the evidence in the literature peroxides and, through the catalysts, free radicals appear to be at work, which the KI corrected. This is an application that recalls its use in oxygen–alkaline pulping and in the prevention of the peroxide defects in microfilm.

Conclusions

• The presence of transition metal compounds as oxidation catalysts can cause rapid degradation of calcium carbonate-alkalized papers under humid conditions. Magnesium carbonate offers better protection than calcium carbonate.

• TAPPI method T-453-ts-63, which uses only the dry oven, gives a satisfactory estimate of the stability of acid paper but has no value in predicting oxidative degradation or the life of a paper containing the oxidation catalysts. The humid oven will find both acid degradation and oxidative degradation.

• Dry storage of paper will not protect against acid but will minimize the effect of oxidation catalysts and oxidation.

• Temperature and humid conditions of storage, and the presence of oxidation catalysts in the paper, as well as the pH and alkaline reserve, must be taken into account in applying the Arrhenius relation to predict the life of paper.

Literature Cited

1. "Papermaking, Art and Craft," p. 9, Library of Congress, Washington, D.C., 1968.
2. Ibid., p. 16.
3. Ibid., p. 18.
4. Levey, M., *Trans. Am. Philos. Soc., New Ser.* (1962) **52**, Pt. 4, 10.
5. Murray, J., "Observations and Experiments on the Bad Composition of Modern Paper," Whittaker, London, 1824.
6. Hansard, T. C., "Typographia," Baldwin, Craddock and Joy, London, 1825.
7. Herring, R., "Paper and Papermaking, Ancient and Modern," 2nd ed. 81, p. 97, Longman, Brown, Green and Longmans, London, 1856.
8. Johnson, R., *Library J.* (1891) **16**, 241.
9. Kingery, R. E., "Permanent/Durable Book Paper," p. 15, Virginia State Library #16, Richmond, 1960.
10. Martens, A., *Mitt. Materialprufungsanst.. Tech. Hochsch. Darmstadt* (1911) **29**, 57–60; *J. Soc. Chem. Ind.* (1911) **30**, 414.
11. Lydenberg, H. M., *Library Journal* (1915) **40**, 240–242.
12. Herzberg, W., *Papierfabrikant* (1914) **42**, No. 17, 478; *J. Soc. Chem. Ind.*, **33**, 545.
13. Kohler, S., Hall, G., *Pap. Ind.* (1925) **7**, 1059–1063; Hall, G., *Pap. Trade J.* (1926), April 8, Technical Section, 185–191.
14. Jarrell, T. D., Hankins, J. M., Veitch, F. P., *Tech. Bull. No. 334*, U.S. Department of Agriculture, Washington, D.C., Sept. 1932 as adapted by Williams, J. C., *Bull. Am. Group, I.I.C.* (1971) **12**, 16–32.
15. Schierholtz, O., U.S. Patent **2,033,452**, 1936.
16. Clapp, V. W., *Scholarly Publishing* (1971) Jan., 107–124.
17. Thomas, J. J., "Deterioration and Preservation of Library Materials," Winger, H. W., Smith, R. D., Eds., pp. 99–107, University of Chicago Press, 1970.
18. Hanson, F. S., *Pap. Ind. Pap. World* (1939) Feb., 1157–1164.
19. Barrow, W. J., "The Manufacture and Testing of Durable Book Papers," Church, R. W., Ed., p. 25, Virginia State Library, Richmond, 1960.

20. Cowling, E. B., "Cellulose as a Chemical and Energy Resource," Wilke, C. R., Ed., pp. 164–168, Interscience, John Wiley & Sons, 1975.
21. Battista, O. A., *Ind. Eng. Chem.* (1962) **54**, No. 9, 20–29.
22. Golova, D. P., Nosova, N. I., *Russ. Chem. Rev.* (1973) **42** (4) 327–338.
23. Ericcson, B., Lindgren, B. O., Theander, O., *Sven. Papperstidn.* (1971) **74**, 757–765.
24. Klienert, T. N., Marraccini, L. M., *Sven. Papperstidn.* (1963) **66**, 189–195.
25. Robert, A., Traynard, P., Martin-Borret, O., U.S. Patent **3,384,533.**
26. Noreus, S. E. O., Samuelson, H. O., U.S. Patent **3,652,386.**
27. Minor, J. L., Sanyer, N., *J. Polym. Sci., Part C* (1971) **36**, 73–84.
28. McCamy, C. S., Pope, C. I., Nat. Bur. Stand. Tech. Note, #261 (1965).
29. Henn, R. W., Mack, B. D., *Photogr. Sci. Eng.* (1969) **13**, 276.
30. Borchardt, L. C., Butler, J. P., *Anal. Chem.* (1957) 414–419.
31. Praskiewicz, R. W., Subt, S. S. Y., Government Printing Office, Washington, D. C., private communication, 1976.
32. Gilbert, A. F., Pavlovova, E., Rapson, W. H., *Tappi* (1973) **56**, No. 6, 95–99.
33. Manoucheri, M., Samuelson, O., *Sven. Papperstidn.* (1973) **76**, 486–492.
34. Trier, G., *Tappi* (1972) **55**, 769–771.

RECEIVED March 24, 1977.

4

Methylmagnesium Carbonate—An Improved Nonaqueous Deacidification Agent

GEORGE B. KELLY, JR., LUCIA C. TANG, and MARTA K. KRASNOW

Preservation Research and Testing Office, Library of Congress, Washington, D.C. 20540

Methylmagnesium carbonate, prepared by carbonation of a solution of magnesium methoxide, is compared with the magnesium methoxide as a deacidification agent for paper. Although the two materials are equally effective in deacidification and in prolonging the life of the paper, the methylmagnesium carbonate is two to 10 times as stable to water, depending upon the solvent used. This stability avoids premature precipitation, minimizes surface deposits, and increases the interval between cleanings of equipment, making the solution much more convenient to use. The use is covered by U.S. Patent No. 3,939,091, February 17, 1976, assigned to the Library of Congress. A royalty-free, nonexclusive license will be available.

The detrimental effect of acid in paper has been well documented (*1, 2, 3, 4*), and numerous treatments have been proposed to alleviate the effect. Schierholz (*5*), Barrow (*6*), and others have proposed methods of neutralizing the acids in paper based on aqueous treatments. However, many papers are sensitive to aqueous treatments, either because of the fragility of the paper or the tendency of the inks or colors to run when exposed to water, and for these papers a nonaqueous deacidification treatment is required.

One of the most widely used nonaqueous deacidification processes is that proposed by Smith (*7*) based on a methanol or methanol–Freon solution of magnesium methoxide. This process is very effective and leaves a good alkaline reserve, but the magnesium methoxide is very sensitive to water, and this leads to inconvenience in the handling and processing of paper as a result of premature precipitation. These inconveniences were recognized, and a better nonaqueous deacidification agent was being sought when a reference to methymagnesium cabonate was found in the literature (*10*). This compound was easily prepared, was soluble in nonaqueous solvents, and had been extensively investigated as a reagent for organic syntheses. It promised a much more nearly neutral treatment than magnesium methoxide and the prospect of hydrolyzing directly to magnesium carbonate. It was therefore decided to investigate its use as a deacidification agent in comparison with magnesium methoxide.

Magnesium compounds are particularly attractive as deacidification agents as they tend to be more soluble than those of calcium or other alkaline earths, which makes their use more convenient and makes the attainment of an adequate alkaline reserve somewhat easier. Magnesium compounds had also been reported to act as stabilizers in oxygen wood-pulping operations by Robert in 1965 (*8*). The stabilizing effect was investigated in detail by Gilbert et al. in 1973, who reported that the effect was a result of inactivation of metallic oxidation catalysts such as iron (*9*). Magnesium compounds therefore appeared to offer the possibility of protecting the cellulose from oxidation as well as degradation. The role of magnesium compounds in paper oxidation was discussed further by Williams (*11*).

Experimental

Methylmagnesium carbonate was prepared by saturating an 8% solution of magnesium methoxide in methanol with carbon dioxide at room temperature (25°C) over 2 hr. The resultant solution was clear and colorless. Portions were diluted 10:1 with various solvents and observed for 24 hr for evidence of precipitation. The methanol solution was evaporated to dryness under vacuum on a steam bath, and a friable, glossy white solid was recovered; solubility in a number of solvents was determined at the ratio of 1 g of solid in 50 mL solvent.

For treatment of papers, an 8% solution of magnesium methoxide was diluted to about 1% (0.116M by analysis) with trifluorotrichloroethane (Freon TF) and divided into two portions. One of these was saturated with carbon dioxide over 3 hr; the other was reserved for comparison. The rate of conversion was followed by periodic pH measurements on the solution and on 2-mL portions of the solution which were diluted to 100 mL with distilled water. Similar portions were also absorbed on filter paper, dried, and the pH of the paper was measured.

The magnesium methoxide and methylmagnesium carbonate solutions were used to treat a series of three papers. Each 8½ $\times$ 11-in. sheet was covered with a separate 25-mL portion of one of the solutions in a shallow enameled pan, saturated, drained, and dried. After treatment, the treated sheets and the untreated controls were conditioned (TAPPI T-402) and tested for physical properties: brightness (TAPPI T-452 modified to use a single sheet against a white, glazed clay backing of 66 brightness); MIT fold (TAPPI T-511); pH and titration (2.5 g

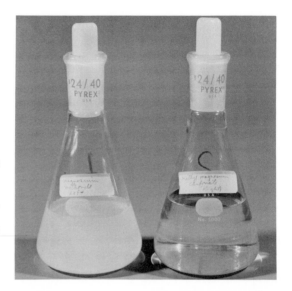

Figure 1. Comparative stability to water of magnesium methoxide and methylmagnesium carbonate in methanol. Left flask: magnesium methoxide plus 0.5 mL water. Right flask: methylmagnesium carbonate plus 5 mL water.

paper was pulped with 250 mL water in a Waring Blendor for 45 sec. The pH was measured on resultant pulp with a pH meter while stirring with a magnetic stirrer. Titration was with standard 0.1N NaOH to pH 7.0 if the paper was acid. If the paper was alkaline, excess standard acid was added, the solution was boiled for 1 min with agitation to expel CO_2, cooled, and back-titrated with 0.1N NaOH to pH 7.0); thickness (TMI Model 549E micrometer, average of 10 samples); tensile strength (TAPPI T-494 modified to 15-mm strip); and accelerated aging (TAPPI T-453 modified to 100°C and extended to 36 days).

The convenience and operating characteristics of the two solutions were judged further by applying the solutions to paper by brushing with a 7-in. wide paste brush, the paper backed with blotting paper to absorb edge run over. Sufficient solution was applied to wet the papers thoroughly and distributed evenly with the brush. The convenience of spraying was judged by spraying the paper with a manual pump-type plastic sprayer (Figure 1), pumping the solution five to seven times twice a day until plugging occurred.

Results and Discussion

Methylmagnesium carbonate is reported by Finkbeiner and Stiles to have the formula $CH_3OMgOCO_2CH_3 \cdot XCO_2$ where X may vary with solvent and temperature (10). While this formula is empirically correct, the structure has not been conclusively established and may be more complex than indicated.

Methylmagnesium carbonate is much more stable to water than magnesium methoxide, as illustrated in Figure 1. The methylmagnesium carbonate solution in methanol was able to absorb 10 times as much water as the magnesium methoxide solution without precipitation, but it does precipitate with larger amounts of water. Pure methanol is not suitable as a solvent for much of the deacidification work since it frequently causes movement of inks and dyes on the paper. To overcome this problem, the working solution is usually the commercial 8% solution of magnesium methoxide diluted to about 1% with a poor solvent such as Freon TF. Such a mixture is satisfactory for most deacidification work and is also recommended with methylmagnesium carbonate. If the Freons should be restricted in the future because of their damage to the ozone layer, the dilution could be made with a variety of other solvents which may include toluene, ether, acetone, tetrahydrofurane, or chlorinated hydrocarbons, which should provide considerable flexibility in choosing a suitable replacement.

In the methanol–Freon solvent mixture the methylmagnesium carbonate is only about twice as tolerant to water (as measured by the volume of water necessary to cause precipitation) as magnesium methoxide, but this appears to be sufficient to eliminate most, if not all, of the problems with water sensitivity. The difference in stability is apparently a result of the lower concentration of carbon dioxide in the methanol–Freon mixture since the Freon is a much poorer solvent for carbon dioxide than is methanol.

The solubility of carbon dioxide in the solvent also affects the rate of reaction in the preparation of methylmagnesium carbonate as shown in Table I. In pure methanol the pH became constant after carbonation for 40 min at room temperature, indicating complete reaction, whereas in the methanol–Freon solvent, the reaction takes about 2 hr.

Table I. Preparation of Methylmagnesium Carbonate

Effect of Carbon Dioxide and Solvent on pH of 0.116M Solutions

Carbona-tion Time (min)	Methanol Solvent			Methanol–Freon TF Solvent[b]		
	pH	Appear-ance	Water Dilution pH[a]	pH	Appear-ance	Water Dilution pH[a]
0	11.9	clear	10.4	11.5	clear	10.7
10	8.5	clear	7.3	11.6	clear	10.7
20	8.3	clear	6.8	8.7	cloudy	10.3
40	8.2	clear	6.8	8.7	cloudy	8.8
80	8.2	clear	6.8	8.7	sl. cloudy	7.7
100				8.7	v. sl. cloudy	7.5
150				8.7	clear	7.4

[a] 2 ml in 200 mL water.
[b] 1 methanol to 7 Freon TF.

In spite of the longer time required, there is an advantage in using the methanol–Freon solvent mixture for the carbonation reaction since it contains a built-in indicator. The mixture becomes cloudy with precipitate and then clears as the carbonation is continued. The reaction is complete when the solution becomes clear again, and it is then ready for immediate use.

Although it would appear that the methylmagnesium carbonate solution with a pH of 7.4 would be a much milder treatment for paper than magnesium methoxide at pH 10.4, this is true only while the paper is in contact with the solution. When the solutions were added to filter paper and dried, the pH was about 10.2 with either treatment. This was a little surprising at first since the methylmagnesium carbonate-treated paper showed effervescence on treatment with acid immediately after drying, indicating that the methylmagnesium carbonate had hydrolyzed to magnesium carbonate, whereas the paper treated with magnesium methoxide required two days exposure to air before it showed noticeable effervescence with acid treatment. However, magnesium tends to form basic carbonates of varying composition depending upon the method of preparation, so it is presumed that the carbonate formed from the methylmagnesium carbonate is of the basic variety. This would explain the equivalence in the pH of the two treated papers as it would require very little magnesium hydroxide present with the carbonate to raise the pH to the indicated level.

If desired, the methylmagnesium carbonate can be recovered as a white, brittle solid by evaporation of the solution under vacuum at temperatures up to $100°C$. Unlike magnesium methoxide, which becomes almost completely insoluble on recovery as a solid, methylmagnesium carbonate solid is very soluble in methanol but tends to dissolve faster if the methanol is presaturated with carbon dioxide. The solid form provides a convenient method of storage or shipment of the material, much like instant coffee.

The effect of treatment with methylmagnesium carbonate and with magnesium methoxide on the properties and aging characteristics of paper was investigated using three papers, a bookpaper, an offset printing paper, and a handmade paper, with varying fiber composition and pH as shown in Table II. Each paper sheet was treated in a shallow tray with a separate 25-mL portion of the appropriate solution of equivalent concentration, sufficient to saturate the sheet. The sheet was then drained and dried to complete the treatment. The pH and alkaline reserve of the treated papers from the two solutions are closely equivalent, as shown in Table III.

The treating operation provided a dramatic illustration of the difference in stability of the two solutions. The magnesium methoxide solution

Table II. Papers Used in Deacidification Treatments

No.	Identification	Composition	pH	Additives
1.	Commercial book	30% bleached southern kraft 70% bleached hardwood kraft	6.5	13 parts clay
2.	Commercial offset	30% bleached · southern kraft 70% hardwood soda	6.1	15 parts clay rosin & starch
3.	Laboratory handmade	33.3% refined rag 33.3% bleached kraft 33.3% bleached sulfite	5.3	1% Neuphor[a] 3% alum

[a] Modified rosin.

formed gelatinous precipitate immediately on contact with the paper and left visible deposits on the surface upon drying. Some of the deposits could be brushed off readily, but they could not be eliminated entirely without damaging the surface of the paper. In the case of handsheets, the deposits were very heavy and were sufficient to have made writing or printing on the sheet difficult to read. This may have been a result of the somewhat rougher texture of these sheets which caused the deposits to adhere more readily than on the smoother commercial papers.

The papers treated with the methylmagnesium carbonate solution showed no precipitation even when allowed to soak in the solution for several minutes and had no visible deposits when they were dried. The texture of the treated papers was also quite different. The treated papers had a pleasant, natural feel, while those treated with magnesium methoxide felt stiff and harsh. The physical properties of the treated papers, the untreated controls, and the solvent-only treated papers, along with the percent fold retention after accelerated aging for 36 days at 100°C, are shown in Table III.

Since the treated papers all ended with essentially the same chemical impregnant, a basic magnesium carbonate, properties were essentially the same from either treatment. There were some minor differences. The surface deposits from the magnesium methoxide showed up as increased paper thickness and in the case of the handmade paper, as significantly higher brightness from the white surface deposits. The solvent alone shows some beneficial effect, presumably a result of washing out of some of the free acid and other impurities in the paper, but the improvement by the solvent alone is very small.

Although the differences in physical properties for the papers treated by the two solutions tend to be minimal, investigation of the techniques

Table III.   Properties

Paper No.	Treatment	pH	Alkaline Reserve $(MgCO_3\%)$
1	None, control	6.5	none
	Mg methoxide	9.1	3.67
	Mg methyl carbonate	8.9	3.17
2	None, control	6.1	none
	Mg methoxide	10.2	3.42
	Mg methyl carbonate	9.8	3.47
	Solvent only	6.5	none
3	None, control	5.3	none
	Mg methoxide	10.3	4.62
	Mg methyl carbonate	10.3	5.12

[a] 36 days at 100°C.

of applying the solutions to paper confirmed that important differences exist in the operating characteristics. The increased stability towards water permits the impregnation of paper by the various methods with greater ease and less tendency towards premature precipitation. The advantage in dipping operations has been discussed previously. With large documents such as posters or maps, dipping is often inconvenient, and for these documents the application may be made with a wide paste brush. The solution is applied and brushed evenly in sufficient amount to thoroughly dampen the paper. The brushes tend to become clogged with gelatinous precipitate after a period of time and need to be cleaned. The period of time between cleanings is about doubled with the use of methylmagnesium carbonate in place of magnesium methoxide, and surface deposits on the paper are also substantially reduced, based on our experience.

The spraying of the solutions was also investigated since magnesium methoxide has been available commercially as a pressure spray package for some time. Considerable difficulty with nozzle plugging has been experienced from these sprayers. Unfortunately, no facilities for filling pressure bottles were available, so a plastic, manual pump-type sprayer, similar to those used to apply window cleaners, was selected as a reasonable alternative (Figure 2). Firm pressure on the pump gave a fine mist with good distribution in a cone-type spray pattern with this sprayer, and the size of the orifice approximated that of the pressure bottles.

Either of the solutions could be sprayed intermittently from these sprayers for a full day with no sign of plugging under the conditions existing in our laboratory (24°C, 45% r.h.). However, on standing over-of **Treated Papers**

MIT Fold (½ kg)		Tensile Strength (kg)		Thickness (mm)	Brightness (%)	Fold Retention after Aging[a] (%)	
MD	CD	MD	CD			MD	CD
558	470	5.43	3.46	0.097	74.5	16	23
532	549	5.51	3.50	0.122	74.6	46	64
483	691	5.10	3.75	0.098	74.0	56	52
565	316	6.18	3.22	0.086	75.4	15	22
670	449	6.83	3.17	0.107	75.4	46	38
575	448	5.60	3.30	0.091	73.0	50	40
593	226	4.91	2.51	0.092	76.6	23	31
5499[b]		6.30[b]		0.188	78.0	1[b]	
5501[b]		5.93[b]		0.200	80.9	54[b]	
5237[b]		6.39[b]		0.194	78.0	48[b]	

[b] Handmade sheet, random fiber orientation.

Figure 2. Pump-type sprayer used in spraying tests

night, the magnesium methoxide sprayer became partially plugged and would not give a good spray pattern. The methylmagnesium carbonate sprayer still worked fine with no sign of plugging.

The magnesium methoxide spray nozzle was cleaned with a fine wire and hard pumping to restore the spray pattern, and the test was continued, spraying the two solutions with five to seven pumpings twice a day on an exactly equal basis. With daily clean out of the nozzle, the magnesium methoxide spray lasted six days before plugging so solidly that the nozzle could not be cleaned. The methylmagnesium carbonate sprayer maintained a good spray pattern for 10 days with no difficulty beyond an occasional, slight interference with the spray pattern on the initial one or two pumps after standing overnight. However, the spray nozzle cleaned itself each time without requiring any probing with a wire. The test lasted 11 days. Here again, the improved performance of the methylmagnesium carbonate in this test is quite clear.

Methylmagnesium carbonate and magnesium methoxide have been extensively tested in the Restoration Office of the Library of Congress. Of the two, methylmagnesium carbonate has been found to be more stable to changes in enivronmental conditions and to have a wider tolerance to many of the different application techniques. While it is perhaps too early to draw too many conclusions about the future uses, it does appear to be most useful in treating materials which cannot, for one reason or another, be subjected to aqueous treatments. Of particular interest is its success in the treatment of fragile manuscript material. In summary, methylmagnesium carbonate offers significant advantages in the treatment of papers because of its much greater stability to water so that premature precipitation is avoided and the time required for cleaning equipment is materially reduced without sacrificing protection of the papers as a result of the treatment.

The use of methylmagnesium carbonate for deacidification has been covered by U. S. Patent No. 3,939,091 issued February 17, 1976.

Literature Cited

1. Jarrell, T. D., Hankins, J. M., Veitch, F. P., Technical Bulletin No. 334, U. S. Department of Agriculture, Washington, D.C. (September 1932).
2. Hanson, F. S., "Resistance of Paper to Natural Aging," *Paper Ind. Paper World*, Feb. 1939, pp. 1157–1164.
3. Hudson, F. L., "Acidity of 17th and 18th Century Books in Two Libraries," *Pap. Technol.* (1967) 8, 189–190, 196.
4. Barrow, W. J., "Permanence/Durability of the Book II," p. 39, Dietz Press, Richmond, 1964.
5. Schierholtz, O. J., U. S. Patent 2,033,452 (March 10, 1936).
6. Barrow, W. J., "Permanence/Durability of the Book III," "Spray Deacidification," Dietz Press, Richmond, 1964.

7. Smith, R. D., "The Non-Aqueous Deacidification of Paper and Books," Ph.D. thesis, University of Chicago, December 1970.
8. Robert, A., Traynard, P., Martin-Borret, O., French Patent No. 1,387,853, February 6, 1965 (*see* also U. S. Patent 3,384,533 (May 21, 1968)).
9. Gilbert, A. F., Pavlovova, E., Rapson, W. H., "Mechanism of Magnesium Retardation of Cellulose Degradation during Oxygen Bleaching," *TAPPI* (1973) **56** (6) 95–99.
10. Finkbeiner, H. L., Stiles, M., *J. Am. Chem. Soc.* (1963) **85**, 616.
11. Williams, J. C., Fowler, C. S., Lyon, M. S., Merrill, T. L., ADV. CHEM. SER. (1977) **164**, 37.

RECEIVED February 9, 1977.

5

Morpholine Deacidification of Whole Books

BERNARD F. WALKER

W. J. Barrow Research Laboratory, Inc., Richmond, Va. 23221

A process for deacidifying whole books has been developed, based on impregnation with a mixture of morpholine vapor and water vapor. Even after accelerated aging at 100°C for 8 days, the paper from processed books maintains a pH close to neutral; the rate of folding endurance loss during accelerated aging is retarded by a factor of about 3.5, showing increased life expectancy for the treated paper. Aging in moist air containing sulfur dioxide indicates that the treated paper also has a degree of resistance to polluted atmospheres. The process is currently being demonstrated at the Virginia State Library in Richmond, Va. on 250 books per day. The equipment is fully automated; present estimates show a total deacidification cost of about $0.32/lb.

The problem of deteriorating books in library and archival collections has been described by many authors; the severity and the urgency of the problem have long been apparent, but more detailed information is available in articles by Lowe (*1*) and Williams (*2*). Several useful deacidification processes are available which can be applied to sheets of paper or to single book pages, but the labor-intensive nature of such page-at-a-time procedures limits their use to relatively small numbers of the more valuable books.

The objective of the present work was to develop a deacidification process which could be applied simultaneously to a substantial number of books and be much more reasonable in time and cost than the single-page procedures. The exploratory phase of the project was started in 1970; the past six years' work have culminated in a process which inexpensively deacidifies about 85 lb of books in 60 min and which substantially retards their subsequent deterioration rate.

From the information generated since 1970 only two main aspects are dealt with here: a description of the process in its current form and the effect of the process on the properties of the paper. The data presented is only a small fraction of the available data but is adequate for illustrative purposes.

Analytical Methods

In testing morpholine-treated paper samples and their corresponding untreated controls, the standard methods of the Technical Association of the Pulp and Paper Industry (TAPPI) were used with few exceptions. In evaluating the permanence of paper, both dry and moist aging procedures were used, both of which were somewhat more elaborate than the dry aging method specified by TAPPI. The residual nitrogen content of treated paper was measured by an Antek digital nitrogen analyzer. Monitoring and controlling the concentrations of free morpholine which could be found in the vicinity of the processing unit and in the air around processed books were done with a Miran infrared spectrometer. During development, the processing parameters were adjusted so that the Occupational Safety and Health Administration (OSHA) requirements for morpholine concentrations in the atmosphere were met fully.

Since the term paper covers a wide range of material compositions and since even a single lot of the same paper shows great variability when the samples tested are small in area (as is the case in testing samples cut from book pages), statistics were used extensively to select the number of replicate tests to be made in relation to the scatter of each test and to evaluate the significance level of the differences between treated and untreated samples. As an example, the folding endurance test on papers of poor uniformity requires a minimum of 50 replicates if the difference between average folds of, say, 250 and 350 is to be just significant at the 95% confidence level. Appropriate statistical programs were developed for use on a Hewlett-Packard 9810A calculator.

Process and Equipment

The process is simple; it consists of placing the books to be deacidified in an air-tight container, then removing most of the air with a vacuum pump to an absolute pressure of 0.5–1.0 torr. A mixture of morpholine vapor and water vapor is admitted to the container for about 10 min, during which the alkaline vapors completely penetrate each book. Evacuation to 2–3 mm Hg removes most of the residual morpholine, and the remaining chemical is flushed out by letting in air to 700 mm Hg and evacuating the chamber to 20 mm Hg; these last two steps are repeated several times. All morpholine removed is disposed of through a water-spray scrubber to the sewer so that at no time during processing can free morpholine escape into the room.

Figure 1 gives an overall view of the appearance of the equipment currently used for 80 lb of books. The unit was manufactured by Vacu-

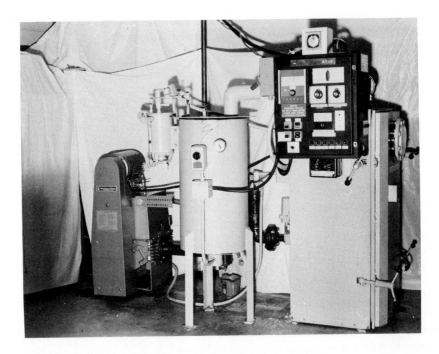

Figure 1.   Deacidification unit

dyne/Altair, Inc. in Chicago. It occupies about 10 ft × 12 ft and will readily fit into a small room. The unit has four main parts: the chamber to contain the books, the evaporator, the control panel, and the vacuum pump. The process controls were subsequently modified extensively by this laboratory.

Figure 2 shows the books loaded onto the shelves with the door open. Figure 3 shows the control panel. The process is initiated by turning the handle in the upper right-hand corner toward "Evacuation." The fully

Table I.   Classification of Books Processed

Years of Publication

Before 1900	1900– 1920	1921– 1940	1941– 1960	1961– Present
1%	8%	15%	29%	47%

Type

Fiction	Nonfiction	Government	Bound Periodicals	Foreign
8%	44%	15%	10%	23%

automated process runs by itself for the 60 min of processing time. Finally, the door is opened, and the books are removed. Automation of the unit permits operation by semiskilled labor.

During developmental work, thermistors taped to several of the book pages inside the processor allowed monitoring of temperature changes at the actual site of deacidification, the paper itself. Temperature changes arising from moisture loss by the paper and from morpholine–water–cellulose interactions could be detected readily. The books used were obtained from the Exchange and Gifts Division of the Library of Congress. Table I shows their distribution by type and by year of publication.

Figure 2. Books loaded ready for processing

Figure 3.   Control panel

Table II.   Effect of Morpholine Treatment on pH of Book Pages

Book No.	Before Treatment	Immediately after Treatment	Stored Several Weeks	Oven-Aged Equivalent of 100 Years
31	5.5	8.4	6.5	6.3
24	5.1	8.0	6.4	6.0
21	5.6	8.2	6.3	6.0
68	5.9	7.8	6.4	6.1
14	5.1	8.0	6.7	6.3
17	5.2	8.2	6.7	6.5

Experimental Data

pH. Table II shows that treatment causes the original pH of about 5 to increase to about 8. After standing several weeks in the room, residual traces of free morpholine dissipate, and the pH stabilizes at about 6.3–6.7. Even after accelerated aging, the average pH remains above 6.0. This numerically modest increase in pH reflects a substantial decrease in acid content.

Fold Loss Rate. A direct way of evaluating the effect of the morpholine process on the stabilization of paper is to measure the rate at which its folding endurance deteriorates before and after treatment. Figure 4 typifies the effect. The two lines are for the same paper aged in a dry oven at 100°C; the line with the lesser slope reflects morpholine-treated

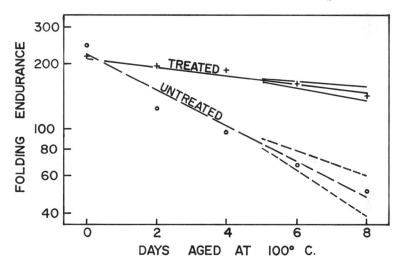

Figure 4.   Effect of morpholine treatment on rate of fold loss

paper and that with the steeper slope is the untreated control. The converging lines are 95% confidence limits around the slopes. In this case, the pH of the paper was raised 1.5 units by the morpholine process, and the change in slope shows that the aging rate was substantially reduced. This graph is a composite of several sets of data from the control book used in comparing a smaller laboratory processor with the present 50-book processor.

Since the reactivity of paper towards deacidifying processes varies greatly with the type of paper and its condition, one would expect that the improvement in aging rate would vary from one paper to another. To illustrate this, Figure 5 shows a small improvement in aging rate, and Figure 6 shows a greater improvement. These last two figures also

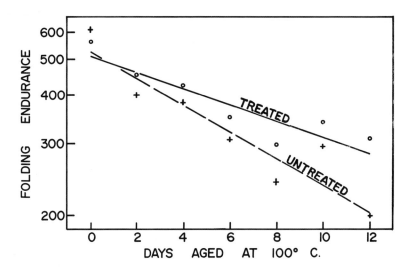

Figure 5. Change in aging rate resulting from morpholine treatment

show the dispersion of the data points about an individual regression line when using 50 replicate fold tests for each point.

Life Expectancy Estimates. If the end of the useful life of a paper is arbitrarily defined as a folding endurance of one double fold, rate-of-fold-loss lines such as those in Figure 4 can be extrapolated until they reach one double fold, and the corresponding accelerated-aging intercepts on the time axis can be compared directly. This gives a measure of the extent of improvement resulting from treatment.

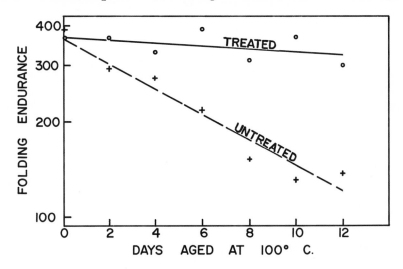

Figure 6. Change in aging rate resulting from morpholine treatment

From the conservator's point of view, it would be useful to convert these accelerated-aging times to equivalent years of natural aging so that estimates could be made of how many additional years of life expectancy are provided by applying the morpholine treatment. Unfortunately, it is not yet possible to do this unequivocally because of the uncertainty of the relationship between accelerated aging at elevated temperatures and natural aging at ambient temperatures. Estimates of the length of natural aging equivalent to 72 hr at 100°C of accelerated aging vary from 18.5 years to 306 years; many published values center around 25 years.

Although the relationship appears to vary widely with the type of paper and the exact test conditions used, it seems certain that a relationship does indeed exist. Thus, as shown in Figure 4, morpholine treatment prolongs the useful life of paper under conditions of accelerated aging and also corresponds to an increased life expectancy under conditions of natural aging. The significance of these findings is that from all the tests made on the morpholine treatment, an average book is estimated to last about 2½ times longer than its untreated counterpart. More recent changes in processing procedure have increased this factor to 3–5.

Paper Property Changes. Tables III, IV, and V show evaluations of possible changes in the properties of paper which might be caused by the morpholine process. As to folding endurance, of the 36 books tested, five showed higher fold after treatment, six showed lower fold, and 25 were unchanged. Table III indicates that the changes resulting from treatment can be either positive or negative. However, as shown in earlier figures, even when the fold strength decreases after treatment, the rate of fold loss also decreases so that after extended aging, the treated sample exhibits the better fold characteristics. Table IV shows changes in tear strength resulting from morpholine treatment. They are insignificantly small. Another set of tests was made for tensile strength; Table V shows no measurable change. The last three sets of data indicate that morpholine treatment does not harm the strength of paper significantly.

Color Changes. Amines can cause color changes in paper; the extent of the possible changes was estimated by measuring brightness according to TAPPI standard T-452. The data are given in Table VI and indicate that before oven aging, brightness reductions do not exceed 3–4 points. This is a consequence of the low concentration of morpholine used in the process; only occasionally is a brightness change observed. Although Table VI shows a detectable change in two of the samples, with the last 3,000 books processed such changes have been apparent in less than 1% of the cases.

Permanence of Deacidification. If paper were composed of chemically inert fibers, one would expect that a brief exposure to the alkaline vapor of morpholine would have no appreciable effect since there would

Table III. Fold Change from Morpholine Treatment

Sample No.		Folding Endurance	95% Confidence Limits	Results
38	Untreated	2019	1752–2286	no change
	Treated	2016	1849–2183	
2	Untreated	116	106–125	no change
	Treated	132	118–146	
5	Untreated	8	7–9	increased
	Treated	12	10–14	
66	Untreated	114	76–151	decreased
	Treated	49	27–70	

Table IV. Effect of Morpholine Treatment on Tear Strength of Book Paper

Book No.		Tear Resistance (g)	95% Confidence Limits	Results
54	Untreated	64	65–63	no change
	Treated	63	64–61	
66	Untreated	28	28–27	no change
	Treated	27	29–26	
19	Untreated	49	50–48	decreased
	Treated	46	48–45	
22	Untreated	49	50–48	no change
	Treated	50	51–49	

Table V. Effect of Morpholine Treatment on Tensile Strength

Book No.		Tensile Strength (kg/m)	95% Confidence Limits	Results
66	Untreated	214	187–241	no change
	Treated	201	184–217	
19	Untreated	384	367–400	no change
	Treated	388	377–399	
21	Untreated	368	354–383	no change
	Treated	381	368–395	
54	Untreated	462	424–501	no change
	Treated	423	395–452	

Table VI. Effect of Morpholine Treatment on Brightness

Book No.		Unaged	Observable Yellowing
10	Untreated	58	none
	Treated	55	
66	Untreated	68	slight
	Treated	64	
54	Untreated	77	slight
	Treated	75	
76	Untreated	83	none
	Treated	83	

be no specific affinity between morpholine and such fibers. However, cellulose has properties which strongly favor the adsorption and retention of morpholine. Since it has a very large specific surface, it contains appreciable amounts of adsorbed moisture and is often acid-sized; even pure cellulose contains acidic groups. Also, under mildly swelling conditions, cellulose can form the so-called "inclusions" with molecules the size of benzene or morpholine. During deswelling of cellulose, such molecules can be more or less firmly held or "included" within the paper structure.

Morpholine itself has three characteristics which favor its adsorption and retention by paper: first, it is an amine, and amines are known to adsorb tenaciously on many surfaces; second, it is alkaline; and third, it has a mild swelling effect (3) on the less-ordered regions of cellulose. When one considers these characteristics of paper and the known characteristics of morpholine, it is easy to see how paper could bind morpholine with some tenacity. Morpholine is probably adsorbed on the large specific surface of cellulose, and it will certainly react with accessible

Table VII. Morpholine Retention by Treated Books Aged in Ambient Air[a]

Book No.	Nitrogen Content Untreated (ppm)	Increase in Nitrogen Content (as Morpholine)	
		1 Mo after Treatment	3 Mo after Treatment
A	713	833	no change
B	529	1440	no change
C	643	1443	no change
D	649	1145	no change

[a] Each sample is an average of 20 tests.

acidic constituents of the paper. As a mild swelling agent, morpholine has the possibility of being included within the cellulose structure. For these reasons, one would expect that morpholine-treated paper would more or less firmly retain some morpholine.

In fact, this does happen. Table VII illustrates tests of morpholine-treated paper corrected for the nitrogen content of untreated controls; a significant increase in residual nitrogen is apparent, which in this case can originate only from retention of morpholine. After a 3-mo additional exposure to ambient air, no change was detected, and it is therefore concluded that exposure to ambient air at normal humidity does not reduce the bound morpholine content.

Resistance to Polluted Atmospheres. There is general agreement that it is desirable for a deacidified paper to have built into it some degree of protection against future inadvertent exposures to acidic atmospheres. The buffering capacity of a paper above pH 7.0 is termed "alkaline reserve." There is no consensus as to the necessary extent of this reserve, but the Preservation Office of the Library of Congress has suggested 3% as a reasonable level for reserve alkalinity, expressed as calcium carbonate.

Using the normal titration method on morpholine-treated paper samples, reserve alkalinity levels of less than 1% are found. However, in view of the previously mentioned possibilities for interaction between cellulose and morpholine and the observed reduction in the aging rate of morpholine-treated paper, it was thought likely that morpholine could be present in a form not immediately titratable but which might still offer some degree of protection against acid attack.

It was therefore considered useful to age under conditions which would simulate the effect of exposure to a polluted urban atmosphere. This was accomplished by aging paper in 60% relative humidity air containing 5 ppm sulfur dioxide, the most common urban air pollutant. Table VIII shows that morpholine-treated paper possesses a significantly improved resistance to acidic atmospheres. The extent of this protection varies; comparing it with the Barrow two-bath process which is a calcium hydroxide–calcium bicarbonate system, it ranges from about the same to half that much. This conclusion is based on the retention of fold during accelerated aging at 60% r.h. and 75°C. About the same degree of protection was conferred upon the tear resistance, which further supports the finding that morpholine-treated paper indeed possesses a reduced sensitivity to acid-induced degradation.

Odor. To arrive at a usable process, it was essential that the morpholine concentration in the air around the processor and around processed books should be reduced to a level where neither odor nor health hazards would be a problem. Measurements of both the odor and the

Table VIII. Resistance of Morpholine-Treated Paper to an Acidic Atmosphere[a]

Paper No. 45 (pH 5.1)

	Untreated	Morpholine Treated	Barrow Two-Bath Treated
Loss	24%	13%	8%
Tear drop	58.0 → 44.3	58.3 → 50.9	61.8 → 56.9
Loss	67%	48%	26%
Fold drop	225 → 75	184 → 95	265 → 195

Paper No. 50 (pH 4.5)

	Untreated	Morpholine Treated	Barrow Two-Bath Treated
Loss	37%	16%	9%
Tear drop	58.3 → 36.5	60.4 → 50.7	62.6 → 56.6
Loss	84%	25%	33%
Fold drop	87 → 14	69 → 53	74 → 50

[a] At 75°C, 60% r.h., and 5 ppm SO_2.

morpholine concentrations would allow the process conditions to be adjusted to meet requirements. Measurements of morpholine concentration were made with the Miran infrared analyzer, calibrated over the range 1–100 ppm of morpholine in air. The applicable OSHA health-related standard is defined as an upper limit of 20 ppm for a weighted 8-hr exposure.

The ability to detect odors varies widely from one individual to another, depending on factors such as age and smoking. It is therefore necessary to express the relationship as a proportion of the population which can detect a given concentration. In Figure 7, the horizontal scale is probability, the vertical scale is concentration. The graph is interpreted to mean for example that 50% of the population can detect 0.7 ppm and that 89% of the population can detect 21 ppm. These data were developed for the project by the Illinois Institute of Technology Research Institute using a smell panel. On the basis of these measurements, process conditions were adjusted to meet two criteria:

1. To satisfy OSHA's requirements, the morpholine concentration in the air around treated books and during processor operation should never exceed 20 ppm.

2. The atmosphere around freshly treated books should never exceed more than 10 ppm.

After making suitable process adjustments, morpholine concentrations were measured around the processing equipment immediately after a batch of books had been treated. From Table IX, it is apparent that the concentrations even immediately after processing are in a range considered safe by OSHA rules. These levels drop to undetectable levels a

Table IX. Morpholine Concentrations around Processor

Area	Morpholine Concentration (ppm)
6″ in front of processor	< 1
Door opened after run	1.5–2.5
Shelf areas inside processor after run	1.5–5
4 ft above work area	< 1–1.5
3″ from freshly treated books	5–6
At nose level above freshly treated books	4.5

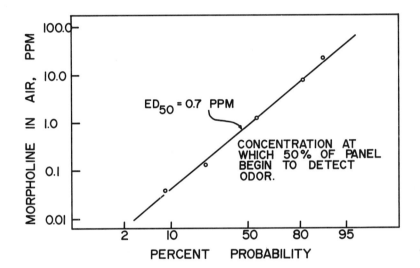

Figure 7.   Odor threshold detectability for morpholine in air

few hours after treatment. Therefore, there is no health hazard associated with the process, and odor has been reduced to a negligible level.

Possible Biocidal Effect. There has been some interest in whether the morpholine process has an effect comparable with that of an ethylene oxide-type fumigation process. Brief tests by a Corning Museum microbiologist in 1973 indicated that the process does have a significant value as a biocidal treatment, but these findings would require much more testing before a firm conclusion could be reached.

Range of Treatable Materials

As has been described, the intensity of the process was adjusted to accomplish deacidification of the paper in bound books without significant damage to book covers, to colored inks, or to the paper itself. As finally developed, no detectable damage exists for more than 99% of the 3,000 books processed. However, the process is not perfect, and occasionally changes in color of book covers are observed. Specifically, some types of colored pyroxylin covers tend to lighten slightly in color; most leather covers darken somewhat, but changes in the colors of printed illustrations, glue-sized papers, and in handwritten colored inks have not occurred. Newsprint sometimes shows a slight yellowing.

Overall, it is believed that these occasional changes are to be expected in a process of this type; they imply that the books to be deacidified should be selected when neutralization and life extension of the paper are the primary objectives and minor appearance changes can be tolerated. All deacidification processes demand that the conservator exercise a degree of judgement, and the morpholine process is no exception.

The process is designed as an inexpensive mass-production application of vapor-phase deacidification, and it would be inappropriate to apply it indiscriminately without pretesting items where book components other than the paper were considered to be of artistic or historical value. Packs of loose sheets enclosed in archival storage boxes have also been processed, and all the material in the boxes and the boxes themselves were completely deacidified. In cases where an item to be processed is out of the ordinary, one can either draw on past experience or make a processing test on similar material of no value.

Cost

The first prototype processor will deacidify about 50 books/hr. Under the specific local conditions of labor, power, and materials cost in Richmond, Va., it is estimated that it costs about $0.32 to deacidify each pound of book. This includes all material and labor costs and a five-year, straight-line depreciation of the equipment cost.

Under escalating conditions of labor and power cost or with a process of larger or smaller capacity, this figure could vary upward or downward by a wide margin. However, we believe it is safe to say that even under the most unfavorable circumstances, a pound of books could be deacidified today for less than $0.50. In comparison, deacidification by the conventional single-page processes costs about $0.25 for each page; xeroxing or microfilming costs $6–9/book.

Advantages of the Process

1. The process deacidifies about 85 lb of books in 60 min at a total cost presently estimated to be about $0.32/lb.

2. The process significantly reduces the accelerated-aging rate of book paper without harming the strength properties. An average improvement ratio of 2.6 has been found.

3. Prototype automated equipment is presently in use.

4. Processing of about 3,000 books indicates that the morpholine process is applicable to 99% of normal books without likelihood of damage.

5. There are indications that the process also fumigates books.

Disadvantages of the Process

1. The process occasionally causes color changes on pyroxylin covers.

2. The process often noticeably darkens the color of leather covers and occasionally causes groundwood papers to show visible yellowing.

3. The process does not strengthen deteriorated paper.

4. A capital investment of about $30,000 in equipment is necessary.

5. The process does not work equally well on every paper in existence.

The last three disadvantages are not unique to the morpholine process; they would probably apply to a greater or lesser extent to any bulk deacidification process. These advantages and disadvantages represent what is considered to be an optimum balance between many factors, including cost, effectiveness, process speed, and potential damage to book covers.

It is of interest to compare these positives and negatives with the requirements for the ideal process, published by the Library of Congress' Preservation Office in John Williams and George Kelly's paper (4) of 1974 entitled "Research on Mass Treatments in Conservation."

Of the nine published requirements, the morpholine process appears to meet seven—those specified for cost, pH, penetration, permanence, odor, lack of toxicity, and uniformity of treatment. It meets the eighth requirement—avoidance of new problems—to only a limited extent because of the occasional color changes of pyroxylin covers and the darkening of leather. The ninth requirement—reserve alkalinity—is not met in a literal sense, but aging in sulfur dioxide indicates it is met in at least one case where it is needed.

Current Status of the Process—January 1977

The laboratory phase of the operation has been completed, and the 50-book/hr unit is undergoing a 6-mo trial at the Virginia State Library in Richmond, Va. The first five weeks of full operation have shown no major problems, and 6500 books have been deacidified without incident.

Acknowledgments

The Barrow Laboratory, in pursuing their objective, has been fortunate in having the continued financial support of the Council on Library Resources, which has funded the project since its inception. Since December 1975, substantial support has also been provided by the National Endowment for the Humanities. The staff of the Laboratory wishes to express their thanks to the Council and to the Endowment for their confidence and for the funds which have made this project possible.

Literature Cited

1. Lowe, David G., "The Case of the Vanishing Records," *American Heritage,* **40,** No. 5:34–35, 107–111 (August, 1969).
2. Williams, Edwin E., "Deterioration of Library Collections Today," *Libr. Q.* (1970) **40,** No. 1:3–17.
3. Betrabet, S. M., *Text. Res. J.* (1966) **36,** 684–686.
4. Williams, John C., Kelly, George B., Jr., "Research on Mass Treatments in Conservation," *Bull. Am. Inst. Conserv.* (1974) **14,** No. 2.

RECEIVED February 8, 1977.

6

Questions Concerning the Design of Paper Pulp for Repairing Art on Paper

ROY PERKINSON

Print and Drawing Conservation Laboratory, Museum of Fine Arts, Boston, Mass. 02115

ROBERT FUTERNICK

Print and Drawing Conservation Laboratory, Fine Arts Museum of San Francisco, San Francisco, Calif. 98121

Three methods for repairing damaged art on paper are described, and questions concerning the design of paper pulp to be used for repairing art works are advanced. The most important criteria for designing paper pulp are dimensional stability consistent with strength; color stability; neutral pH; the potentiality for adding coloring agents not easily faded by light; a means of incorporating materials to vary opacity; and that small quantities of paper pulp be made readily accessible.

We would like to describe one of the techniques of repairing holes and tears in prints and drawings which has recently attracted interest among art conservators and discuss some of the related questions which have yet to be answered. Perhaps by sharing some of our concerns, we who are not chemists may benefit from their suggestions.

There are three methods which are most commonly used for repairing damaged works of art on paper, that is, lithographs, drawings, etchings, and woodcuts. The first method is the most direct. It involves selecting a suitable paper of high quality, such as handmade Japanese paper, and affixing it to the art work with starch paste, in effect bridging the hole or tear. This may help to consolidate the damaged area but does little to improve the appearance of the picture since the damage may still be quite obvious.

The second method of repair is much more time consuming and tedious if it can be accomplished at all. It presupposes that the conservator has on hand a great variety of papers of various ages, colors, thicknesses, and surface characteristics. The conservator must carefully pare down the edges of the damaged area, working on the back of the sheet, so that the edges nearest the hole have been reduced to scarcely a few fibers in thickness. Then a repair piece is selected which, as nearly as possible, is identical to the paper of which the art object is composed. (For this purpose it is considered more important to match transmitted and reflected color, surface texture, gloss, and thickness than to match the exact fiber composition.) This too is pared down at its edges so that when the repair is completed, the combined thickness of the insert and the art work is no greater than either alone. The success of this demanding procedure depends not only on the skill and perseverance of the conservator but also on the good fortune of finding precisely the correct piece of scrap paper. In spite of the difficulty of this method, it has its advocates, and the result may be a repair which blends so well with the picture that only an expert can detect its presence.

Because the first method is not always very satisfactory from the aesthetic standpoint and because of the limitations of the second, conservators have sought to expand their repertoire with alternative procedures. One possibility which has attracted recent interest is the use of a suspension of paper fibers to fill losses in a way that is analogous to the manufacture of paper. The paper pulp to be used for repairing an art work, for instance, can be obtained by the maceration of handmade rag-fiber paper in an ordinary food blender.

Machinery and techniques have been developed in both Europe and the United States for applying pulp repair techniques to the field of book conservation. Such apparatus is designed to facilitate the repair of damaged leaves of books and to make possible repairs which are more compatible with the original, both aesthetically and mechanically. The Library of Congress, among others, has devoted considerable effort to developing mechanized techniques for applying pulp to damaged documents and book pages and is completing a catalog of paper samples corresponding to various combinations of paper fiber mixtures, which will assist in the selection of an appropriate color of paper for the necessary repairs.

A color "palette" for various shades of browns (obviously the most useful for repair of aged papers) has sometimes been achieved through the use of different kinds of unbleached fibers such as unbleached kraft, linen, or cotton. At this point, however, it should be pointed out that pulp designed for use in book repair may differ in its requirements from that used on art objects. Pulp used on art objects must withstand continual exposure to light without significant alteration in color. Unbleached kraft, linen, or cotton fibers tend to become lighter with prolonged exposure to light and would therefore be unsatisfactory for this purpose. Folding endurance might be considered one of the prerequisites for pulp for book repair, but it is probably of less importance for art objects.

What then are the requirements for paper pulp to be used for repairing art works? Among the most important criteria would be:

1. Maximum dimensional stability consistent with strength.
2. Color stability of the fiber stock itself.
3. Neutral pH.
4. Potentiality for the addition of suitable coloring agents not easily faded by light.
5. A means of incorporating materials to vary opacity.
6. That small quantities of pulp supplies be made readily accessible.

With regard to the first requirement, there are two aspects of dimensional stability which must be considered: shrinkage upon initial drying and the expansion and contraction characteristics of the paper *after* drying in response to continuing fluctuations in humidity. As anyone in a paper mill knows, fibers must first be subjected to a mechanical treatment called "beating" before they will be capable of bonding or attaching sufficiently to each other to form a sheet of paper with the desired properties. There is no need to describe this process in detail, but it is important in this context because it is responsible, more than any other single treatment of the fibers, for determining the final properties of a sheet of paper, including the extent to which it will react to changes in the moisture content of the surrounding atmosphere. When fibers are subjected to prolonged beating, they will form a paper which will not only contract dramatically upon drying but also will continue to react strongly to variations in atmospheric humidity.

A good illustration of the results of using highly beaten pulp for repairs is seen in Figures 1 and 2. We tried producing pulp from cuttings of cotton cloth by beating them in a ball mill, a rotating cylindrical device containing ceramic balls. As the mill turns, the balls tumble over and over, macerating the cotton cloth and converting it to pulp. We found that it required a long time to produce pulp in this way and that as a result the majority of the fibers has experienced too much beating. Some of this pulp was flowed into the losses in a damaged print available for experimentation (Figure 1), but after drying, the pulp had contracted to such an extent (Figure 2) that it caused the print to buckle. Clearly, if fibers are beaten before use to help develop strength, the beating must be carefully limited. It would be useful if further study and more systematic experimentation could be done to help determine the degree of beating which would be most appropriate for the needs of the art conservator.

The second requirement suggested above was that the basic fiber stock should have good color stability. One of the problems with using colored fibers such as raw linen or unbleached kraft pulps is their tendency to become lighter on exposure to light, while some bleached fibers may tend to become significantly darker. Slight color changes are no doubt unavoidable—the same is of course true for the art works themselves—but before a particular fiber stock is selected for use in repair it should be tested to determine whether it is reasonably stable in color.

Coloring of paper pulp is a problem which requires further study. As mentioned previously, most coloring agents used in commercial paper manufacture are easily faded by light. Many cannot be used under conditions of neutral pH. Those conservators fortunate enough to have

Figure 1.   Damaged print available for experimentation

Figure 2.   A repair made with too highly beaten pulp

a plentiful supply of scraps of aged papers of various colors have "recycled" these to obtain different hues, but not everyone has access to enough expendable material for this procedure. Moreover, the brown color of old papers may be bleached when removed from storage and exposed to light. Mineral pigments have long been considered the most lightfast means of coloring paper, but the technology for using them has yet to make its way into the field of art conservation. The difficulties of attaching the pigment to the fibers has raised questions concerning the feasibility of this coloring method since it would obviously not be acceptable for the coloring matter to tend to bleed into the surrounding area of the picture. A procedure involving treatment of the fibers with lightfast, fiber-reactive textile dyes or synthetic, ultrafine organic pigments, followed by drying, thorough washing, beating, and rewashing, may deserve additional experimentation. It should be remembered that *exact* reproducibility of color is much less important for our purpose than it is in the paper industry. After all, some final color compensation will often have to be applied by the conservator; an initial base color helps achieve the goal of simulating the color of the original art paper.

The fifth requirement mentioned above was that a means be devised for varying the opacity of the repair paper formed from the pulp. Some machine-made papers of the 19th and 20th centuries are particularly difficult to simulate with pulp repair techniques because of their compactness, uniform formation, and opacity. From the manufacturer's standpoint, opacity can be varied by a number of means, such as selection of the type of fiber stock, degree of beating, chemical treatment, pressure exerted on the paper at various stages of its manufacture, and addition of opacifying agents. Not all of these possibilities are open to the conservator, who may have to manipulate a small quantity of pulp into place in a fragile art work, but it might be useful for conservators to experiment with many more kinds of fibers to try to expand the range of papers which can be simulated. As an example, we prepared three samples of paper from cotton linters, bleached softwood kraft, and bleached hardwood kraft. The sheets had the same thickness but differed noticeably in their opacity, with the cotton linters having the least opacity and the hardwood kraft the greatest. (The pulp was obtained from dried, unrefined fibers redispersed in a blender for about one minute. The paper was then formed on a small handsheet mold made in the lab.)

The use of opacifying agents in conjunction with pulp for repairs also needs further study. Small quantities of kaolin, titanium dioxide, and diatomaceous earth, for example, can be added by careful manipulation during the course of applying the pulp itself. In this way it is not necessary to use fixing agents which will bond the additive to the fibers, although in commercial practice much of the additives might be lost during formation and drainage on the screen without the use of a retention aid.

Certainly the use of pulp for repair is in its infancy. Improvements in production techniques and increased craftsmanship will no doubt follow developing interest in this subject. Whatever new procedures are found in the future, however, it is hoped that the materials used would not be accessible only to the conservator with costly, highly specialized equipment. Some commercial papermills and at least two manufacturers of handmade paper have provided pulp of a few different kinds to conservators, but there is little or no economic incentive to produce the variety of pulps needed, so these sources of supply may not be available in the future. Perhaps demand could be consolidated and the supply ensured if certain basic standards for pulp could be agreed upon.

Bibliography

Alkalaj, Stella, "The Chemical Laboratory for Hygiene, Conservation and Restoration of Damaged Written Materials in the National Library of Cyril and Methodius, Sofia," *Restaurator* (1969) **1** (2) 87–91.
Belen'kaya, N. G., "Methods of Restoration of Books and Documents," "New Methods for the Restoration and Preservation of Documents and Books," pp. 24–49, Israel Program for Scientific Translations, Ltd., 1964.
Brannahl, Günter, "Papiergussverfahren [Procedures for the Application of Paper Pulp]," *Proc. Conf. of Graphic Restorers 2nd, 1971*, Vol. 69, Biblos-Schriften, Vienna, 1972.
Keyes, Keiko Mizushima, Farnsworth, Donald S., "Practical Application of Paper Pulp in the Conservation of Works of Art on Paper," pp. 76–86, preprints of papers presented at the fourth annual meeting of the American Institute for Conservation, 1976.
Nyuksha, Yu. P., "The Technology of Conservation and Restoration of Library Materials," *Restaurator* (1975) **2** (2) 65–79.
Röckel, Franz, "Vom Blattbildner zum Anfaserungsegerät [From Sheet-former to pulp-caster]," *Proc. Int. Conf. Graphics Restorers, 2nd, 1971*, Vol. **69**, pp. 77–85, Biblos-Schriften, Vienna, 1972.
Trobas, Karl, "Ein Neues Mehformat-Anfaserungsegerät [A New Multi-format Casting Apparatus]," *Proc. Int. Conf. Graphics Restorers, 2nd, 1971*, Vol. **69**, pp. 101–109, Biblos-Schriften, Vienna, 1972.

RECEIVED June 28, 1977.

An Evaluation of Recent Developments for the Mass Drying of Books

GEORGE M. CUNHA

New England Document Conservation Center, Abbott Hall, School St., Andover, Mass. 01810

Serious flooding disasters which have ravaged some of the world's libraries and record centers have initiated investigations into methods for the mass drying of books. A technically sound, an aesthetically satisfactory, and an economically feasible procedure is required. Draining and air drying books—in open or in moving air—is an effective method, but it can be time consuming, and mold growth presents serious problems. Freeze stabilization has been instituted to combat mold growth problems and to give officials time to plan subsequent drying procedures. The author describes these procedures, summarizing work done on actual water-damaged books resulting from flooding disasters, and he calls for collaboration among scientists, conservators, and librarians to resolve the wealth of problems caused by these disasters.

The great 1966 flood in Florence focused world attention on problems of protecting cultural property, but that tragic event was only one in a long, sad history of great damage of the records of our heritage. Experiences at Florence and equally serious water-damage disasters since (accidents at the University of Corpus Christi Library, 1971; Temple Law Library, 1972; Federal Records Center, St. Louis, 1972; and Corning Museum of Glass, 1972) did initiate investigations of methods for the mass drying of books that hopefully will result ultimately in procedures that will be technically sound, aesthetically satisfactory, and economically feasible. The reason for mass drying wet books is first to salvage out-of-print volumes and secondly, if possible, to recover books still in print at a cost that is less per volume than their repurchase price. Table I shows

Table I. Hypothetical Costs with Restoring
100,000 Library Volumes (1)

Category	Number of Items	%	Dollar Cost per Item	Dollars Required for Restoration Category
Discard	10,000	10	—	—
Replacement	20,000	20	10.00	200,000
Restoration				
Minimum	10,000	10	1.00	10,000
Intermediate	50,000	50	50.00	500,000
Complete	10,000	10	500.00	5,000,000
Total Cost				$5,710,000

the estimated costs for the rehabilitation of a library of modest size by presently available methods ($5,710,000.00), emphasizing the importance of continuing at high priority the quest for more efficient methods for mass treating water-damaged books (1).

The salvage of water damaged books includes removing water, preventing mold growth, minimizing physical damage to the pages and covers, removing accumulations of mud, reducing stains, and protecting printing ink and colored illustrations. The cardinal requirement, however, for successful wet book recovery is the development of better methods for removing moisture from great numbers of books. Following the flood damage resulting from Hurricane Agnes in 1972, a conference was called at the Library of Congress at which scientists, conservators, librarians, and archivists discussed previous and recent techniques for fire- and water-damaged materials. This conference coincided with the Temple University Klein Law Library disaster in which Robert McComb and Peter Waters of the Library of Congress staff served as consultants.

As a result of the recommendations made at the 1972 conference and following the Klein Law Library disaster, the research and testing office of the Library of Congress undertook a high priority research program to investigate the mechanisms and the safety parameters of all known and experimental drying techniques. This research (as yet unpublished) was aimed at finding a mass method of drying which was not only economical but would cause minimal damage to cellulose and related material. It was as a direct result of this research that the Library of Congress was able to recommend acceptable methods of freeze vacuum drying. As a further result, the first mass drying under controlled conditions was carried out in collaboration with the General Electric Space Systems

Center at Valley Forge, Pa. (9). It was the Library of Congress' recommendation for the safety limits of cellulose-type materials which made possible the success of this project and others which have followed. After the St. Louis fire at the Military Records Center, the Library of Congress was again involved in vacuum–air purge drying operations, this time in collaboration with McDonnell Douglas Aircraft Corp. (7).

In addition to the important work at the General Electric Space Center and the McDonnell Aircraft Corp. in collaboration with the Library of Congress, organized investigations were conducted at the Corning Museum of Glass (4–6) and the Massachusetts Institute of Technology (14, 15) on freeze drying, vacuum drying, combinations of thermal and vacuum drying techniques, the use of dielectric and microwave energy, solvent extraction, and the reevaluation of the traditional methods of air drying and interleaving book pages for the removal of water.

Results to Date

For centuries the generally accepted method for drying water-damaged books has been first to drain them as much as possible and then stand them on edge to dry in the open air. This method, still in wide use today, is effective particularly if the books when partially dry are interleaved with unprinted newsprint, paper towels, or other absorbent paper to assist the drying process. The advantage of air drying is that it is not expensive, particularly if volunteer help is available. The disadvantage of air drying is that it is time consuming, and if temperature and humidity are high, there is a good probability that mold growth with all its attendant problems will take place before the drying operation is completed. The use of fungicide-impregnated (particularly thymol) interleaving papers will help reduce mold growth, but this will always be a major problem in the process of air drying water-damaged books even in temperate zones.

At Florence (3) books were tumbled in sawdust to faciltate water removal; truckloads of books were sent to wind tunnel-like drying sheds and other industrial drying facilities with various heating arrangements to accelerate moisture evaporation; books were spun in centrifuges at raised temperatures in addition to being air dried with interleaving. The consensus of those who participated in this work was that air drying in moving air at 122°–140°F and an r.h. of 35–50% was the best method then available for drying paper (3). Air drying with or without controlled temperature and humidity is still the most freqeuntly used recovery technique.

Because of the problem of mold, wet books in any quantity are now usually individually wrapped and in those countries that have freezers, frozen as soon as they can be recovered from a disaster area. This freeze stabilization, as it is called, is also a holding process giving conservators, curators, and administrators time to plan subsequent action.

Subsequent to freeze stabilization, wet books can be thawed and air dried with or without interleaving or they can be vacuum dried in heated chambers (5). The moisture in frozen books can be sublimed by freeze drying (10) or removed by a vacuum/thaw/outgassing process (8), with microwave energy (6, 14), with dielectric energy (6), or by solvent extraction with or without vacuum assistance (5).

Brief descriptions are offered below for those drying processes which are receiving attention by scientists and conservators.

Air Drying Books. Frozen (or unfrozen but wet) books are (A) placed flat on open shelves; as room air temperature thaws the ice, the surplus water drains from the book and evaporates (5). (B) Frozen (or unfrozen but wet) books are stood on end on a table in a current of room temperature air. As frozen (or wet) pages open naturally, they are interleaved with absorbent paper (changed frequently) until books are dry (5).

Vacuum Drying Books. (A) Frozen (or wet) books are placed in a chamber and heated by warm air. Vacuum is applied to remove water vapor as the ice thaws (5, 7). This is sometimes called the "purged air" system. (B) Frozen (or wet) books are placed in an unheated chamber. Moist air is evacuated and replaced with dry heated air (0% r.h.). When the replacement air becomes saturated with moisture, it is evacuated and the process repeated until the books are dry (4, 5). (C) Thawing books are put in a chamber. Vacuum is applied and then controlled at a pressure of about 5 torr. Heat is then applied to books through shelves to replace latent heat of vaporization. As moisture is released from books in vapor form (outgassing), it is collected by pumps and reverted to ice on cooled condensers in the chamber. After most of the water leaves the books, the book temperature is increased gradually from 32°F to 80°–85°F; the chamber is opened after 48 hr, the books are removed from the shelves, and the condensers are defrosted (4, 5, 10).

The vacuum drying methods take advantage of the greater vapor pressure of water in the liquid phase in contrast to the lower vapor pressure of ice or water at its melting point (4): vapor pressure of H_2O at 0°C = 4.6 mm; vapor pressure of H_2O at 4.4°C = 6.3 mm (potential efficiency increase of 37%); vapor pressure of H_2O at 10°C = 9.2 mm (potential efficiency increase of 100%).

Freeze Drying Frozen Books. Specific information is available on the freeze drying of books by Flink and Hoyer (15). They investigated the application of radiant heat at 45°C to frozen books in a chamber kept at a constant pressure of 200 mtorr. Water vapor was continually removed until the weight of the books (on a balance in the chamber) became constant. Average drying time was 1½–2 days per batch of books (a batch = about 10–20 books) where the limitation was on the size and not the number of books. It is generally considered that freeze drying is impractical primarily because of the costs that would be involved in building and operating equipment for mass treatment. However, freeze drying with laboratory equipment of single books of great rarity and value is a logical solution.

Microwave Drying of Books. Microwave energy covers a wide spectrum of electromagnetic radiation of short wave lengths. Commercial units operate at 915 or 2450 MHz. Energy from magnetrons or Klystron tube oscillators is transferred to the drying chamber by a wave guide (6). Water, having a dipole moment, is sensitive to microwave (and dielectric) frequencies and tries to align itself with the direction of the applied voltage. Heat develops in this alignment process, and frozen water first melts then evaporates (6). Microwave (and dielectric) energy unfortunately generates heat more readily in materials other than paper in books—i.e., leather, covers, certain adhesives, metal of any sort such as paper clips, wire staples, and even gold and silver foil used in some book illustrations—creating serious limitations in the use of this method for mass drying (5).

Drying Books with Dielectric Energy. (A) Dielectric heating applies to a wide range of electromagnetic frequencies. Commercial units are designed to operate at frequencies of 13.56, 27.72, and 40 MHz (6). Jones, Lawton, and Parker contend that 27-MHz radio frequency provides better moisture leveling in paper than 2450-MHz microwave energy (17, 18). Dielectric systems ordinarily use a negative grid triode tube as a variable power control.

Dielectric (and microwave) energy sources transfer energy (heat) directly by radiation to the water molecules primarily without an intermediate transfer medium, thus raising the temperature of an object more uniformly than conductive or convective methods. Dielectric current is kept constant, and plate current (or electrode separation space) can be varied according to the size of the frozen material being thawed (6). Theoretically, this should be an advantage in the mass drying of books by reducing the time for thawing and vaporizing water and compensating for the variations in weight, thickness, etc. of frozen volumes. Actually, this method does not work well because of: (a) rapid evaporation of water vapor within books, (b) charring of other materials (leather, metallic lettering, adhesives), (c) charring of the paper itself (excessive drying), and (d) the requirement for shielding, etc. for personal safety. Fischer and Duncan used incremental bursts of dielectric (and microwave) energy in their experiments to minimize vapor explosions and charring with some success (5, 6).

Removing Water from Frozen Books by Solvent Extraction. SOLVENT EXTRACTION/AIR DRY. Frozen books are submerged in a precooled anhydrous solvent in a sealed container and stored in a freezer. As the ice dissolves the water/solvent mixture is replaced periodically until all water is removed. Books saturated with solvent are then interleaved with absorbent paper and air dried (5).

SOLVENT EXTRACTION/VACUUM DRY. It is the same procedure as above, but when water has been completely replaced by solvent, the books are placed in a vacuum chamber and brought back to their original weight by evaporating the solvent in a reduced pressure chamber. (Solvent extraction is out of the question for most modern books, which are usually printed with highly soluble (in solvents) offset printing ink.)

Interpretation

Fischer and Duncan (*4, 5, 6*), after the heavy damage to the library at the Corning Museum of Glass during Hurricane Agnes in 1972, made a systematic study of all of the drying methods. Two specific groups of contemporary books, one containing only coated and the other only uncoated paper, were placed through a simulated flood and drainage period and frozen in order to have standard frozen samples for studying which drying technique would be best for the museum's collection. Their conclusions are that while no mass drying treatment investigated is a panacea, certain techniques warrant further investigation. They have rated the methods for mass drying books using these criteria for evaluating the finished product (*5*).

(1) *Visual appearance*

(a) Distortion of the book structure—i.e., the text, the spine, the covers

(b) Appearance of individual pages—i.e., sticking, staining, bleeding of print, dye transfer from illustrations and illuminations, cockling of paper, and dimensional changes

(2) *Physical properties*

(a) Tensile breaking strength and tensile energy absorption

(b) Tear strength of dried paper

(c) Thickness of the dried paper

(d) Acidity of the dried paper

Fischer and Duncan rate the various drying processes in this order of decreasing suitability (*4*):

(1) Freeze/thaw/vacuum dry with controlled heat assistance

(2) Interleave/air dry

(3) Solvent extraction/air dry

(4) Solvent extraction/vacuum dry

(5) Drained/air dried

(6) Vacuum/warm air purged

(7) Microwave drying

(8) Vacuum without warm air purge

(9) Dielectric drying

Some of Fischer and Duncan's observations supporting the above ratings (based on the one type of coated- and the one type of uncoated-paper books) are:

(A) Drying techniques that work well on uncoated paper do not necessarily work well with coated stock (*4*).

(B) Freeze/thaw/vacuum drying technique is particularly effective with catalogs and journals containing coated paper (*4*).

(C) Water penetration in coated book pages may not be uniform, particularly if books were tightly packed on shelves.

(D) Books loosely packed on shelves absorb more water than those tightly packed.

(E) Weight of a wet book is an indication of water absorption and a means for measuring effectiveness of drying.

(F) The one type of coated paper used in this study absorbs 80% more water than the one type of uncoated paper used (2).

(G) If proper environmental conditions are selected, the one type of uncoated-paper book showed that almost all absorbed water will be released by draining in 120 hr (4).

(H) The water absorbed by the book cover may exceed the water absorbed by the text (4).

(I) The mechanism by which water is absorbed in a book highly depends on the composition and texture of the paper as well as the cover (2).

(J) Absorption of water by coated paper can be more rapid than that for uncoated paper.

(K) Drying newly made paper on high speed rolls in a paper mill leaves stresses in the paper which are released when the paper is later wet, as in a flood, and redried. This is probably one major source of cockling (4).

(L) Freezing has no known negative effect on paper (4); however, the binding of a book may be damaged as a result of expansion of water during freezing.

(M) Better results can be obtained when drying with interleaving wet books if they are frozen first (4). This does not apply to vacuum drying.

(N) Quickness in freezing coated-paper books after recovery from a disaster area helps to reduce blocking—i.e., sticking together of pages— upon subsequent drying. Blocking can take place before freezing as well as in subsequent drying operations (4).

(O) Blocking is sometimes caused by uneven or excessive heating in mass drying operations. The thawed ice dissolves starch and casein, constituents of some coated-paper stock. Both being adhesives, they then stick the pages together during the final stages of drying. Evidence exists that this happens when the temperature in a book exceeds 10°C. However, when temperatures are kept below 4.4°C, there is no sticking as a result of the freeze–thaw drying operation.

(P) Rewetting blocked book pages and immediate freezing, followed by drying, sometimes makes it possible for the stuck pages to be separated.

(Q) Microwave and dielectric energy has not been successfully applied to drying of books printed on coated paper—i.e., starch, casein, clays, etc. (5).

(R) Microwave and dielectric energy is not suitable for mass drying of books because of the invariable presence of metal in the form of clips, staples, foil, and even iron and copper in the paper itself and the higher reaction to this energy by leather, some adhesives, etc. (6).

(S) Uncontrolled heating by microwave and dielectric energy can cause coated-paper pages to balloon (or burst). Water inside each page is converted to vapor more rapidly than it diffuses to the surface of each page (6).

(T) Successful mass drying requires efficient movement of water/ water vapor from the pages to their edges and equally efficient removal of water vapor from these edges to the immediate surroundings.

(U) Special problems arise in drying photographs. Mass drying via freeze–thaw vacuum drying is possible if the emulsion has not been degraded by microbiological attack.

(V) Success in applying microwave and dielectric energy for destroying all fungi in books and book paper has not been demonstrated (6).

Peter Waters, based on his experience at the National Records Center fire in St. Louis, the fire at Temple University, and elsewhere, is satisfied that freeze and vacuum drying operations do not damage cellulose in paper (8) and that these methods are the best now available for mass drying of books.

Shoulberg, reporting on his experience with freeze/thaw/vacuum drying experiments only (9), observes:

(a) Except for moisture content and shrinkage because of the water, the book's condition coming out of the vacuum chambers has not basically changed.

(b) Temperature control is of major importance. Sticking of coated paper is accelerated at high drying temperatures.

(c) Freeze/thaw/vacuum drying will not kill fungi (11), and subsequent vacuum fumigation is required.

(d) Arrangement of books on shelves in a vacuum chamber is critical from the point of view of heat transfer into the books and movement of water out of them (12).

(e) The controlling time factor in the mass drying of books is the diffusion rate of water vapor through the pages (13).

(f) The size of books and composition and texture of the paper affect the rate of water diffusion from the interior to the edges of books.

(g) Handling techniques and equipment available (shelves holding boxes, wrapping materials, dollies, trucks, etc.) are a major consideration in developing mass drying techniques.

(h) Mass drying does not remove mud and dirt from frozen books.

(i) Mass drying by the freeze/thaw/vacuum drying processes aids in removing smoke and mold odors.

Flink and Thomas in their report on the use of microwave energy (14) (200 watts at 2450 MHz) and flowing air for water vapor removal admit that to avoid charring of book paper, the drying operation had to be stopped before the books became "bone dry."

Summary

During the past 10 years there has been considerable investigation of methods for mass drying of books ranging from reevaluation of the centuries-old "air drying in the sun" methods to experiments with high frequency electromagnetic energy. Only one of the newer mass drying techniques (the freeze/thaw/vacuum drying process) is an improvement over the long-practiced air drying methods. One of the major advantages of the freeze/thaw/vacuum drying process is that the water-damaged books can be held in the frozen state for unlimited periods of time, enabling librarians to reconsider the on-the-spot decisions made at the time of the disaster, to compare replacement vs. restoration costs, and to reach an understanding with insurance underwriters, etc. before proceeding with the recovery.

There is still an urgent requirement for further in-depth scientific and engineering studies of the mass drying of books made with different types of papers, and procedures must be developed that will result in a high rate of recovery of books in usable condition without further expensive restoration. This major problem calls for collaboration among scientists, engineers, librarians, and conservators to uncover and pursue avenues heretofore overlooked. It is suggested that the following matters warrant priority consideration.

(A) *For the scientist*

1. Can book paper, adhesives, covering materials, etc. be designed to be highly resistant to water damage so that books printed in the future will be more receptive to mass recovery techniques?

2. Develop control of the absorption of water during paper manufacture, during its subsequent history in books on library shelves, and finally during drying operations.

3. Improve methods for transferring heat to the interiors of wet books during mass drying.

(B) *For the engineer*

1. Investigate more economical ways to fumigate and sterilize books while they are undergoing mass drying.

2. Determine whether it is possible before mass drying to wash mud-damaged frozen or wet books.

3. Consider deacidification of books during a mass drying operation.

4. Evaluate approaches to paper reinforcement during a mass drying operation by impregnating it with resins introduced into the drying chamber in gaseous form.

5. Assess whether it is possible to devise mechanical methods (pressing) to return distorted frozen books to their original condition during mass drying operations.

(C) *For the librarian*

1. What can the library profession do to make available in library records more information on the past history, composition of paper, construction details, etc. of the books in research libraries?

2. What can the library profession do in regard to establishing "salvage criteria" for the books in research and special libraries—i.e., rarity, value, replaceability, priority for salvage, etc.?

These matters for examination by librarians are of equal importance to the answers we seek from scientists and engineers. What would be the purpose of attempting to salvage 100% of a library that is 80% replaceable at reasonable cost when the effort could be better applied to the recovery, if they were identifiable, of the 20% of the books that are nonreplaceable.

Literature Cited

1. Fischer, D. J., "Restoration of Flood-Damaged Materials in a Special Library," *Conserv. Admin.*, p. 188, New England Document Conservation Center, North Andover, Mass., 1975.
2. Ibid., p. 143.
3. Horton, C., "Saving the Libraries of Florence," *Wilson Libr. Bull.*, June 1967, pp. 1035–1043.
4. Fischer, D. J., Duncan, T., "Conservation Research: Flood-Damaged Library Materials," *Bull. Am. Inst. Conserv.* (1975) **15** (2) 28–48.
5. Fischer, D. J., "Simulation of Flood for Preparing Reproducible Water-Damaged Books and Evaluation of Traditional and New Drying Processes," ADV. CHEM. SER. (1977) **164**, 105.
6. Fischer, D. J., "Conservation Research: Use of Dielectric and Microwave Energy to Thaw and Dry Frozen Library Materials," ADV. CHEM. SER. (1977) **164**, 124.
7. Waters, P., "Mass Treatment after a Disaster," *Conserv. Admin.*, New England Document Conservation Center, North Andover, Mass., 1975.
8. Ibid., p. 115.
9. Shoulberg, R., "Stabilization Using Freeze-Drying," *Conserv. Admin.*, New England Document Conservation Center, North Andover, Mass., 1975.
10. Ibid., p. 154–163.
11. Ibid., p. 167.
12. Ibid., p. 156.
13. Ibid., p. 154.
14. Thomas, D., Flink, J., "Microwave Drying of Water Soaked Books," *J. Microwave Power* (1974) **9** (4) 349–354.
15. Flink, J., Hoyer, H., "The Conservation of Water-Damaged Written Documents by Freeze Drying," *Nature* (1971) **234** (5329) 420.
16. Williams, N. H., "Moisture Leveling in Paper, Wood, Textiles, and Other Mixed Dielectric Sheets," *Symposium on Microwave Power*, 1966.
17. Jones, P. L., Lawton, J., Parker, I. M., "High Frequency Paper Drying, Part I," *Trans. Inst. Chem. Eng.* (1974) **52**: 121–131.
18. Lawton, J., "High Frequecy Paper Drying, Part II," *Trans. Inst. Chem. Eng.* (1974) **52**: 132–135.

RECEIVED March 16, 1977.

Simulation of Flood for Preparing Reproducible Water-Damaged Books and Evaluation of Traditional and New Drying Processes

DAVID J. FISCHER

Milton Roy Co., P.O. Box 1899, Sarasota, Fla. 33578

One of the consequences of the tropical storm Agnes, June 1972, reached as far north as Corning, N.Y. The Corning Museum of Glass' library, the library of record for the world's glass scholars, sustained extraordinary damage when flooded by waters from an adjacent river. All of the library's damaged collection was frozen. A team developed a plan, which included special research projects, for the restoration of this collection. A simulation of the flood and assessment of traditional and new methods of drying frozen books were undertaken. One of the major achievements was the successful application of a freeze–thaw–vacuum drying process to the museum's frozen, coated-paper catalogs, journals, and books.

Tropical storm Agnes struck Corning, N.Y. on June 23, 1972. This upstate region had been subjected to torrential rains as Agnes changed from hurricane to tropical storm designation, causing flash floods west of Corning on the Canisteo river. Three rivers, the Canisteo, Cohocton, and Tioga join at Painted Post to form the Chemung which flows through the heart of the city located in a narrow valley. Although the Chemung continued to rise at an alarming rate on Thursday, June 22, the N.Y. State Department of Environmental Conservation advised the river would crest 5 ft below flood stage at 3:00 A.M. Friday morning. At 3:00 A.M. on Friday, the Harrisburg National River Forecast Center reported the Chemung would reach flood stage within 2 hr. At 5:00 A.M. the 23.5-ft dikes were topped by a river cresting at 27–28 ft. The devastation was staggering. Dikes built to contain a 100-year-frequency flood were no deterrent to this 500–1000-year flood precipitated by Agnes.

The Corning Museum of Glass, only one block from the river, was ravaged. Water reached a height of 5⅓ ft inside the museum's main floor. Approximately 525 of the 13,000 glass objects were broken. The Museum library, the library of record for the world's glass scholars, sustained extraordinary damage: approximately 6500 of a total collection of 13,000 volumes and 3,000 of the 6,000 periodicals were under water, as were 600 volumes in the rare and special book collections.

The river deposited a thick layer of mud as it receded. To stop all biological growth and to preserve the library's contents, all books, file drawer materials, object catalogs, photographs, and journals were frozen. This action permitted the staff to consider and to evaluate restoration methods.

A restoration team—a paper conservator, librarians, and a scientist with assistants—was assembled. The extent of the damage was determined, the library materials were inventoried, and a plan was developed for restoration of the collection. The conservator and the scientist worked with a variety of damaged materials to formulate the technical requirements for the restoration program. Equipment for thawing, washing, deacidifying, drying, and fumigating was ordered and received with the necessary work tables to set up a system. Traditional hand-restoration procedures were applied to the flood-damaged books. An applied research program was also instituted. Attention was focused on the following procedures: drying, mud removal, separation of stuck coated-paper pages, deacidification and buffering, and fumigation and sterilization.

To assess each new technique thoroughly, the following plan was developed. Two groups of identical books (each group had the same title, author, publisher, and edition number) were bought for experimental research from one book store at one time. One group of identical books was selected to represent the easiest type to restore (1). These books contained only uncoated paper. Selection of the other group (2), the most difficult to restore, was made after experimentation established that severe sticking and excessive dye transfer would occur after the pages were wetted and dried. This group of books contained only coated paper and colored illustrations.

The conservation experiments required books uniformly damaged by flood water. A simulated flood, drainage, and book-freezing sequence was developed so that it would be applied to these two groups of books resulting in a minimal variation in damage. The composition of the uncoated and the coated paper was held basically constant in these studies. Future extension of this research effort should consider varying the composition of the uncoated and coated papers. Different fibers, sizing, adhesive coatings, and their fillers are all significant composition variables which will influence the quality of the restoration result. When coated paper is involved, the coating (starch, casein, or different latexes) itself as well as the coating filler (clay, inorganic oxides, or carbonates) must be given specific consideration in perfecting a restoration procedure for the paper in a book.

Simulation of the Flood for Preparing Reproducible Water-Damaged Books

The initial preparation of standard flood-damaged books excluded the use of mud. A high of 25°C and a low of 21°C were designed for the temperature of the flood waters inside the museum since accurate measurements were not available. The times when the water first touched and receded from the books on the bottom shelves as well as how long the water was at its peak height were estimated. A single value of 16–17 hr was determined as a typical period of floodwater contact with the library's books.

Two extremes in book location on the shelves were considered and evaluated for influence on the amount of water absorption. A book placed loosely on the shelf so that it would float freely and sink in the flood waters was used as an indicator of minimum packing pressure. The tightly packed storage condition was established by placing a book between two 1.3-cm Plexiglas plates which were clamped together. Losses of water from books stored under these two extremes of pressure were determined for both short and extended drainage times. The high-pressure position was established by tightening C-clamps on each of the four corners of the Plexiglas plates. A uniform torque of 4.0 kg-cm was applied as each clamp was tightened. This value was assigned as typical of the maximum pressure that the books had sustained on the library shelves. Both the uncoated- and the coated-paper books, mentioned earlier, were used in these studies.

The primary measurement made on each book before and after it encountered the simulated flood was its weight. In special cases, physical property measurements were made on the pages in the book. Photographs of the books before, during, and after the simulated flood recorded the sequence.

The length of the drainage period after the simulated flood was difficult to determine. The first flood-damaged book was probably frozen 39 hr after the flood waters receded; the last books were placed in a freezer 114 hr later. To simulate the exact conditions, the temperature, relative humidity, and movement of the air in contact with the wetted books would have to be programmed. These problems coupled with the urgent need to supply identical, flood-damaged samples for experimentation necessitated a compromise in exact duplication of the Corning flood and drainage sequence. Rather than perfect the operation of chambers for rigidly controlling the environment of the wetted books during an extended drainage period, a decision was made to use the shortest possible drainage time—5 hr—which might be encountered in future water disasters before freezing of books would be initiated. This was duplicated precisely for preparing identical, flood-damaged books.

After the books had been processed—i.e., weighed, dry, wetted, and drained—they were inserted in Ziploc plastic bags, sealed, and immediately placed in the freezer at −23°C. The weight of the frozen book was essentially that of the drained book. As a precaution, each book was weighed as it was removed from the freezer before the restoration process was initiated. The application of drying techniques to both wetted and frozen books was followed by weighing the books and noting their return to the original dry weight.

Results from the Simulated-Flood Investigations

Table I shows the overall variation in the weights when the simulated-flood procedure was applied to similar pairs of identical books over an 8-mo period. The simulated flood was applied to these books as if they were loosely packed on the shelf—i.e., stored with minimum pressure applied to them. The relationship of each book's dry weight with the temperature and relative humidity of the room appears to have been comparable. The variability of the wetting action of both types of books is also similar; however, the variances (the standard deviation squared) associated with the weights of the drained books are significantly different (statistical significance reported at the 95% confidence level unless otherwise noted) by use of an F-test (3). Since the handling of book pairs—i.e., one uncoated- and one coated-paper book—was the same in preparing samples for subsequent restoration studies, it might be concluded that drainage water from the books containing uncoated paper could be different from books with coated paper.

An extended-drainage-time study was conducted. Two pairs of the coated- and uncoated-paper books were used. The flood and drainage studies with these four books were implemented twice; approximately 4 mo intervened. One book in each pair was held in the tightly packed position and the other in the loosely packed position throughout the water contact and drainage period. Weights of the dry, wetted, and drained books, with corrections made for clamps and Plexiglas plates, were recorded. The ranges of room temperature and relative humidity

Table I.   Book Weights during Simulated-Flood Sequence

| | | Weights (g) and % [c] | | | |
Condition of Book	Type of Paper	Mean	Range 95% C.L.	N	Standard Deviation
Dry	Uncoated weight	294.7	292.4, 297.0	17	2.3
	%	—	— —	—	—
Wet [a]	Uncoated weight	535.3	513.8, 556.8	16	21.5
	%	82.7	75.7, 89.1		6.7
Drained [b]	Uncoated weight	491.2	474.7, 507.7	17	16.5
	%	66.6	61.6, 71.6		5.0
Dry	Coated weight	429.6	427.3, 431.9	16	2.3
	%	—	— —	—	—
Wet [a]	Coated weight	965.3	946.3, 984.3	15	19.0
	%	125.1	120.9, 129.3		4.2
Drained [b]	Coated weight	921.2	912.7, 929.7	16	8.5
	%	114.4	112.3, 116.5		2.1

[a] Loosely packed book, 16–17 hr in floodwater.
[b] Book lying on side, 5 hr of drainage.
[c] Percent increase in weight as a result of treatment.

were noted for both series. When the coated- and uncoated-paper books were tightly packed, they appeared to absorb comparable amounts of water (Table I). Even after 120 hr in their drainage position, they retained comparable amounts of water, about half of the amount that was absorbed. To track the loss of water during drainage, regression analyses were applied to the percent increase in weight of each book as a result of water absorption (Table II).

The loosely packed coated- and uncoated-paper books absorbed more water than the tightly packed books—approximately five times as much for the coated- and twice as much for the uncoated-paper books. In both series of experiments more than 93% of the water absorbed in the loosely packed, uncoated-paper books evaporated during a 120-hr drainage period. These experimental results could explain why several of the actual frozen, flood-damaged, uncoated-paper books, after thawing, contained only small amounts of water. They were perhaps the last uncoated-paper books to be packed and frozen after the flood waters receded.

Table II. Equations, Regression Analysis for % Increase in Weight of Books as a Result of Water After Simulated Flood and during Drainage

Series	Type of Paper in Book	Type of Packing on Shelf	Equations, % Increase in Weight as a Result of Water as a Function of Drainage Time (hr)	R^{2c}
1st[a]	Coated	tight	$\% = 25.6335 - 0.0517t - 0.6220\sqrt{t}$	.9968
	Uncoated	tight	$\% = 39.3250 - 0.06023t - 1.4014\sqrt{t}$	.9979
	Coated	loose	$\% = 126.031 - 0.4443t - 2.3936\sqrt{t}$	.9992
	Uncoated	loose	$\% = 78.2493 + 0.528t - 12.9423\sqrt{t}$	.9871
2nd[b]	Coated	tight	$\% = 30.2738 + 0.0064t - 1.5221\sqrt{t}$	.9950
	Uncoated	tight	$\% = 33.4342 + 0.0579t - 2.3768\sqrt{t}$	.9761
	Coated	loose	$\% = 117.5865 - 0.3800t - 2.0376\sqrt{t}$	.9986
	Uncoated	loose	$\% = 99.1620 + 0.5338t - 14.5164\sqrt{t}$	.9890

[a] 22–28°C; 23–32% r.h.
[b] 23–26°C; 50–60% r.h.
[c] Square of correlation coefficient relates the fit of the equation with the actual data. Ideally the value would be 1.0.

The independent studies on loss of the moisture from the books by sublimation while in the freezer could not account for the amount of water being lost.

The loosely packed, coated-paper books under equivalent 120-hr drainage conditions lost approximately 67% of the absorbed water. It was difficult to remove the water from this type of coated-paper book regardless of the drying technique. If the book was not frozen, the individual pages had to be interleaved shortly after removal from the flood waters; otherwise, severe sticking of pages would occur and make diffusion of the remaining water to the outside edge of the book difficult.

The need to determine how the flood water was distributed throughout the books suggested the following experiment. The mull or super of each of two pairs of coated and uncoated books was cut with a sharp knife so that the covers of each book would be separated from the text. This operation also allowed the separated cover and text to be put back together very easily. Thus, each book was returned to its original structure and volume after the individual weight of the cover and text were recorded. Pairs of books were then placed in the tightly and loosely pack positions, and the simulated-flood conditions were applied. After the 16-hr period, the books were removed from the water and held vertically at a slight angle until all excess water had drained from the book. When the water flow decreased to a slow drip, weighings were undertaken—first, the combination of cover and text and then the individual cover and text sections. The increase in the weight as a result of absorption of water was then determined for each section as well as for the total book.

Before reviewing the specific results of these experiments, two observations made during this study should be reported. To remove the books from the compressed Plexiglas plates at the end of the submersion period, a reverse torque of 15–20 kg-cm for the coated and 11–14 kg-cm for the uncoated books had to be applied to the C-clamps. This increased amount of torque required to release the clamps was a result of pressure from the expansion of the paper while it was wet. In the case of the coated-paper book, an actual bowing of the center of the Plexiglas plates clamped against this book was observed.

The absolute weights of water absorbed in the text and cover sections of each book under both extremes of pressure during storage and while undergoing the simulated flood were documented. The amounts of water absorbed by the coated- and uncoated-paper tests were comparable when the books were tightly packed. The cover on the uncoated-paper book appeared to absorb slightly more water than the cover on the coated-paper book. Individual results for each study are given; only two trials were undertaken (Table III). Covers on these books were identified with the paper in the text. Their composition, cloth over cardboard, was completely independent of the kind of paper in the text. More specifically, the cloth cover for the coated-paper book was rough in texture and appeared to be more porous. Both types of cloth covered a heavy cardboard base.

Table III.   % Increase in Weight for Text and Covers of Books as a Result of Water Absorbed during 16-hr Simulated Flood

Location of Water in Book	Type of Paper in Book	% Increase in Weight as a Result of Water[a]			
		Tightly Packed Books		Loosely Packed Books	
		Trial 1[b]	Trial 2[c]	Trial 1[b]	Trial 2[c]
Text	coated	13.3	9.8	107.8	105.4
	uncoated	18.0	14.8	21.8	29.4
Cover	coated	53.8	43.9	137.9	145.1
	uncoated	96.4	71.4	166.9	225.9[d]
Combination	coated	22.8	17.8	116.1	115.3
	uncoated	41.3	31.1	65.0	87.5[d]

[a] Water absorption measured immediately after removal from flood water.
[b] Temperature range 22°–26°C; r.h. range 34–37%.
[c] Temperature range 19°–22°C; r.h. range 28–29%.
[d] Slit in cover may cause excess of absorbed water.

The amount of water taken up by the coated- and uncoated-paper text was quite different when the books were loosely packed. The covers on both types of books absorbed comparable amounts of water in this storage position. More water saturated both text and covers when loosely packed than when tightly packed. The percent increase in the weight resulting from water as shown in Table III reveals that the material in the covers used in these books held more water than the paper in the text. The percentages calculated for the overall water content in the total book clearly emphasize the advantage of having books tightly packed on shelves to minimize the risk of water damage. This was true for both the coated- and uncoated-paper books.

The identification of water distribution throughout flood-damaged books was carried beyond the weighings made after the 16-hr flood interval. After these weighings, the covers were placed around the appropriate text. In the first trial, involving the tightly packed books, the Plexiglas plates were pressed against the respective books, and torque equivalent to that which was recorded when the book was removed for the initial weighings was applied to each C-clamp. During the second study, after the 16-hr flood covers were weighed and placed around the text, the original tightly packed books were drained without being compressed, placed in a horizontal position equivalent to that used in both studies for drainage of the loosely packed books. The change in weight after the 5-hr drainage interval is documented in Table IV.

Table IV. Amount of Water Retained after 5-hr Drainage

		Weights (g)			
	Type of Paper in	Trial 1 [a]		Trial 2 [a]	
Distribution of Water	Book	Drained	Δ [e]	Drained	Δ [e]
Text, tightly packed	coated	364.0 [c]	−3.5	3.55.0 [d]	−3.0
book	uncoated	234.5 [c]	−1.5	235.0 [d]	−1.0
Cover, tightly uacked	coated	143.0 [c]	−9.0	134.5 [d]	−8.0
book	uncoated	143.0 [c]	−21.0	126.5 [d]	−17.5
Text, loosely packed	coated	662.0	−18.0	658.5	−10.5
book	uncoated	251.0	−0.0	264.0 [b]	+2.0
Cover, loosely packed	coated	232.0	0.0	227.0	−9.5
book	uncoated	200.0	−25.5	221.5 [b]	−55.5

[a] Room conditions in Table III notes b and c.
[b] Note d in Table III applies.
[c] After the 16 hr flood, the weights were recorded, and the text was placed inside the cover. The Plexiglass plates were applied with torque on the C-clamps equal to that required for their release.
[d] Drainage positions were equivalent to those used for the loosely packed book.
[e] Δ is the change in weight in grams experienced after a 5-hr drainage.

Differences in water loss by those uncoated- and coated-paper texts previously flooded in the tightly packed book position may exist. The amount of the loss, 1 g and 3 g, respectively, is very small. The loss of water from the coated-paper text of the loosely packed books seems to be greater than for the uncoated-paper, loosely packed books. Drainage of water from the loosely packed coated-paper text appears to be greater than that noted for coated-paper text in the tightly packed book position.

Although it was clear that the tightly packed book position might be advantageous during a flood, it was less clear that this placement would be valuable during drainage. Greater water drainage losses seemed to occur among the coated-paper texts in the loosely packed books compared with the tightly packed books. The previous history may be important since the effect of pressure during drainage is not reflected in a significant difference (-3.5 g and -3.0 g) for the coated-paper text of the previously flooded, tightly packed-book position but may be reflected in a difference in the larger values (-18.0 g and -10.5 g) for the previously flooded, loosely packed books. The large losses of water from the cover, as opposed to the text water loss, of the uncoated-paper book in both the tightly packed and loosely packed book positions raise a question. What happens to the water when it drains from the cover? Because this experiment was not designed to eliminate the possibility of water from this source permeating the text during drainage, we cannot identify the absolute loss of water from the text for this period.

A review of the individual coated pages in the tightly packed books used in this study revealed that water only penetrated to a depth of 1 cm from the outside edge of the book. This result suggested that the swelling in the margin area of the pages created a pressure which precluded further diffusion of water to the inside of the coated-paper text during the flood. This observation during the controlled experiment clarified an earlier discovery of this limited-wetting phenomenon in many of the actual flood-damaged coated-paper books. The books must have been tightly packed on their shelves throughout the flood, removed after the water receded, and frozen before water could uniformly penetrate the entire text. An inspection of the uncoated-paper pages in the tightly packed book, referred to in Table IV, showed that they were uniformly wet. This was consistent with observations made after thawing and checking the actual flood-damaged uncoated-paper books. The pages in these books were uniformly wet unless they had drained dry in their loosely packed position.

Evaluation of Traditional and New Drying Techniques

After a systematic analysis of drying procedures, it was decided to apply a priority for conducting a comparative study of traditional and new approaches to drying books. How does one determine whether a new process for drying a book is equivalent to or better than a traditional method? A systematic visual examination of the book's structure as well as the quality of printed matter and illustrations are criteria that can be applied. Furthermore, physical property measurements of the strength of the paper in the book can be made. If such statistics compiled for the treated and the control (unflooded) books are compared, the results should allow one to draw conclusions about the merits of each drying method.

Preparation of Books and a Brief Description of the Drying Process

Again, two types of books (1, 2), easy and difficult to dry, were used in these investigations. Each book was sent through the standard simulated-flood sequence: it was placed in water 16 hr, drained 5 hr, put in a Ziploc bag, frozen, and stored in a freezer below −14°C. All of the previously prepared simulated flood-damaged books remained in the freezer until the drying process was applied. After the experiment in drying was conducted, the book was equilibrated with library-shelf storage conditions, again sealed in a Ziploc bag and refrozen. This precaution was necessary to minimize subsequent aging. Several days prior to the actual evaluation of the quality of the drying processes, the books were removed from the freezer, thawed, and equilibrated with room temperature. The control books, also stored in the freezer, were removed with the treated books and handled in the same manner.

Brief summaries of the drying processes used in this study are listed below. Each process was sufficiently developed so that reproducible results could be obtained if the samples going through the process were of the same quality. The removal of water from the flood damaged books was considered complete when the original dry weight of the book was reestablished.

Dielectric Drying (A, B). A single frozen book was placed between the horizontal electrodes of a 27-MHz dielectric heater. A plastic foam support was placed on the bottom electrode with the book face down on this support. The upper electrode was positioned above the book to prevent arcing between the electrodes. Incremental bursts of energy were applied to the book to melt the ice and to volatilize the water. To minimize the possibility of arcing between the electrodes, the cover of the book was removed before complete drying in our initial investigations (A). Later, more advanced techniques were developed to allow retention of the cover during drying (B).

Microwave Drying. A single frozen book was placed on a plastic form support inside a 2450-MHz microwave oven. Increments of energy were applied, melting ice and volatizing the water. The cover of the book was removed before drying to minimize the concentration of excess energy in the cover and to prevent localized charring.

Vacuum Dry (1A, 1B). The frozen books were placed horizontally on the floor of the chamber. The heated walls melted the ice. A vacuum pump was applied to evaporate the water from the books. Pumping was continued until the books returned to their original weight. The process produced for drying 1B was exactly the same as 1A; however, the samples were dried in separate independent experiments. The book dried in the 1A experiment was frozen, while the book dried in the 1B experiment was placed in the drying oven immediately after the standard drainage period.

Vacuum Dry–Air Cycle. The frozen books were set on their bottom edge in a chamber; the air in the chamber was removed. Dry heated air (0% relative humidity) was allowed to enter and to circulate around the books until atmospheric pressure was attained. When the moisture content of this circulated air became high, it was removed by evacuation. This cycle was repeated until the books were dry. ΔT_S and ΔT_L designate smallest and largest acceptable temperature differences between the heated input air and that in the ambient room.

Freeze-Thaw, Vacuum Drying (1A, 1B). The frozen books were laid with the spine vertical on metal shelves inside a large chamber. A controlled amount of heat was applied to the shelves to thaw the ice and to allow the water to evaporate. A vacuum was established to remove the water from the books. Progress in removing water from the books was checked by noting the return of the book's weight to its original value.

Freeze-Thaw, Vacuum Drying (2). The frozen books were arranged separately in a horizontal position on the shelves of a small "freezer dryer." The temperature of the shelf was set above freezing and held constant to supply energy for thawing the ice and evaporating the water. A vacuum to remove the water vapor was applied until the book became dry.

Interleaving-Air Drying (1A, 1B, 1C). Both frozen and newly flooded and drained books were grouped horizontally on a table. Air at room temperature was circulated around them. As soon as the frozen books thawed enough to be opened, dry newsprint was placed between each page. The newsprint sheets were changed approximately four times before the weight of the book was reduced to its original dry value. The same drying technique was applied to the A, B, and C samples which were dried on different occasions. Samples A and B were not frozen before the drying technique was implemented.

Solvent Extraction (1A, 1B). A single frozen book was set in a container and submerged in precooled anhydrous solvent. The container was then sealed and stored in a freezer. As the ice dissolved, the water–solvent mixture was replaced with anhydrous solvent until the moisture content in the book was reduced to that known for the original preflooded book. At this point, excess solvent was removed, and the book was interleaved with newsprint and stored at room temperature. During this storage, fresh paper was interleaved several times to remove the solvent. Both samples A and B were treated by the same technique; however, it was used at two different times. In this set of experiments, absolute anhydrous ethyl alcohol was used.

Solvent Extraction, Vacuum Drying. The same procedure as described in the solvent-extraction technique was used except that the treated book was not interleaved but was placed immediately in a vacuum chamber. The book was then brought to its original weight by evaporation of the solvent.

Drained-Air Dried (1A, 1B). Individual frozen books were laid on their side, not stacked, while room temperature air was gently circulated around them. Gradually the ice thawed, and the water drained from the books and evaporated. By weighing the books periodically, one could determine when all of the flood water was removed. Both samples A and B were treated by the same technique; however, it was used at two different times.

Criteria for Evaluating Books Dried by Different Processes

A decision was made that the results from the visual examination of the treated books were to be rated equally with the evaluation of the physical property measurements of the paper inside the books. Each treated flooded book was to be rated by comparing it with a control book which had not been subjected to any wetting and subsequent drying treatment. Table V gives an outline of the criteria chosen for this comparative study. If an individual feature in the visual evaluation was found equivalent to the control, a maximum value of two was assigned for the rating. If a feature was found inferior to that of the control but the book could still be used in normal library circulation, the rating was one. If the book was unacceptable for use in the library, the rating was zero. The structure of each book was rated according to the following criteria:

• Volume—Does the volume of the book appear equivalent to the control? Has it changed slightly or drastically?

• Spine—How do the curvature of the spine and the quality of the sewing compare with the control? Have they changed slightly or drastically?

• Cover—Is the appearance of the cover and back edge equivalent to the control? Has attachment of the cover to the text been degraded? If a change is noted, is it slight or drastic?

Comparison of the individual pages included the following inspection:

• Sticking of Pages—If any pages were sufficiently stuck so that they could not be separated or when separated, the print or illustration was damaged, a rating of zero was given. When this occurred, all other features concerning the appearance of the pages were rated zero since we assumed that such sticking would cause intermixing of the surface coatings and whatever else was on them.

• Staining of Base Paper—Did the combination of the simulated flood and drying technique change the color of the surface of the base paper— i.e., the nonprinted or nonillustrated areas?

• Bleeding of Print—Did the print expand, contract, bleed from, or diffuse into the adjacent area?

• Dye Transferal, Illustrations—Did the ink or dyes present in the illustration fade, run, or diffuse into the other colors or the adjacent area of the base paper?

• Cockling—Was the surface of the paper uniformly dried? Were irregularities slight or extensive?

Since the environmental history of the book would influence the results obtained from physical property measurements made on the paper, each book was preconditioned in a standard atmosphere (*4*) before any paper samples were removed. The following physical property measurements were made on the same pages throughout each of the control and dried books: tensile breaking strength (*5*); tensile energy of absorption (*6, 7*); internal tear resistance (*8*); thickness (*9*); and hot-water extractable acidity or alkalinity (*10*).

Arrangements were made with an accredited testing laboratory to make these measurements according to standard TAPPI procedures. If the physical property was not different from that of the control, a maximum rating of two was given. Duncan's Multiple Range Test (*11*) was applied to all the properties of the pages in the treated and control books. Whenever a significant difference was observed in the ranking for a physical property, a rating of one was given. If the property were so altered that the book could not be returned to library circulation, the rating was zero. The maximum rating of two was also assigned when a physical property had improved.

Evaluation of Drying Results and Visual and Physical Property Examination

Visual Examination. Since the visual evaluation in this study involved considerable judgment, a panel of evaluators was recruited. The panel included two librarians, a paper conservator, a scientist, and a staff member familiar with the quality of library books in circulation. Each member was given a description of the major and subcategories listed in Table V. Panelists were shown examples of books illustrating each of the criteria to be rated. After several training sessions to develop consistency in ratings, the panel rated the complete set of dried books which had received different restoration treatment.

To establish the final visual rating for each book, the average was determined from the individual ratings and entered into Table VI. This table lists the individual visual and property rating results for both the uncoated- and coated-paper books. A maximum visual rating of 16 for a book was not achieved. The highest value acquired for a coated-paper book was 10.0. A higher value of 13.0 was obtained for an uncoated-paper book. It is important to remember that this visual evaluation included

Table V. Evaluation of Dried, Flood-Damaged Books

Examination Criteria	Machine or Cross Direction of Test	Maximum Points Per Feature	Accumulative Total
Visual quality			
book structure			
volume	—	2	2
spine	—	2	4
cover	—	2	6
individual pages			
sticking of pages	—	2	8
staining of base paper	—	2	10
bleeding of print	—	2	12
dye transferring illustrations	—	2	14
cockling	—	2	16
Physical property measurements			
tensile, break	MD	2	18
tensile, energy absorption	MD	2	20
tensile, break	CD	2	22
tensile, energy absorption	CD	2	24
thickness	—	2	26
tear	MD	2	28
	CD	2	30
Total acidity or basicity	—	2	32

not only the effect of the drying process on the book but also the inherent flood damage.

The influence of the sticking of the coated-paper pages on the overall rating is readily understood by a review of the numbers for the coated-paper books in the third column of this table. This rating clearly identified the drying processes which did not cause sticking of the coated-paper category and suggested which drying process would be most useful in restoration efforts.

Physical–Chemical Property Examination. Initially, physical property tests were made on the control books only to establish the inherent variability of the paper in the books and the testing procedure. With this information the number of replicas required to determine statistically significant differences in each tested property was apparent. Physical property measurements were then scheduled for the paper in the dried books. To identify the variability from book to book more carefully, additional control books were sent to an accredited paper testing laboratory for measurement at the same time the dried books were being tested. A one-way analysis of variance (12) was applied to all physical property tests on the books. The analysis confirmed that there was a significant

Table VI. Evaluation of Drying Processes

Drying Process	Type of Paper	Visual Rating	Property Rating	Final Process Rating
Freeze-thaw, vacuum (1B)	uncoated	13.0	16.0	52.4
	coated	9.4	14.0	
Freeze-thaw, vacuum (1A)	uncoated	12.1	16.0	48.9
	coated	8.8	12.0	
Interleave-air, frozen (1C)	uncoated	11.4	16.0	48.6
	coated	9.2	12.0	
Freeze-thaw, vacuum (B)	uncoated	12.0	16.0	48.0
	coated	10.0	10.0	
Solvent extraction (1B)	uncoated	9.9	16.0	45.8
	coated	8.9	11.0	
Interleave-air, not frozen (1B)	uncoated	10.5	16.0	45.8
	coated	8.3	11.0	
Solvent extraction (1A)	uncoated	9.7	16.0	45.2
	coated	9.5	10.0	
Interleave-air, not frozen (1A)	uncoated	9.9	16.0	44.7
	coated	8.8	10.0	
Solvent extraction, vacuum	uncoated	10.5	15.0	42.9
	coated	7.4	10.0	
Drained-air (1B)	uncoated	12.8	16.0	31.2
	coated	2.4	0.0	
Vacuum-air cycle, ΔT_S	uncoated	11.9	16.0	30.4
	coated	2.5	0.0	
Vacuum-air cycle, ΔT_L	uncoated	12.1	16.0	29.9
	coated	1.8	0.0	
Vacuum, not frozen (1B)	uncoated	11.1	16.0	29.5
	coated	2.4	0.0	
Drained-air (1A)	uncoated	11.8	16.0	29.0
	coated	1.2	0.0	
Microwave,[a] 2450 MHz	uncoated	12.2	16.0	29.0
	coated	0.8	0.0	
Vacuum, frozen (1A)	uncoated	11.6	15.0	28.7
	coated	2.1	0.0	
Dielectric,[a] 27 MHz (1A)	uncoated	12.2	15.0	27.8
	coated	0.6	0.0	
Dielectric,[b] 27 MHz (2B)	uncoated	11.2	16.0	27.6
	coated	0.4	0.0	

[a] Covers removed.
[b] Covers attached.

difference among the books. Duncan's Multiple Range Test (*11*) was then used to rank and to arrange the individual sets of physical property data into homogeneous groups. A lower rating of one was assigned to those physical properties of the dried paper not included in the groups of data containing control book information. A rating of zero was given to those properties which changed to such a degree that the book could not be returned to use—e.g., coated paper pages sticking so tightly that measurements on individual pages could not be made.

The results of rating physical–chemical properties for all the uncoated and coated books are given in the fourth column in Table VI. A maximum value of 16 was obtained for the uncoated-paper book; a value of 14 was obtained for the coated-paper book. The zero rating values assigned to the physical property measurements for the coated-paper books clearly identified the limitations of these processes for drying this type of coated paper.

Observations and Discussion of the Drying Results

To develop the best guideline for determining which processes offered the greatest potential for drying books with these two extremes in paper, the visual and physical–chemistry property ratings for both the uncoated-paper and coated-paper books were added together (Table VI). The magnitude of the sum of these four numbers listed in decreasing order gives an overall view of what this exploratory evaluation revealed about the process for drying these extremes in book paper. These processes were applied under conditions which were known to have reproducibly dried other types of books. However, none of these processes was studied to ascertain specific conditions which could best dry the type of paper in these books.

Several general observations can be made. The freeze-thaw, vacuum-drying process appears to have great promise for drying not only uncoated- but coated-paper pages. The results of drying the paper in the coated-paper books are significant; only those processes rated above 40 dried the coated paper without producing the sticking problem. The other processes with a rating of 31.2 or below during drying caused severe sticking. The final process rating results for the freeze-thaw, vacuum (1A, 1B) and (2) processes represent values from both large and small units. Scaling up did not cause any major differences in the quality of the dried product. These two units differed in capacity by a ratio of 1000. The results, 48.9 and 52.4, for the freeze-thaw, vacuum (1A, 1B) process in the large unit reveal the range of variability that this unit gives in drying identical books at two different times.

How do these freeze-thaw, vacuum-dry processes compare with the traditional approaches of drained-air and interleave-air drying? The drained-air drying process has a low rating, between 29.0 and 31.2. Since coated paper without interleaving sticks tenaciously, the drained-air drying process appears inferior to the freeze-thaw, vacuum-drying process. The traditional interleave-air process for drying books, especially when the books have been previously frozen, gives results (48.6) comparable with the freeze-thaw, vacuum dry process. It is impossible to identify any important difference in the quality of the products dried by these two processes.

Reproducibility of the drying was checked in random fashion with several other processes: interleave-air, solvent extraction, dielectric, and drained-air dry. In every case, the final replicated process rating results were close to the initial value. On two different occasions, the interleave-air drying process was applied to the flooded and drained, but not frozen, books. The final process ratings, 45.8 and 44.7, were close. A higher final process rating of 48.6 was obtained when this technique was applied to a similar pair of books that were frozen and thawed before being interleaved. Is the difference random error, or does this higher value suggest that there may be an advantage to freezing books before interleaving? Further study is required to establish the validity of this suggestion.

Another drying process which can be applied successfully to separating coated paper is solvent extraction. The reproducibility of its application at two different times is emphasized by the similarity of the final process ratings, 45.2 and 45.8. If this process is modified to include vacuum drying rather than interleaving as a final step, the overall process rating appears to be reduced to 43.9 if random error can be ignored. The remainder of the drying processes, those with a final rating of 31.2 and below, did not effectively dry this coated paper. Application of the vacuum-air cycle drying process, first at a small and then at a higher ΔT, resulted in very close final process rating values, 30.4 and 29.9. The microwave and dielectric drying processes are also in this category since they cannot be used successfully for drying books containing this coated paper. This undesirable result was not an accident since it happened on different occasions with several types of coated paper.

Summary and Conclusions

Simulation of the flood to determine its effect on the quality of paper in books as well as the structure of the book itself is reproducible. The simulation of the drainage conditions is also reproducible for books manufactured with the same materials. There is evidence that the rate of water loss from the books is associated with the type of paper in the text of the book. Evidence exists that comparable amounts of water are absorbed by books containing either coated or uncoated paper when they are packed tightly on a shelf and inundated by flood waters. Loosely packed, coated-, and uncoated-paper books absorb more water than tightly packed books. Therefore, the application of pressure by tightly packing books on a shelf can keep the absorption of water to a significant minimum during a disaster.

After books are subjected to a flood, the loosely packed, uncoated-paper books can release almost all the water absorbed during a 120 hr drainage period if the environmental conditions are equivalent to, or more favorable than, those prevalent during this drainage study. Such results can be expected only if mold or biological growth does not take place in the books.

The absorption of water by the covers of books can be important. The total amount of water in the cover can exceed that of the paper in the text, depending upon the materials that are used in the cover and text and the thickness of the book. The pressure generated by the expansion of coated paper while absorbing water is impressive. If books containing this type of paper are placed under pressure prior to being covered by water, the partial expansion of the coated paper can limit and in many cases stop penetration of water into the interior of the book.

Freeze-thaw vacuum, interleave-air, and solvent extraction processes offer the greatest potential in drying these types of coated- and uncoated-paper books after they have been wetted and frozen. The drained-air, vacuum-air cycle, vacuum, microwave, and dielectric drying processes work well on uncoated paper, but they fail to dry books containing this type of coated paper. Small and large units for freeze-thaw, vacuum drying have been used successfully to remove water from these frozen coated and uncoated books.

As a result of the above investigations (excluding the freeze-thaw, vacuum 1B run), a recommendation was made by the author and the conservator to apply the freeze-thaw, vacuum dry process to the majority of the actual frozen flood-damaged books, periodicals, and catalogs containing coated paper. In essence, the application was a success; however, one must study the article in the AIC bulletin (13) and the Corning Museum of Glass book (14) to understand better how this process was applied and how the results were measured for this complex distribution of damaged materials. Many bound coated items were saved because of the application of this process.

Acknowledgments

Thomas W. Duncan was the book and paper conservator at the Corning Museum during these investigations. He is presently associated with the New England Document Conservation Center, North Andover, Mass. The author is grateful for his direct assistance in planning and implementing these investigations. The following organizations and individuals also contributed to the research, process development, and paper tests which aided in the completion of this survey; specific references to their contributions were not made since much of their work is unpublished: Kimberly Clark Corp. (R. H. Boehm, director, Research and Development; J. F. Wade, manager, Test Development and Testing Laboratories); Library of Congress (John C. Williams, research officer and Peter Waters, restoration officer, Preservation Office); Corning Glass Works (W. H. Armistead, vice president of Corporate Research; Janet Johnson, statistician); General Electric Co. (Richard Shoulberg, applications engineer); McDonnell Douglas Corp. (Emil Wang, branch manager; H. F. McKinney, group engineer). The author is especially indebted to R. H. Brill and J. H. Martin of the Corning Museum of Glass for their encouragement to pursue these investigations. Special appreciation is due Carolyn Horton, New York, Peter Waters, Washington, D.C., Marilyn Weidner, Philadelphia, Pa., and William de Alleaume, Albany, N.Y. for their advice and the confirmation of the need to undertake this study.

The majority of the funds required for conducting this research was obtained from the U.S. National Museum Act and the National Endowment for the Arts.

Literature Cited

1. Underwood, R. M., "The Complete Book of Dried Arrangements," Bonanza Books, New York, 1952.
2. Abbate, F., "American Art," Octopus Books, Milan, Italy, 1966.
3. Dixon, W. J., Massey, F. J., Jr., "Introduction to Statistical Analysis," p. 110, McGraw-Hill Book Co., New York, 1969.
4. Technical Association of the Pulp and Paper Industry, "Standard Conditioning and Testing Atmospheres for Paper, Board, Pulp Handsheets, and Related Products," T-402os-70, TAPPI, Atlanta.
5. Ibid., "Tensile Breaking Strength of Paper and Paperboard," T-404ts-66.
6. Ibid., "Stretch of Paper and Paper Board," T-457os-46.
7. Ibid., "Tensile Breaking Properties of Paper and Paper Board (Using Constant Rate of Elongation)," T-449os-70.
8. Ibid., "Internal Tearing Resistance of Paper," T-414ts-65.
9. Ibid., "Thickness (caliper) of Paper and Paper Board," T-411os-68.
10. Ibid., "Hot-Water Extractable Acidity or Alkalinity of Paper," T-428sa-67.
11. Dixon and Massey, "Introduction to Statistical Analysis," pp. 156–167.
12. Hicks, C. R., "Fundamental Concepts in the Design of Experiments," Holt, Rinehart and Winston, Inc., New York, 1964.
13. Fischer, D. J., Duncan, T., "Conservation Research: Flood-Damaged Library Materials," *Bull. Am. Inst. Conserv.* (1975) **15** (2) 28–48.
14. Martin, J. H., "The Corning Flood: Museum under Water," Corning Museum of Glass, Corning, N.Y., 1977.

RECEIVED January 19, 1977.

9

Conservation Research: Use of Dielectric and Microwave Energy to Thaw and Dry Frozen Library Materials

DAVID J. FISCHER

Milton Roy Co., P.O. Box 1899, Sarasota, Fla. 33578

One of the consequences of tropical storm Agnes, June 1972, reached as far north as Corning, N.Y. The Corning Museum of Glass' library, the library of record for the world's glass scholars, sustained extraordinary damage when flooded by waters from an adjacent river. All of the library's damaged collection was frozen. A team developed a plan, which included special research projects, for the restoration of this collection. The problems associated with the logistics in thawing frozen catalogs, journals, and books for identifying them as well as for recording the type of damage which would necessitate restoration was immense. The use of dielectric heaters for thawing solved this problem. Only limited use of this process, however, was possible for completely drying books.

On June 23, 1972, Corning, N. Y. was battered by an unusually severe flood, one which might occur only once during a 500–1000-year period. Although there were countless problems caused by the flood, the damage to the collections housed in the library of the Corning Museum of Glass demanded special attention.

All flooded paper materials—books, periodicals, documents, rare books, files, and records—were frozen as quickly as possible to prevent biological growth. A restoration effort to save the library's contents and a parallel on-site applied conservation research program were established. The goal of this research program was to develop, whenever possible, new techniques and to improve traditional methods for restoring flood-damaged library materials (1).

124

Need for Fast Thawing and Drying Methods

Table I outlines removal of the items from the freezer and decisions on degrees of restoration and preservation that each should receive. A trial run through the sequence clearly showed that traditional air thawing was the step which seriously limited the total amount of work that could be done. A method for initially thawing each item quickly so that it could be identified and its restoration outlined was needed. The conservator and the librarians asked the scientist to find which high-speed thawing methods could be used most efficiently.

When the extent of damage was determined for the thawed book, a decision was then made on whether to go ahead immediately with the restoration process, including the best drying approach, or to again freeze the book. The latter approach was taken in the majority of the cases since the special restoration techniques that were required could only be supplied when the appropriate talent became available.

Dielectric and Microwave Energy

Dielectric and microwave energy of the appropriate frequency can transfer energy directly via radiation (2, 3, 4) without an intermediate transfer medium. This energy transfer and application can raise the temperature of an object more uniformly than the conduction and convection methods. More specifically, use of either dielectric (5) or microwave (6) radiation to interact directly with water molecules had the potential to accelerate the thawing and drying of our frozen, flood-damaged library and archival materials.

The term "dielectric heating" can be applied to a wide range of electromagnetic frequencies. Commercial dielectric units are available for operation at frequencies of 13.56, 27.12, and 40 MHz. These frequencies can be used with government approval if the proper shielding and grounding precautions are taken. Their application for drying paper, wood, and textiles has been discussed by Williams (7), Jolly (8), Hankin et al. (9), and Anderson et al. (10). Results on drying books have been published by Thomas and Flink (11, 12). Microwave radiation covers a narrow spectrum of electromagnetic radiation which involves shorter wavelengths. Commercially available units operate at approved frequencies of either 915 or 2450 MHz. To operate these systems safely, radiation leakage must be prevented.

Additional background information on the drying can be obtained by studying the publications by P. L. Jones, J. Lawton, and I. M. Parker (13) and J. Lawton (14). They analyzed results from drying paper by both radio and microwave frequencies using laboratory-scale apparatus and conclude that the 27-MHz radio frequency provides a greater mois-

Table I.   Restoration and Preservation of Library Materials

```
                        ┌─────────────────┐
                        │    Items in     │
                        │  freezer truck  │
                        └─────────────────┘
                                 │
                        ┌─────────────────┐
                        │ Remove for partial│
                        │thawing, identification│
                        └─────────────────┘
                                 │
┌──────────────┐  ┌─────────────────┐  ┌──────────────────┐
│Hold for immedi-│  │ Library staff selects│  │Special collection│
│ate replacement │  │and recommends action│  │   restoration    │
└──────────────┘  └─────────────────┘  └──────────────────┘
                                 │
┌──────────────┐  ┌─────────────────┐
│Replacement ac-│  │ Receipt of items by│
│tion not known;│  │conservator for storage│
│hold in freezer │  │ in freezer and future│
└──────────────┘  │      action      │
                  └─────────────────┘
┌────────┐  ┌────────┐
│Actually│  │Restore │
│replace │  └────────┘
└────────┘
              ┌──────────────────┐  ┌──────────────────┐
              │Minimal cleaning, │  │Restoration action│
              │drying, etc. for  │  └──────────────────┘
              │   microfilming   │
              └──────────────────┘
                        ┌────────────┐
                        │ Fumigate,  │
                        │ sterilize  │
                        └────────────┘
                        ┌────────────────┐
                        │Receipt of items by│
                        │  library staff  │
                        └────────────────┘
                        ┌────────────────┐
                        │Microfilm operation│
                        └────────────────┘
              ┌──────────────────────────┐
              │Return of items to library│
              └──────────────────────────┘
┌────────┐ ┌────────────┐ ┌────────────┐ ┌──────────────────┐
│ Books  │ │Temporary or│ │ Storage of │ │Selection of binding│
│shelved │ │ short-term │ │ microfilm  │ │for restored items │
└────────┘ │ packaging, │ └────────────┘ └──────────────────┘
           │   boxing   │
           └────────────┘
```

ture leveling effect than the microwave frequency of 2450 MHz. This further supported the intention to use the 27-MHz frequency. Their study, however, does not include trying to dry paper that has either print or pigmented illustrations on it.

Electrical Energy Converted to Heat

Molecules having dipole moments become sensitive to specific high frequencies. The magnitude of the dipole moment plus other environmental factors create sensitivity to specific frequencies. Water has such a dipole moment. Placed in certain oscillating voltage fields, it becomes sensitive to dielectric and microwave frequencies by trying to align itself with the direction of the applied voltage. When the direction of the field changes several million times a second, there is friction between the water molecules and heat develops. The amount of alignment of the molecules—i.e., polarization—is proportional to the field intensity or voltage gradient established between the electrodes.

The frozen materials were placed between the electrodes of the dielectric heater. Application of radiation energy raised the temperature of the frozen water, causing it to melt and then to evaporate. Details on the type of dielectric and microwave equipment used in these investigations can be found in the Appendix. Choice of frequency was based on those that were available immediately in commercial units.

Oscillators to maximize interaction with water and to minimize interaction with the surrounding material in the books were not constructed for two reasons. The time and funds required to build such a unit were not available. Williams' publication (7), however, indicates that most of the interaction at 27 MHz and 2450 MHz, the primary frequencies used in this investigation, was with the water rather than the materials in the paper.

Microwave energy is applied differently from dielectric energy. It is transmitted to an enclosed application chamber by a wave guide, a rectangular pipe. There is microwave interaction with water molecules in frozen books placed in this chamber. Generated heat raises frozen water's temperature to cause melting and evaporation.

The successful application of either microwave or dielectric energy for drying requires that water, as it is evaporated, be removed from the paper and book. Air with low relative humidity is forced through the chamber to facilitate water vapor removal from the object. Since interaction of the water molecules at different locations in the chamber may not be uniform, each frozen flood-damaged item was inverted and partially rotated between each burst of energy. Radiation leakage from both types of equipment is possible; therefore, special precautions for complete shielding and grounding were taken. The doors to the chamber of the microwave and dielectric units were used as a safety device. Closed doors released the electrical power to the chamber or the electrodes. Power was automatically cut when the doors opened.

Exploring Operation Limits—Dielectric and Microwave Heaters

Exploratory experiments in thawing and drying randomly selected materials from the museum's collection were conducted. Frozen flood-damaged books and file materials that the librarians knew could be discarded or replaced were chosen for the initial experiments. The dielectric grid current was kept constant as the plate current or electrode separation space was varied according to the size of the frozen library materials and an estimate of the water they contained.

Some of the problems that arose while operating the dielectric and microwave equipment are listed in Table II. Books with leather covers, bindings applied with some synthetic adhesives, or excessive amounts of frozen mud on the spine or back edge could not be dried by either the

Table II. Limitations on Use of Process

Equipment		Detection of Problems
Dielectric	Microwave	
*		Arcing
*	*	Arcing, flashing
*	*	Arcing
*	*	Burnt odor
*	*	Arcing, flashing
*		Burnt odor
*	*	Burnt odor
*	*	Ballooning or bubbles
*	*	Arcing, flashing
*		Burnt odor

dielectric or microwave heaters. Burning or charring was observed at each of these sites. Any section of the frozen item which offered a better electrical conducting path than the paper or water yielded more readily to the high frequency current. This current, if unchecked, raised the temperature enough to cause charring and burning.

These preliminary tests indicated an erratic response by the frozen book to the radiation. Equivalent drying did not occur with similar damaged materials. Whether the irregularities were caused by the material or the equipment's performance was not evident. After the initial experiments with both dielectric and microwave heaters, the dielectric apparatus was chosen for additional experiments. This decision was based primarily upon this equipment's having the higher power capability.

Some books could be thawed in several minutes with this equipment, but the results of these preliminary studies about its use for complete drying raised serious questions. Therefore, during the early part of the restoration period, a decision was made that the equipment only be used for thawing. Specific restrictions were placed on equipment operation:

Dielectric and Microwave Heaters

Damage to Book, Paper

Cause	Location	Type
high conductivity of adhesives	spine	burning of synthetic, sometimes animal, and casein glues
high conductivity of materials	covers and book edge	burned sections
levitation of top cover and pages during final stages of drying	top cover	burned sections
paper clips, metal folder clasps inside frozen packets	paper around metal	charring of the paper
conductivity of leather	cover	burned and charred
Thermofax	complete sheet	burned
staples, metal eyelets	area around metal	burned paper
too much energy applied	covers and coated-paper pages	inflated covers and split sheets
conductivity of mud	cover and book edge	burned area
localized eddy currents	metallic pigment, especially gold in illustrations	charred area

• The upper electrode must always be placed at least 2.0 cm above the frozen item.

• Any burst of energy applied to the frozen items should not exceed one minute.

• Mud on the covers should be removed as much as possible before or during examination of the item between bursts of energy.

• If a need existed to remove small amounts of water after the thawing, the covers of the books should be removed.

• All paper clips, eyelets, or any metallic pieces attached to the frozen items should be removed immediately after thawing before any additional energy was applied.

Systematic Investigations

Typical Water Loss and Temperature Profile of Books while Thawing and Drying. *The Connoisseur, An Illustrated Magazine for Collectors,* Volumes 13, 21, and 25 (1908) had been partially damaged in the flood. After replacements had been received, the damaged books were available for experimentation. The three volumes, equivalent in size and composition, underwent a simulated flood, drainage, and freezing (1) to examine the drying characteristics of two 27-MHz units and one 12-MHz dielectric heater to see if there were differences in the efficiency of these units. A summary of the water absorbed and removed in drying these books is recorded in Table III.

In each drying operation the electrode separation and grid control current were the same. Any differences in plate current and water removal were the result of different heaters and frequency. Energy in 45-sec bursts was applied to each of these volumes after the leather covers were removed. The texts were rotated and turned after each burst of energy to aid in uniform interaction of the field with the sample. After each burst, the weights of the text as well as the highest temperature in the book were recorded. The amount of water removed per burst of energy was low at first and then increased to a maximum of 172 g as the temperature inside the book exceeded 90°C. A specific plot of energy

Table III. Water Content and Its Removal

Volume	Dry Weight (g) Original	Dry Weight (g) No Cover	Wet Weight (g) With Cover	Wet Weight (g) No Cover	% Increase With Cover	% Water Removed, Text Only
13	1,118	1,005	2,057	1,792	84	78
21	1,136	1,032	2,055	1,878	81	82
25	1,056	962	1,854	1,674	75	74

removed per burst vs. the numbered burst allowed the performance of each dielectric dryer to be compared. The 27-MHz heaters were found to be more effective units for removal of water than the 12-MHz heater. The trend in the magnitude of the water lost per burst followed the increase in temperature measured inside the book after each burst of energy. The maximum amount of water removed per burst took place when the peak temperature was reached. During subsequent bursts the amount of water per burst decreased rapidly while the temperature inside the book decreased at a much slower rate.

During those bursts when large amounts of water were released, the volatilized water, in its rush to leave the pages, forced the book open. Therefore, the upper electrode had to be placed approximately 2 cm above the book. This placement minimized the chance that the rising water vapor could cause a short between the electrodes.

Need for Calibrating Heater Efficiency. A material which would absorb water, allow water to interact uniformly with the dielectric and microwave frequencies, and be similar in composition to paper was desired. Cellulose sponges, 3M brand ($19.5 \times 11.4 \times 4.0$ cm) were obtained, tested, and used instead of books with unprinted or nonillustrated paper to check the reproducibility of the drying equipment. However, preliminary wetting and drying of these sponges, using a 27-MHz heater, showed that the original salt solution suspended in the sponge by the manufacturer had to be leached out if the sponges were to give reproducible results while drying. The salt's migration in and out of the cellulosic matrix during drying was not predictable. Only when deionized water was absorbed by the sponges could each heater be evaluated on an equivalent basis. The number of constant bursts of energy required to remove a standard amount of water from the same sponge was chosen for characterizing the heater's performance and consistency.

Additional Comparison of 12-MHz with 27-MHz Dielectric Heaters. Between six and nine 45-sec bursts of energy were required to remove a standard amount of deionized water from a wetted sponge for a 12-MHz heater, while a range of three to eight 45-sec bursts of energy were required by the 27-MHz heater to remove the same weight of water from comparable wetted sponges. Thus, the 27-MHz heater appeared to be more efficient when conditions were set with both units for the fastest possible drying without arcing.

In later experiments the number of bursts required to remove a standard 150 g of water was increased when the temperature of the sponge was lowered and water at $0°C$ was added. Again the 27-MHz heater was found to be more efficient than the 12-MHz heater. The same conclusion was drawn when tests were conducted when the water in the sponges was frozen.

Microwave Investigations

Characterization of the Oven. The microwave oven described in the Appendix was, after exploratory studies, used in the following investigations. Deionized water at 25°C was added to two prewashed and rinsed sponges until they weighed 250.0 g each. The wetted sponges were frozen. One sponge was taken from the freezer, immediately placed on the foam plastic tray, and placed in the microwave oven. The only adjustment possible to vary the energy to the sample was the length of the energy burst. After exploratory experiments, a 45-sec burst was selected. Nineteen bursts were required to remove 150 g of water from this frozen sponge, which was rotated and turned upside down after each burst. The amount of water lost and the temperature of the sponge after each burst were determined and recorded. This procedure was duplicated with the second frozen sponge. Between 18 and 19 bursts were required to remove 150 g of water from this sponge. With replication in performance established, the equipment could be used to dry the standard, flood-damaged research books (1). The number of bursts of energy required to remove an equivalent amount of water from these standard books was much greater than that required with the available 27-MHz dielectric dryer. Subsequent studies with special packages of equivalent paper confirm these results so the general use of microwave drying was dropped, except for special experimentation.

Drying of Special Research Books. Two research books, one containing only coated (Francesco Abbate, *American Art*, Octopus, 1966.), the other only uncoated paper (R. M. Underwood, *The Complete Book of Dried Arrangements*, Bonanza, 1952.), were chosen for a comparison study of drying techniques (1). They went through the simulated flood, drainage, and freezing sequence (1). During earlier experience with the microwave oven, covers charred or burned if they were not removed. Therefore, each cover was carefully separated from the text of the book after thawing and before the text was dried.

The text of the frozen coated-paper book was put in the oven and dried. After each burst, the text was turned and rotated. Its inside temperature and incremental water loss were noted. A total of 48 bursts was applied to this frozen 682-g text to remove water until its dry weight of 321.0 g was reached. An inspection showed that all the coated-paper pages in the text were stuck, a condition similar to that which resulted when the 27-MHz heater was used to dry the same type of book (1).

The text of the frozen uncoated-paper research book was dried in the next experimental run with this oven. Eight 45-sec bursts of energy were required to remove the water from this lightly wetted 244.5-g text. The amount of water absorbed by this text during the simulated flood was small since it was in the tightly packed position (1). Its dry weight was 201.0 g. An inspection of each page revealed that the dried product was excellent and equivalent to that obtained when a similar frozen book was dried by the 27-MHz heater.

Applications of Dielectric Heating

The 27-MHz dielectric dryer was used initially to thaw all of the frozen office correspondence and file drawer materials. This was extremely valuable since quick access to these records was necessary for two reasons: (1) getting the Museum operational as soon as possible and (2) establishing a sound basis for insurance claims on all property, including the glass and library collections.

The following applications, however, are specific examples of the use of the dielectric heater for conducting research and treating frozen flood-damaged books. These discussions do not necessarily follow a chronological sequence and involve slight variations in using the heater throughout the 2-year period.

General Restoration Effort. During the summer of 1973 about 400 frozen flood-damaged books, whose value did not justify restoration, were to be microfilmed. These books had been isolated earlier because they had few, if any, coated-paper pages. The job of not only thawing but also drying all of these books with the dielectric heater was assigned to the assistant conservators. Each of these frozen books was put, one at a time, on a standard foam plastic tray placed on the bottom electrode. The upper electrode was lowered to a level of 2.0 cm above the top of the book. Various bursts of energy were then applied. A single 27-MHz unit was used for these books. The conservator's assistants decided the length of time for the energy burst. No single burst, however, was to exceed 2.0 min. A sponge was used to remove excess mud from the book after it was thawed and before it was dried. This was a precautionary measure to eliminate paths by which high current arcing could occur. The 400 books were dried in fewer than 20 working days. The speed with which the books (containing a variety of paper) dried was impressive. Evidence of charring was observed in two books only, a result which could not be explained; repeated checks of the 27-MHz heater by drying the standard cellulose sponge showed that it was operating in a consistent manner.

One book, *Sequestre de Villeroy Tableaux Anciens et Modernes, Objects d'Arts et d'Ameublement* (21.5 × 27.0 cm, 65 pages), was given two 30-sec bursts of energy to produce thawing. Mud was washed from the pages before dielectric drying continued. Six 1-min bursts dried it. During the last burst, arcing was observed with localized charring along its path. The current entered the center of the spine and came out the back of the book 4 cm from the back edge. Minute charring was observed on page 54. The amount of charring increased in subsequent pages with the maximum on the final page. The initial point of penetration and the subsequent path of the current through the book gave no clue to the cause.

There may be one explanation: during the flood, excess glue, present on the spine, could have migrated between the signatures towards the center of the individual pages. High concentration of such glue could provide a low resistance path for this frequency of dielectric current. Studies of the operational limits of this dielectric heater uncovered several examples of this type of current shorting, which in turn resulted in a charring of the paper. In earlier cases, the migrated glue was visible. Such glue was not visible in this book.

The second book, *Jahrbuch des Veriens fur Ort und Heimat Kunde in der Grafschaft Mark, Verbunden mit dem Markischen Museum zu Mitten an der Ruhr* (15.0 × 20.5 cm, 281 pages) was given two 1-min bursts of energy for thawing so that the covers could be removed. Dielectric heater treatment was continued without mud removal since there were only trace amounts. During the third 1-min burst of energy, charring began at pages 24 and 25. The amount of charring decreased as pages were turned in both directions away from these pages. Charring ceased at pages 12 and 34. Later weighing and air drying of this book revealed that charring happened when water equivalent to 29% of the book's dry weight was present. Such charring had never been observed before in books containing this amount of water.

There were many pages with illustrations in this book. Why charring started on pages 24 and 25 could not be determined. Perhaps a small amount of conducting dirt or mud could have been deposited on the highly inked area of the pictures. If so, high eddy currents could have caused a localized hot spot and the burning of the paper. Human error did not contribute to this charring or burning. These experiences, plus the previously observed limitations of the dielectric heater technique, especially in drying coated paper, precluded general use of this unit for drying library materials which were not expendable.

Unique Use. A critical new need developed after *De visione perfects sive de amborium visionis axium concursu in eadem objets puncto* (Cherubim d'Orleans, Pere, 1678) was thawed. The cover was removed, and the threads were cut from the signatures. The wetted paper was so weak that the pages could not be separated. Heavy blotting board was placed on each side of the text, and a special dielectric drying approach was applied. The text was placed in the dielectric heater between plastic trays (sandwich technique). Energy bursts of 30-sec were applied until most of the water in the book was removed. When approximately 110% of the book's dry weight was approached, the book was removed from the dryer. The pages were strong enough so that each signature and page could be separated for normal air drying. Dielectric radiation to remove water from this paper until it was strong enough to be separated helped save this 1678 text.

Special Research Books. The sandwich technique, placing the wetted book between two inert plastic trays, was used to dry the flooded, drained, and frozen coated- and uncoated-paper research books (*1*) in an improved 27-MHz heater. The covers of these books were not removed in applying this drying procedure.

One frozen uncoated-paper research book weighing 480.5 g was dried by applying 20 30-sec bursts. The final weight of the dried book was 287.5 g. The sandwich technique used for this book, cover intact, gave excellent results.

A replica of the previous flooded, drained, and frozen uncoated-paper research book was dried by again applying the sandwich technique in another 27-MHz heater. The frozen weight of the book was 449.0 g; the dry weight was 290.0 g. Only 14 30-sec bursts, contrasted to the earlier 27-MHz heater's 20 bursts, were required to thaw and to dry this book. The appearance of the dried cover and text was equivalent to that observed previously. The sandwich technique was applied successfully.

Attention was turned to drying coated paper. A check on the heater performance by drying the earlier rewetted calibrated sponge was made. The flooded, drained, and frozen coated-paper research book was then placed between the electrodes of the dryer with foam plastic trays above and below. Arcing was a problem after the book was thawed. The current passed through the front and back covers and edge. After 12 30-sec bursts, the cover was found to have charred appreciably. It was removed from the text. Although none of the pages of the text was charred, there was evidence of pages sticking. The text was then dried without any arcing, and a thorough examination of the pages of the dried product showed that every one had stuck. The text was completely blocked and worthless. Since this result was the same as that obtained after dielectric heating of other coated-paper books, a similar experiment with this coated-paper research book was not conducted.

Summary and Conclusions

Dielectric (12- and 27-MHz) and microwave (2450-MHz) radiation can be used successfully for high-speed drying of uncoated paper when the electrical conductivity of pigments, adhesives, and cover materials is less than that of the paper. In these investigations, the 27-MHz frequency was found to be more effective than the 12- or 2450-MHz frequencies.

Drying of the books or periodicals containing coated paper was *not* successful in these investigations. In almost every case, the pages stuck

together. If high rates of energy were applied, individual pages bal-
looned or split as the water inside the page became a gas. The rapid
rate at which this gas formed greatly exceeded the rate at which it
could penetrate the coated adhesive surface of the page and evaporate
from the outer surface. Therefore, gas inside the page expanded, causing
the outside surfaces of the page also to expand, resulting in the appearance of a partially inflated balloon. This behavior was also observed with
several book covers.

High-speed thawing and drying of file materials, correspondence,
etc. were achieved when all paper clips, metal eyelets, carbon paper, and
Thermofax sheets were removed. Drying of books with covers in place
was more difficult. Microwave radiation was not successful, but dielectric
energy with the sandwich technique could dry some of these books.
Excess mud had to be removed, or arcing would occur through this lower
conductivity path during the application of energy. Leather bindings
charred or burned regardless of how short the energy bursts.

These conclusions may appear different from the results described
by N. Ya. Solechnik (15) where dielectric radiation treatment of leather
with gold embossments and clasps in the binding plus ordinary and
colored photographs took place without damage. The purpose of the
experiments covered in Solechnik's report was to fumigate and to sterilize
wetted books, not to dry them. He mentions that the maximum increase
in moisture content of the paper treated was approximately 6%. At this
moisture level the results of a 10-min treatment could be quite different
from the results in these investigations. The water content in the frozen
flood-damaged books in the majority of cases in these studies was in
excess of 150% of the dry weight of the book. Under the ideal application of dielectric energy with the sandwich technique, more than 200 g
water/min could be evaporated from wetted paper.

The critical need for equipment which would quickly thaw frozen
materials was satisfied by use of these dielectric heaters. The librarians
and conservator could identify the extent of damage to each item and
effectively plan the restoration required. The economical application of
dielectric and microwave drying to coated-paper books needs a major
breakthrough to bring about success.

The major contribution of dielectric energy to the restoration effort
was its use in thawing all file materials and nonrare books and pamphlets.
They could be identified by the librarians, and their restoration could be
planned by the conservator. Use of dielectric energy offers an efficient
method of drying those books which could be replaced if charring might
occur. The frequency of damage for this technique as applied to
uncoated-paper books was 0.5%.

Acknowledgments

Thomas W. Duncan was the book and paper conservator at the museum during these investigations. He is presently associated with the New England Document Conservation Center, Andover, Mass. The author is grateful for his direct assistance in planning and implementing these investigations.

Special thanks are due the administrators of the U.S. National Museum Act for their initial support and recognition of the need to conduct this conservation research simultaneously with the actual restoration of the flood-damaged materials and the subsequent support of the National Endowment for the Arts.

The author is indebted to R. H. Brill and J. H. Martin of the Corning Museum of Glass for their encouragement of this investigation. The author is also grateful to Robert McComb, Physical Scientist, and Peter Waters, Restoration Officer of the Preservation Office, Library of Congress, for their encouragement and advice on the usefulness of dielectric and microwave energy for drying wetted library materials.

Appendix

(1) *Dielectric units*

27-MHz: Thermex unit; Chemetron Corp.; model CP 30B424X; three units (serial # 72-127-T4, 72-127-T4, and 71-190T); input 240 V, 3 phase, 60 cycle, 42 amps, 14.5 KVA; power factor 0.96; 8 KW output.

12-MHz: Thermex unit; Chemetron Corp.; model CP 30B424; serial # 72-127-T5; input 460 V, 3 phase, 60 cycle, 22 amps, 14.5 KVA; power factor 0.96; 8 KW output.

(2) *Microwave unit*

Radarange; Amana Corp.; model 44-4, Mfg. P 71100-2M, serial # L53425720; 110 V A.C., 14.5 amps, 1600 watts, 2450-MHz.

Literature Cited

1. Fischer, D. J., "Simulation of Flood for Preparing Reproducible Water-Damaged Books and Evaluation of Traditional and New Drying Processes," ADV. CHEM. SER. (1977) **164**, 105.
2. Cable, J. W., "Introduction to Dielectric Heating," Reinhold Publishing, 1954.
3. Edgar, R., "Microwave Systems," *Industrial Microwave Processing,* Ratheon Co., Waltham, Mass., 1972.
4. von Hippel, A., "Dielectric Materials and Applications," Wiley, New York, 1954.
5. Preston, M., "Dielectric Heating Frequencies—A Comparison," Fitchburg Industrial Products, technical brochure, May 1971.
6. Wade, L., "Varian-Microwave Energy for Industrial Processing," Varian Associates, Palo Alto, Calif.

7. Williams, N. H., "Moisture Leveling in Paper, Wood, Textiles and Other Mixed Dielectric Sheets," *Symposium on Microwave Power,* March 1966.
8. Jolly, J. A., "Consideration in the Use of Microwave Energy for Wood Drying," *Second Annual Seminar on Industrial Microwave Technology,* March 1969.
9. Hankin, J. W., Leidigh, W. J., Stephansen, E. W., "Microwave Paper Drying Experience and Analysis," *Tappi* (1970) **53** (6) 1063–1070.
10. Anderson, N., Hedvall, R., Berggren, B., Fahraeus, P., "Microwave Drying of Paper," *Svensk Paperstidning,* **75,** 663–671.
11. Thomas, D., Flink, J. M., "Rapid Drying of Water Soaked Books Using a Microwave Tunnel Dryer," *Restaurator* (1975) **2,** 66–80.
12. Thomas, D., Fink, J. M., "Microwave Drying of Water Soaked Books," *J. Microwave Power,* **9** (4) 349–354.
13. Jones, P. L., Lawton, J., Parker, I. M., "High Frequency Paper Drying Part I—Paper Drying in Radio and Microwave Frequency Fields," *Trans. Inst. Chem. Eng.* (1974) **52,** 121–131.
14. Lawton, J., "High Frequency Paper Drying Part II—The Effect of Non-Uniform Field Distributions in the Radio Frequency Drying of Paper," *Trans. Inst. Chem. Eng.* (1974) **52,** 132–135.
15. Solechnik, N. Ya., "New Methods for the Restoration and Preservation of Documents and Books," Office of Technical Services, OTS 64-11054, pp. 1–23, U. S. Dept. of Commerce, Washington, D. C., 1964.

RECEIVED April 25, 1977.

Conservation Research: Fumigation and Sterilization of Flood-Contaminated Library, Office, Photographic, and Archival Materials

DAVID J. FISCHER

Milton Roy Co., P.O. Box 1899, Sarasota, Fla. 33578

One of the consequences of tropical storm Agnes, June 1972, reached as far north as Corning, N.Y. The Corning Museum of Glass' library, the library of record for the world's glass scholars, sustained damage when flooded by muddy waters from an adjacent river. All of the library's damaged collection was frozen to prevent microbiological attack. A team developed a plan, which included special research projects, for the restoration of this collection. One of the major, successful projects was a process for not only fumigating but sterilizing the collection.

On June 23, 1972 the city of Corning, N.Y. was hit by a devastating flood. The muddy waters rose to a height of five feet, four inches on the main floor of the Corning Museum of Glass. As the waters receded, a layer of mud was deposited on the museum's priceless glass collection, its library of record, archives, slide and film collection, and office files. Because the mud contained microbial contaminants as well as eggs from various insects, all of the flood-damaged materials except the glass objects were frozen to preserve them from attack by these biological species. This freezing action also permitted the museum's staff to consider restoration plans specifically designed for each of these damaged items.

Even though some of the museum holdings were not directly in contact with the flood waters, all became contaminated during subsequent removal from the museum and transfer to temporary storage areas. Since the humidity and temperature were not controlled in these storage areas, there was serious concern about the possibility of biological growth in these materials. A random check of the storage area, books in the collection, and correspondence in the office files substantiated this concern. Insect, fungal, and bacterial growth were found, and an immediate method to solve this problem was required. Starch, casein, and cellulosic materials, constituents of paper formulations, were being utilized by some of these species.

Approach to Fumigation and Sterilization of Contaminated Books

As restoration planning evolved, concern for the stored, nonfrozen contaminated materials increased. The use of insecticides was considered initially; however, the suggestion was eliminated after discussions were held with several groups of paper conservators. They felt that such compounds might leave residual halogens in the paper. Such halogens ultimately contribute to an acidic environment which in turn accelerates aging of the paper.

This need to treat biological contamination necessitated the search for and purchase of appropriate equipment that could be operated by the museum staff. To minimize capital expenditures and as a result of the need for quick delivery and of the fact that only a small amount of space was available, a modified Vacudyne Fumigator (VDF) designed for use in libraries was selected. It was manufactured with an extra-large vacuum pump and had heating elements installed in its side walls. The unit was sold (Vacudyne Altair, Chicago Heights, Ill.) as an instrument to establish conditions for kill of insects and mold, not as a sterilizer for kill of bacteria. Since ethylene oxide could be used in its chamber, however, modification of its normal operating sequence was considered to develop a sterilizing treatment for the books. Ethylene oxide, when used under the proper conditions, is not only a fumigant but also an effective sterilizing agent. It is used extensively by the pharmaceutical industry to sterilize various plastics and bandages.

Fumigating to destroy book worms, silverfish, moth, larvae, mold, and fungal contaminants proceeds under milder conditions than those required for killing the bacteriological contaminants. Since it was necessary to sterilize all of the museum's books to eliminate subsequent damage resulting from biological growth or transfer of contaminants by users to other books as well as to the users themselves, the following experimental approach was developed. To obtain the maximum amount of information on the quality of sterilization with the least effort, attention was focused primarily on identifying conditions for kill of what was believed to be one of the most resistant bacterial species. After being procured, this species was to be placed in the center of closed books, the location most difficult for gas penetration. If process conditions could be identified for kill at this location, the assumption that all other less resistant forms of biological life would also be killed was believed to be valid. Time and money would be saved by not conducting the latter experiments. A survey of the museum's problems confirmed that mold and bacterial growth were even more of a threat than insect growth.

Experimental Considerations

Fumigation. The initial effectiveness of the VDF was determined by conducting a series of experiments which varied the amount of air being evacuated before the ethylene oxide mixture was allowed to enter, the time of exposure, and the temperature of application to the books. The dimensions of the chamber in the fumigator were 1.2 m $\times$ 0.92 m $\times$ 0.46 m. A normal library cart with three shelves would be moved in and out of the chamber. When these shelves were stacked with books, approximately two-thirds of the volume inside the chamber was filled by the books and the cart. After loading the chamber and closing the door, a preselected program—evacuation of air, injection of gas for treatment, evacuation of gas, and back-filling with air—was begun.

Ethylene oxide at a composition of 12% by weight with UCON refrigerant 12 (Oxyfume-12, Union Carbide Corp.) is nonflammable and can be used safely in a closed system. The effectiveness of this commercial mixture depends on the amount of ethylene oxide present, the temperature of its application, the time of exposure, and the relative humidity in the chamber ($1, 2, 3$).

Microbiological Tests and Controls. Because *Bacillus subtilis* is a rugged, resistant microbiological species, spore strips (Castle Co., Rochester, N.Y.) of this bacteria were chosen for the study. The investigation was supplemented by use of additional biological samples involving actual microbiologically attacked pages from badly damaged books; colonies of mold and bacteria had been allowed to mature intentionally for use in these experiments. Later in this paper, these samples which were placed inside books are described as muddy-moldy pages. Cultures of *Escherichia coli* and *Aspergillus sp.* were also used in the experiments.

Positioning of Biological Test Samples. Spore strips and sections of muddy-moldy pages were placed initially inside closed books. All samples were held at the center of the page with pressure sensitive tape. When kill was not observed, the samples were again attached to a page in the book which was now set on its bottom edge and left partially opened during treatment.

During the final experiment, when better conditions for kill were identified, special attention was given to the positioning of biological samples. They were attached to pages in the center of books which were then placed between two 1.27-cm Plexiglas plates. Four C-clamps, one placed at each corner of the plates, were tightened with equivalent torques, 40 kg-cm, to ensure the uniform application of pressure to each book. This amount of torque was chosen to duplicate the pressure exerted on books when they are tightly packed on the library cart shelf. Five different locations on the cart, one at the outside edge of the top and bottom shelf and one in the center, were used for the books containing biological samples.

Trypticase soy agar and Sabouraud's agar, in petri dishes, were streaked with *E. coli* and *Aspergillus sp.* and placed on top of books packed on the cart. The cart was placed in the chamber and exposed to ethylene oxide for 4 hr. These petri dish samples were used for a special part of the second series of experiments.

Microbiological Media. Trypticase soy broth (liquid), trypticase soy agar for bacteria, and Sabouraud's agar for fungi were used as media. Although the agar media are identical to and nutritionally comparable with the liquid media, the agar was added as a solidifying agent for cultivation of bacteria or fungi on a semisolid surface.

Culturing of Test and Control Samples. Both control and treated spore strip samples were cultured at 37°C in trypticase soy broth for 48 hr to determine kill. Swab samples, taken from sections of the surface of the muddy-moldy pages before and after exposure to ethylene oxide, were placed in 1 mL of $0.001M$ phosphate buffered saline solution at pH 7.0 for plating on appropriate media. These samples were taken from a 6.45-cm² section.

To determine the effect of adding moisture to dried contaminated pages, 1 mL of the phosphate buffered saline solution at pH 7.0 was added to a section of each of several muddy-moldy pages before treatment with ethylene oxide. Swabs were taken from these selected areas before and after the gaseous treatment. Duplicate plates were made of all samples.

Process Conditions for Ethylene Oxide. Exposure to ethylene oxide lasted 4, 6.5, and 15 hr. To keep the relative humidity at the necessary percent (*1, 2, 3*), water vapor was added to the chamber of the VDF. Exposure of the books to ethylene oxide occurred at either room temperature or at an elevated temperature. When the maximum temperature in the chamber in the latter case was set for approximately 40°C, it took about 60 min to get to 33°C and 3 hr to reach the maxium value. The temperature changes of the gas throughout the chamber after closing the chamber door were determined by placing a series of thermocouples both inside and outside of the books at different positions on the cart. A maximum difference of 11°C was recorded upon entry of the gas into the chamber between a pair of these thermocouples positioned on the bottom shelf. The difference was reduced to 1°C after 8 min of exposure. Temperatures at the various positions were monitored throughout the entire experiment.

A comparable discrepancy was observed for the extreme in the chamber's gas temperature after entry of ethylene oxide. Temperature measurements were made between the gas occupying the volume just adjacent to the gas inlet (located at the bottom and rear of the chamber) and the volume in the center of the chamber. The initial disparity in temperature as a result of injecting the gas was reduced to almost 4°C after 7 min of exposure.

The evacuation level and the volume of the books and cart in the chamber controlled the amount of ethylene oxide present in the chamber. The first series of tests was made when the air pressure in the chamber was reduced to a value of 15 in. Hg. At this pressure, a solenoid valve was opened to release the ethylene oxide mixture. Gas continued to enter until a pressure of 1 in. Hg was attained; then the valve was shut. When the second and third series of experiments were conducted, evacuation in excess of 28 in. Hg took place before the solenoid valve was opened for entry of the ethylene oxide into the chamber. After the desired exposure time had elapsed, the chamber was evacuated to this pressure again and then filled with filtered air before it was opened.

Experimental Results and Discussion

Series I. The initial series of experiments was conducted by placing the spore strips inside closed books at five different locations on the cart and exposing for 4 hr and 14 hr at room temperature. The limit of the evacuation pressure was set at 15 in. Hg. Approximately 50 books were positioned on the cart, occupying about two thirds of the volume inside the chamber. None of the spores was killed by these treatments. Furthermore, when the chamber was opened, the UCON refrigerant 12 could be detected. These two results suggested that (1) an increase in the total amount of ethylene oxide was required to facilitate kill and (2) the VDF program should be modified so that gas left after treating the books could be removed before the chamber door was opened. One change in the VDF program satisfied both needs. The level of evacuation was adjusted to a pressure of 28 in. Hg before ethylene oxide entered the chamber and before the chamber was back-filled with air.

Series II. In this series of experiments both spore strips and muddy-moldy pages were used, some placed in books which were partially opened and set on their bottom edges while they were being treated. Moisture was added to some sections of the completely dried, contaminated pages. The results listed in Table I show that spores of *B. subtilis* were not killed in 15 hr when located inside closed books. When a book was left partially open to permit ready access of ethylene oxide, all spores were killed.

Table I.   Treatment of Spore Strips at Room Temperature

Treatment Time (hr)	Number of Individual Samples[a]	Location of Spore Strips	Results after Incubation	
			Unexposed Strip[b]	Exposed Strip
4	5	Inside closed books	+	+
15	5	Inside closed books	+	+
15	5	Inside partially opened books, standing on edge	+	−

[a] One at outside edge of top and bottom shelf and one at the center of the cart.
[b] Growth = + and no growth = −.

Table II.   Treatment of Muddy-Moldy Pages at Room Temperature

Treat-ment Time (hr)	Number of Individual Samples	Location of Sample	Bacteria and Fungi Counts/6.45 cm²			
			Bacteria		Fungi	
			Before	After	Before	After
4	5[a]	Inside closed book	TNTC[c]	TNTC	TNTC	TNTC
4	5[a]	Inside partially opened book	TNTC	TNTC	TNTC	TNTC
4	2[b]	Placed in open petri dish[d]	60	0	TNTC	0
15	5[a]	Inside partially opened book	TNTC	0	TNTC	0

[a] One at outside edge of top and bottom shelf and one at the center of the cart.
[b] Located at outside edges of top shelf on cart.
[c] TNTC = too numerous to count.
[d] Sample moistened with 1 mL phosphate buffer.

The results described in Table II suggest that a necessary minimum amount of moisture encouraged kill of fungi and bacteria at short exposure times; kill was observed on the moistened muddy-moldy pages put in the petri dishes on top of the books within 4 hr. If the pages were dry, a 15-hr exposure was required for kill of these same species. The latter findings, involving exposure of muddy-moldy pages taped to pages in partially opened books, supported the data noted in Table I for similar exposure and kill of spores.

Table III.   Treatment of Cultures Streaked on Nutrient at 4-hr Exposure

Species	Nutrient	Number of Samples	Growth after Incubation[a]	
			Before	After
Escherichia coli	Trypticase soy agar	5	+	−
Aspergillus sp.	Sabrouraud's agar	5	+	−

[a] Growth = + and no growth = −.

An additional experiment (*see* Table III) used streaks of moist vegetative cells of bacteria and moist fungal species placed on nutrients in petri dishes. Again it appears that only a 4-hr treatment at room temperature was required to kill these moist species. However, this conclusion assumes kill by direct contact with the gaseous ethylene oxide as contrasted to subsequent kill because of ethylene oxide being absorbed by the agar and gradually released thereafter. Similar dehydrated froms (*see* Table II), present on dry muddy-moldy pages, required 15 hr of exposure. The necessary moisture content and its location appear critical. The presence of water at a site other than biological could produce a reaction with ethylene oxide which would eliminate its chance to sterilize.

Series III. During these tests, conditions comparable with the second series were maintained except that the chamber was heated. It is obvious from a review of Table IV that a 6.5-hr exposure is sufficient to kill the spores in the most tightly packed books. There was a high percentage of kill of bacteria and fungi on the muddy-moldy pages (Table V) placed in the same books and treated at the same time, but the kill was not total. These facts imply that longer exposure times are required for complete kill when contamination is excessive, mud is present, and the surface of the page is dry. Complete kill was obtained when a 15-hr (Table V) exposure was applied to muddy-moldy pages with populations of contamination comparable with those treated during the 6.5-hr exposure at the same elevated temperature.

Table IV.   Treatment and Evaluation of Spore Strips at Elevated Temperature

Evaluation of Growth after Different Exposure Times

Type of Book Storage	Position on Cart[b]	4 hr Controls[a]	4 hr Exposed	6.5 hr Controls	6.5 hr Exposed	15 hr Controls	15 hr Exposed
Partially opened	1	+	−	+	−	+	−
"	2	+	−	+	−	+	−
"	3	+	−	+	−	+	−
"	4	+	−	+	−	+	−
"	5	+	−	+	−	+	−
Clamped shut	1	+	−	+	−	+	−
"	4	+	+	+	−	+	−

[a] Growth = + and no growth = −.
[b] 1, 2: edges of top shelf; 3: center of intermediate shelf; 4, 5: edges of bottom shelf.

Table V. Evaluation of Treated Muddy-Moldy
Pages at Elevated Temperatures

Type of Book Storage	Position on Cart	Exposure Time (hr)	Bacteria and Fungi Counts/6.45 cm²			
			Bacteria		Fungi	
			Before	After	Before	After
Partially opened	1	4	TNTC[a]	0	TNTC	0
	2	4	TNTC	0	TNTC	0
	3	4	TNTC	0	TNTC	0
	4	4	TNTC	0	TNTC	0
	5	4	TNTC	0	TNTC	0
Clamped shut	1	4	TNTC	TNTC	TNTC	0
	4	4	TNTC	TNTC	TNTC	0
Closed, lying on side	2	4	TNTC	0	TNTC	0
	3	4	TNTC	50	TNTC	0
	5	4	TNTC	0	TNTC	0
Partially opened	1	6.5	TNTC	0	TNTC	20
	2	6.5	TNTC	70	TNTC	10
	3	6.5	TNTC	0	TNTC	10
	4	6.5	TNTC	10	TNTC	30
	5	6.5	TNTC	50	TNTC	10
Clamped shut	1	6.5	TNTC	80	TNTC	60
	4	6.5	TNTC	300	TNTC	0
Closed, lying on side	2	6.5	TNTC	50	TNTC	0
	3	6.5	TNTC	0	TNTC	10
	5	6.5	TNTC	180	TNTC	10
Clamped shut	1	15	TNTC	0	TNTC	0
	4	15	TNTC	0	TNTC	0
Closed, lying on side	2	15	TNTC	0	TNTC	0
	3	15	TNTC	0	TNTC	0
	5	15	TNTC	0	TNTC	0

[a] TNTC = too numerous to count.

During the Series III experiments, ATI Sterilization Indicator Tapes, #00180 (Aseptic-Thermo Indicator Co., North Hollywood, Calif.) were mounted beside all spore strips and muddy-moldy pages placed in the books used for the 6.5- and 15-hr treatments. The color change from yellow to dark blue suggested that an environment for potential sterilization existed in each case. The tapes could not guarantee micro-environmental sterilization conditions when excessive growth had left biological debris or when mud had been deposited. Such factors may control reactions with ethylene oxide or limit its diffusion to the active biological site.

Summary

Sterilization of spore strips and muddy-moldy pages in books treated at room temperature was accomplished in 15 hr when the books were set on their edges and left partially open. The importance of sufficient moisture is obvious from the results of treating the muddy-moldy page for 4 hr after being dampened. A convenient practical way to ensure the supply of the necessary amount of moisture to each biological site on each page still needs to be developed.

If library books which had not been exposed to muddy water or had not experienced excessive bacterial and fungal growth are involved, a 6.5-hr treatment under the conditions listed in Series III is sufficient to sterilize even tightly closed books. Treatment of the most seriously contaminated books (muddy-moldy pages) required an excess of 6.5 hr and less than 15 hr of processing when the conditions outlined in the Series III investigations were met.

The use of the higher vacuum, allowing a greater amount of ethylene oxide to enter the chamber, facilitated kill of the biological species. After treatment and back-filling with filtered air, traces of the UCON refrigerant 12 gas were not detected upon opening the chamber door at the end of the sterilization sequence. The results from the above investigations with books led to the successful application of this process for sterilizing the library holdings, archives, office files, film, and photographic prints of the Corning Museum of Glass.

Acknowledgments

Robert E. Kephart, Professor of Microbiology at the Corning Community College, conducted all of the biological tests. The author is grateful for his direct assistance in planning and implementing these investigations. The author is also indebted to R. H. Brill and J. H. Martin of the Corning Museum of Glass for their encouragement of these investigations. Appreciation is due Robert M. Organ, Chief of Conservation, Analytical Laboratory at the Smithsonian Institute, for his information on uses of ethylene oxide.

Part of the funds for conducting this research were obtained from the National Museum Act and the National Endowment for the Arts.

Literature Cited

1. Ernst, R. R., Shull, J. J., "Ethylene Oxide Gaseous Sterilization—Concentration and Temperature Effects," *Appl. Microbiol.* (1962) **10**, 337–341.

2. Gilbert, B. L., Gambill, F. M., et al., "Effect of Moisture on Ethylene Oxide Sterilization," *Appl. Microbiol.* (1964) **12**, 496–503.
3. Opfell, J. B., Wang, Y., et al., "Penetration by Gases to Sterilize Interior Surfaces of Confined Spaces," *Appl. Microbiol.* (1964) **12**, 27–31.

RECEIVED April 15, 1977.

11

Design of a Liquified Gas Mass Deacidification System for Paper and Books

RICHARD DANIEL SMITH

Wei T'o Associates, Inc., P.O. Box 352, Park Forest, Ill. 60466

The Wei T'o Nonaqueous Book Deacidification System, an in-progress pilot project at the Public Archives of Canada, is presented in terms of institutional background, system selection, characteristics of liquified gas systems, and current system design. The manual aqueous (magnesium bicarbonate) and nonaqueous (magnesium methyl carbonate: magnesium methoxide mixture with carbon dioxide in methanol and trichlorotrifluoroethane) deacidification solutions used at the Public Archives extend potential record life but are limited to unique, valuable records because of treatment cost. The system was chosen as a pilot project test because its chemistry was accepted, a history of successful use existed, and mechanical problems of handling liquified gas solvents appeared solvable. Deacidification of paper using liquified gas solvents to dissolve, carry, and deposit deacidification agents function analagously to chlorofluorocarbon refrigeration cycles. Successful treatment requires vacuum drying books to 0.5% moisture or lower, solution impregnation at pressures up to 200 psig, and flash drying to deposit the deacidification agent throughout the materials treated.

This report on the Wei T'o Nonaqueous Book Deacidification System at the Public Archives of Canada is divided into: (1) institutional background, (2) system selection, (3) characteristics of liquified gas systems, and (4) current system design. The focus on deacidification (neutralization of paper and impregnation of an alkaline buffer) occurs because most deterioration is caused by acid-catalyzed hydrolysis of cellulose (*1, 2*).

Institutional Background

The Public Archives of Canada, established in 1872, is a federal department of the government of Canada with many responsibilities. Among the latter are acquiring from many sources all significant archival material of every kind, nature, and description relating to all aspects of Canadian life and to the development of the country and for providing suitable research services and facilities to make this material available to the public (3). Its eight collecting divisions are the Manuscript Division, Public Records Division, Library, Machine Readable Records, National Map Collection, Picture Division, National Photographic Collection, and National Film Archives (including historical sound recordings).

The Records Conservation Section, staffed with 20 persons, of the Administration and the Technical Services Branch currently provide conservation and restoration services for paper materials to the Public Archives and National Library of Canada. Studies, both within and without the Public Archives, indicate the present collection is deteriorating more rapidly than the Records Conservation Section can restore it. Moreover, the collections are growing at increased rates, and the stability of materials to be acquired is projected as no better than materials already in the collection.

The obvious solution of expanding the Records Conservation Section was established as unrealistic in terms of rate of collection deterioration, personnel availability, and treatment cost. The collections are estimated to lose 50% of their folding endurance (a measure of capability of paper to resist wear from patron use) every 7.5 years. The leaves of many books are too weak for rebinding 60 years after the date of publication and break if turned after 100 years (4). The Section has been unable to recruit qualified conservators for existing positions, and the competition for available conservators is increasing as more institutions establish conservation programs. The manual aqueous (magnesium bicarbonate) and nonaqueous (magnesium methyl carbonate: mixture of magnesium methoxide and carbon dioxide in methanol and trichlorotrifluoroethane) deacidification treatments used by the Section are known to alleviate this deterioration, but cost restricts their application to unique, exceptionally valuable materials.

Thus, on examination, the Public Archives found itself meeting its acquisition and service missions but failing to maintain its general collection in useable condition. The Public Archives of Canada investigated alternate approaches for extending the useful life of its collections because the techniques practiced by the Records Conservation Section gave no promise of bringing the rate of records deterioration under control.

System Selection

The Wei T'o system was selected for pilot trial because it appeared to best meet the requirements of the Public Archives of Canada (5–9). The deacidification of paper is not a preservation panacea but a partial treatment known to extend the potential life of paper. For example, deacidification does not strengthen deteriorated and embrittled paper, an increasingly important aspect of the conservation problem. The impregnation of 3–5% by weight of resin strengthening agents throughout a book is considered a straightforward operation for a liquified gas process but a difficult task for a vapor phase process. The analysis suggests that if it is necessary to use liquified gases for strengthening paper, the same procedure should be used for deacidification.

Storage of archival library, and museum holdings at reduced relative humidities and temperatures functions similarly to deacidification in reducing the rate at which the chemical reaction, given in Figure 1, proceeds. Clearly, the reaction demonstrates acid attack, producing a chemically equivalent but partially hydrolyzed cellulose, and cannot proceed if water or energy are removed. The availability of water and energy to enter into the reaction can be reduced by controlling the relative humidity and storage temperature. The choice between cold storage as a form of preservation and deacidification itself can be made on the basis of cost. Cold storage and the mass nonaqueous deacidification process being reported on were evaluated as equal in cost 30 months after treatment for a 1,000,000-volume library in a 1970 study (10). Thereafter, the annual maintenance and operation costs made preservation through air conditioning increasingly more expensive at a projected rate of \$0.10/volume/yr.

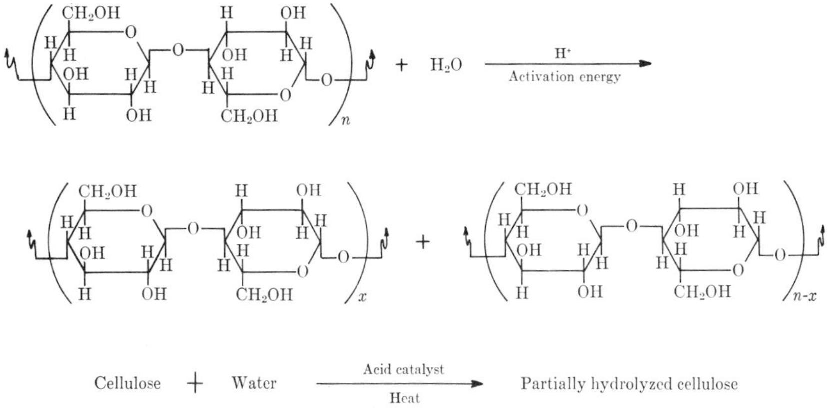

Figure 1. Acid-catalyzed hydrolysis of cellulose

The fact that holdings of the Public Archives and National Library of Canada are working collections, available for regular patron use, which may be called upon for loan and exhibition indicated the system chosen should provide protection when materials are outside institutional control. These missions raised questions about cold storage because new facilities would be required, possibly distant from use points, and restrictions on patron use introduced.

The Records Conservation Section has five years of satisfactory experience treating a variety of unique works with Wei T'o solutions. A survey of conservators and scientists in other institutions verified the chemistry was sound and the results were aesthetically acceptable. The problems to be resolved were mechanical, involving equipment choice rather than the chemistry of the treatment (11). The hazards inherent to the system could be isolated and controlled at the treatment site. The solvent, approximately 90% dichlorodifluoromethane and 10% methanol by volume, has a maximum allowable concentration of 982 ppm in air (12), a level many times more than expected in workroom air. Incorporation of solvent recovery equipment not only reduces unit treatment cost but avoids a potential detrimental effect on the ozone layer in the upper atmosphere by dichlorodifluoromethane.

Peripheral benefits of the choice include a reduction in oxidative degradation as magnesium compounds, particularly magnesium hydroxide, sequester the trace metals, iron, copper, and cobalt, which catalyze oxidative degradation (13, 14, 15). The elimination of iron also reduces the probability of foxing (staining) caused by mold interacting with iron in damp storage conditions or records wet by water from burst pipes (16). In summary, the system was chosen because (1) the chemistry of the process was accepted, (2) a history of successful use existed, and (3) the problems to be resolved appeared solveable.

Characteristics of Liquified Gas Systems

The concept of using liquified gases to dissolve, transport, and deposit deacidification agents in paper and books was pioneered at the Graduate Library School, University of Chicago (9, 10). Liquified gas systems are seen as combining the merits of traditional liquid and vapor phase deacidification methods. Liquid deacidification solutions are used to protect more acidic papers because they introduce larger quantities of deacidification agent than available vapor phase systems do. The solvents are introduced as liquids and removed as vapors to facilitate rapid drying and the deposition of deacidification agent throughout the treated aggregates of paper, that is, books. Typically, magnesium methoxide, the preferred agent, is prepared in methanol at concentrations of 8–10%

and subsequently diluted with dichlorodifluoromethane to a 0.5–1.0% concentration. These concentrations introduce four to 10 times more deacidification agent than required to neutralize the 0.1% by weight sulfuric acid equivalent typically found in deteriorated paper. Prior to introducing the solution, the books to be treated are vacuum dried to low levels of dryness, that is, under 0.5% moisture.

The liquified gas solution, maintained separately in anhydrous condition, is impregnated in books at pressures ranging from 70–200 psig. The treatment does not require a dwell or soaking time, but the solution must contact intimately the materials undergoing treatment. After draining the solution surrounding the wetted materials, the solvents are flash dried (removed rapidly by pressure reduction) to deposit the deacidification agent throughout the books. Control during this stage is critical because the solution tends to migrate towards the periphery of the books before evaporating since the temperature of the books drops as a result of the heat consumed in vaporizing the solvents. Migration is minimized by supplying heat during drying or by reducing the pressure to maintain the pressure differentials. The alkaline buffer deposited is expected to vary from a minimum near the spine or bound margin to a maximum at the head, tail, and fore-edge margins of the leaves in treated books. This variation is considered advantageous because the heavier concentration is deposited in the edges of the leaves where acidic gases are preferentially adsorbed from polluted air.

Another way to visualize the treatment process is to contrast it to the refrigeration cycle in home air conditioners, freezers, or refrigerators. Schematics of the system and a home refrigerator are presented as Figures 2 and 3. In Figure 2, the liquid refrigerant, typically dichlorodifluoromethane (Genetron 12, Freon 12, or Halocarbon 12) flows as a self-propelled liquid from the receiver to the evaporator. The pressure drops, and the refrigerant evaporates, thereby taking up heat and cooling the refrigerator. The low pressure gas (roughly 20 psig) is drawn into the compressor and compressed to perhaps 100 psig. This high pressure gas gives up heat in the condenser and condenses into a liquid to complete the cycle by flowing back into the receiver.

These same functions are the fundamental treatment blocks of the Wei T'o System as shown in Figure 3. In addition, the continual recycling is broken at the receiver. This introduces a requirement for two receivers. One receiver, called the storage tank, holds the deacidification solution. The other receiver receives the condensed solvent gases precisely as in the refrigeration cycle. A turbine pump is incorporated to move the solution to the process tank, the analog of the evaporator in the refrigerator. However, the books are thoroughly wetted in the process tank, and excess solution is drained back to the storage tank prior to the process

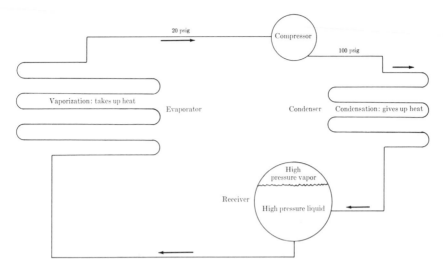

Figure 2. Refrigeration cycle

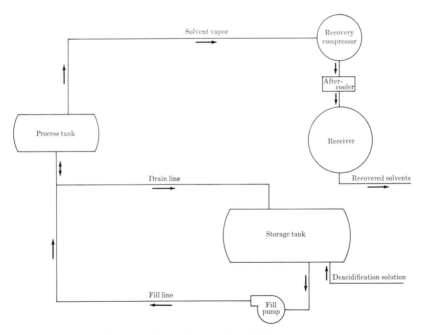

Figure 3. Liquified gas deacidification system

tank functioning as an evaporator. The liquid solution impregnated in books is flashed (vaporized rapidly) to produce a drying effect throughout the wetted books. The vapor is recovered through condensation by compression and cooling just as in refrigeration. The condensed solvents in the present system will be transferred to cylinders and transported elsewhere for recycling into fresh deacidification solution.

Where possible, the equipment and operating procedures were selected for additional benefit. For example, the vacuum pump and exit port of the vacuum drier were enlarged for emergency use in drying water-wet books. In future, additional treatments such as impregnating selected resins to strengthen weakened paper are to be tested.

Current System Design

The system originated in June 1974 when Wei T'o Associates was asked to prepare a design for consideration. Arrangements were made with an American engineering firm to undertake construction in January 1975. This first system did demonstrate feasibility of the process, but the quality of treatment was not satisfactory. Certain components proved unreliable, and concern existed as to whether the system met safety requirements. These operational problems are believed to have caused the engineering firm to become unwilling to complete the system. This attitude plus funding considerations and the need for local maintenance and repair service led to a decision to complete the system in Canada. The initial step of identifying experienced Canadian engineering firms who were available, qualified, and interested in undertaking completion occurred in autumn 1976. During winter and spring 1977, the entire system was reviewed in terms of chemical processing, refrigeration fabrication standards, and component selection. The modified system which resulted is divided into three sections: (1) warm air and vacuum drying; (2) deacidification (includes evacuation, solution impregnation, deposition and drying, and solvent recovery); and (3) auxilary operations for presentation in this progress report.

The water contained in air-dry books, 4–10% by weight, if not removed before treatment, is swept out of the books by escaping vapor to contaminate the recovered solvents. Removal before treatment offers the advantages of introducing a more uniformly deposited, tightly held deacidification agent, reducing contamination of the solution returned to the storage tank and increasing the savings in solvent recycling, and the capability of using recovered solvent vapor to equalize pressure between the process and storage tanks. Approximately 50% of the water in air-dry books is removed by drying for 24 hr in an electric, forced-air bench drier at 140°F. The water remaining is removed in a heated-shelf (120°F) vacuum drier operated at 2 mm Hg or less overnight. The vacuum is returned to ambient pressure with air at 1–2 ppm of water when books are removed from the vacuum drier. Two wire-frame, perforated metal floor baskets measuring 10 in. by 18 in. are placed in the process tank for each of the five to six deacidification cycles per day. The books, dried to at least 0.5% by weight of water, are handled in baskets for convenience in controlling exposure during drying and deacidification and preventing damage in handling. The fragility—i.e., embrittlement—caused by drying is a relative matter and is far less than the loss of strength that occurs from wetting paper with water. Deacidified books are brought back to full strength through gradual moisture regain prior to their return to the collection.

The major steps in the deacidification process are presented schematically in Figure 4. Following the loading of two book baskets, the process tank door is secured and the preset cycle is started with air evacuation to 1–2 mm Hg. The pressure is then equalized with the storage tank by introducing the recovered solvent vapor from the receiver. The fill pump is started, and the process tank liquid filled. A small quantity of solution is allowed to flow through the process tank, but the bulk is returned to the storage tank through the bypass line. Impregnation pressure is controlled by adjusting the pressure regulating valve. The fill pump is turned off, and the excess solution is drained back into the storage tank when the books are thoroughly wetted.

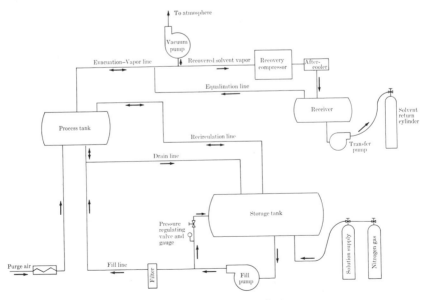

Figure 4. Current system design

The vapor filling the process tank and vapor from the solution wetting the treated books is recovered by an oil-free compressor to approximately 7 psig. The books are brought rapidly to a damp dry condition by removing additional vapor with a vacuum pump. This small quantity of vapor is exhausted to the atmosphere because the cost of its recovery is not justifiable at this time. The damp dry books in baskets are placed in closed corrugated boxes for 24–48 hr to complete drying, moisture regain, and return to room temperature. Thereafter, the deacidified books are inspected for appearance and quality of treatment prior to returning them to the colletcions.

The auxiliary operations include (1) a supply of solution (prepared elsewhere) in 140 lb-net refrigeration cylinders and its transfer to the storage tank by nitrogen gas pressure, (2) pumping of the recovered solvents from the receiver to refrigeration cylinders for transportation and beneficiation elsewhere, and (3) a self-contained hot water system for heating the shelf vacuum drier. The period required for a book to be treated and be returned to the collection is estimated at two weeks. This allows a one-week backlog for efficient batching of like books and one week to pass through the two-day drying, one-day deacidification, and two-day recovery and inspection cycles. Deacidification cycles of about 60 min are anticipated. Most of this time is required for air removal, solvent recovery, and evacuation. Solution impregnation and removal requires only five to 10 minutes. A daily production of 150 deacidified books measuring 6 in. by 9 in. by 1 in. is expected from the five to six cycles anticipated.

Experience to date indicates equipment selection and system design are important considerations in liquified gas deacidification systems. Operations using magnesium alkoxides or similar materials sensitive to trace quantities of moisture should be conducted under anhydrous conditions, and in-line design constructions leading to vapor locks should be avoided. Components must be selected for exposure to an anhydrous, methanol/dichlorodifluoromethane, alkaline alkoxide solution.

Acknowledgments

The author gratefully thanks the Public Archives of Canada for permission to publish this article and the Dupont Co., Wilmington, Del., and Dupont of Canada, Ltd., Kingston, Ontario, for guidance in handling liquified gas refrigerants.

Literature Cited

1. Clapp, V. W., "The Story of Permanent Durable Book Paper, 1115–1970," *Restaurator Supplement No. 3*, 1972.

2. Smith, R. D., "A Comparison of Paper in Identical Copies of Books from the Lawrence University, the Newberry, and the New York Public Libraries," *Restaurator Supplement No. 2*, 1972.
3. Public Archives of Canada, Publication Catalogue No. SA2-5070, p. 1, Ottawa: Ministry of Supply and Services, 1976.
4. Smith, R. D., "Maps: Their Deterioration and Preservation," *Special Libraries* (February 1972) **63:** 59–68.
5. Smith, R. D., "Treatment of Cellulosic Materials," U.S. Patent No. 3,676,-182, Washington, D.C., July 11, 1972.
6. Smith, R. D., "Preserving Cellulosic Materials Through Treatment with Alkylene Oxides," U.S. Patent No. **3,676,055**, Washington, D.C., July 11, 1972.
7. Smith, R. D., "Treatment of Cellulosic Materials," Canadian Patent No. **911, 110**. Ottawa, October 3, 1972.
8. Kelly, G. B., Jr., "Composition for Use in Deacidification of Paper," U.S. Patent No. **3,939,091**, Washington, D.C., February 17, 1976.
9. Smith, R. D., "New Approaches to Preservation," "Deterioration and Preservation of Library Materials," Winger, H. W., Smith, R. D., Eds., University of Chicago Press, Chicago, 1970.
10. Smith, R. D., "The Nonaqueous Deacidification of Paper and Books," Ph.D. dissertation, pp. 194–195, University of Chicago, Chicago, 1970.
11. Kelly, G. G., Jr., et al., Adv. Chem. Ser. (1977) **164,** 62.
12. American Conference of Governmental Industrial Hygienists. "General Exact Solution for Mixtures of *N* Components With Addictive Effects and Different Vapor Pressures," "Threshold Limit Values of Airborne Contaminants and Physical Agents," pp. 43–45, ACGIH, Cincinnati, Ohio, 1971.
13. Williams, J. C., et al., Adv. Chem. Ser. (1977) **164,** 37.
14. Ericsson, B., "Oxygen Oxidation in Aqueous Alkaline Medium," Ph.D. dissertation, Kungl Tekniska Höskolan, Stockholm, 1974.
15. Sinkey, J. D., "The Function of Magnesium Compounds in an Oxygen–Alkali–Carbohydrate System," Ph.D. dissertation, Institute of Paper Chemistry, Appleton, Wisc., 1973.
16. Waters, P., Restoration Officer, Preservation Office, Library of Congress, Washington, D.C., personal communication.

Received June 24, 1977.

Care and Preservation
of Textiles

Care of Fabrics in the Museum

NOBUKO KAJITANI

The Metropolitan Museum of Art, 5th Ave. at 82nd St., New York, N.Y. 10028

Preservation includes all activities that contribute to guaranteeing the life of museum objects, whether on exhibition, in storage, or being handled. Essentially, it is a study of the chemical, physical, and photochemical compatibility of the object with all aspects of its environment and an approach to controlling the interaction among them to maintain the intrinsic quality of the object. Fabrics are highly susceptible to degradation caused by mechanical, chemical, and photochemical action. The allocation of an independent area, maintenance of optimum climatic conditions, minimal exposure to illumination, good organization, and establishment of maintenance procedures to minimize handling and contamination are, therefore, essential. People responsible for their care must have visual and tactile sensitivities, be neat and clean, and not mind tedious routines necessary for their care.

The primary function of a museum is to preserve the objects of our past (1). This can only be accomplished after comprehensive study by a combination of museum professionals of the history, art history, ethnography, and aesthetic value of the objects as well as of their technical, physical, and chemical condition. Such study constitutes the foundation of preservation philosophy, science, and technique.

Preservation—as opposed to conservation—includes all those "dos and don'ts" that contribute to guaranteeing the life of the objects, whether they are on exhibition, in storage, or being handled, studied, or treated. "Care" and "maintenance" are used synonymously with "preservation" throughout this paper. Conservation, on the other hand, refers to "radical treatment" in a laboratory setting. The purpose of such treatment is usually to bring the object back to an appearance as similar as possible to the original and to stabilize its condition, often by adding new material. Thus, conservation is part of preservation, but preservation is not part of conservation. Essentially, both preservation and conservation of works of art are, *first*, studies of the chemical, physical, and photochemical compatibility of the object and other matter and elements with which it is in contact, and, *second,* approaches to controlling the interaction among them to maintain the intrinsic quality of the object.

Fabrics of the past must be studied from various points of view. They cannot be understood and appreciated fully by studying only one of their many aspects or by just looking at them. Their role in a social, commercial, technological, and agricultural context must be reviewed along with their history and art history, both as isolates and in comparison with objects in other media within their cultural settings; their scientific and technical aspects must also be examined.

Unlike most other works of art, the majority of fiber-made objects in the museum was not at the time of manufacture deemed "high art." Instead, they were intended to serve utilitarian purposes in clothing, bedding, and furnishing for people of all social levels. They were often used repeatedly until they were in tatters. What seems an insignificant fragment is in fact significant and reflects an intricate background. Although very few come with historical and personal documentation, museum fabrics themselves provide ample opportunity to research knowns and explore unknowns.

Although originally created for household use, museum fabrics no longer have that function and must be respected as works of visual art. Translating the museological philosophy of preservation into action means that costumes should not be tried on, chair seats should not be sat upon, curtains should not be hung in windows without protection against the light, objects should not be placed on displayed tablecloths, and floor coverings should not be walked upon. Nothing should be casually touched while being studied by scholars or while being prepared for storage even if the object was in a pile at an antique shop until that morning. In the museum, we have the power to change mere rags and tatters into meaningful objects.

Being organic material, fabrics respond more critically to maintenance procedures and the environment than do most works of art in other media. Their care rests on microscopic as well as macroscopic considerations of fibers and dyes. Their physical and chemical characteristics, pliability and absorbency, are extremely sensitive to environmental fluctuations; they are highly susceptible to degradation by soil, light, climate, and physical motion. To guarantee the life of a museum fabric, we must understand the nature of the material, its condition, and its visual impact as a museological object, and we must establish and practice a long-range preservation program.

Preservation of works of art, particularly fabrics, demands a never-ending effort (2) which, of necessity, will outlast the involvement of an individual museum staff member. The optimum setting and procedures for preservation must, therefore, be part of museum policy and not tied to the tenure of a given person.

Personnel

Seven position titles—trustee, director, curator, conservator, exhibition specialist, restorer, and caretaker—are most often encountered in museums. People in these positions are expected to carry out the functions of acquisition, study, conservation, and presentation with due consideration of the impact of these functions on preserving the collection. Indeed, only with the combined effort of these workers can preservation be guaranteed. Often one person must carry out more than one function; in other cases, a number of people share one function. In all instances, however, their responsibilities do intertwine, so that everyone concerned must work together in good faith.

Maintenance of an impeccably clean storeroom and good physical organization that are essential for the preservation of the fabric collection is impossible without qualified personnel. Selection of a caretaker (not to be confused with the person responsible for the upkeep of the museum building) is likely to be very difficult. As the museum fabric field is not an established professional area, it is best to train an individual according to his or her ability and development. At the outset, he must be sensitive in touch and vision, have a strong sense of cleanliness and neatness, and also an ability to tolerate tedious routines. The position should not be filled casually by any job applicant who comes along.

I discuss the work of a good fabrics caretaker, but it should go without saying that anyone—museum staff member or visiting scholar—must observe the same precautions in handling the fabrics as does the caretaker.

Individuals working with museum fabrics must be willing to conform to certain dress and behavior standards for protecting the collection. For example, everyone must wear work clothes that permit easy movement without disturbing the surroundings or the objects with sleeves, belts, bows, ties, and frills. Since dust and other soiling matters dominate the surfaces of the objects, smocks and aprons should be worn and must be periodically changed. Pins, neckties, bracelets, rings, and necklaces must be removed. Hair must not hang loose, and nails should be trimmed short and smooth. For the protection of the worker, comfortable shoes that provide some support should be worn because the worker stands most of the time. Although this sounds officious, saliva from chattering mouths causes problems—one must turn away from a museum fabric to talk.

Four major health problems (3) may be encountered by those working with the fiber medium: eye damage from engaging in minute and microscopic work; back or neck trouble from working for prolonged periods in one posture; internal and external disorders caused by natural and synthetic solvents and their by-products; and various reactions induced by dust. Eyes, the back, and arms must be periodically rested or therapeutically exercised. Some forms of insecticide and dry-cleaning fumes based on petroleum or of synthetic origin are bound to be present where fabrics are stored. Even if the irritant is only a residual, those who are vulnerable or have a history of allergies, internal disorders, and skin ailments must not work with museum collections.

A museum with a fabric collection should have an advisory committee composed of people with expertise in the hand-processing of fabrics, textile engineering, textile processing, dry-cleaning science, fiber science, dye chemistry, textile history, history, and art history. The committee will provide assistance in formulating long-range research projects and in solving preservation problems. The members' current knowledge of rapidly advancing areas of study is vital for a collection.

Museum Fabrics

Fabrics have been the objects closest to all people throughout history; they were not just for the "upper crust" of a society as were a majority of museum acquisitions. The production of fabrics, from farming or gathering raw materials for yarn and dyes to the preparation of fiber, yarn making, coloring, fabric manufacturing, finishing, and trading, has always been assumed by a group of specialists in widely distributed areas. Fabric-making processes have been incorporated into people's daily lives, which are controlled by nature, socioeconomic conditions, cultural trends, trade, and the progress of science and technology, contributing to the well-being of individuals and communities.

The first step in caring for museum fabrics is to understand them as materials: physical and chemical properties of fibers, yarns, and fabrics; the fabrication method and technique; the design layout and color trend; factors related to use; and the pre- and postacquisition state. Subsequent studies should try to date the objects and determine technical and material peculiarities of each provenance and establish history and classification of fabric technology. Here, briefly, the nature of natural fibers and dyes is discussed since they form the majority of museum fabrics at present.

The natural fibers (4, 5) used to form the primary elements from which fabrics are constructed can be classified in two ways: (a) according to their physical form—continuous length, limited length, and processed and (b) according to their chemical composition—protein, cellulose, and mineral—indicating the fiber's animal, plant, or mineral origin, respectively. A continuous length is obtained from cocoons made by the larvae of certain types of insects and from bast, leaf, and bark fibers from plants. Limited-length fibers are external hairs of mammal's, seed hairs of plants, and fibrous minerals. Materials which are processed into fiber-like forms are parchment, membrane, or leather from mammals, paper from plants, and metal from minerals, each of which is prepared in a variety of ways. Each group has characteristic physical and chemical properties which determine the appropriate type of care.

Silk filament is obtained from the cocoon of lepidopterous insects, generally a cultivated species, *Bombyx mori* L. The chemical nature of silk is essentially protein, consisting of bundles of various amino acid molecules; it is also porous, a characteristic of all fibers. Being protein, silk is easily affected by strong alkalis and various inorganic acids. When wet, it loses about 20% of its strength. In a humid climate, silk swells, gaining up to 30% of its weight without feeling wet to the touch. Climatic control, therefore, is important in the storage of silks; any handling must be done carefully.

The morphological features of silk include a pair of fibroin filaments in the center surrounded by serecin, a gummy substance. Fibroin filaments are very fine and smooth and possess a pleasant handle and glorious luster. Serecin, being a gummy substance, dulls fibroin's softness and sheen. To enhance the luster and softness, which are the most highly prized properties of silk, serecin is removed by various methods, most commonly by mechanical action while the silk is moist or by boiling. These processes are known as degumming, and either yarn or fabric is so treated. Both treatments can be accelerated if alkalinity is increased. The degree of degumming determines the shine. Dyes and mordant penetrate silk quite readily, but the dyes are generally not as lightfast as on wool.

External hair of animals, generally called wool, was spun into yarn and woven into fabrics. Like silk, wool is essentially protein; it is composed of various amino acids, a majority of which are keratin. (Unfortunately, the keratin contains sulfur, which attracts certain insects that thrive on wool and contribute to the scarcity of historic woolen fabrics.) The outstanding morphological characteristic of wool fiber is its external scales that overlap in one direction toward the tip of the fiber. The scales can be chemically, mechanically, and temporally damaged and can disappear as the wool deteriorates. Outside of the scales is a membranous layer, the epicuticle; inside them is the bulk of the wool fiber, the cortex, which consists of millions of double-pointed, needle-like cells neatly laid in a lengthwise configuration. In the center is a hollow channel called the medulla.

Because of its physicochemical nature, wool fiber accepts dyes and mordants better than any other fiber. This is the reason for the richness and fastness of most colors associated with wool. Wool, being protein, is easily affected by alkalis and by strong acids. It is unique in having a crimp, which contributes to its good spinning property. Wool fabric can be felted, creased, stretched, and shaped into a desired form and handle by the action of water, steam, agitation, high temperature, and increased acidity or alkalinity. In a humid atmosphere, wool readily absorbs moisture up to 20% of its own weight; when it is wet, it loses physical strength.

Among many bast fibers used in fabrics, flax—called linen after it has been spun and woven—was once the most common. Being cellulose, it withstands moderate alkaline conditions but is easily affected by acids. Microscopic morphological characteristics of flax include ridges running along the length and cross-marks at many points; a canal runs through the center. To function as a water carrier from the ground to the leaves in the flax stalk, the flax fiber (and the linen made from it) is sensitive to humidity: moisture penetrates and moves quickly in the fabric, changing its dimensions, weight, and strength. Linen has practically no affinity for metallic oxides and most dyes. Harvested flax must undergo various fiber extraction processes. Natural wetting extraction does not appreciably damage fiber, but the chemical extraction process recently introduced by some profit-oriented industries tend to reduce fiber longevity. Thus, if linen is to be used as a conservation or preservation material, it must be carefully selected.

Cotton is seed hairs that protect the seeds in their pods from desiccation in the dry season and from moisture in the rainy season. Under the microscope, cotton appears as a collapsed, tubelike fiber twisted at irregular intervals. In its natural state it repels water because of a waxy substance covering the fiber. Once the wax has been removed, cotton becomes the most absorbent fiber known to man. Cotton is cellulose; it withstands moderate alkaline conditions but is easily affected by acids. Because of twist in the fiber, cotton lacks glossiness. "Mercerization," a chemical process, gives luster to cotton fiber by straightening the twist.

By itself a subject of study, metallic yarn used in the past comes in a number of varieties that reflect the level of technology and trade of the time. A majority of metallic threads has been made into yarn by cutting prepared metallic material into strips that were then wound around a core thread of silk or linen. The metallic materials used were either gold or silver leaf adhered to membrane, parchment, leather, or paper or plain soft metal. Membrane is adversely affected by water and alkaline conditions. Metals often contain silver and their corrosion can completely cover the surface.

There are two major yarn types: (a) relatively long fibers to unlimited length (or filaments) produced by combining, splicing, or knotting and (b) limited-length fibers produced by spinning. Silk filaments and relatively long fibrous materials such as flax, ramie, and other bast fibers are generally made into yarn by combining several fibers, then splicing or overlapping ends while adding twist and moisture. A mass of loosened, relatively short fibers such as cotton, wool, and hair is made into yarn by spinning (6); a portion of the mass is drawn out with a certain speed and force and simultaneously twisted. Although both methods are essentially the same, techniques and tools vary in each geographical area according to the handle of raw material and the quality of yarn desired. The balance of drawing out speed, number of twists, and amount of fed-in fiber determine the quality of yarn as do the quality and type of raw material. These first two processes create yarn "singles," two or more of which can be combined or plied.

Either of two twisting directions may be used to form yarn, Z or S, as may be seen by examining the trend of twist from a vertical position. When two or more single yarns of the same twist are twisted together again—i.e., plied—generally in opposite directions, the resultant plied yarn has greater tensile strength but less flexibility than its component yarns. The type and quality of the fiber used and how it is made into yarn and then into fabric determine the type and quality of fabric produced.

There are two types of colorant, pigment and dye (7). Pigments are for the most part inorganic compounds, which come in colors, which are insoluble in water, and which have no affinity for fibers. After being ground into small particles and mixed with a binding medium, they are used to color the surface of any type of material. When applied to fabrics, they affect the surface only, immediately showing the intended colors; any affinity they have for the fabric depends on the binding medium, which is often water soluble. On the other hand, dyes are for the most part organic compounds, soluble in water, and they sometimes vary from the final color desired. Most cellulose or protein fibers will take up dyes when immersed in a dye bath of dyes dissolved in water. Depending on the chemistry of the particular dye, various processes are carried out before and/or after dyeing that make the dye compound insoluble and fast in the fiber and at the same time bring out the desired colors. The penetrating, rich tone characteristic of dyed colors, particularly when transformed from yarn into fabric, sharply contrasts the flat tone of pigment colors.

Certain types of organic compounds in plants and insects have been discovered to be usable as dyes. Most dye compounds of this kind occur only during a particular growth stage and some of them only in plants from a specific locality. The dye-containing part of the plant, cultivated or wild, must be gathered at its appropriate growth stage. Special physical and chemical treatment is required to extract the colorant, to transfer the colorant to the fiber, and to bring out the desired color from the colorant. Harvesting the plant at the optimum stage for dyes is only the beginning of an extremely complex process that includes extracting the dye compound, weighing the relationship among dye, fiber, metallic oxides, and color-inducing agent for their temperature, the hydrogen ion concentration level, and specific gravity. The order of dyeing procedures will depend on this relationship as well as on the material of utensils used, the quality of the yarn to be dyed, quantity of dyes in the plants, climatic conditions during the course of dyeing, water for the dye bath, and so forth.

Thus are the basic elements for making fabric prepared. Countless methods and structures of interworking such elements into fabric—e.g., weaving—have been developed throughout history (8). Depending on the abundance or scarcity and the type of raw material, various fabrics were developed in each geographical area to meet the need for protection against weather; over time, many elaborations of the basic fabric types have been developed.

Interworked structures have been produced by various tools and techniques. What appear to be identical structures may have been executed by different tools and techniques. Moreover, identical fabric structures may present entirely different appearances and handles because of (a) the use of dissimilar materials, (b) the use of different tension during the manufacturing process, or (c) postfabrication treatment such as finishing, dyeing, and laundering.

Each fabric, an interworked composition consisting of the elements described above, exhibits its own physical characteristics: texture, handle, and weight. In addition, museum fabrics exhibit effects created by age and past care. These physical characteristics must be fully understood to know how to deal with the fabric and to provide it with the optimum preservation environment.

Care of Fabrics in the Museum

Introduction. The life of the major components of fiber-made objects—fibers and dyes—is determined by various controllable and uncontrollable factors. Intrinsic elements that affect the longevity of museum fabrics are: material (whose quality is affected by plant's or animal's growing processes), processing of fibers, yarn making, coloring, fabric manufacture, finishing, and construction into a utilitarian form. Extrinsic elements are: use, storage conditions, cleaning, handling, displaying, and so on. All of these factors combined may accelerate fabric destruction by oxidation, acidification, photochemical degradation, and mechanical damage. Methods to combat intrinsic degradation—which has not yet been fully researched—must be carefully and ethically performed step by step, but elimination of extrinsic causes must be accomplished immediately.

Deterioration of fiber-made objects progresses at all times and can easily be hastened by negligence caused by our lack of scientific and technical knowledge of fabric materials and their environment. The deterioration, however, can be significantly slowed—and preservation of the present state enhanced—if a fabric is provided with chemical and physical stability, laid flat on a supportive platform made of chemically inert material in an environment wtih clean air under proper climatic control and with no light.

Museum fabrics are, however, constantly exposed to the threat of deterioration in exhibition galleries and storage areas and while being transported, studied, and treated. Mechanical handling, unsuitable contacting material, climate, contaminants, and light all contribute to physical, chemical, and photochemical deterioration. To retard or prevent such deterioration, we must provide an optimum environment founded on the premise that all museum fabrics should remain unadulterated, pliable, and absorbent for as long as possible and free from any conservation treatment. To determine the optimum environment for a particular museum fabric, the fiber, yarn, colorants, fabric structure, and handle must be studied from various points of view so that the fabric can be given chemical stability and physical support with well-selected preservation materials and techniques. Only proper maintenance of a "good" environment will insure the long-range preservation of museum fabrics.

Museum fabrics may have to undergo conservation treatment to correct preacquisition condition, but they should not have to be treated in the laboratory because of improper maintenance in the museum. In the conservation laboratory, a fabric will be thoroughly examined and revived to come as close as possible to its original beauty. The revival process itself, however, can subject the fabric to the greatest of dangers, which may lead to visual improvement but scientific and ethnographic disaster. For instance, often a soiled fabric can be revived with a wet-cleaning solution only with the loss of its original surface appearance and handle. The conservator must decide if the gains of cleaning outweigh the losses. The choice of backing, mounting, and consolidating treatment will depend on the extent of fiber degradation as well as on a thoughtful consideration of the post-treatment situation. The more competent the caretaker and the more ideal the storage and exhibition conditions, the more likely it is that the museum fabrics can remain unadulterated and that drastic treatment be avoided.

Although there are rare exceptions, one rule that applies in handling over an object for conservation laboratory work is "all or nothing under a long-range plan." A fabric should not be subjected to repeated washings nor should it be mended by more than one method. All treatment should be envisioned under a long-range plan that has been adopted in light of the fabric's condition and the projected posttreatment maintenance program. On the other hand, a rule in preservation work is "everything as soon as and as much as possible." No museum fabrics will be harmed by any attention given to their preservation—from the most basic actions of eliminating light or keeping up slight air circulation in the storeroom to the use of elaborate vibration-free storage units or germ-free air purifiers. Every small action practiced by maintenance personnel counts in preserving fabrics.

After carrying out each day's standard preservation routines—i.e., checking temperature and relative humidity and cleaning the work area and storeroom—the caretaker should work on museum fabrics categorically from problem to problem. Caretakers should familiarize themselves with the type of object, problem, and maintenance procedure to achieve quality work with maximum efficiency. This may mean, for instance, handling all the weighted silks in the collection and methodically preparing them with uniform storage procedures or airing all woolen fabrics seasonally to check systematically for insect infestation. Work haphazardly assigned according to exhibition plans and personal whims of curators only harms objects and drives caretakers to perform mediocre work.

Atmosphere. Steady temperature and relative humidity levels are important for preserving organic material (9) but are very difficult to maintain. Sudden changes as well as extremes of either one are damaging to fabrics. Acceptable ranges for a fabric collection in the eastern United States are said to be a relative humidity of 45% to 55% ± 5% and a temperature between 55° and 66°F. The temperature can be adjusted as long as the relative humidity is maintained at a particular level throughout the year. In general, however, other factors are also involved. For instance, if the temperature rises above 68°F, there is a chance of insect infestation, and if the relative humidity goes over 70%, fungus growth may occur (10).

It is essential for everyone to be concerned about providing a stable climate, particularly in the storeroom where a fabric collection will remain for most of its life (11). Needless to say, rooms must be kept clean and air-conditioned; a steady but slight air circulation should be maintained. Stagnant air in an isolated area in a room or storage unit increases fiber deterioration and may attract insects. Drafts, on the other hand, may blow in damaging air-born dust.

Windows must function properly. They should be of weather proof construction, ultraviolet-ray (uv) filtered, and draped to prevent the entry of unnecessary heat, dust, and light. Light bulbs and fixtures should be properly positioned and lights turned on for as few hours as possible to reduce emission of heat and light.

Illumination. All types of rays around us cause photochemical degradation of fibers and dyes (*12, 13*), and museum fabrics can be adversely affected by seemingly normal use of artificial light. Ultraviolet and infrared (ir) rays, which do not enhance our ability to view objects, are particularly harmful. In addition to the type of light, the fabric's strength and exposure time regulate the degree of photochemical damage. It is essential to keep a fabric collection in darkness as long as possible and to control seriously and conscientiously the use of light in the storeroom, study room, conservation laboratory, and exhibition galleries. Photochemical damage caused by ordinary use of light in the course of a year or two is not easy to discern with our eyes, but once inflicted, the damage cannot be reversed.

Both ultraviolet and infrared rays are emitted by sunlight, uv by fluorescent lights, and infrared by incandescent lights. Direct sunlight should not come into the museum building. Every window and fluorescent lighting fixture should have a uv filter, which should be changed periodically according to the manufacturer's instructions. Such filters do not completely protect fabrics against photodegradation; they only help slow down such deterioration. Heat caused by the infrared rays emitted from incandescent light bulbs is a problem in the museum environment. Lighting fixtures that direct the heat backward are available, but if an ordinary lighting system has to be used, distance must be kept between the object and the incandescent light.

Visible light also harms fabrics and dyes. Windows should be prepared with light-shielding draperies, which should be opened only during visiting hours. This precaution is particularly important in historical houses where the interior is decorated with fabrics. To avoid "weathering"—i.e., deterioration caused by a combination of light soil and drastic fluctuations of temperature and humidity such as occur at windowside—displayed curtains should be hung inside a protective curtain. (Regular fabrics transmit uv rays, but uv-shielding draperies are available.) Period rooms created in a large museum building should make use of false windows, where simulated daylight can be readily controlled by turning lights on only during visiting hours. Skylights should never be built: while uv rays may be eliminated by installing filters, the level of daylight on bright sunny days is far beyond the bearable level. Exposure from sunrise to the gallery's opening and from the gallery's closing to sunset, plus days on which the museum is closed, in effect trebles exposure hours. If skylights already exist, they should be covered completely and a lighting system should be installed. If overhead ambient light is needed, install lighting fixtures above the lower skylight ceiling and cover the entire skylight and lighting system with a roof.

Photochemical degradation occurs the moment fabric is exposed to light. Exposure to light is an unavoidable occurrence for museum objects, but reduction of exposure level and time is feasible and essential since degradation is determined by the level of illumination multiplied by the duration of exposure. Thus, if a fabric is exposed to 30 ft-c, it will suffer as much photochemical damage in 100 days as another fabric exposed to 10 ft-c for 300 days. The level in the exhibition area must be restricted to 10 ft-c. (A minimum of 3 ft-c is necessary for human eyes to distinguish different colors (14).) In the galleries, three types of lighting are necessary: ambient lighting for installation and maintenance; spot lighting for exhibition; and night lighting for the safety of night watch personnel. The whiter (as contrasted with yellow) the light, the more visible the objects are to human eyes, even at the same foot-candle level.

For successful gallery illumination, an important factor to take into account is relative light strengths. Human eyes need time to adjust when foot-candle levels change. For instance, on walking from the bright outdoors into a gallery lighted in 10 ft-c, one would be almost blinded for a short time. If one were led gradually through lobbies and galleries displaying inorganic objects, light levels for fabrics would be acceptable to one's eyes. Equally, when the foot-candle level in a display case is set low enough for the safety of fabrics, if an overhead light set at a higher level is used for ambient light, the fabrics will be almost invisible to viewers. The surrounding areas must be lighted at the same level or, preferably, more dimly than the fabrics on exhibition. Those "fashionable" track lighting systems in museums, if positioned properly, actually permit the control of illumination that is needed for preservation.

Since visual perception of colors is altered and the degree of shadow varied according to the type of light bulb used, it is important to select the appropriate bulb for a particular fixture in a particular position. Also, once turned on, produced light should not be wasted. The viewer's eye level and focal point on the displayed fabric must be calculated to determine the position and angle of light bulbs. Such calculations are best consigned to an expert concerned about preservation who specializes in museum illumination.

Lighting for photography causes considerable damage to fabrics. If a fabric is to be photographed, do it once: repeated photography must be avoided not only because of the harm it causes but also because it necessitates mechanical handling and disturbance of climatic stability. Flash bulbs should not be used. (Electronic flash is known to be less harmful, but it still exposes museum fabrics to high light intensity.)

Work Areas. The fabrics' storeroom should not be combined with the curator's office, the study room, the conservation laboratory, or the maintenance worker's room, so as to avoid exposing the collection to unnecessary light and changes in atmospheric conditions caused by people going in and out, as well as to lessen casual touching of fabrics.

Because of their nature, it is essential for fabrics to be physically separated from art objects made of such materials as metals, porcelain, glass, paper, and wood. The caretaker should not handle solid objects made of those materials interchangeably with fabrics because handling requirements are totally different. As contact is inevitably made with museum fabrics, it is essential to have a wash basin in both the maintenance room and the study room.

A proper working environment, proper equipment, and proper maintenance materials should be provided. Because of the perishability of fabrics, a worker must move around a fabric that rests on a worktable instead of remaining in one position and shoving or moving the museum fabric around. The height of the worktable, therefore, must be comfortable for a standing person, approximately 36 in. from the floor. An adjustable-height chair with a foot rest should be available for use at the worktable. Flooring should be selected to make a provision for the comfort and health of people who work standing up most of the time. Ambient light is needed in the workroom as well as an auxiliary lamp-magnifier illuminator. (The type suited to use with a stationary object has the magnifier mounted on a movable arm and the arm on a free-standing base.) Type and level of light must be carefully selected to aid work while minimizing harm to the museum fabric. For overhead ambient light, a fluorescent light that emits the smallest possible amount of uv, in combination with an incandescent light, is recommended. Such a combination represents a compromise between the two opposing characteristics of these lighting types, shadow and influence on the perception of colors. A partitioned walk-in closet is needed for the ever-increasing amount of preparation materials. Wall color in the work area, traffic route, acoustics, and positions of electrical outlets all affect work efficiency and safety of objects.

Physical Organization of the Collection. The physical organization of a collection can make it more usable and easier to monitor and enable the long-range plans for research, exhibition, and preservation to be carried out satisfactorily.

Developing the physical organization requires people in at least three areas of expertise: historical/ethnographic, material/technological, and maintenanceship. While organizing, the basic catalog information should be compiled and a long-range preservation plan proposed. Revisions of the catalog and the preservation plan may become necessary as the program of preservation/conservation proceeds and exhibition/deterioration progresses. Initially, each item should be designated according to its condition, extent of deterioration and soiling, and so forth, and recommendations should be advanced as to proper handling and what to watch for in terms of preservation. The "when," "how," "what," and "then" of a long-range, comprehensive preservation plan, which includes conservation treatment, will become apparent as these recommendations are developed.

In the storeroom, three separate catalog files must eventually be set up: (a) in numerical order by accession numbers, with storage locations noted; (b) categorized according to present form—costume, fragment, bed cover, and so forth—and filed chronologically within each group; and (c) categories of technical information such as surface patterning technique, interworked single element, woven, embroidered, and so on. Condition should also be noted: very fragile, fragile, fair, and good, with descriptions of wear, tear, soiling, dye-oriented deterioration, yellowing by oxidation, and insect attack. Previous conservation work should also be described. There are endless ways to describe and categorize fabrics, and every single fabric could be described according to all of them. A photographic record is a crucial aid for curators and students in order to organize their research, but more importantly it eliminates unnecessary handling of each fabric.

Storage systems and units and the location and size of the study room and the caretakers area near the storeroom are largely dictated by available funds, architectural restrictions, the estimated number of visiting students per week, the frequency with which each object is to be handled, and the available number of caretakers. The collection can be organized in such a way as to enhance preservation regardless of the elaborateness of storage facilities available, but this is unlikely to be accomplished unless the museum fully embraces the preservation philosophy set forth in this paper.

Preservation preparation materials such as a variety of conditioned papers' desized unbleached muslin, cardboard, tubes, boxes, polyethylene sheeting, and nonstatic thermoplastic sheets *must* be provided, regardless of cost, to create the basic safe storage environment. Adequate funds must be allocated yearly to freshen and launder preparation materials.

Preservation Practices. Each time a museum fabric is touched by our hands, whether it is being moved, studied, or treated, the fabric is exposed to the threat of mechanical and chemical degradation as well as to photochemical deterioration. Because of their physical and chemical characteristics, fabrics change shape upon contact with our hands, a fact to be kept in mind at all times by people working with museum fabrics. Fabrics are also penetrated by soils from the surfaces with which they come into contact.

Soils that we encounter in maintaining a museum fabric collection are hand grime, airborn dust, and particles of fiber from the museum fabric itself. Because fabrics are by nature the best wiping material, museum fabrics, particularly cottons, pick up soils just as any wash cloth does. Therefore, all surfaces that are in contact with fabrics must be kept immaculately clean.

The hand is the surface with which fabrics most often come into contact. No matter how often we wash our hands while handling fabrics, grime always comes back sooner or later, mixes with dust, and then is transferred onto the museum fabrics. Clean hands are essential. It cannot be emphasized too strongly that immediately before handling and after every interruption, hands should be washed in the vicinity where fabrics are being handled. (A moistened paper towel should be used if hand washing is not possible.) Hands should be completely dry before handling fabrics.

The worktable is another surface with which museum fabrics often come into contact. Hard, nonporous materials such as wood, formica, and glass must not be used as a worktable surface. Because of their nonabsorbent nature, they collect hand grime and other oily matters; museum fabrics placed on such a surface naturally serve as a wiping cloth and clean the soiled worktable. (Many fabrics in museums suffer the results: the reverse side is extensively soiled while the obverse is still clean.)

The worktable, therefore, should be prepared by covering it first with cotton padding (dry-cleaner's ironing board padding, which comes as wide as 96 in.), then with desized, unbleached muslin (dry-cleaner's ironing board cover) stretched over it. Use another sheet of muslin on the top and replace daily wtih a fresh, clean one. The cotton muslin, being absorbent, will pick up hand grime. Once settled on the cotton muslin, the grime will not transfer onto museum fabrics. The padding underneath gives the unbleached muslin cover stability, preventing sliding on the table surface, and it provides the cushioning effect needed when rolling a museum fabric onto a tube for storage. (The abrasive muslin surface of the worktable will not be in contact with the surface of the museum fabric; the fabric must be procedurally placed on a supportive paper. *See* next paragraph.)

Mechanical damage from abrasion, tension, and vibration can be caused by the cumulative effects of the simple motions that occur during routine actions such as pulling, dragging, stretching, folding, and rubbing. Museum fabrics, therefore, should be handled as little as possible, and when handled, should be touched as little as possible. By establishing a system aimed at eliminating unnecessary touching and handling, damage and soiling can be drastically reduced. To this effect, museum fabric must always be placed on a supportive paper. This preparation gives stability to the museum fabric and permits the supportive paper, not the museum fabric, to be moved and turned around. If it becomes necessary to touch the museum fabric, it is done wtih as little manipulation as possible.

There are many environmental causes of chemical damage that can occur during daily maintenance: unsuitable contacting material, air pollution, climatic instability, and air stagnation. Rooms where museum fabrics are kept must be clean and neat; materials for surfaces that come into contact with museum fabrics should be properly selected and prepared and kept clean.

Photochemical damage occurs whenever fabrics are exposed to light of any strength or any type. Such damage, whether to fiber or dyes, is not easily recognizable during the course of daily maintenance since it occurs slowly. Once inflicted, however, the effect is often so severe that the fabric cannot be revitalized by conservation laboratory work. Therefore, fabrics must be stored in pitch darkness and their exposure to light restricted to study, conservation work, and limited exhibition only.

Good preparation for storage is a key to good preservation. Storage preparation should be done only by a responsible, trained caretaker. This gives the caretaker an opportunity to check the condition of the museum fabric, preparation material, and storage units. Under no circumstances should visitors be allowed to prepare fabrics for storage.

While in storage, museum fabrics should be in direct contact only with chemically inert and physically suitable storing materials—acid-free paper or properly treated, unbleached muslin. Acid-free tissue paper and other papers should be commercially buffered and, preferably, made of fiber instead of pulp. Of fabric storage preparation materials, unbleached cotton is generally the best; it should be washed to remove starch sizing (15) and other undesirable matter before use. If it has been sent to commercial cleaners, it should be rewashed in conditioned water by the caretaker to assure removal of cleaning agents used by the cleaners. To decide whether to use paper or fabric in storage preparation, the characteristics of each should be compared with the museum fabric and the environmental situation assessed. For example, regarding surface smoothness: paper is slippery and cotton is nonslippery; pliability: paper is less pliable and cotton is more so; absorbency: paper is less absorbent than cotton.

The fabric in a storage unit must be arranged for easy access, and each fabric should have been prepared independently and uniformly so that when it is necessary to take out one museum fabric, others need not be touched, thus eliminating chances for accident and unnecessary handling. The location of each stored fabric should be indicated in the card file; the accession number of each piece should be clearly written on the package in the same position as accession numbers on other packages; and each package must be easily located.

If the museum fabric is resilient enough to tolerate bending motion, it can be rolled. Rolling a museum fabric is, however, not simply winding a fabric around a tube; it is an operation that requires skill and the proper work surface. The padding and surface-resistant cotton muslin on the worktable give stability to the museum fabric and the rolling tube. Indeed, such a covered worktable is the only surface on which pliable fabrics can be properly rolled around a solid tube.

To begin with, one must distinguish sheer from heavy, oddly shaped from square, short from long, heavily textured from slippery, and stiff from stretchy and then decide whether to roll right side in or out, with or without paper or padding in between. Generally, all museum fabrics should be rolled in the direction of the warp. First roll the tube with buffered, acid-free paper. Then start rolling with another piece of soft acid-free paper or desized, unbleached muslin. After rolling it on a few times around, place the edge of the museum fabric on top of the loose end of the paper, overlapping for a distance that is at least as long as one full circumference of the tube. This insures that the edge of the fabric will not be creased. While rolling, the tube is snugly caught by the padded cotton surface and by controlled pressure of hands, making the already-rolled museum fabric stay properly around the tube. As the rolling continues, a ridge will gradually be created in the museum fabric yet to be rolled. Pull the rolled tube back as much as necessary to remove the ridge without loosening the rolled fabric on the tube or pulling the unrolled portion too tightly. Be sure the warp and weft are in the right position relative to each other as well as to the tube. One must learn to roll the tube horizontally and directly in front of oneself to be able to watch for any mishaps and adjust accordingly as the procedure advances. The tension of the rolled museum fabric should be neither too tight nor too loose and must be adjusted according to the type and condition of each museum fabric. The padded worktable gives one the needed physical control. The accession number should be clearly written on the outside wrapping. A card and/or photograph may be added for additional identification.

If the museum fabric is fragile, it should not be bent. To avoid any motion or vibration whatsoever, it should be supported on a solid surface and covered for protection against moving air. If it has been mounted permanently by having been sewn on to a stretcher, then the mount should be covered with a plexiglass box (unlike glass, thermoplastic materials are air-permeable). To protect the museum fabric as fully as possible, it is necessary to consider that the mount has become an integral part of the museum fabric. The mount should be encased in a blackout cover and stored flat. For temporary storage, an unmounted fabric may be placed on a solid board that has been covered with a buffered paper, covered with transluscent paper or nonstatic thermoplastic, and laid unstacked in a drawer. The drawer must be pulled in and out gently so as not to cause vibration and movement of air.

Considering the damage that clearly occurred in the past during long-term storage, it is obvious that museum fabrics should never be creased and folded. For costumes and other three dimensionally constructed objects, light weight, acid-free tissue paper should be crushed and stuffed wherever there is a crease.

The fumes of frequently used insecticide, such as paradichlorobenzene, are often heavier than air. The crystals should be packaged and placed on the ceiling of a cabinet or a box. Objects made of leather, skin, fur, feathers, intestine, wax, and certain resins should be stored elsewhere as they may be adversely affected by volatile insecticides. It has been reported that ethylene oxide fumigation affects certain natural dyes (16). As there are so many factors yet to be investigated regarding the effects of fumigation on museum fabrics and particularly on dyes, this treatment should be done with utmost caution.

Fabrics to be transported should have sturdy cardboard or tube supports and should be protected. When handling a rolled museum fabric, touch only the tube and do not grab the museum fabric. Carry and store tubes horizontally, never vertically. Fabrics laid flat on a support or a mount should be kept horizontal at all times. Floors of hallways and rooms should be smooth, and the truck or dolly used for transport should be equipped with swivelling, rubber-covered casters and shock absorbers. Secure museum fabrics on the truck and move slowly. If the fabric is to be carried by hand, the object must be placed in a box or a case. One should never carry them exposed or hanging free.

Conclusion

Since museum fabrics are, for the most part, made of organic material—fibers and dyes—they respond more critically to maintenance procedures and environment than do most works of art in other media.

Their pliable and absorbent physical and chemical nature makes them very sensitive to degradation during handling, storing, studying, and displaying.

In addition to appropriate funding, which is all too rare, effective preservation of museum fabrics depends upon the functioning of a well thought out, collective working system in a museum as well as on the qualifications of individuals, particularly a caretaker. For dealing with museum fabrics a caretaker must have well-developed visual and tactile senses and a strong proclivity for cleanliness and neatness. He must have the incentive to understand museum fabrics with logical approaches to basic science and technology. His respect for museum fabrics—expressed in sensitive and sensible care of a collection—should be in turn respected by his colleagues in the museum.

Taking care of museum fabrics is the most tedious part of museum work, yet it can be the most important and rewarding one. It enables one to establish communication with the distant past as well as to extend it to future generations. And, as a matter of course, through his daily direct contact with museum fabrics, the caretaker is closer than any person today to those who engaged in producing and caring for them in the past.

Acknowledgments

I am indebted to James W. Rice, Chemist Consultant, Textile Museum, and Joseph V. Columbus, Conservator, National Gallery of Art, both in Washington, D. C., for their long-time guidance and assistance in textile conservation. My thanks also go to Susan Gould for her valuable editorial work on my manuscript.

Literature Cited

1. "Professional Practices in Art Museums," Association of Art Museum Directors, New York, 1971.
2. "Conservation of Cultural Property in the United States," National Conservation Advisory Council, Washington, D. C., 1976.
3. Carnow, B. W., "Health Hazards in the Arts and Crafts," Chicago, 1974; obtainable by writing to Dr. Bertram W. Carnow, Box 3, Hubbard Woods, Winnetka, Ill. 60093. *See* also various publications available from Hazards in the Arts, 5340 North Magnolia, Chicago, Ill. 60640.
4. Mauersberger, H. R., "The Textile Fibers," 6th ed., John Wiley & Sons, New York, 1954.
5. Koch, P. A., "Microscopic and Chemical Testing of Textiles," Chapman & Hall, London, 1963.
6. Fannin, A., "Handspinning," Van Nostrand Reinhold, New York, 1970.
7. Yoshioka, T., "Tennen Senryō no Kenkyū (Natural Dyes)," Mitsumura-Suiko, Tokyo, 1974.
8. Emery, I., "Primary Structures of Fabrics," Textile Museum, Washington, D.C., 1966.

9. "Museum Climatology: Contributions to the London Conference, Sept. 1967," Thomson, G., Ed., International Institute for Conservation of Historic and Artistic Works, London, 1968.
10. Hueck, H., "Textile Pests and Their Control," "Textile Conservation," Leene, J., Ed., Smithsonian Institution, Washington, D. C., 1972.
11. Thomson, G., "Textiles in the Museum Environment," "Textile Conservation," Leene, J., Ed., Smithsonian Institution, Washington, D. C., 1972.
12. Feller, R., "The Deteriorating Effect of Light on Museum Objects," "Museum News Technical Supplement," No. 3, Washington, D. C., 1964.
13. van Beck, H. C. A., Heertjes, P. M., "Fading by Light on Organic Dyes on Textiles and Other Materials," Stud. Conserv. (1966) 11, No. 3, International Institute for Conservation of Historic and Artistic Works, London.
14. Crawford, B. H., "Just Perceptible Color Differences in Relation to Level of Illumination," Stud. Conserv. (1973) 18, No. 4.
15. AATCC Technical Manual, American Association of Textile Chemists and Colorists, Research Triangle, North Carolina, 1976.
16. Arai, H., Tokyo National Research Institute of Cultural Properties, verbal communication, 1976.

RECEIVED May 13, 1977.

Some Techniques of Textile Conservation Including the Use of a Vacuum Hot Table

PAT REEVES

Conservation Center, Los Angeles County Museum of Art,
Los Angeles, Calif. 90036

Textiles, as are many objects of art, are subject to the deteriorative effects of dirt, acidity, light, humidity, and mishandling. The steps by which they are conserved are detailed, including a discussion of the problems inherent in their restoration. The use of the vacuum hot table—a recent technique—is exemplified in the treatment of embroideries and two Civil War flags, and the use of adhesives is discussed in regard to this technique.

Since most of my readers are not professional textile people at home among tabby weaves, compound silks, ikats, and double-cloth, I try to keep my textile terminology simple. I mention some of the problems we face in working with ancient textiles, some of the answers we have come up with, and the solutions for which we are still searching. It seems chemists have shown a bit of favoritism to painting, metal, and paper conservators and not to the textile conservator. Those in textiles do need chemical help, and I hope we can work together more closely in the future.

A definition of art conservation has been stated by Ben Johnson, Head Conservator at the Los Angeles County Museum of Art: "Conservation can be defined as the application of science to the examination and treatment of objects of art and to the study of the environments in which they are placed. Art restoration is the portion of conservation which deals primarily with the treatment of objects. It should be understood that restoration does not imply an attempt to return the object to its original state but rather to prevent deterioration of the original materials while respecting their integrity (1)."

I must point out something which is implied in this definition: all of our work is reversible. At any time, we can stop a process if it is not working, reverse it, and try another way. (Later I give you an example of this.) Also, if a chemist discovers a better way of doing something next year, we can reverse what we have done and use the new formula.

Textiles suffer from the same perils as do other objects of art: dirt, acidity, light, humidity, and mishandling. In many ways textiles are inherently more fragile than other objects. The degree of fragility depends to a great extent upon the fibers from which they are created. Silk deteriorates more rapidly than does wool, cotton, or linen. The dyes with which they are colored and the mordants with which the colors are set can accelerate deterioration. Dirt is abrasive and in some cases has latent chemical properties which can cause damage. Therefore, it is necessary that textiles be cleaned before they are mended and mounted for display or storage.

Normally, the first step in textile conservation is the examination of the piece to determine the fibers from which it was made and the technique by which it was created. One determines the spin of the yarns, whether Z or S, and the number of wefts and warps per inch. Next, one tests for colorfastness: first with distilled water, then with glycerin and water, and finally with a neutral detergent and water. If the colors run with any of these solutions, obviously the piece cannot be washed, and one tests with dry-cleaning solvents and other chemicals.

Before washing, the textile is encased in nylon tulle, well basted with a long running stitch for protection in the necessary handling. It is then soaked in a 25% solution of glycerin and distilled water for a few hours overnight. During the process, dirt is loosened and emulsified and the fibers are relaxed. After thorough rinsing, the textile is then gently bathed in neutral detergent and distilled water. This process sometimes must be repeated. The final step in cleaning is another thorough rinsing in distilled water and a pH test.

When the textile has dried on a padding material, it is transferred to a work board of suitable size. My work boards are made of Homosote (a form of pulp-board) covered with Contact paper. The nylon tulle is removed, clipping each basting thread and removing it with forceps. With the aid of guide lines and T-squares, the piece is steamed and blocked, which simply means aligning the warps and wefts in the position in which they left the loom originally.

After blocking, the decision is made as to the means of support to be provided. If the textile is strong enough to hang freely, it is lined with a suitable washed cotton. The lining must support the textile as well as protect it from dust and contact with the wall. The support is achieved by sewing the textile to the lining vertically (and sometimes horizontally) every few inches. The stitches, of course, are invisible on the face of the textile. In this manner the weight of the textile is distributed and is not being pulled only from the top. It is hung in one of two ways: by using Velcro at the top or making a sleeve for a hanging rod.

If the textile is not to hang freely, it is then mounted on a strainer which has a washed cotton fabric stretched very tightly over it. The textile is sewn and mended down to this mounting fabric and then enclosed in a 3-sided Plexiglas box, making sure the Plexiglas does not touch the textile. The back of the strainer is covered with a washed cotton flannel, which allows the textile to "breathe" but still acts as a dust and moisture barrier.

Some problems are inherent in the way the textiles are woven or embellished. That is, one can anticipate the manner in which they will deteriorate and how they can be protected against themselves. One example of this we find in large European tapestries. Most of them are made with warps running horizontally, instead of vertically, as in most other textiles. The warps are heavier and stronger than the wefts, but the tapestry hangs by its finer wefts. After many years of hanging, the wefts begin to break and sag, leaving exposed warps. This kind of inherent deterioration can be anticipated and measures taken against it. Tapestries should have vertical strips of cotton sewn invisibly to the back of the tapestry, giving support to distribute the weight. The lining also helps in this manner and is useful in balancing the tapestry to avoid getting ripples in it.

Embellished textiles are those on which the decoration is applied after the fabric has left the loom. The most comomn examples are embroidery and needlepoint. Embroidery almost always is done with a greater tension in the stitches than in the textile, resulting in an uneven surface tension. This means that the unembroidered areas will pucker and crease. Each pucker and crease will eventually break the fibers, resulting in a split in the fabric. The method I have devised to help prevent this kind of damage is to pad the unembroidered areas lightly from the back using a washed cotton flannel. Just enough padding is added to eliminate the puckers and creases.

Another similar problem often occurs with flags, particularly American flags. They are made of strips of different colors sewn together. The sewing usually will have more tension than the fabric. In ironing even a new flag, one must watch for ripples between the stitchings. In an old flag, when the fabric between the stitching has stretched and sagged from age, the problem is aggravated.

In the past when I have had a textile too fragile to withstand a needle, I have pasted a very light silk lining to it, using Japanese rice paste, which is harmless and easily reversible. This method had the advantage of preserving a piece which was otherwise hopeless, but it also had certain disadvantages: it was somewhat stiff and would not always lie flat even though it was dried under weights.

Today, instead of the Japanese rice past method, I am using the vacuum hot table (2) with a heat-activated adhesive, which is also harmless and reversible. I am stressing here the use of the vacuum hot table in the treatment of textiles as it is a fairly recent technique for us. The vacuum hot table was designed for painting conservators and used by them in re-lining old paintings. The first published account I know of in the use of this table for textiles is by Sheila Landi (3) of the Victoria and Albert Museum in London. Another reference is by Kathryn Scott (4).

One recent successful use of the vacuum hot table was in the treatment of an American Civil War flag. The flag was brought to me in such a tattered and fragile state that I could not even remove it from the brown paper bag which contained it. I transferred the contents of the bag into a nylon-mesh laundry bag. I was able to determine that the fabric was a fine wool and to test the blue and red colors which were found to be fast in water. I soaked the flag (still in the mesh laundry bag) in a glycerin–water solution for several hours. The solution was very dark and dirty at the end of the soak. The flag was then rinsed, washed, and rinsed, washed again and rinsed. By the end of the final rinse, the water was clear and the pH neutral.

Only after the soaking and washing did I remove the flag from the laundry bag and place it on a clean sheet on my table. While it was still damp, I straightened it out enough to be able to measure it (Figure 1). Because of the many losses in the flag, it was decided to line it with the same colors—actually, to make a new flag for the lining. A suitable cotton fabric was found and dyed exactly to match the original. The "lining flag" was made to fit precisely under the old flag.

The usual procedure would have been to thumb-tack the lining to a frame and spray it with adhesive. Because of the extensive losses in the old flag, however, large areas of the "lining flag" would be shown, covered with unabsorbed adhesive. The solution to this was to take an inexpensive cotton fabric, wash it, thumb-tack it to a frame, and loosely baste the original flag to it, wrong side up. The cotton fabric simply served as a support for the old flag while it was sprayed with the adhesive (Figure 2).

After the adhesive had dried, the basting stitches holding the flag to the cotton backing were removed, and the old flag was placed right side down on the "lining flag." It was adjusted properly and the most fragile areas adhered with the use of a tacking iron. It was then moved to the vacuum hot table and covered with silicon paper, to prevent the adhesive from contacting the table, and a membrane which made pos-

Figure 1. Flag first laid out on the table

Figure 2. Flag and temporary lining being sprayed with adhesive

sible the vacuum. Sand bags were placed around the edges of the table to ensure a perfect vacuum, and the table was set at 65°C (150°F). At the conclusion of the treatment, a sleeve was put at the top of the flag and the lining on the wrong side so that it could be hung (Figure 3).

The flag done on the hot table was successful only because the old flag was so tattered and stringy that it could be made smooth on the lining. The new flag (which formed the lining) was seamed on the sewing machine with a very low tension.

On another Civil War flag we were not so successful. This flag was intact enough that it needed only to be lined with a thin silk. Because it was so nearly intact, however, and the fabric between the seams had stretched and sagged, it could not be made to lie flat. We were unaware of the problem since it was possible to iron the flag by hand, leaving a

Figure 3.   Flag at conclusion of treatment

few ripples but no creases. The vacuum table was not so accommodating. It made every ripple into a sharp crease. It was indeed a mess. We then put the flag face down on a plain table and applied Picrin, a dry-cleaning solvent which is called a "volatile dry spotter," to the back of the lining which reversed the adhesive. That lining was thus easily removed and discarded. Another lining was cut and hand-sewn to the flag along every seam, adjusting ripples as we went. The torn areas were mended to the lining.

An embroidery with very high tension is not a suitable problem for the vacuum hot table. The vacuum causes the piece to become absolutely flat and will make permanent creases and transform the puckers into creases. This does not apply to all embroideries, however. I have successfully done some on the vacuum hot table.

The textiles most successfully treated on the vacuum hot table are those which are smoothest and have the least texture. Highly textured pieces are more difficult. For example, a Peruvian tapestry-woven piece was too fragile to sew so it was treated on the vacuum hot table with a thin silk lining. This worked marvelously for the loose wefts on the back of the textile. On the surface, however, the loose and raveling wefts were not improved because they had not come in contact with the adhesive, the surface wefts being, as it were, the top part of a sandwich composed of weft, warp, weft. In attempting to sew down the loose surface wefts, the fragile and rotten warps broke at the first stitch, which was the sign to stop immediately.

The answer was to put the piece back on the vacuum hot table, this time adhering the almost invisible silk to the face of the textile. This was not as pleasing aesthetically as I would have liked, but at least the piece is safe and will last for many years. Otherwise it would have totally disintegrated in a few years. In another Peruvian piece of similar structure, there was no problem because the warps were strong enough to withstand the sewing down of loose surface wefts which were not held by the adhesive.

The adhesive I use is Beva 371-B (5). I find it most satisfactory and have not had reason to try any other. At the Victoria and Albert Museum a polyvinyl acetate emulsion is used. At the present time, experiments are being carried out testing various adhesives and their effects on textiles when used on the vacuum table. This is being done by Christine Daulton, working under Joyce Stoner Hill, at Virginia Commonwealth University in Richmond. The adhesives she has chosen for her experiments and testing are: polyvinyl alcohol, polyvinyl acetate, Rhoplex N-850, Beva 677, Beva D-8, and both high and low ethyl hydroxyethyl-cellulose.

In conclusion, the use of the vacuum hot table is not the answer to every textile conservation problem. It is one useful tool in the repertory. Each work of art, by definition, is unique. Therefore, each textile must be individually treated, using the method most applicable to the problems.

Literature Cited

1. *Anal. Chem.* (1972) **44** (1), 25A.
2. "Vacuum Hot Table," Peter Koch, Apparatebau, Hannover, West Germany.
3. *IIC Stud. Conserv.* (1973) **18** (4).
4. *AIC Bull.* (1974) **14** (2).
5. Formula for Beva 371B: Elvax Resin Grade 150, 500 g; Ketone N. Resin, 300 g; Celloyn 21, 40 g; toluene, 1000 g.

RECEIVED January 7, 1977.

14

Preservation of Natural Textile Fibers—
Historical Perspectives

TYRONE L. VIGO[1]

Southern Regional Research Center, New Orleans, La.

The development of methods and tests for preserving natural textile fibers is surveyed. The effect of the environment in which the textiles are stored or exposed, chemical, physical, and biological agents responsible for their degradation, and test methods for evaluating their performance and extent of damage are discussed. Emphasis is on cotton, wool, and silk, with selected references on other cellulosic fibers such as jute and linen.

The use of natural vegetable and animal fibers dates back to ancient times. Despite the advent of synthetic textile materials, natural fibers still account for the greater part of world fiber consumption, and their care and preservation are of paramount importance. This survey discusses methods for preserving natural fibers, identifies causes of degradaiton attributable to textile processing and the environments in which fibers exist or are stored, and evaluates methods of assessing their ability to withstand degradation and of determining the extent and nature of damage in the textile. Emphasis is on cotton for the vegetable fibers and on wool for the animal fibers, with selected studies on linen, jute, and silk. Since the literature on this subject is formidable, only the most relevant, current, and informative reviews, books, and references are included. The reader should delve more deeply into particular aspects of this complex and interesting subject by consulting specific references cited. Discussion of degradation is arbitrarily divided into (1) environmental, (2) chemical agents, (3) physical agents, (4) biodeterioration, and (5) test methods.

[1] Present address: USDA Textiles and Clothing Laboratory, 1303 W. Cumberland Ave., Knoxville, Tenn. 37916.

Environmental Degradation

The influence of the environment on degradation of natural textile fibers is well documented. Most research has been directed towards assessing how well materials withstand weathering or outdoor exposure although there has been increased emphasis on preservation of textiles in storage, particularly as objects of art in museums.

Weathering. The weathering of materials, whether they be textiles, metals, or building materials such as wood or stone, is an extremely complex process (1). In a comprehensive survey (2) outdoor degradation of cellulosic fibers, particularly cotton, is attributed to sunlight, microorganisms, atmospheric pollutants, climate, alternate wetting and drying, wind, dust, rain, and other natural causes. In practice, simulation of all of these factors in accelerated weathering tests has been difficult. Most investigations, therefore, concentrated on one of the variables—e.g., biodeterioration or photochemical degradation. However, some studies determined the serviceability of the textile materials by actual outdoor exposure. These weathering studies are discussed, with specific agents receiving attention later in this survey.

The first weather-resistant treatment for cellulosic textiles is considered to be an 1884 patent for the mineral dyeing of cotton with lead chromate (3); however, it was not recognized as an effective weather-resistant finish until 1910. This is perhaps anticlimatic since the ancient Egyptians effectively preserved mummies by burial in an arid climate by wrapping them with linen containing salt, carbonates, and resinous materials, thereby incorporating many of the necessary features for optimum textile preservation (4). It was less than 50 years ago that fluidity and tensile strength measurements were proposed to distinguish between photochemical degradation and biodeterioration of cotton textiles resulting from outdoor exposure (5); this suggestion was confirmed experimentally about 10 years later (6). Extensive studies were made by Grimes (7, 8) on the effect of climatic conditions on weathering of undyed and dyed cotton fabrics; further recommendations for uniform exposure because of location and seasonal variations were made by Dean and Worner (9).

Although numerous finishes have been effective in protecting cellulosic textiles from environmental biodeterioration, many of these treatments prevent mildew and rot at the expense of accelerating photochemical degradation of the fabrics. The most successful weather-resistant finishes use a mildewproofing agent in combination with a light-resistant agent (such as a pigment) and a binding agent (such as a nitrogenous resin or synthetic coating). A selected list of chemical approaches for obtaining weather-resistant cellulosics is shown in Table I.

Table I.   Weather-Resistant Finishes for Cellulosic Fabrics

Major Ingredients

uv Resistance	Antimicrobials	Binders & Other Agents	Reference
Various pigments	copper salts	chlorinated paraffins	10
Various pigments	copper salts	urea–formaldehyde resins	11
Chromic oxide	copper salts	—	12
Light-stable vat dyes	acetylation	—	13
—	metal salts	urea and melamine–formaldehyde resins	14
Chromic oxide	copper metaborate	zirconyl ammonium carbonate	15
Titanium oxide	—	polyvinyl chloride	
Chrome yellow	tributyltin oxide	melamine–formaldehyde resins	16
—		aluminum salts; soap/wax	17

Most comparative weathering studies of natural and synthetic fibers were conducted on yarns between 1950 and 1970 (*18–24*). The ability of the fibers to withstand outdoor exposure was influenced by the locations selected for their weathering and by the construction of the yarn. Acrylic yarn, however, generally exhibited the best resistance, whereas jute and silk gave the poorest. Variability of outdoor weathering was observed with cotton and other cellulosic fibers, wool, nylon, and polyester. A comprehensive study of comparative weathering evaluated all of the important cellulosic fibers, wool and silk, and many of the synthetic fibers. Fiber properties such as strength, extensibility, abrasion resistance, and degree of polymerization were related to outdoor performance (*20, 21, 22*). Of the natural fibers evaluated, the order of decreasing resistance to outdoor exposure was:

hemp > cotton > linen > ramie > wool > jute > silk

One of the more recent studies on cotton, polyester, and nylon (*24*) demonstrated that cotton was superior to the synthetics in outdoor performance in areas of low air pollution but that its performance was reduced considerably in areas of high air pollution. Specific effects of air pollutants are discussed later under chemical agents causing fiber degradation.

In addition to the studies on weathering of processed wool, there has also been interest in the weathering of wool as it grows on the backs of sheep. Excessive weathering of fleece presents a technological problem because it leads to uneven dyeing in the upper tips of the fibers. Von Bergen (*25*), by comparing the solubility of the fibers in alkai, demonstrated that wool from the backs of sheep had much greater fiber damage than from the underside or belly of the animals. A later study (26) revealed that such damage was a result of the destruction of disulfide bonds rather than of the hydrolysis of main peptide chains of the fiber. This conclusion was confirmed by observing that the cystine content in the tips of the wool fiber decreased to the same extent when it had been weathered on sheep as when unweathered fibers were exposed on rooftops (27).

Storage. The deleterious effect of the environment during storage and display of textiles, although not as drastic or as rapid as that in outdoor exposure, presents similar problems in preservation. Again, photochemical and biological degradation are the most important factors. John Mercer, the father of textile chemistry, may have been the first to make recommendations for preserving textile goods during storage; in 1843 he suggested the use of chromium salts and dry surroundings to prevent growth of mildew on calico stored in ships embarking on long voyages (28).

The effects of degradation on cotton, linen, and wool fabrics stored for two to four years at temperatures of 78°F and 102°F (the latter simulating attic conditions in summer) were investigated in some detail (29). Degradation of cellulosic fabrics was measured by changes in fluidity, breaking strength, and copper number and in wool fabrics by changes in cystine content. All fabrics stored in diffused light deteriorated much more than fabrics stored in the dark at the same temperature; exposure to diffused light at 78°F produced as much degradation as storage at 102°F in the dark. For optimum preservation, it was recommended that all fabrics be stored in the dark at low temperatures, free of finishing material. The importance of low relative humidity in preventing biodeterioration of cellulosics by microorganisms and of wool by insects in museums was stressed in a later study (30). Relative humidities of under 50% with temperatures under 10°C were considered suitable for preventing biodeterioration in stored museum textiles; however, wool fabrics displayed at room temperature would require moth- or insect-proofing treatments.

Specific studies on the storage of cotton and other cellulosics began in the early 1920s when it was noted that cotton with moisture content above 9% in storage offered a surface conducive for rapid growth of fiber-degrading microorganisms (31). The tendering of cotton fabrics dyed with Sulfur Black was related to the production of sulfuric acid during conditions of normal warehouse storage (32, 33); treatment with alkaline solutions to minimize such degradation was recomemnded (34). Linen specimens dating back to 2000 B.C. showed mechanisms of aging similar to those of modern linen undergoing accelerated ageing; however, on degradation, the ancient linen had much shorter cellulose chain lengths than the modern material (*35*).

Some of the chemical strategies used in weatherproofing have been applied to the preservation of cellulosics for indoor storage and display. The historical Wasa sails of 1628 were preserved by copolymerizing acrylates and styrene onto this material (*36*). Antimicrobial treatment of cotton goods by polymerization in situ of a urea–mercury compound with formaldehyde or immersion in a quaternary ammonium salt solution protected the fabric for up to three years' storage provided it did not need to be laundered (*37*).

The difficulty of cleaning cotton fabrics that were soiled and then stored for several weeks or months before laundering has been noted (*38*). Detailed information on preparation of historical textiles for storage and display (identification, cleaning, and restoration) is given in two excellent reviews (*39, 40*) as well as in other papers in this volume.

In addition to protection of wool fabrics from insects, other factors that influence its storage stability have been investigated. The pH of wool extracted with water has been related to its durability; a pH of 2.7–9 at room temperature and of 3–8 in moist heat did not cause damage on storage (*41*). Wool fibers, when wet with water and left in air at 20°C and 65% relative humidity, became stiffer up to three years and beyond; a mechanism for this effect was postulated (*42*). Wool goods, both dyed and undyed, may be protected from fading and yellowing during display by using a packaging film of polyvinyl chloride containing a benzotriazole uv absorber (*43*).

The major problem in the storage and display of silk is its poor light resistance. This photochemical lability becomes even more acute in silk fibers weighted with tin or other metal salts. A series of studies demonstrated that even storage in the dark decreased tensile properties of tin-weighted silk, and the rate of degradation was directly dependent on the extent to which the fiber was weighted (*44, 45, 46, 47*). A more recent study shows that yellowing and deterioration of silk in humid atmospheres may be prevented by treatment with a thiourea resin (*48*).

Chemical Degradation

Natural fibers may be adversely affected by sunlight, air pollutants, acids and alkali, bleaches and other oxidizing agents, and chemical finishing processes. However, the effects of photochemical degradation are by far the most problematic in the conservation of textiles and therefore have received the most attention.

Photochemical degradation of natural fibers depends on the atmospheric conditions in which the textiles are exposed, stored, or displayed, on the chemical nature of the fiber, and on the types of dyes and additives present in the fiber. As early as 1548, fading of dyed fabrics in sunlight was observed, but not until 1837 was it discovered that fading could be arrested on cotton, wool, and silk fabrics if the materials were exposed to light in a vacuum (49). Gebhard later confirmed this observation (50) and postulated a mechanism involving the production of peroxide-containing species to account for the fading of dyed fabrics in humid environments.

The effect of light on undyed and dyed cellulosic textiles has been extensively reviewed from the 1920s to the present time (3, 51, 52, 53, 54). Witz in 1883 (55) was the first to relate the accelerated degradation of bleached cotton fabrics in sunlight to the oxidation of the cellulose by residual hypochlorite. Although undyed cotton fabrics are not rapidly degraded by the near ultraviolet radiation present in sunlight, impurities in the fiber can cause photosensitization. Scouring cotton fabrics to remove impurities (56) improved weathering and sunlight resistance. The formation of quinoid structures by degradation of the lignin present in jute is believed to contribute significantly to the poor stability to light of that cellulosic fiber (57).

Despite numerous investigations on the photosensitization or photo-tendering of cellulosic fibers by vat and other dyes, there is still no agreement on the mechanism by which this degradation occurs. The two currently proposed mechanisms are not always consistent with many of the anomalies observed in the lightfastness of dyed cellulosics. One mechanism postulates oxidation of the fiber by production of singlet oxygen from reaction of the dye in the triplet state with molecular oxygen (58), whereas the other attributes fiber oxidation to reaction of the activated dye with the cellulose by a hydrogen-atom abstraction process (59). Giles concluded (60) by a statistical analysis of over 16,000 commercial evaluations of lightfastness of dyed fibers that (a) fastness was generally higher on fibers having high moisture regain, provided the regain value was at least 4% and (b) solid material incorporated into the fibers such as resins used for durable press and surfactants generally reduced the dyefastness of the fiber.

Earlier treatments to protect cellulosic fabrics from sunlight usually involved the application of pigments or mineral dyes (3). An intensive screening of many chemical compounds produced over 100 pigments, inorganic salts, and oxides that protected cotton fabric against sunlight (61, 62, 63). However, the type and amount of metal salts applied to cellulosics can have either beneficial or detrimental effects on the ability of the fibers to withstand actinic degradation. The rutile form of titanium dioxide is effective in protecting cotton fabrics outdoors, whereas the anatase form of this compound greatly accelerates degradation (64);

copper and zinc salts can either protect or degrade cotton fibers depending on the amount of metal present (65).

Other approaches for protecting cellulosics against actinic degradation have included chemical substitution, graft polymerization, and the use of ultraviolet absorbers. Benzoylation was effective in improving resistance of cotton to weather and radiation (66); a similar benefit was obtained by the graft polymerization of acrylonitrile onto jute (67). When jute fabric was covered with a film containing a benzophenone uv absorber (68), it was unaffected by sunlight. Ultraviolet screeners have been used to improve light resistance of all types of materials (69). Some of the more recently used absorbers for cellulosic fabrics have been allyl-substituted phenols (70) and a nickel-ketoxime chelate, a known triplet-state quencher (71).

The effect of light on wool has recently been reviewed (72, 73). Although it has been known for some time that sunlight may either bleach or yellow wool (74), only in recent years was it discovered that photobleaching of wool is caused by the visible violet region of sunlight (75). The advantages of photobleaching over wet-peroxide bleaching of wool during processing have been described (76). Photochemical degradation of wool in ultraviolet light was found to be retarded by alkali and accelerated by acids (77). The yellowing of wool has been attributed to oxidation of the amino acids tyrosine and tryptophan when it was photosensitized with fluorescent brightening agents (78), but it was observed that yellowing occurs in the range of 300–400 mμ where these amino acids are transparent (79). Other investigators claim that yellowing is a result of formation of carbonyl compounds from suint, a natural grease present in wool fiber (80).

Several types of chemical agents have been used to protect wool against yellowing by sunlight and fluorescent brightening agents. Treatments effective against sunlight included tetraalkyltitanates (81), substituted benzophenones (82), and thiourea–formaldehyde resins (83). Because of the photochemical nature of brightening agents, the types of compounds useful in protecting wool fibers against photosensitization are limited. Although reducing agents such as thioglycolic acid (84) and phosphonium salts (85) as well as copolymers of vinyl acetate/chloride (86) were effective for this purpose, none of them were particularly durable to laundering and dry cleaning.

The yellowing of silk in sunlight has been related to the discoloration of tryptophan formed by oxidative decomposition of silk fibroin (87). Silk is similar to wool in its response to sunlight—i.e., photobleaching by visible light and maximum degradation (244–275 mμ) and yellowing (309–322 mμ) at other wavelengths (88). Stability of silk to light also depends on the pH of its water extract; a pH value of 10 afforded the best photochemical protection (89). Recent studies have utilized the adsorption of copper ions (90), grafting of acrylates and acrylonitrile (91), reaction with expoxides (92), and use of benzotriazole uv absorbers (93) to protect silk from sunlight.

The detrimental effect of air pollutants on natural fibers was noted in weathering studies by Race (94). He attributed degradation of cotton fabrics to sulfur dioxide present in the air. Salvin has extensively reviewed and analyzed effects of pollutants on textile fibers and considers particulate matter, sulfur dioxide, oxides of nitrogen, and ozone as the major agents causing fiber damage (95). He also observed that in many instances fiber degradation attributable to air pollution has been incorrectly ascribed to photochemical action. Other conclusions drawn were: (a) sulfur dioxide is particularly damaging to undyed cellulosics and nylon but not to other fibers and (b) dyed cellulosics and wool are most sensitive to fading by nitrogen dioxide, moderately affected by ozone, and only mildly sensitive to sulfur dioxide.

The last type of chemical degradation to be considered is that encountered by natural fibers in their purification by agents such as acids, alkali, and bleaches. Several excellent reviews and books are available on this subject (96, 97, 98, 99), all of which stress the proper choice of temperature, pH, and other reaction conditions to optimize removal of impurities from fibers while minimizing damage.

Although hypochlorite was first used to bleach cellulosics, hydrogen peroxide is presently used as a commercial whitening agent not only for cellulosics but for wool, silk, and many synthetic fibers. The greatest destruction of cellulosics with hypochlorite is known to occur in neutral solutions (100); however, chelating agents effectively prevented damage to cellulose by hypochlorite at pH 7 and by other oxidizing agents (101) to a lesser extent. Bleaching of cotton with peroxide is maximum at alkaline pH, precisely the conditions under which most fiber damage occurs, presumably because of oxidation by molecular oxygen (102). The advantages of using peroxide activators and stabilizers for bleaching cellulosics have been discussed (103). Contrary to previous opinions, a recent article advocates addition of metal salts to alkaline peroxide to optimize bleaching and minimize fiber degradation; a mechanism for this beneficial effect has been proposed (104).

The adverse effects of alkali on wool cause reduction in its dry strength only after fiber solubilization and considerable loss in its cystine content (105). Because of its sensitivity to alkali, wool is preferentially given a peroxide bleach with added formic acid; silk does not degrade nearly so much under alkaline conditions and may be bleached at pH 10 with peroxide, using stabilizers such as sodium silicate (98).

Physical Degradation

The two main factors that contribute to the physical degradation of fibers are mechanical damage and thermal decomposition. Degradation resulting from wear is not usually a major concern in the preservation and storage of textiles. However, durable press treatments developed for cotton fabrics in the past 30 years generally have reduced resistance to abrasion and will cause wear much more rapidly than unmodified cotton on repeated laundering (*106*). Some of the more innovative approaches to overcome this problem have been the wet fixation of resins on the fiber (*107*) and the free-radical cross-linking of cellulosics, by silicones to produce permanent press fabrics with lubricity (*108*). Abrasion resistance of a variety of natural and synthetic fibers was compared by collecting data from 14 types of wear tests ranging from actual-wear trials to laboratory evaluations; most tests showed wool to be slightly superior to cotton, with both fibers being quite superior to silk (*109*). Inherent mechanical properties, fabric construction, and types of chemical finishing agents applied have been cited as major factors that contribute to abrasion resistance (*106, 110*).

Although wool has adequate abrasion resistance, it is dimensionally unstable and requires shrinkproofing and antifelting treatments. At least six different mechanisms have been proposed to explain the felting of wool fibers (*111*). Most antifelting treatments have utilized oxidizing agents, particularly chlorine, but overoxidation can cause fiber damage (*111*). Other approaches for preparing dimensionally stable wool include interfacial polycondensation (*112, 113*) and the subjection of the fiber to high energy sources such as a glow discharge (*114*).

The thermal degradation of textiles is influenced by the environment in which they exist as well as by impurities, additives, and finishing agents in the fiber. Damage to all fibers by heat and secondary influences such as ultraviolet light and biological attack occurs more rapidly in humid atmospheres. Cotton and silk can withstand higher temperatures than can wool without adverse effects on their fiber properties.

Cotton may be stored at temperatures as high as 125°C (257°F) for up to six hours even at high relative humidity and retain 80% of its breaking strength; however, above this temperature, fiber degradation becomes more severe (*115*). The thermal behavior of cellulosics at 140°–200°C was investigated; carboxyl and carbonyl groups and resins in the fibers and pulp accelerated thermal degradation (*116*). Current research on the thermal degradation of cotton and other cellulosics emphisizes understanding how decomposition occurs so that the fibers may be more effectively flameproofed (*117*).

Thermal degradation of wool continues to be a subject of considerable interest. The effect of dry heat on this fiber has been reviewed (118) with the observation that temperatures as high as 140°C cause yellowing but no marked decrease in mechanical properties. The use of metal salts or cross-linking agents to improve heat resistance was also suggested (118). Wool undergoes rapid degradation above 100°C when water is present (119). Investigations on the hydrothermal degradation of wool at 50°–100°C indicate that decomposition of disulfide groups increases with increasing time and temperature (120). Steam causes the hydrolysis of polypeptides (121), and air accelerates fiber degradation at 100°–150°C (122). When silk was heated above 125°C, a decrease in amino acid content was observed (123).

Biodeterioration

Damage to cellulosics by biological attack is usually attributed to microorganisms, whereas wool is more susceptible to destruction by insects. In some circumstances, however, either destructive source may cause biodeterioration in any of the natural fibers.

The principles and mechanisms by which the microbial decomposition of cellulose occurs as well as methods of evaluating textile susceptibility are discussed in detail by Siu (124). A more recent article discusses mechanisms by which organisms cause enzymatic hydrolysis of cellulose and lists representative cellulolytic species; the three classes of destructive microorganisms are bacteria, actinomycetes, and fungi although yeasts, algae, and myxobacteria have also been implicated (125).

There has been a variety of approaches for imparting antimicrobial activity to cellulosic fibers, many of them developed as part of a weather-resistant finish (Table I). Metal salts, organometallics, resins, sulfur and nitrogen compounds, and chemical modification of hydroxyl groups by acetylation or cyanoethylation are typical methods used to impart antimicrobial activity (125). A survey made in 1966 lists all commercial products available for protecting materials against biodeterioration— trade names, active ingredients, end uses, and names of manufacturers are tabulated (126).

The resistance of cellulose to microbial attack when it was treated with resins was attributed to chemical bonds formed between the fiber and the resin; this was ascertained by treating cotton with a variety of phosphonium salt-resin compositions having different degrees of cross-linking and homopolymerization (127). Some of the more recent approaches for producing antimicrobial fibers include the use of reactive dyes (128) and mixtures of zirconyl and copper salts (15) on cotton and the bromination of jute (129).

Since termites are notorious for their ability to digest wood and attack almost any type of material, including textiles, there is great interest in developing chemical treatments to combat them. The most effective method to date has been the use of arsenic compounds (*130*). Cockroaches may also damage textiles in storage, particularly if sizing is present on the fiber. Insecticides such as Dieldrin and lindane have been recommended (*131*) for incorporation into paints, varnishes, and lacquer to discourage entry of this pest in ships and other storage areas.

Although wool is not as susceptible as cellulosics are to microorganisms, this fiber may be subject to attack by mildew and bacteria if it contains impurities such as suint, sizing, and soaps or if it is stored in warm humid environments (*132, 133*). However, the storage of purified wool under cool, dry conditions will minimize this type of damage. The same is true of silk; if all of the sericin is removed during its degumming process, silk is fairly resistant to microorganisms (*134*). Despite these tendencies, there has been a great increase in research activity on effects of bacteria and fungi in wool. This subject has recently been reviewed (*132, 133, 135*). Generally, the same microbiota that cause cellulolytic degradation will damage wool fibers (*135*). The same strategies for imparting antimicrobial activity to cellulose have been advocated and practiced for mildewproofing wool, namely, treating with halophenols and organometallics and chemically modifying the fiber (*135*). The point was stressed that mildewproofing agents are not necessarily mothproofers or vice versa (*133*).

The attack of wool by several species of moths and beetles remains an important technological problem. A study on damage to several types of fibers by larvae of two representative species of moths, *Tinea pellionella* and *Tineola bisselliella,* showed that only wool was extensively degraded; unscoured silk and regenerated cellulosics suffered moderate damage, and other fibers were only slightly affected (*136*). The development of mothproofing and related subjects may be explored by reading the books of Moncrieff (*137*) and McPhee (*138*). Three methods of applying mothproofing agents to wool are described: spraying of the fiber and its surroundings, storage of the textiles with volatile chemicals, and permanent mothproofing by chemical finishing or modification of the fiber (*139*). Only the latter method is considered practical. Presently, there are three commercially available mothproofing agents, one of which is Dieldrin, a chlorinated hydrocarbon. The other two are aromatics having chloro and sulfonic acid groups (*140*). All of these are advantageously applied from acidic dyebaths. Although Dieldrin is the most efficient of the three, there is some concern about transfer of this insecticide on treated wool to humans (*141*). The search for new effective

Table II. Current Approaches for Mothproofing Wool

Type Compound	Reference
Thioureas	143
Organotins	144
Insect-growth regulators	145
Organophosphates and phosphonates	146
Quaternary ammonium salts	147
Zinc acetate	148
Synthetic pyrethroids	149

mothproofers continues. Some of the recent approaches evaluated and investigated are shown in Table II.

Test Methods

Performance. Although wear and field trials and actual storage of textiles are the ultimate in predicting the ability of treated fibers to withstand degradation, such studies are tedious and time-consuming. Accelerated performance tests have therefore been devised to relate fiber preservation to actual storage and exposure conditions.

There are currently four AATCC tests approved for evaluating weather resistance of fabrics, two based on actual outdoor exposure and the other two being accelerated tests where fabrics are exposed to a carbon-arc lamp with or without wetting of the fibers (150). Whether the xenon arc or carbon arc represents the best light source for simulating fading of dyed fabrics to sunlight remains a subject of continual debate (151, 152). Use of a mercury–tungsten fluorescent source for accelerated fastness tests has also been advocated (153). New lightfastness standards have recently been recommended because the current blue wool fabrics used as standards do not fade consistently (154). A violet polyester fabric standard has been proposed to replace the wool standards; the synthetic fiber standard appears to be advantageous in that it has a linear rate of fade, good reproducibility on repeated exposure, and other favorable characteristics (155).

The increasing emphasis on evaluating detrimental effects of air pollution on fibers is reflected by the development of tests for exposure of fabrics to ozone at low and high humidities (156). Predicting the aging of textiles in storage has also been a matter of concern. A test has been devised to expose all types of textile materials at 50% relative humidity and 70°C and relate fiber changes occurring in five days to the changes after a year of natural aging (157).

Although the significance of fiber mechanical properties such as breaking and tearing strength, extensibility, and tenacity has been established, abrasion or wear resistance of textiles is still measured by a variety of techniques. Generally, there are four types of laboratory wear evaluations: flat, flex, tumble, and edge abrasion (*110*). Relating the data from only one of these tests to actual wear performance is not usually meaningful, probably because of the complex nature of fatigue and mechanical degradation of fibers. The thermal or heat resistance of cellulosic (*117*) and wool (*158*) fibers is now evaluated by instrumental methods such as differential thermal analysis, thermogravimetric analysis, and differential scanning calorimetry.

The fungus resistance of textiles is usually evaluated by direct inoculation of the fabrics with the organisms *Chaetomium globosum* or *Aspergillus niger* and/or soil burial of the fabrics (*159*). In either case, tensile strength determinations are made at various periods to assess the resistance of the fabric to mildew and rot. The soil burial test is rather severe compared with most fabric exposure and storage conditions and has been criticized for its poor reproducibility. Careful selection of soils used in this type of testing has been advocated to minimize this problem (*160*). Insect resistance of textiles, specifically against the pests causing the most problems, clothes moths and carpet beetles, is determined by the amount of excrement left on the fabric and by loss in fabric weight (*161*).

Damage Assessment. Damage to cellulosic fibers is usually a result of depolymerization by acids, biological attack, and oxidation caused by heat, bleaches, or sunlight. The more classical methods of evalauting chemical damage of cellulose involve change in fiber dyeing characteristics, alkali solubility, and copper number, but ultimately tensile strength and fluidity measurements offer the most reliable criteria (*162*). Measurements of degree of polymerization and alkali swelling as well as the use of microscopy to detect transverse fiber cracks are considered the most sensitive methods for detecting enzymatic hydrolysis of cellulose (*163*). The detection of free radicals in photosensitized or phototendered fibers by electron spin resonance techniques has been used to assess photochemical damage (*164*). Infrared spectroscopy (*165*), chemiluminescence (*166*), and polarography (*167*), have also been used to determine chemical damage in cellulosic fibers. A recent study utilized an iodine–sulfuric acid test to differentiate damage in jute resulting from weathering, heat, acids, and hypochlorite oxidation. Other tests such as copper number, fluidity, alakli solubility, carboxyl group determination also aided in distinguishing the types of damage undergone by the jute fiber (*168*). The use of microscopy to distinguish between chemical and biological degradation of cotton and between oxidation and acid damage to wool by application of fiber swelling agents has been investigated (*169*). The rate of loss of tensile properties such as breaking strength and tearing strength is often used as criteria in evaluating damage resulting from wear. Mechanical degradation, particularly that associated with abrasion, is also determined by microscopy and fabric weight loss (*110*).

The most common type of damage in wool fabrics is that caused by alkali, photoyellowing, oxidation, insects, and mechanical factors; degradation by acids and microorganisms is less frequently observed. Photodegradation of wool has long been related to decreases or changes in amino acid content (*77*). Electron spin resonance techniques were used to detect free radicals produced during ultraviolet exposure of this fiber (*73*). Damage by alkali (*105*) and heat (*120*) was also correlated with decrease in sulfur and amino acid composition of wool. Numerous chemical tests have been devised over the years to assess wool damage. The alkali and urea–bisulfite solubility methods are the ones most frequently used. The alkali solubility test is particularly suitable for determining damage from light exposure, oxidative bleaches, and antifelting treatments (*170*). Differences in dyeing behavior are also utilized to ascertain the type and extent of damage to wool fibers (*170*). The species of moth or beetle causing damage to woolen goods may be determined by observing the shape of their mandible imprints under a microscope (*171*).

As with cotton and other cellulosics, the use of the electron microscope has aided the evaluation of mechanical degradation and wear of wool fabrics. Scale removal and fibrillation were more representative of normal wear, whereas a variety of fiber faults were observed on wool fabrics abraded by laboratory testers; such faults included longitudinal splitting, transverse fracture, and abraded fibrils (*172*).

Conclusion

To effectively preserve natural textile fibers, one must consider the environment in which they are stored, the causes of their degradation, processes and finishing techniques used in the textile industry at the time the fiber or fabric was made as well as recognize the most current methods available for preventing or minimizing fiber degradation. Development and refinement of methods for addressing fiber damage and predicting fiber life offer numerous research opportunities and challenges for those concerned with the conservation of natural fibers.

Acknowledgment

I am indebted to Dorothy B. Skau, Librarian of the Southern Regional Research Center, for her invaluable assistance in locating and recommending literature sources.

Literature Cited

1. "Deterioration of Materials: Causes and Preventive Techniques," Greathouse, G. A., Wessel, C. J., Eds., Reinhold, New York, 1954.
2. Howard, J. W., McCord, F. A., *Text. Res. J.* (1960) **30**, 75.
3. Brysson, R. J., Berard, W. N., *Am. Dyest. Rep.* (1971) **60**, 27.
4. Lucas, A., *Survey Dept., Paper 12, Chem. Abstr.* (1912) **6**, 10105.
5. Searle, G. O., *J. Text. Inst.* (1929) **20**, T162.
6. Thaysen, A. C., Bunker, H. J., Butlin, K. R., Williams, L. H., *Ann. Appl. Biol.* (1939) **26**, 750; *Chem. Abstr.* (1940) **34**, 21804.
7. Grimes, M. A., *Texas Agr. Expt. Stn. Bull.*, No. 474, Feb. 1933.
8. Grimes, *Texas Agr. Expt. Stn. Bull.* No. 506, May 1935.
9. Dean, J. D., Worner, R. K., *Am. Dyest. Rep.* (1947) **36**, 405.
10. Heffner, L. L., *Text. Res. J.* (1954) **24**, 272.
11. Report of Southeastern Section, Am. Assoc. Text. Chem. Color., *Am. Dyest. Rep.* (1947) **36**, 705.
12. Rose, G. R. F., Bayley, C. H., *Text. Res. J.* (1954) **24**, 792.
13. Berard, W. N., Gremillion, Jr., S. G., Goldthwait, C. F., *Text. Res. J.* (1956) **26**, 81.
14. Berard, W. N., Gauthreaux, G. A., Reeves, W. A., *Text. Res. J.* (1959) **29**, 126.
15. Conner, C. J., Danna, G. S., Cooper, Jr., A. S., Reeves, W. A., *Text. Res. J.* (1967) **37**, 94.
16. St. Mard, H. H., Hamalainen, C., Cooper, Jr., A. S., *Text. Ind. (Atlanta)* (1970) **134** (1) 152.
17. Miller, G., "Biodeterioration of Materials," Vol. 2, Walters, H. A., Hueck-van der Plas, E. H., Eds., Wiley, New York, 1972, p. 279.
18. Ray, Jr., L. G., *Text. Res. J.* (1952) **22**, 144.
19. Fels, M., *J. Text. Inst.* (1960) **51**, P648.
20. Lünenschloss, J., Stegherr, H., *Text. Prax.* (1960) **15**, 931, 1011.
21. Lünenschloss, J., Kurth, H., *Text. Prax.* (1960) **15**, 1146, 1283.
22. Lünenschloss, Kurth, *Text. Prax.* (1961) **16**, 52.
23. Moncrieff, R. W., *Text. Manuf.* (1967) **93**, 442.
24. Little, A. H., Parsons, H. L., *J. Text. Inst.* (1967) **58**, 449.
25. von Bergen, W., *Am. Soc. Test. Mater., Proc.* (1935) **35** (II), 705.
26. McMahon, P. R., Speakman, J. B., *Trans. Faraday Soc.* (1937) **33**, 844.
27. Zahn, H., Blankenburg, G., *Text. Res. J.* (1962) **32**, 986.
28. Parnell, E. A., "Life and Labours of John Mercer," Longmans, Green & Co., London, 1886, p. 248.
29. Rogers, R. E., Hays, M., *Text. Res. J.* (1943) **13**, 20.
30. Hueck, H. J., *TNO Nieuws* (May, 1965) **20** (5), 301; *Chem. Abstr.* (1965) **63**, 12251g.
31. Fleming, N., Thaysen, A. C., *Biochem. J.* (1921) **15**, 407.
32. Griboedov, I. D. N., Milkhallov, T. A., *Tr. Leningr. Tekst. Inst.* (1955), No. 6, 64; *Chem. Abstr.* (1958) **52**, 17723h.
33. Rakhlina, S. S., Kozlova, L. P., *Nauchna.-Issled. Tr. Tsentr. Nauchna.-Issled. Inst. Khlopchatobum. Promsti.* (1959) **2**, 33; *Chem. Abstr.* (1963) **58**, 14176e.
34. Sadek, S. E., Galil, F., *Am. Dyest. Rep.* (1968) **57** (15), 544.
35. Kleinert, T. N., *Holzforschung* (1972) **26** (2), 46; *Chem. Abstr.* (1972) **77**, 49886x.
36. Bengtsson, S., "Conserv. Archaeol. Appl. Arts, Preprint Contrib. Stockholm Congress," Leigh, D., Moncrieff, A., Oddy, W. A., Eds., *Int. Inst. Conserv. Hist. Artistic Works Abstr.*, London, 1975, p. 33; *Chem. Abstr.* (1976) **84**, 88743n.
37. Maurya, M. S., Padya, G., Krishna, B., *Curr. Sci.* (1973) **42** (5), 168.
38. Utermohlen, Jr., W. P., Wallace, E. L., *Text. Res. J.* (1947) **17**, 670.

39. Leene, J. E., "Textile Conservation," Smithsonian, Washington, D. C., 1972.
40. Lehman, D., *Melliland Textilber.* (1967) **48** (11), 1298.
41. Engler, A., Schefer, W., *Text. Rundsch.* (1963) **18** (2), 57.
42. Rigby, B. J., Mitchell, T. W., Robinson, M., *J. Macromol. Sci. Phys.* (1974) **B10** (2), 255.
43. Garrow, C., King, M. G., Roxburgh, C. M., *Text. Inst. Ind.* (1970) **8** (7), 198.
44. Forbes, W. M., Mack, P. B., *Rayon Melliland Text. Mon.* (1936) **16**, 719.
45. D'Olier, A. A., Mack, P. B., *Rayon Melliland Text. Mon.* (1936) **17**, 102.
46. Roberts, N. M., Mack, P. B., *Rayon Melliland Text. Mon.* (1936) **17**, 21.
47. Ibid., 103.
48. Nishi, H., *Nippon Sanshigaku Zasshi* (1958) **27**, 269; *Chem. Abstr.* (1959) **53**, 18494e.
49. Forrester, S. D., *J. Soc. Dyers Colour.* (1975) **91**, 217.
50. Gebhard, J., *J. Soc. Dyers Colour.* (1910) **26**, 163.
51. Cunliffe, P. W., *J. Text. Inst.* (1924) **15**, T173.
52. Appleby, D. K., *Am. Dyest. Rep.* (1949) **38** (4), 149.
53. Robinson, H. M., Reeves, W. A., *Am. Dyest. Rep.* (1961) **50** (1), 17.
54. Bentley, P., McKellar, J. F., Phillips, G. O., *Rev. Prog. Color. Relat. Top.* (1974) **5**, 33.
55. Witz, G., *Bull. Soc. Ind. Mulhouse* (1883) **43**, 334.
56. Reeves, W. A., Robinson, H. M., Brysson, R. J., Berard, W. N., *Canvas Prod. Rev.* (1959) **35** (7), 32.
57. Callow, H. J., Speakman, J. B., *J. Soc. Dyers Colour.* (1949) **65**, 758.
58. Egerton, G. S., Morgan, A. G., *J. Soc. Dyers Colour.* (1971) **87**, 268.
59. Bamford, C. H., Dewar, M. J. S., *J. Soc. Dyers Colour.* (1949) **65**, 674.
60. Giles, O. H., *J. Soc. Dyers Colour.* (1967) **73**, 127.
61. Brysson, R. J., Berard, W. N., Bailey, J. V., *Text. Res. J.* (1957) **27**, 209.
62. Brysson, R. J., Berard, W. N., Bailey, J. V., DuPré, A. M., *Canvas Prod. Rev.* (1957) **32** (12), 36.
63. Anonymous, *Canvas Prod. Rev.* (1959) **34** (12), 38.
64. Henson, W. R., Kelly, P. G., *Nature* (1956) **177**, 1241.
65. Wicks, Z. W., *Int. Rev.* (1953) **12** (2), 35.
66. Arthur, Jr., J. C., Mares, T., George, M., *Text. Res. J.* (1965) **35**, 1116.
67. Trivedi, I. M., Mehta, P. C., *Cellul. Chem. Technol.* (1973) **7** (4), 401.
68. Gantz, G. M., Sumner, W. G., *Text. Res. J.* (1957) **27**, 244.
69. Lappin, G. R., "Ultraviolet-Radiation Absorbers," *Encycl. Polym. Science Technol.*, Mark, H. F., Gaylord, N. G., Bikales, N .M., Eds., Interscience, New York, 1971, **14**, p. 125.
70. Perlina, R. V., Nikiforova, I. S., Bronovitskii, V. E., *Strukt. Modif. Khlopk. Tsellyul.* (1972) No. 5, 287; *World Text. Abstr.* (1974) **6** (16), 6148.
71. Imperial Chemical Industries, British Patent **1,321,645** (1970).
72. Bendak, A., *Am. Dyest. Rep.* (1973) **62** (1), 46.
73. Bendak, *Am. Dyest. Rep.* (1976) **65** (5), 37.
74. von Bergen, W., *Melliland Textilber.* (1926) **7**, 451.
75. Launer, H. F., *Text. Res. J.* (1965) **35**, 395.
76. Launer, *Text. Res. J.* (1971) **41**, 311.
77. Smith, A. L., Harris, M., *J. Res. Natl. Bur. Stand.* (1936) **17**, 97.
78. Graham, D. R., Statham, K. W., *J. Soc. Dyers Colour.* (1956) **72**, 434.
79. Bendit, E. G., *J. Text. Inst.* (1960) **51**, T544.
80. Hoare, J. L., Stewart, R. G., *J. Text. Inst.* (1971) **62**, 455.
81. Lundgren, H. P., *Proc. Int. Wool Text. Res. Conf. Aust. 1955 C* (1956) 374.
82. Rose, W. G., Walden, M. K., Moore, J. E., *Text. Res. J.* (1961) **31**, 495.
83. Milligan, B., Tucker, D. J., *Text. Res. J.* (1964) **34**, 681.
84. Tucker, J. E., *Text. Res. J.* (1969) **39**, 830.

85. Holt, L. A., Milligan, B., Wolfram, L. J., *Text. Res. J.* (1974) **44**, 846.
86. Holt, Milligan, Wolfram, *Text. Res. J.* (1975) **45**, 257.
87. Okamoto, S., Imai, S., *Sen'i Gekkaishi* (1957) **13**, 139; *Chem. Abstr.* (1959) **52**, 5830b.
88. Enomoto, M., Setoyama, K., *Sen'i Gekkaishi* (1972) **28** (4–5), 147; *Chem. Abstr.* (1972) **77**, 115808b.
89. Harris, M., Jessup, D. A., *J. Res. Natl. Bur. Stand.* (1931) **7**, 1179.
90. Shimizu, F., Aidi, G., *Sen'i Gekkaishi* (1970) **26** (7), 316; *Chem. Abstr.* (1971) **74**, 127272y.
91. Polesskaya, S. F., Korchagin, M. V., *Zh. Vses. Khim. Ova.* (1974) **19** (1), 111; *Chem. Abstr.* (1974) **81**, 50848a.
92. Shiozaki, H., Tanaka, Y., Setoyama, K., *Nippon Sanshigaku Zasshi* (1974) **43** (5), 391; *Chem. Abstr.* (1975) **82**, 141470h.
93. Kuwahara, A., Wantaba, T., Machida, Y., *Nippon Sanshigaku Zasshi* (1974) **43** (6) 445; *Chem. Abstr.* (1975) **83**, 133176x.
94. Race, E., *J. Soc. Dyers Colour.* (1949) **65**, 56.
95. Upham, J. B., Salvin, V. S., "Effect of Air Pollutants on Textile Fibers and Dyes," EPA-650/3-74-008, Research Triangle Park, N.C., 1975.
96. Marsh, J. T., "An Introduction to Textile Bleaching," Wiley, New York, 1948.
97. Bell, T. E., "Bleaching," *Encycl. Polym. Sci. Technol.*, Mark, H. F., Gaylord, N. G., Bikales, N. M., Eds., Interscience, New York, 1965, **2**, p. 438.
98. Peters, R. H., "Textile Chemistry," Vol. II, Elsevier, New York, 1967.
99. Dickinson, J. C., *Wool Sci. Rev.* (1975) **51**, 43.
100. Glibbens, D. A., Ridge, B. P., *J. Text. Inst.* (1927) **18**, T135.
101. Shenai, V. A., Date, A. G., *J. Appl. Polym. Sci.* (1976) **20** (2), 385.
102. Elöd, E., Vogel, F., *Meilliland Textilber.* (1937) **18**, 64.
103. Ney, W., *Text. Prax. Int.* (1974) **29** (11), 1552.
104. Steinmiller, W. G., Cates, D. M., *Text. Chem. Color.* (1976) **8** (1) 30.
105. Elöd, E., Nowotny, H., Zahn, H., *Kolloid Z.* (1940) **93**, 50.
106. McNally, J. P., McCord, F. A., Text. Res. J. (1960) **30**, 715.
107. Hollies, N. R. S., Getchell, N. F., *Text. Res. J.* (1967) **37**, 70.
108. Welch, C. M., Bullock, J. B., Margavio, M. F., *Text. Res. J.* (1967) **37**, 324.
109. Morton, W. E., Hearle, J. W. S., "Physical Properties of Textile Fibers," Textile Institute, Manchester, 1962, p. 403.
110. Galbraith, R. L., "Abrasion of Textile Surfaces," "Surface Characteristics of Fibers and Textiles," Schick, M. J., Ed., Part I, Marcel Dekker, New York, 1975, p. 193.
111. Makinson, K. R., "Surface Properties of Wool Fibers," "Surface Characteristics of Fibers and Textiles," Schick, M. J., Ed., Part I, Marcel Dekker, New York, 1975, p. 109.
112. Whitfield, R. E., Miller, L. A., Wasley, W. A., *Text. Res. J.* (1961) **31**, 704.
113. Whitfield, R. E., Remy, D. E., Pittman, A. G., *Text. Res. J.* (1967) **37**, 655.
114. Pavlath, A. E., Lee, K. S., *Text. Res. J.* (1975) **45**, 742.
115. Wiegerink, J. G., *J. Res. Natl. Bur. Stand.* (1940) **24**, 639.
116. Phillipp, B., Baudisch, J., Stöhr, W., *Cellul. Chem. Technol.* (1972) **6**, 379.
117. Kilzer, F. J., "Thermal Degradation," "Cellulose and Cellulose Derivatives," Bikales, N. M., Segal, L., Eds., Part V, Wiley-Interscience, New York, 1971, p. 1015.
118. Anonymous, *Wool Sci. Rev.* (1970) **39**, 40.
119. Stirm, K., Rouette, P. L., *Melliland Textilber.* (1935) **16**, 4.
120. Sweetman, B. J., *Text. Res. J.* (1967) **37**, 384.

121. Ibid., 844.
122. Watt, I. C., *Text. Res. J.* (1975) **45**, 728.
123. Kato, Y., Hagiwara, M., *Nippon Sanshigaku Zasshi* (1973) **42** (3), 224; *Chem. Abstr.* (1974) **80**, 4721k.
124. Siu, R. G. H., "Microbial Decomposition of Cellulose," Reinhold, New York, 1951.
125. Desai, A. J., Pandey, S. N., *J. Sci. Ind. Res.* (1971) **30** (11), 598.
126. Hueck-van der Plas, E. H., *Int. Biodeterior. Bull.* (1966) **2** (2) 69.
127. Kaplan, A. M., Mandels, M., Greenberger, M., "Biodeterioration of Materials," Walters, A. H., Hueck-van der Plas, E. H., Eds., Vol. 2, Wiley, New York, 1972, p. 208.
128. Amin, S. A., Abdou, L. A. W., Kamel, M., *Text. Res. J.* (1975) **45**, 67.
129. Sengupta, S. R., *Colourage* (1975) **22** (18), 35.
130. Becker, G., "Biodeterioration of Materials," Walters, A. H., Hueck-van der Plas, E. H., Eds., Vol. 2, Wiley, New York, 1972, p. 249.
131. Singh, I. D., Perti, S. L., Tandon, R. N., "Biodeterioration of Materials," Walters, A. H., Hueck-van der Plas, E. H., Eds., Vol. 2, Wiley, New York, 1972, p. 301.
132. Lewis, J., *Wool Sci. Rev.* (1973) **46**, 17.
133. Lewis, *Wool Sci. Rev.* (1973) **47**, 25.
134. Howitt, F. O., "Bibliography of Silk," Hutchinson's, London, 1946.
135. Agarwal, P. N., Puvathingal, J. M., *Text. Res. J.* (1969) **39**, 38.
136. Kuwana, Z., Nakamura, S., *Text. Res. J.* (1963) **33**, 649.
137. Moncrieff, R. W., "Mothproofing," Mapleton, Brooklyn, N.Y., 1950.
138. McPhee, J. R., "The Mothproofing of Wool," Merrow, Watford Herts England, 1971.
139. Dusenbury, J. H., "The Molecular Structure and Chemical Properties of Wool," "Wool Handbook," von Bergen, W., Ed., Vol. 1, 3rd ed., Interscience, New York, 1963, p. 299.
140. Anonymous, *Wool Sci. Rev.* (1965) **27**, 1.
141. Anonymous, *Wool Sci. Rev.* (1965) **28**, 33.
142. Freeland, G. N., Hoskinson, R. M., Sasse, W. H. F., *J. Text. Inst.* (1972) **63**, 643.
143. Hoskinson, R. M., Russell, I. M., *J. Text. Inst.* (1973) **64**, 144.
144. Hoskinson, Russel, *J. Text. Inst.* (1974) **65**, 455.
145. Hoskinson, Russel, *J. Text. Inst.* (1975) **66**, 193.
146. Hoskinson, R. M., Mayfield, R. J., Russell, I. M., *J. Text. Inst.* (1976) **67**, 19.
147. Nahta, P., *Text. Chem. Color.* (1973) **5** (9), 204.
148. Koenig, N. H., Friedman, M., U. S. Patent **3,927,969** (Dec. 23, 1975).
149. Bry, R. E., Simonaitis, R. A., *Text. Chem. Color.* (1975) **7** (2), 36.
150. Am. Assoc. Text. Chem. Color. Tech. Man., **51**, AATCC, Research Triangle Park, N.C., 1975, p. 237.
151. Park, J., *Rev. Prog. Color. Relat. Top.* (1975) **6**, 71.
152. Hindson, W. R., Southwell, G., *J. Soc. Dyers Colour.* (1973) **89**, 254.
153. Park, J., Smith, D. J., *J. Soc. Dyers Colour.* (1974) **90**, 431.
154. Babiarz, R. S., Schuler M,. J., *Text. Chem. Color.* (1976) **8** (5), 24.
155. AATCC Research Committee, *Text. Chem. Color.* (1976) **8** (6), 16.
156. *AATCC Tech. Man.*, **51**, (1975) 144.
157. Schefer, W., *Schweiz. Arch. Angew, Wiss. Tech.* (1966) **32** (11), 369; *Chem. Abstr.* (1967) **67**, 33726c.
158. Crighton, J. S., Findon, W. M., Happey, F., *Appl. Poly. Symp.* (1971) **18**, (2), 847.
159. *AATCC Tech. Man.* (1975) **51**, 268.
160. Turner, R. L., "Biodeterioration of Materials," Walters, A. H., Hueck-van der Plas, E. H., Eds., Vol. 2, Wiley, New York, 1972, p. 218.
161. *AATCC Tech. Man.* (1975) **51**, 271.

162. Dean, J. D., "Chemical Changes in Cotton Fabrics During Processing and Use," "Chemistry and Chemical Technology of Cotton," Ward, Jr., K., Ed., Interscience, New York, 1955, p. 698.
163. Reese, E. T., Mandels, M., "Enzymatic Degradation," "Cellulose and Cellulose Derivatives," Bikales, N. M., Segal, L., Eds., Part V, Wiley-Interscience, New York, 1971, p. 1087.
164. Baugh, P. J., Phillips, "Photochemical Degradation," "Cellulose and Cellulose Derivatives," Bikales, N. M., Segal, L., Eds., Part V, Wiley-Interscience, New York, 1971, p. 1063.
165. Zhbankov, R. G., Komar, P. V., Ivanona, N. V., Garbuz, N. I., Balabaeva, M. O., *Khim. Teknol. Proizvodnykh. Tsellyul. Dokl. Vses. Nauchno. Tekh. Soveshch.* (1971) 286; *Chem. Abstr.* (1973) **78**, 17881w.
166. Pugachevskii, G. F., Plesha, I. V., *Mekh. Svoistva. Iznosostoikost Tekst. Mater. Dakl. Vses. Nauchno. Konf. Telzst. Materialoved. Soobschch. Zarub. Gostei, 7th, 1970* (1971) 293; *Chem. Abstr.* (1972) **77**, 21310f.
167. Kotylar, G. I., Kushnir, E. G., Polikarpov, I. S., *Tekst. Promst.* (1974) **34** (12), 64; *Chem. Abstr.* (1975) **82**, 87493c.
168. Young, F. S., *J. Text. Inst.* (1974) **65**, 476.
169. Bigler, N., *Textilveredlung* (1975) **10** (4), 134.
170. Golub, S. J., "Physical and Chemical Testing," "Wool Handbook," von Bergen, W., Ed., Vol. 1, 3rd Ed., Interscience, New York, 1963, p. 763.
171. Ott, D. J., *Am. Dyest. Rep.* (1955) **44**, 3515.
172. Anderson, C. A., Robinson, V. N., *J. Text. Inst.* (1971) **62**, 281.

RECEIVED January 14, 1977.

15

Conservation of Textiles Manufactured from Man-Made Fibers

S. H. ZERONIAN

Division of Textiles and Clothing, University of California, Davis, Calif. 95616

The different types of man-made fibers which predominate currently in apparel and home furnishings are reviewed and problems to be faced in preserving them discussed. The influence of environmental factors on the properties of man-made fibers are examined and comparisons are drawn between their stability and that of natural fibers. Methods are surveyed for the identification, or estimation, of damage to man-made fibers that may have occurred during use. Precautions that need to be taken in the cleaning and display of fabrics are indicated.

From the successful attempts in the second half of the 19th century to produce artificial fibers (1), a huge man-made fiber industry has been created. It only requires a cursory visit to a department store to appreciate the large amount of man-made fibers used currently in apparel and in home furnishings. This is also borne out by the available statistics (Table I). The data presented in this table (2) indicate that for consumer end uses the trend in the United States is for cotton and wool to be replaced by man-made fibers. By 1974 appreciably more noncellulosic man-made fibers and textile glass fibers were being used than cotton.

Up to the present time conservators were interested in preserving textiles made from natural fibers. With time, however, as present day materials incorporating man-made fibers are collected, concerns will arise as to their preservation and display. In this chapter, I survey the different types of man-made fibers, discuss environmental factors that can degrade them, and indicate methods for the identification or estimation of such damage. Also, I indicate where precautions need to be taken in their cleaning and display.

Table I.   U.S. Consumption of Fibers by End-Use
Market in 1968–74 (2)

	1974		*1971*		*1968*	
	$lb \times 10^6$	% [a]	$lb \times 10^6$	% [a]	$lb \times 10^6$	% [a]
Cotton						
Apparel	1515	35.8	1660	41.1	1802	44.7
Home furnishings	969	28.4	1230	36.9	1362	45.0
Other consumer-type products	377	29.1	413	34.8	410	46.3
Wool						
Apparel	88	2.1	131	3.2	315	7.8
Home furnishings	28	0.8	84	2.5	106	3.5
Other consumer-type products	8	0.6	31	2.6	33	3.7
Rayon and Acetate						
Apparel	387	9.1	570	14.1	651	16.2
Home furnishings	264	7.7	383	11.5	482	15.9
Other consumer-type products	236	18.2	256	21.6	255	28.8
Noncellulosic Man-Made Fibers [b] *and Textile Glass Fibers*						
Apparel	2241	53.0	1678	41.6	1262	31.3
Home furnishings	2153	63.1	1636	49.1	1077	35.6
Other consumer-type products	674	52.1	486	41.0	188	21.2

[a] The percentages show the share of each fiber in the specified end use each year.
[b] Includes acrylic, anidex, modacrylic, nylon, olefin, polyester, saran, Spandex, TFE–fluorocarbon and vinyon.

Textile Organon

The first man-made fibers of commercial importance were the cellulosics. With respect to regenerated cellulose fibers, viscose rayon predominates. Between 1900 and 1967, world production of viscose rayon rose from 1000 tons to 2,700,000 tons (3). Cellulose derivative fibers did not go into commercial production until the 1920s. At that time cellulose acetate was manufactured. Cellulose triacetate fiber was brought into commercial production in the United States in 1954 (4).

The first noncellulosic (synthetic) fiber to be of major importance for textile apparel was nylon. In the United States, nylon 66 was commercially produced in 1939 (4). Nylon 6, another polyamide which is produced also on a large scale, was obtained on a pilot plant scale in the same year in Germany (5). Modacrylic and acrylic fibers were commercially produced in the United States in 1949 and 1950, respectively (4). Polyester fiber was invented in England in 1940 (1) and went into commercial production in the United States in 1953 (4). Polyester production is higher than that of any other man-made fiber at this time (Table II).

Table II.   U.S. Man-Made Fiber Production in 1975 (6)

Fiber (Generic Name)	Amount Produced (lb × 10⁶)
Polyester	2995.1
Nylon[a]	1857.3
Textile glass	540.1
Acrylic and modacrylic	524.6
Olefin[b]	442.9
Rayon	435.7
Acetate and triacetate[c]	313.3
Other[d]	65.4

[a] Includes aramid.
[b] Yarn and monofilament only; staple plus tow included under "other."
[c] Does not include fiber produced for cigarette filtration purposes.
[d] Includes saran and Spandex yarn; also, olefin and vinyon staple and tow.

Textile Organon

With respect to the other fibers in Table II, glass fiber and textile-grade multifilament polypropylene came into commercial production in the United States in 1936 and 1961, respectively (4). A number of generic types have not been mentioned in this brief outline of the foundations of the man-made fiber industry since their utilization in the United States is relatively small, either because they are utilized for specialized end uses or because they have not reached their full potential as yet.

In recent years, the man-made fiber industry, in addition to inventing new polymers for fiber production, has spent considerable efforts to modify existing generic type fibers in order to alter both their physical appearance and their aesthetic properties. For example, man-made fibers can be given bulk and stretch by texturizing, a process which utilizes mechanical forces and heat. Again, variations have been brought about in fiber cross sections, luster, crimp, dyeability, and static propensities. Thus, for the organic fibers listed in Table II, within each of the generic classes there are a wide variety of fibers manufactured by different companies under various trademarks. A summary of properties of many fiber types has been published (7). Outstanding books on man-made fibers include Moncrieff's (3) and those edited by Mark et al. (8, 9).

Chemically, deterioration of textiles during aging occurs by pathways including oxidation and photodegradation. The observed loss in strength of fibers or yarns by heat exposure and by weathering can give indications of the permanence of fibrous materials. Few studies are available from which comparisons can be made between the stability of man-made and natural fibers. While specific results will be given here, comparisons have to be made with caution because the performance of man-made fibers can vary widely within, as well as between, generic groups. Also, it is not known how well the results of laboratory studies correlate with performance under service conditions.

In one study (*10*) tests were made on yarn manufactured from unscoured polyester, nylon, high tenacity rayon, acrylic, acetate, and glass fiber which had been exposed to heat and air. The conclusions were that the breaking strength and tenacity of glass fiber yarn were virtually unaffected by exposure to 1800 hr of dry heat at temperatures up to 177°C. The polyester and acrylic were unaffected by such exposures at temperatures up to 121°C but the breaking strength and tenacity of the other fibers were reduced. The retained breaking strength of the acetate and high tenacity rayon for this exposure were 66% and 47%, respectively. Depending on the type, the retained breaking strength of nylon varied from 24% to 81%. Note that, unlike polyester, the retained breaking strength of the acrylic fiber was affected somewhat by scouring. In another study (*11*) a comparison was made between natural and man-made fibers of the effect on the percent strength retained after 1000 hr of exposure to air at 121°C. The samples were all scoured. Wool was not affected by the exposure. The retained strength of the acrylic was either 97% or 78%, depending on the type, and that of polyester was 93%. The nylon retained 33% of its strength while high tenacity rayon and cotton retained about 20%. Acetate and silk were completely degraded by the exposure. An indication of the comparative heat resistance of polypropylene fiber is shown by the results of another study (*12*). In this study, the percent strength loss of glass, polypropylene, polyester, and acrylic fibers were compared after thermal exposure. After five days exposure at 100°C, the polypropylene fiber lost no strength, but when the temperature was raised to 130°C, the strength retention was 80%. In contrast, the strength retention after 20 days exposure at 130°C for glass, polyester, and acrylic was 100%, 95%, and 91%, respectively. It appears from the cited data that when fibers are heat-aged at relatively low temperatures, the strength retention performance of glass and polyester equals that of wool and is superior to that of cotton. The performance of acrylic fiber is almost as good as that of polyester or glass. These conclusions can only be tentative as the strength retention can be affected by the heating conditions and can vary widely between fibers of different types but within the same generic group. Continuing research and development may have improved performance in some of the man-made fibers since the quoted data was obtained. Again, performance will vary within a generic group. The presence, absence, or type of degradation inhibitors in a man-made fiber will depend on the specific end use intended for the fiber.

When comparisons are made of the resistance to photodegradation of different fibers, it is important that exposure conditions are identical.

The strength loss suffered by a textile fiber subjected to weathering can be dependent on many factors including: geographical location (*13*); atmospheric contaminants (*14*); temperature and relative humidity (*15*); and the time of year. With respect to time of year, however, it has been claimed that discrepancies caused by seasonal changes can be eliminated by relating fiber strength loss to ultraviolet radiation rather than total radiation (*16, 17*). The strength loss of a fiber is influenced also by whether the sample is exposed directly to sunlight or is exposed under window glass (*18*) since window glass will filter out shorter wavelengths of ultraviolet radiation. Correlations between outdoor exposures and exposures to artificial light sources can be difficult since indoor sources of ultraviolet radiation do not duplicate natural sunlight and differ greatly among themselves in spectral energy distributions (*19*).

Fiber characteristics also matter when comparisons are being made between the light resistance of fibers of different generic classes. Factors other than the chemical composition of the polymer can affect light resistance. For example, the physical characteristics of the fiber can have an effect. Light resistance, as measured by strength retention, increases with fiber diameter probably because less radiation penetrates the interior (*18*). The cross-sectional shape of a fiber can influence reflection, refraction, and transmission of radiation striking the fiber and thus can affect the light resistance of the fiber (*18*).

Modification of the polymer or the presence of additives can effect the light resistance of a fiber. This is extremely important for textile conservation since fibers being produced currently by the man-made fiber industry may perform differently from those produced in earlier years. For example, a company bulletin, published first in 1960, reported that the resistance to chemical decomposition by fluorescent light or by sunlight of many of the nylons they manufactured had been improved (*20*). Titanium dioxide, which is used as a delustrant during the manufacture of fibers, can decrease their light resistance (*13, 15, 18, 21, 22, 23*). Dyes (*18, 24, 25*) and finishes (*25, 26*) are other important factors.

The form in which the materials are exposed is also relevant (*27*). The inner parts of a coarse yarn or heavy fabric may be relatively undamaged while the outside is degraded; thus, the strength retention of such samples may be higher than that of a finer yarn or lighter fabric. Yarn twist can also have an effect since low-twist yarns are damaged a little more rapidly than higher-twist samples (*28*).

So it is difficult to draw comparisons between the performance of fibers on sunlight exposure. Available publications containing data obtained with undyed materials show that acrylic fibers consistently have excellent resistance to photodegradation whether exposed to direct sunlight or to sunlight behind glass (*13, 18, 28, 29, 30*). The comparative performance of other man-made fibers and natural fibers varies in these reports because of the factors discussed above.

All pollutants can also cause deterioration of fiber properties. The effect of such pollutants as ozone, sulfur dioxide, and nitrogen dioxide on individual fibers is discussed later.

During long-term use, deterioration which appears as yellowing may occur in some man-made fiber. For some fibers, it is caused by their intrinsic chemical properties. The causes and methods of alleviating such yellowing are also discussed later. However, sometimes fabric yellowing may be related to additives such as optical brighteners; cationic, anti-static, and soil-release finishes; softeners; or resinous agents. For example, yellow discoloration has occurred on occasion with pastel-colored or undyed, white fabrics either in storage or on display. The problem occurs primarily with nylon, acetate, or permanent press (polyester-cotton) materials. It appears to be related to the additive rather than the fiber since testing has shown that many of the additives yellow on exposure to oxides of nitrogen (*14*). High relative humidity can also be an important factor. Washing the fabrics sometimes removes this type of yellow discoloration.

Problems may arise in cleaning synthetic fibers (*14*). Sooty soils are particularly troublesome as they are tenaciously bound to fiber surfaces. These soils may contain unsaponifiable hydrocarbons, typically found in Los Angeles-type air pollution. Such soils are not easily removed from man-made fibers by laundry detergents but may yield to dry-cleaning. Nylon, despite repeated laundering, takes on a yellowish hue when exposed to sooty soils (*14*). Contributing to soiling problems of many man-made fibers is their tendency to acquire electrostatic charges that attract oppositely charged particles. Finish components on permanent-press, polyester-cotton materials attract soil particles and hold them tenaciously (*14*). Many of these problems are now being overcome by modifications made by the textile industry in fiber properties and by the use of antistatic and soil-release finishes.

The first task facing the conservator is to identify the fiber. Several methods are available: burning test (*3, 31, 32*), longitudinal and cross-section examination by light microscope (*3, 31, 32, 33*), solubility tests (*3, 31, 32, 33*), staining tests (*3, 31*), and fiber density (*3, 31, 32, 33*). Instrumental techniques include infrared spectroscopy (*32, 33, 34*), differential thermal analysis (*32, 34*), and gas chromatography (*32, 34*). Techniques for quantitative analysis of blends have been established also (*35*). In any textile conservation work it is important to know the effect of different chemicals on the fibers. Reports have been published which indicate the effect of a number of different bleaching and stripping agents (36) and inorganic and organic chemicals (37, 38, 39) on man-made fibers.

Some of the generic classes of fibers are now discussed individually, including methods of chemical and morphological characterization of damage. Methods of minimizing damage are also reviewed. Discussions of polymer stabilization can be found in References 40, 41, and 42. Because physical testing techniques would essentially be the same for all fiber classes, they are not discussed here. Normally, the most useful indices for conservation work would be breaking strength and extension at break of the fabric, yarn, or fiber.

Cellulosics

Rayons. Rayons are composed essentially of regenerated cellulose. Considerable changes in viscose technology over the years have resulted in improved performance (43). For example, viscose rayon in the 1940s and early 1950s had low wet strength, but since then rayons have been produced with improved wet strength. Viscose rayons can be separated into the following groups: regular; intermediate; high tenacity, low wet modulus; and Polynosic. (In Europe polynosic is a generic name.) The different types of rayons have been described in many publications and reviews (3, 4, 7, 8, 43). Delustrants such as titanium dioxide may be added during fiber manufacture. Rayons are available in various cross-sectional shapes (43) and longitudinally straight or crimped.

A defect of regular rayon fabric in the absence of a cross-linking finish is its solubility in alkali with consequent loss of strength and dimensional stability. These defects have been largely overcome in the "high performance" rayons. Mitchell and Daul (43) reported that regular textile grade rayon staple fiber accounts for 70–80% of the output of the rayon industry.

Many of the numerous methods available for analyzing cellulose have been described in detail in a single volume (44). A critical review of methods for determining carbonyl groups has been written (45). Among other methods, carboxyl content can be measured by the methylene blue method (46) and an empirical measure of the reducing power of cellulose can be obtained by the copper number method (47). Molecular weight determinations can be made by viscometry using a number of different solvents. Standard methods are available for determining fluidity (48) or intrinsic viscosity (49) in cupriethylenediamine hydroxide. These parameters may be converted to degree of polymerization (DP) by suitable conversion constants. Note that the fluidity method was withdrawn as an ASTM standard in 1970. Recently, cadoxen [tris(ethylenediamine)cadmium hydroxide] has been used as a solvent for cellulose. The rate of degradation, caused by atmospheric oxygen, of cellulose in this solvent is negligible (*50*). Thus cadoxen can be used relatively easily for accurate determinations of DP (*51*).

Staining methods with the aid of a light microscope can be used to determine damage. The presence of microorganisms can be demonstrated by lactophenol blue or by a 1% aqueous solution of gentian violet (*52*). An alcoholic solution of gentian violet (*53*) can be used to establish fiber inclusions and mechanical or chemical damage. Both mechanical and microbial damage to the surface of viscose fibers can be determined using a solution of Chlorazol Sky Blue FF (*54*). Schwertassek (*55*) has used an iodine sorption test to detect photodegradation.

Descriptions of the chemical and physical properties of rayon can be found (*3, 43*). Rayons have good resistance to dry-cleaning solvents, and both oxidizing and reducing bleaches may be used with suitable precaution (*31*). Perspiration can degrade the fibers on prolonged exposure.

Rayons can vary from slightly susceptible to very susceptible to mildew and some other microorganisms. Bacteria decomposing cellulose have been discussed (*56*) and methods of preventing microbiological degradation noted (*57*). Rayons are resistant to moths and silverfish but some types are destroyed by termites and roaches (*43*). Although moth larvae will not attack all-viscose fabrics, they will eat viscose rayon mixed with wool, but they cannot digest the rayon and will excrete it unchanged (*3*).

Photodecomposition can occur, accelerated by titanium dioxide. Direct photolytic breakdown of cellulose can take place under the influence of 2537-Å radiation (*58*). Radiation of wavelengths greater than about 3400Å cannot induce degradation of cellulose directly. Certain dyes and substances such as titanium dioxide, however, can cause photosensitized deterioration of the cellulose in the presence of oxygen and moisture (*58*). Müller (*59*) and Reumuth (*60*) have concluded that photodegraded material surrounds the titanium dioxide particles in light-damaged, delustered viscose rayon. In order to minimize photodegradation, the use of 2-hydroxybenzophenone derivatives as ultraviolet absorbers for cellulose has been explored (*61*).

Air pollutants can cause damage to rayons. Artificial weathering tests have indicated that as the strength of the rayon decreases, its fluidity and reducing power as determined by copper number increase, but the carboxyl content decreases (*62*). When these tests were made with air contaminated with 0.1 ppm sulfur dioxide, an additional loss in strength was found over that caused when the weathering tests were made in pure air (*62*).

Resins may influence phototendering of rayons. Wood (26) has reported that viscose rayon fabrics treated with urea formaldehyde or thiourea formaldehyde resin are protected from the degradative effects of mercury vapor lamp radiation. The mechanism of the protective effect is not fully understood as yet. Possibly resins can quench free radicals formed during irradiation. Work with resin-treated cotton indicates that simultaneous scission of cellulose chain molecules and resin–cellulose bonds occurs on exposure to light (63).

Rayons on aging may show a tendency to yellow. The cause of yellowing of cellulose is complex. The factors involved have been investigated (64, 65). Alkaline borohydrides which reduce carbonyl groups and lactone groups to alcohols lessen the yellowing of cellulose (65, 66). Oxidizing bleach can restore whiteness also (64).

The cautions noted earlier in attempting to predict performance in ageing from heating experiments are supported by the work of Kleinert et al. (67). They compared heat-accelerated aging of rayon with prolonged storage in the dark at 20°C and found the former to be much more severe.

Acetate and Triacetate. Cellulose acetate fiber is made from partially acetylated cellulose whereas the cellulose triacetate fiber is made from almost completely acetylated cellulose; by the Federal Trade Commission definition, the latter must have not less than 92% of the hydroxyl groups acetylated (4). The fibers can be manufactured with different diameters and cross-sectional shapes (68). The fibers are bright unless a delustrant such as titanium dioxide has been added during the manufacturing process. Acetate and triacetate fibers can be produced with an exceptionally high degree of whiteness which is not significantly altered by exposure to indoor climatic conditions over a long time (68). The fiber can be colored by incorporation of pigments in the dope prior to spinning. Such yarn is exceptionally colorfast.

Many of the methods available for analyzing cellulose acetate or triacetate, including the degree of acetylation and DP, have been described in detail (44). Alternate methods for determining degree of acetylation have been developed also (69, 70, 71).

Typical chemical and physical properties of these fibers have been discussed (68). In slightly acidic or basic conditions at room temperature, acetate and triacetate fibers are very resistant to chlorine bleach at the concentrations normally encountered in laundering (68). Acetate and triacetate fibers are not affected by the dry-cleaning solutions normally used in the United States and Canada, but triacetate is softened by trichloroethylene (68). Delustering can be accomplished by hot soap solutions (72) so caution needs to be applied during cleaning of acetate fabrics. The immediate cause of delustering by hot soap solutions is the formation of numerous fine holes through the fiber thickness. Luster can be recovered by applying heat (3).

Based on soil burial tests, the resistance of triacetate to microorganisms is very high, approaching that of polyester, acrylic, and nylon fibers (68). Acetate fiber is less resistant. For example, soil burial tests indicate that after a burial of six weeks triacetate retains 90% of its strength whereas acetate retains less than 50% (68). Neither acetate nor triacetate fiber is readily attacked by moths or carpet beetles although these larvae have cut through acetate to get at wool or have damaged acetate that was contaminated with foreign substances containing starch (68).

The color of cellulose acetate dyed with some disperse dyes is subject to gas fading. Treatment of the dyed material with diethanolamine or melamine can overcome the problem (3). Similarly, with cellulose triacetate, gas fading of dyes can occur. It has been stated that protection can be obtained by the application of an inhibitor (3).

The strength of acetate yarn upon exposure to dry heat (120°C) for 500 hr is reduced by 58%. That of triacetate yarn is reduced by 30% at 130°C (68). In another publication (73) heat aging experiments indicate that the strength retention of triacetate is greater than cotton, which in turn is greater than nylon. Experimental details, however, are lacking in the aging conditions and the type and form of the fibers.

Dubyaga et al. claim that photodegradation of cellulose triacetate is accompanied by breakdowns in the acetyl groups and in the pyranose ring at the C_1—C_2 linkages and by oxidation at C_6 (74). According to Sprague and Horner the following generalizations on light stability appear justified. Acetate and triacetate fibers, when exposed under glass, behave similarly to cotton and rayon; namely, they are somewhat more resistant than unstablized, pigmented nylon and silk and appreciably less resistant than acrylic and polyester fibers. In comparison with under-glass exposures, the light resistance of acetate and triacetate is decreased by direct weathering (68). As with other fibers, the photochemical degradation of cellulose acetate is increased by titanium dioxide and water (15). Haziness has been found in delustered acetate after exposure to light. The haziness was attributed to the production of small gas bubbles, probably of carbon dioxide (59). Some pigments increase light resistance (68). The light stability of acetate fibers is increased also by such compounds as 2,4-dioxybenzoquinone, diphenylamine, and β-naphthylamine (75).

Synthetic Man-Made Fibers

Nylon. Nylon fibers are made predominantly from either poly(hexamethylene adipamide) (nylon 66) or polycaproamide (nylon 6). In order to reduce transparency, increase whiteness, and prevent undesirable gloss in finished fabrics a delustrant (titanium dioxide) is added during the fiber manufacturing process (76). Pigments can also be added to the polymeric mass prior to filament spinning. Typical light stabilizers for use with nylon are manganese salts (76). Nylons can be produced with a variety of cross-sections (76), and they are available as staple or in filament form. Filament yarn may be textured.

Methods for determining amine and carboxyl end-groups have been described (77, 78, 79, 80). A variety of techniques can be used to determine DP (81, 82). Chain scission can also be described empirically by fluidity (83) or relative viscosity (84) measurements. Tests developed to detect aldehyde, carbonyl, peroxide, and pyrrole groups in photodegraded nylon have been described (21). Mödlich et al. (85, 86) have discussed the identification and differentiation of damage in polyamide fibers by such tests as dyeing reactions, behavior to zinc chloroiodide, swelling and dissolution in sulfuric acid, and microscopical examination. A rapid colorimetric method has been described to detect degradation of nylon caused by acids. In this method an aqueous solution of a mixture of a blue and yellow dye is applied to the clean fiber which has been stripped of dye. The tint of the stained fiber changes from yellow via green to blue with increasing degree of acid damage (87). Staining tests to detect photodegradation utilize Procion Black HGS (88) and ninhydrin (89). Ninhydrin can also be used to detect chemical damage. The quantitative uptake of Color Index acid blue 1 can be used for assessing degradation by light or acid (90). Setting conditions also affect the results. Bobeth and Kandler (91) have obtained an estimate of the setting conditions with Rhodamine G. The fibers are examined under a fluorescence microscope. Samples set by hot air and steam can be differentiated.

The chemical and physical properties of nylons have been extensively described (76). Nylon will not support mildew or bacteria. Moth larvae may bite their way through nylon if imprisoned. In soil burial tests, it was found that nylon 6 retained more than 95% of its strength after six months. By contrast, wool and cotton were rotten after one month (3). Nylon may be affected by chlorine bleach, and strong oxidizing bleaches can damage it (31).

Reports on long-term performance of man-made fibers are few. However, an analysis has been made of 20 nylon climbing ropes that had been used for up to 18 years, and it was found that significant deterioration had occurred. Note, however, that the deterioration was related to the amount and type of use and not to age. Loss in strength was a result primarily of fiber abrasion of the rope surface, and there was no evidence of significant light degradation (92).

Thermal oxidation of nylon 6 has been reviewed (5). When heated in the presence of oxygen, nylon 6 decreases in tensile strength and becomes yellow in color. A strong ultraviolet absorption band develops with an inflection at 2400Å. Heat decreases the number of amine end-groups whereas hydrolysis would be expected to increase them (78). The mechanism of photochemical degradation of nylon has been reviewed (93). Titanium dioxide decreases the resistance of nylon to light of wavelength greater than 3000Å; thus, it is connected with photooxidation rather than photolysis (21).

Swallow (25) has reported on the effects of dyes on the weathering of nylon textiles. Among the conclusions he draws are that (a) some of the dyes used in the tests usually afforded better protection than the others in the conditions studied; (b) fading of high tenacity nylon webbings dyed with 25 different dyeings gave a good indication of strength loss when the change in color was moderate, but with extra-high tenacity threads fading gave no useful information on strength loss in any of the conditions examined; (c) extra-high tenacity threads increased in strength by 5% after storage of nine months; and (d) in dyestuffs of the same Color Index number but from four different manufacturers, one gave slightly better strength retention (3%) than the others. This study supports the statement made earlier that the properties of fibers can vary within generic types as well as between them. Also, it appears that nominally similar materials may, in fact, behave differently when weathered.

Photodegradation can be reduced. A comprehensive range of ultraviolet absorbers for application to nylon fabric has been evaluated (94). Schwemmer has discussed how trivalent chromium stabilizes the peptide linkages and improves the resistance to light of nylon (95). Improved light resistance can be obtained by treatment with 0.5% phenol solution at temperatures below 60°C (96). Reaction of amino end-groups with copper by treatment with aqueous copper sulfate is effective as is reaction with acetic anhydride, phenyl isocyanate, acrylonitrile, and acrylic esters (96). Protection against thermal degradation as well as photodegradation is claimed to be conferred on nylon by treatment at 95°C in an aqueous bath containing a halogeno-1,3,5-triazine derivative and sulfuric acid (97).

The air must be kept clean when displaying nylon textiles. There are indications from outdoor exposure studies that the degradation of nylon may be accelerated if the ambient atmosphere is polluted (98), and Trávníček (99) has discussed reports of witnesses concerning damage to nylon resulting from sulfur dioxide-laden soot. As nylon 66 is exposed outdoors, its strength and relative viscosity fall. After a loss in strength of about 40%, however, the relation between retained strength and relative viscosity differs for samples exposed in urban-industrial areas from those exposed in cleaner air (*100*), indicating that the mechanism of degradation differs in polluted atmospheres. In artificial weathering studies it has been shown that the degradation of nylon 66 by exposure to light and air is increased if the air is contaminated with sulfur dioxide (*101, 102*). Ozone and nitrogen dioxide may also affect the properties of nylon (*101*).

Fiber morphology can be affected during photochemical degradation. Surface damage, such as pitting, can be detected by scanning electron microscope. A review of work in this area has been published recently (*103*).

Yellowing may be a problem with nylon. It has been found that delustered nylon 66 fabric turns yellow on storage after photodegradation (*104*). This yellowing tendency was diminished by treatment with borohydride. The gradual yellowing of polyamide fibers which accompanies their aging in the atmosphere has been shown to be a result of reaction at the amine end-groups of nylon. Treatment with thermosetting formaldehyde-based resins, as used in textile finishes, increases the tendency to discolor, but reaction with urea blocks the amine ends and confers a measure of protection against yellowing (*105*). Phenylphosphinates added before fiber formation reduce the tendency of nylon to yellow (*106*).

Polyester. The most common polyester in use is derived from the homopolymer poly(ethylene terephthalate). Many types of this fiber contain a delustrant, usually titanium dioxide. Optically brightened polymers are quite common. The optical brightener, such as specially stabilized derivatives of either stilbenes or phenylcoumarins, can be added to the polyester before formation of the fiber (*107*). Some commercial fibers contain minor amounts of copolymerized modifier to confer such properties as basic dyeability. A wide range of polyester fibers is used for consumer end-uses. Both staple fiber and filament yarn are available. Filament yarns with noncircular cross-sections are made (*107*).

Methods for determining carboxyl end-groups and hydroxyl end-groups in polyesters have been described in detail (*77*). Estimation of carboxyl end-groups by hydrazinolysis has been described by Zahn et al. (*78*). These authors also describe methods for analysis of comonomers in polyesters. Infrared spectroscopy has also been used for measuring end-group concentrations (*108*). DP determinations can be made from viscosity measurements in *o*-chlorophenol (*109*) or in phenoltetrachloroethane solution (50:50) (*110*). At times it may be sufficient to express results simply as relative viscosities (*101*).

For some fibers such as nylon and cotton, photodegradation can be observed either by measuring losses in breaking strength or by measuring the decrease in viscosity of solutions of the photodegraded material. In the case of polyester fiber, however, Little and Parsons have reported that the intrinsic viscosity of polyester fibers is insensitive to photochemical attack (*100*). Again, in the studies of Zeronian et al. (*101*) a large loss in strength (34%) of polyester yarn by photodegradation was accompanied by only a small drop in relative viscosity (from 1.72 to 1.67). However, the number of carboxyl end-groups more than doubled from 21–47 g equiv/10^6 g polymer. Thus, if only small amounts of material are available, it is recommended that end-group analysis be used to quantitatively determine photochemical degradation for this polymer. With respect to stains for studying fiber deterioration, *N,N*-dimethyl-paraphenylenediamine hydrochloride has been used for detecting weathering damage in polyester fibers (*111*).

Summaries of chemical and physical properties of different polyester fibers are available (*107*). Polyesters display excellent resistance to conventional textile bleaching agents and are most resistant to cleaning solvents (*107*). Mold, mildew, and fungi may grow on finishes applied to polyester fabrics but do not attack the fiber itself (*3*). Again, insects that devour natural fibers normally do not affect polyester fibers although they may cut their way out of the fabric if trapped.

The resistance of polyester fibers to aging is generally considered excellent (*107*). A review discussing work on the degradation, including thermal degradation, of polyester has been published (*112*). During thermal degradation of the polymer, the concentration of hydroxyl groups tends to decrease and carboxyl group content increases. After most of the hydroxyl end-groups have been consumed, anhydride groups can be formed by the reaction of vinyl end-groups with carboxyl groups and by dehydration of the carboxyl groups.

Work on the photodegradation of poly(ethylene terephthalate) has been reviewed recently (*113*). Reducing the luster of polyester fiber by titanium dioxide increases its susceptibility to photodegradation. As in the case of nylon, fiber morphology can be affected during photochemical degradation. Both light and electron microscopy have been used to detect damage on the surface of photodegraded polyester fibers (*103*). The light resistance of polyester fabrics and dyeings on them can be improved by impregnation with specified benzophenones or substituted acrylonitriles (*114, 115*).

Polyester fabric does not appear to be greatly affected by air pollutants. Clibbens (*98*), in reviewing the study by Little and Parsons (*100*) on the weathering of polyester fabric at eight different sites ranging from rural to urban areas, noted that the polyester did not appear to be significantly affected by the atmospheric variable. The effect of contamination of the air with sulfur dioxide, ozone, or nitrogen dioxide on the properties of polyester fabric has been reported in an artificial weathering study (*101*). Sulfur dioxide and ozone did not appear to affect the fabric but there was some evidence that nitrogen dioxide was affecting its properties.

Acrylics. Manufacturers of acrylic fibers have not generally published or confirmed the chemical composition of their fibers (*116*). Acrylic fiber will generally contain 85–94% acrylonitrile; the balance is made up of comonomers having a specific function, such as to provide dye affinity for specific dye classes or to regulate diffusion of dye into the fiber. A list of typical comonomers has been published (*116*). Acrylic fibers may also contain heat (*117*) and light stabilizers (*116*). They may also contain a delustrant such as titanium dioxide. Some products contain optical brightening agents. These materials probably never exceed 4–5% of the total composition. The cross-sectional shapes of the fibers vary (*116*).

The chemical analysis of acrylic fibers has been discussed in detail by Heidner and Gibson (*118*). The DP of polyacrylonitrile can be obtained from viscosity measurements and from other conventional methods for determining molecular weight. Cernia (*117*) has discussed the relation between viscosity and molecular weight for polyacrylonitrile. Methyl methacrylate in acrylonitrile copolymers has been determined iodiometrically by using a variation of Zeisel's method for alkoxy groups (*119*). A procedure has been described by which acid groups in acrylics can be measured by nonaqueous titrimetry (*120*). A flame-photometric method has been used for determining acid groups and verified by sulfur analysis, potentiometric titration, and a dye adsorption method (*121*). Differential infrared spectrophotometry may be used for detection of end-groups— i.e., sulfate or sulfonate—in polyacrylonitrile (*122*). The ultraviolet absorption of polyacrylonitrile in solutions has been assigned to ketonitrile groups present to only a small extent but possibly important in the thermal degradation of acrylic materials (*123*). Kjeldahl nitrogen determinations together with the use of the Wieniger reaction mixture have been used to assess photochemical degradation in polyacrylonitrile fibers (*124*).

A summary of typical chemical and physical properties of acrylic fibers has been published (*116*). Acrylic fibers are unaffected by soaps and other chemicals used in washing and drycleaning. Biological attack is negligible. As stated earlier, acrylic fibers have excellent resistance to sunlight deterioration; however, surface damage is possible by light exposure. In artificial weathering studies, pitting has been found on the surface of acrylic fibers (*103*). There is a possibility that air pollutants such as nitrogen dioxide, ozone, or sulfur dioxide may affect the tensile properties of acrylic fibers, but there is as yet no conclusive evidence (*101, 102*).

Modacrylic Fibers. Commercial modacrylic fibers contain either vinyl chloride or vinylidene chloride copolymerized with acrylonitrile; other monomers may also be present (*125*). The cross-sectional shapes of different modacrylic fibers vary.

Molecular weight characterization of modacrylic fibers is difficult because of the limited number of solvents available and inhomogeneties in composition between individual polymer chains that affect solution properties, particularly if the comonomers are ionic in character. Dimethylformamide and dimethylacetamide are suitable for measurement of molecular weight of polyacrylonitrile, but errors are introduced when copolymers are analyzed (*126*). Bortniak et al. (*127*) have analyzed modacrylic fibers quantitatively in microgram quantities by using pyrolysis gas chromatography.

Typical physical and chemical properties of commercial modacrylic fibers have been published (*125*). Modacrylics are not affected by bleaches in the concentrations used for spot and stain removal (*31*). They are immune to attack by rot, mildew, bacteria, and insects such as moths and carpet beetles (*125*). Fungi may grow in dirt in an unlaundered Dynel fabric, but washing out the dirt removes the mildew with no effect on the fabric.

Modacrylic fibers have good resistance to sunlight. These fibers, however, change color on sunlight exposure. Initially, bleaching occurs followed by slight yellowing, turning to a tan color on prolonged exposure (*125*). Air pollutants do not appear to be as harmful to modacrylic materials as to some other fibers. There is evidence from artificial weathering studies that the presence of nitrogen dioxide, ozone, or sulfur dioxide in the air does not cause additional deterioration to the tensile properties of modacrylic fiber (*101*).

Conclusions

The preservation of textiles made from man-made fibers requires attention to similar factors as textiles made from natural fibers—i.e., temperature, humidity, light conditions, and air purity. In some instances, preservation should be easier. Synthetic fibers and cellulose derivative fibers, for example, would be less prone to insect damage than natural fibers. As in the case of the natural fibers, there are well-established techniques for determining the type and extent of damage that has occurred to man-made fibers during use. This will assist in determining cleaning and preservation techniques.

There is continuing research and development to improve the properties of existing man-made fibers and of the finishes and dyes to be applied. This work could alleviate some of the problems such as yellowing mentioned in this review, but these problems will still remain in fabrics now produced. The textile industry is dynamic. Thus conservators will need to continually update their knowledge of the properties of existing man-made fibers and of recently invented fibers which may become as important as those described in this review in the future.

Literature Cited

1. Hague, D. C., "The Economics of Man-Made Fibres," George Duckworth and Co., London, 1957.
2. *Text. Org.* (1975) **46** (11), 164.
3. Moncrieff, R. W., "Man-Made Fibres," 6th Ed., John Wiley & Sons, New York, 1975.
4. Man-Made Fiber Fact Book, Man-Made Fiber Producers Association, Inc., Washington, D.C., 1974.
5. Sbrolli, W., "Nylon 6," in "Man-made Fibers: Science and Technology," Mark, H. F., Atlas, S. M., Cernia, E., Eds., **2**, 227, Interscience, New York, 1968.
6. *Text. Org.* (1976) **47** (1-2), 4.
7. "Textile Fibers and Their Properties," Burlington Industries, Inc., Greensboro, N. C., 1970.
8. "Man-Made Fibers: Science and Technology," Mark, H. F., Atlas, S. M., Cernia, E., Eds., **1–3**, Interscience, New York, 1967–68.
9. "Encyclopedia of Polymer Science and Technology," Mark, H. F., Gaylord, N. G., Bikales, N. M., Eds., **1–16**, Interscience, New York, 1964–1972.
10. "Heat durability and Heat Shrinkage of Yarns," *Du Pont Bull.* (1959) X-111.
11. "Comparative Heat Resistance of Fibers," *Du Pont Bull.* (1956) X-56.
12. Galanti, A. V., Mantell, C. L., "Polypropylene Fibers and Films," Plenum Press, New York, 1965.
13. Fels, M., *J. Text. Inst.* (1960) **51**, P648.
14. Upham, J. B., Salvin, V. S., "Effects of Air Pollutants on Textile Fibers and Dyes," *U.S. NTIS Ad. Rep.* (1975) PB-241–507.
15. Egerton, G. S., Shah, K. M., *Text. Res. J.* (1968) **38**, 130.
16. Singleton, R. W., Kunkel, R. K., Sprague, B. S., *Text. Res. J.* (1965) **35**, 228.
17. Singleton, R. W., Cook, P. A. C., *Text. Res. J.* (1969) **39**, 43.
18. "Light and Weather Resistance of Fibers," *Du Pont Bull.* (1966) X-203.
19. Hirt, R. C., Schmitt, R. G., Searle, N. D., Sullivan, A. P., *J. Opt. Soc. Am.* (1960) **50**, 706.
20. "Resistance to Light," *Chemistrand Bull.* **1.13**, revised 1964.
21. Moore, R. F., *Polymer* (1963) **4**, 493.
22. Taylor, H. A., Tincher, W. C., Hamner, W. F., *J. Appl. Polym. Sci.* (1970) **14**, 141.
23. Lock, L. M., Frank, G. C., *Text. Res. J.* (1973) **43**, 502.
24. Egerton, G. S., Assaad, N. E. N., *J. Soc. Dyers Colour.* (1970) **86**, 203.
25. Swallow, J. E., "Effects of Dyes and Finishes on the Weathering of Nylon Textiles," *U.S. NTIS Ad. Rep.* (1975) AD-A016642.
26. Wood, F. C., *J. Text. Inst.* (1939) **30**, P142.
27. West, K., *J. Text. Inst.* (1962) **53**, P204.
28. Little, A. H., *J. Soc. Dyers Colour.* (1964) **80**, 527.
29. "Tech-Talk," *Chemstrand Bull.* (1965) **TT-17**.
30. "Acrylics Outdoors," Monsanto Report, October 1968.
31. Lyle, D. S., "Modern Textiles," John Wiley & Sons, New York, 1976.

32. "Identification of Textile Materials," 6th Ed., The Textile Institute, Manchester, 1970.
33. "Fibers in Textiles: Identification," *AATCC Tech. Man.*, American Association of Textile Chemists and Colorists, Research Triangle Park, N. C., **46**, 51.
34. "Analytical Methods for a Textile Laboratory," *AATCC Monogr.* 3, 2nd Ed., American Association of Textile Chemists and Colorists, Research Triangle Park, N. C., 1968.
35. "Analysis of Textiles: Quantitative," *AATCC Tech. Man.*, American Association of Textile Chemists and Colorists, Research Triangle Park, N. C., **46**, 41.
36. "Resistance of Fibers to Bleaching and Stripping Agents," *Du Pont Bull.* (1968) X-225.
37. "Comparative Chemical Resistance of Fibers," *DuPont Bull.* (1956) X-48.
38. "Resistance of Fibers to Organic Chemicals," *Du Pont Bull.* (1966) X-215.
39. "Resistance of Fibers to Aqueous Solutions of Various Salts," *Du Pont Bull.* (1967) X-216.
40. Scott, G., "Atmospheric Oxidation and Antioxidants," Elsevier Publishing Co., New York, 1965.
41. "Polymer Stabilization," Hawkins, W. L., Ed., Wiley-Interscience, New York, 1972.
42. Rånby, B., Rabek, J. F., "Photodegradation, Photooxidation, and Photostabilization of Polymers: Principles and Applications," John Wiley & Sons, New York, 1975.
43. Mitchell, R. L., Daul, G. C., "Rayon," *in* "Encyclopedia of Polymer Science Technology," H. F. Mark, N. G. Gaylord, N.M. Bikales, Eds., Vol. 11, p. 810, Interscience, New York, 1969.
44. "Methods in Carbohydrate Chemistry," Whistler, R. L., Ed., Vol. III, Cellulose, Academic Press, New York, 1963.
45. Nevell, T. P., "The Hydrolytic and Oxidative Degradation of Cellulose," *in* "Recent Advances in the Chemistry of Cellulose and Starch," J. Honeyman, Ed., p. 75, Heywood and Co., London, 1959.
46. Davidson, G. F., *J. Text. Inst.* (1948) **39**, T65.
47. Nevell, T. P., "Determination of Reducing End-Groups," *in* "Methods in Carbohydrate Chemistry," R. L. Whistler, Ed., Vol. III, p. 43, Cellulose, Academic Press, New York, 1963.
48. "A.S.T.M. D539-53," *ASTM Stand.*, Part 25, American Society for Testing and Materials, Philadelphia, 1969.
49. "A.S.T.M. D1795-62," *ASTM Stand.*, Part 21, American Society for Testing and Materials, Philadelphia, 1974.
50. Henley, D., *Sven. Papperstidn.* (1960) **63**, 143.
51. Brown, W., Wikstrom, R., *Eur. Polym. J.* (1965) **1**, 1.
52. Rollins, M. L., Tripp, V. W., "Light Microscopy of Cellulose and Cellulose Derivatives," *in* "Methods in Carbohydrate Chemistry," R. L. Whistler, Ed., Vol. III, p. 335, Cellulose, Academic, New York, 1963.
53. Jolliff, E. C., *Text. Res. J.* (1959) **29**, 279.
54. Ford, J. F., *J. Text. Inst.* (1960) **51**, T157.
55. Schwertassek, K., *Faserforsch U. Textiltechnik* (1953) **4**, 181 and (1962) **13**, 195.
56. Heyn, A. N. J., *Text. Res. J.* (1957) **27**, 591, and (1958) **28**, 444.
57. Gascoigne, J. A., *Chem. Ind. (London)* (1961) 693.
58. Phillips, G. O., "Photochemistry of Carbohydrates," "Advances in Carbohydrate Chemistry," Wolfrom, M. W., Ed., **18**, p. 9, Academic, 1963.
59. Müller, J., *Melliand Textilber.* (1952) **33**, 742.
60. Reumuth, H., *Melliand Textilber.* (1952) **33**, 743.
61. Head, F. S. H., Lund, G., *J. Soc. Dyers Colour.* (1969) **85**, 61.

62. Zeronian, S. H., *Text. Res. J.* (1970) **40**, 695.
63. Zeronian, S. H., Miller, B. A. E., *Text. Chem. Color.* (1973) **5** (5) 89.
64. Rochas, P., Gavet, L., *Bull. Inst. Text. Fr.* (1957) **69**, 85.
65. Sihtola, H. et al., *Pap. Puu* (1958) **40**, 579, 582, 627, 634 and (1959) **41**, 35.
66. Virkola, N. E., Sihtola, H., *Nor. Skogind* (1958) **12**, 87.
67. Kleinert, T. N., Moessmer, V., Apuchtin, A., *Text. Rundsch.* (1957) **12**, 124.
68. Sprague, B. S., Horner, L. I., "Cellulose Esters, Organic Fibers," "Encyclopedia of Polymer Science and Technology," Mark, H. F., Gaylord, N. G., Bikales, N. M., Eds., **3**, 419, Interscience, New York, 1965.
69. Howlett, F., Martin, E. J., *J. Text. Inst.* (1944) **35**, T1.
70. Nevell, T. P., Zeronian, S. H., *Polymer* (1962) **3**, 187.
71. Mitchell, J. A., Bockmann, C. D., Lee, A. V., *Anal. Chem.* (1957) **29**, 499.
72. Marsden, R. J. B., Urquhart, A. R., *J. Text. Inst.* (1951) **42**, T15.
73. Laughlin, K. C., "Fibers of Cellulose Triacetate," "Man-Made Fibers: Science and Technology," Mark, H. F., Atlas, S. M., Cernia, E., Eds. (1968) **2**, 103.
74. Dubyaga, V. P. et al., *Vysokomol. Soedin Ser. B* (1968) **10**, 465.
75. Rogovin, Z. A., Kostrov, Yu. A., "Cellulose Acetate Fibers," "Man-Made Fibers: Science and Technology," Mark, H. F., Atlas, S. M., Cernia, E., Eds. (1968) **2**, 81.
76. Snider, O. E., Richardson, R. J., "Polyamide Fibers," "Encyclopedia of Polymer Science and Technology," Mark, H. F., Gaylord, N. G., Bikales, N. M., Eds., **10**, 347, Interscience, New York, 1969.
77. Price, G. F., "Techniques of End-Group Analysis," "Techniques of Polymer Characterization," Allen, P. W., Ed., page 207, Butterworths, London, 1959.
78. Zahn, H., Kusch, P., Müller-Schulte, D., Nissen, D., Rossbach, V., *Text. Res. J.* (1973) **43**, 601.
79. Heidendahl, R., *Dtsch. Textiltech.* (1970) **20**, 459.
80. Richter, W., Herlinger, H., Schlack, P., Sommermann, F., *Chemiefasern* (1970) **20**, 199.
81. Head, F. S. H., *J. Polym. Sci.* (1969) A-1, **7**, 2456 and (1970) **8**, 3651.
82. Burke, J. J., Orofino, T. A., *J. Polymer Sci. Part A-2* (1969) **7**, 1.
83. Boulton, J., Jackson, D. L. C., *J. Soc. Dyers Colour.* (1945) **61**, 50.
84. Smith, A. S., *J. Text. Inst.* (1957) **48**, T86.
85. Mödlich, H., *Text. Praxis* (1959) **14**, 1041.
86. Bubser, W., Mödlich, H., *Text. Praxis* (1959) **14**, 1152.
87. Scharf, R., *Text. Faserstofftech.* (1955) **5**, 573.
88. Kato, K., *Text. Res. J.* (1962) **32**, 181.
89. Kratzsch, E., Hendrix, H., *Melliand Textilber* (1964) **45**, 1129.
90. Swiss Standards Association, *Text. Rundsch.* (1963) **18**, 674.
91. Bobeth, W., Kändler, L., *Faserforsch. Textiltech.* (1957) **8**, 444.
92. Weiner, L. I., Sheehan, L. J., *U. S. Govt. Res. Dev. Rep.* (March 1966) **AD 631**, 428.
93. Fox, R. B., "Progress in Polymer Science," Jenkins, A. D., Ed., Vol. I, 47, Pergamon Press, New York, 1967.
94. *Am. Dyest. Rep.* (1966) **55**, 1065.
95. Schwemmer, M., *Text. Rundsch.* (1956) **11**, 1, 70, 131.
96. Hashimoto, T., *J. Soc. Text. Cellu. Ind. Jpn.* (1958) **14**, 321, 484.
97. Imperial Chemical Industries, B.P. 892, 379, May 2, 1958.
98. Clibbens, D. A., *Text. Inst. Ind.* (1968) **6**, 20.
99. Trávníček, Z., *Proc. Int. Clean Air Congr., 1st, 1966*, p. 224, The National Society for Clean Air, London, England (1966).
100. Little, A. H., Parsons, H. L., *J. Text. Inst.* (1967) **58**, 449.

101. Zeronian, S. H., Alger, K. W., Omaye, S. T., Proc. Int. Clean Air Congr., *2nd, 1970,* Englund, H. M., Beery, W. T., Eds., p. 468, Academic Press, New York, 1971.
102. Zeronian, S. H., Alger, K. W., Omaye, S. T., *Text. Res. J.* (1973) **43,** 228.
103. Zeronian, S. H., "Effect of Photochemical and Environmental Degradation on the Surface Properties of Textile Fibers," "Surface Characteristics of Fibers and Textiles," Schick, J. M., Ed., Part I, p. 365, Marcel Dekker, New York, 1975.
104. Marek, B., Lerch, E., *J. Soc. Dyers Colour.* (1965) **81,** 481.
105. Steiger, F. H., *Text. Res. J.* (1957) **27,** 459.
106. Du Pont, British Patent **902, 905,** and **902, 907,** Aug. 28, 1959.
107. Farrow, G., Hill, E. S., "Polyester Fibers," "Encyclopedia of Polymer Science and Technology," Mark, H. F., Gaylord, N. G., Bikales, N. M., Eds., **11,** 1, Interscience, New York, 1969.
108. Ravens, D. A. S., Ward, I. M., *Trans. Faraday Soc.* (1961) **57,** 150.
109. Furrer, E., *Text. Rundsch.* (1958) **13,** 129.
110. Conix, A., *Makromol. Chem.* (1958) **26,** 226.
111. Gray, V. E., Wright, J. R., *J. Appl. Polym. Sci.* (1963) **7,** 2161.
112. Buxbaum, L. H., *Angew. Chem. Int. Ed. Engl.* (1968) **7,** 182.
113. Wiles, D. M., "The Photodegradation of Fibre-Forming Polymers," "Degradation and Stabilization of Polymers," Geuskens, G., Ed., p. 137, Applied Science Publishers, London, 1975.
114. Standring, P. T., Penmore, G. W., *J. Text. Inst.* (1960) **51,** T336.
115. Strobel, A. F., *Am. Dyest. Rep.* (1961) **50,** 583.
116. Davis, C. W., Shapiro, P., "Acrylic Fibers," "Encyclopedia of Polymer Science and Technology," Mark, H. F., Gaylord, N. G., Bikales, N. M., Eds. (1964) **1,** 342.
117. Cernia, E., "Acrylic Fibers," "Man-Made Fibers: Science and Technology," Mark, H. F., Atlas, S. M., Cernia, E., Eds. (1968) **3,** 135.
118. Heidner, R. H., Gibson, M. E., Jr., "Acrylic and Modacrylic Fibers," "Encyclopedia of Industrial Chemical Analysis," Snell, F. D., Hilton, C. L., Eds., **4,** 219, Interscience, New York, 1967.
119. Volkova, L., Kvasha, N. M., Sidorkina, E., *Volokna Sint. Polim.* (1970) 290.
120. Kirby, J. R., Baldwin, A. J., *Anal. Chem.* (1968) **40,** 689.
121. Grigoriu, A., Grindea, M., *Ind. Text.* (1973) 24 ,555.
122. Matsubara, I., *Bull. Chem. Soc., Jpn.* (1960) **33,** 1624.
123. Kirby, J. R., Brandrup, J., Peebles, L. H., *J. Macromolecules* (1968) **1,** 53.
124. Fester, W., Hendrix, H., *Forschungsber. Landes Nordrhein Westfalen, n1157* (1963).
125. Kennedy, R. K., "Modacrylic Fibers," "Encyclopedia of Polymer Science and Technology," Mark, H. F., Gaylord, N. G., Bikales, N. M., Eds., **8,** 812, Interscience, New York, 1968.
126. DeBoos, A. G., *Text. Prog.* (1974) **6** (3) 12.
127. Bortniak, J., Brown, J. C., Sild, S., *J. Forensic Sci.* (1971) **16,** 380.

RECEIVED December 6, 1976.

16

Reinforcing Degraded Textiles

Part I: Properties of Naturally and Artificially Aged Cotton Textiles

G. M. BERRY, S. P. HERSH, P. A. TUCKER, and W. K. WALSH

School of Textiles, North Carolina State University, Raleigh, N.C. 27607

To provide a substrate suitable for evaluating the potential of various polymeric materials as consolidants and reinforcing agents for protecting fragile textiles, three techniques for artificially aging fabrics are examined: acid hydrolysis, heating, and irradiation with high-voltage electrons. A comparison of the strength, extent of oxidation, crystallinity, molecular weight, and fracture mechanics of the degraded fabrics with those of several pre-Columbian cottons indicated that none of the artificially aged fabrics duplicated the ancient samples in all properties. However, strength levels could be controlled to match those of the archaeological cottons, and those degraded fabrics which were matched in strength loss were judged to be suitable substrates for the initial resin reinforcing studies.

A wide range of natural and synthetic materials has been used in textile conservation to consolidate, reinforce, and protect fragile textiles of historic and artistic value (1, 2, 3). Weak, brittle, and even powdering fabrics can benefit from treatments which enable the cloth to be handled without causing further damage. Ideally, any treatment applied to a valuable object should be reversible so that, if necessary, the item can be restored unaltered to its original condition. Many conservators, however, recognize that when treatment is essential for the survival of an article, consolidation can be carried out even if the treatment is not reversible. Note that some polymers, such as poly(vinyl alcohol) and cellulose nitrate, whose applications were thought to be reversible in the past and thus accepted by a number of conservators, proved in time not only to be irreversible but also harmful (4, 5). This present study is not concerned with reversibility but only with preservation methods for decayed textiles that threaten to disintegrate unless consolidated. We hope that reversible systems will be studied in the future. This study also does not consider the joining of the object to a supporting substrate, but only self-, internal consolidation. Thus, the adhesive characteristics of the materials applied are not examined.

The ideal finish or treatment should increase the strength and flexural endurance of the object without altering its appearance or hand. Therefore, strength, flexibility, and appearance are the main criteria that are considered in judging the acceptability of a proposed consolidant. Long-term stability, an equally important factor, cannot be judged adequately in the limited time frame of this report.

This work was done to study the use of modern synthetic resins as textile consolidants, and the initial results are described in this and the following chapter (Part II). Before consolidants could be tested, however, model fabrics that adequately mimic naturally degraded textiles had to be developed. The preparation of a suitable model or models is hampered since natural degradation undoubtedly involves several mechanisms. The present condition of an ancient textile depends on many factors such as the history of the original fiber, the method of spinning, weaving, dyeing and finishing, and the deleterious influences encountered during the life of the material.

Textiles deteriorate naturally by oxidation, heat, mechanical stress, radiation, moisture, and microbiological and enzymatic attack (6,7). The major effects of deterioration are strength loss, decreased molecular weight, increased solubility, increased oxidation, changes in crystallinity, and alterations in appearance and hand. Model aged fabrics were prepared by high-voltage electron irradiation, thermal degradation, and acid hydrolysis. To assess how well the artificial degradation mimics the properties of naturally aged fabrics, the properties of archaeological samples had to be determined since suitable information was not available. Thus, Chapter 16 in this series describes the characterization of archaeological samples and the preparation of model fabrics. Chapter 17 evaluates consolidants applied to model degraded fabrics.

Experimental

Fabric Samples. ARCHAEOLOGICAL. Two groups of ancient samples were available for examination. The first consists of two fabric fragments from a Chancay grave site in central Peru. They date from about A.D. 1200. A photograph of one of these is given in Figure 1. These fabrics are identified as the "A.D. 1200" samples. The second group of samples is from the Gramalote site in northern Peru and date from the Initial Period, about 1000 B.C. This group consists of three samples. The first

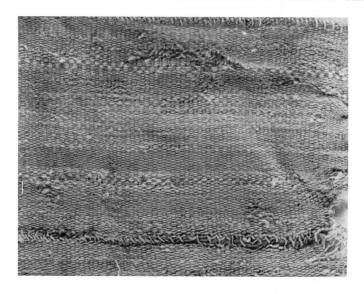

Figure 1.   Fabric fragment from a Chancay burial site, ca. A.D.
1200

was taken from an architectural site at the dig and consists mostly of white yarns and fibers. Henceforth, these samples are referred to as "architectural." The other two sets, referred to as test "pit 8" and "pit 9" samples, are from refuse pits at the same site. Pit 9 comes from a depth of 41–60 cm, and pit 8 is from a depth of 101–120 cm.

CONTEMPORARY. The fabric used for the degradation and resin application studies was a standard 80 × 80 count, 3.5 oz/yd² print cloth. It was machine washed in a 0.1% solution of Triton X-100, a nonionic detergent, before treating. The contemporary fibers were standard USDA calibration cotton.

Test Methods. FABRIC TENSILE STRENGTH. The grab method described in ASTM method D1682-64 was used to measure the tensile breaking load of the fabric on a Scott CRE tester (8). All measurements of strength and stiffness were made in a standard atmosphere for testing textiles (70 ± 2°F and 65 ± 2% r.h.) after conditioning at least 72 hr. Normally, five replicate measurements were made of each sample in the filling direction only. Since only one fabric was involved, breaking strengths were not normalized for linear density or cross-sectional area.

FIBER TENSILE STRENGTH. The breaking strength of single fibers was determined on an Instron tensile testing machine using a ¼-in. gage length and a 0.2 in./min elongation rate. This short gage length minimized the effect of weak spots along the fiber. The linear density of the individual fibers was measured on an Insco Co. Vibroscope to calculate the breaking strength in normalized units of gf/den (9). Usually, at least 15 fibers were broken to determine the average tenacity of each sample. Measurements were made after conditioning in a standard atmosphere for at least 72 hr. When fibers were too brittle to be removed from yarns, the entire yarn was broken at zero-gage length. When yarns had to be broken, the linear density of the yarn was measured by pulling the crimp out of the yarn, measuring its length, and then weighing the sample (*9*).

FABRIC TEAR STRENGTH. The tearing strength was measured on an Instron tensile testing machine using ASTM test method D2261-71 (*8*). This test uses the tongue (single-rip) method of testing. Usually, the average of five tests is reported for each sample. All measurements reported were made in the filling direction.

EXTENT OF OXIDATION VIA TURNBULL'S BLUE TEST. This test has been used for some time as a qualitative test for carboxyl groups in cellulose. To develop the blue color indicative of the presence of carboxyl groups, the procedure described by Sundaram and Iyengar (*10*) was followed. First, a 1.0% solution of ferrous sulfate is added to the cotton sample. Any carboxyl groups on the cellulose react with the ferrous sulfate to form the ferrous salt. The excess ferrous ions are then washed out. The sample is next treated with potassium ferricyanide which reacts to form the potassium salt of the cellulose and ferrous ferricyanide, a blue compound known as Turnbull's Blue. To obtain a semiquantitative measurement and a ranking index of the amount of Turnbull's Blue on the treated samples, reflectance curves were measured on the sample before and after treatment using a GE Hardy recording spectrophotometer against a MgO standard. Typical reflectance curves are shown in Figures 5–7. The relative amount of blue pigment on the fabric was then estimated from the K/S value, the ratio of the absorption to scattering coefficients (*11*). The K/S value was calculated for the wavelength of minimum reflectance (680 nm) from the Kubelka-Munk equation:

$$K/S = (1 - R^2)/2R$$

where R is the percent reflectance. The K/S ratio gives a value proportional to the concentration of pigment on the sample which was then used to estimate the extent of oxidation.

For example, consider Figure 5 which shows the reflectance curves measured on the contemporary print cloth. The calculated K/S values are 0.005 and 0.178 before and after the Turnbull's Blue reaction, respectively. The net increase in blue pigment is $0.178 - 0.005 = 0.173$ (arbitrary units). For cotton degraded by exposure to 100 Mrads of high-voltage electron radiation (shown in Figure 6) the net increase in K/S value upon formation of Turnbull's Blue is $0.752 - 0.012 = 0.740$ unit. Thus, if the concentration of carboxyl groups in the untreated cotton is taken arbitrarily to be 1, the concentration in the degraded fabric relative to the undegraded fabric would be $0.740/0.173 = 4.28$, the value that appears in Table I.

EXTENT OF OXIDATION VIA INFRARED SPECTROSCOPY. Infrared spectra were determined using the KBr pellet technique described by O'Connor et al. (*12*) on a Perkin-Elmer 521 grating infrared spectrophotometer. Cut fiber was ground in a Wiley mill to pass a 20-mesh screen, and pellets were then formed after mixing 3.3 mg cellulose with 350 mg KBr. Although the absorption band at 1724 cm^{-1} is normally assigned to carbonyl groups from ketones, aldehydes, and carboxyl groups, any moisture present will form hemiacetals and/or aldehydrates which will eliminate aldehyde carbonyls from the 1724-cm^{-1} band. Thus, this band can effectively be

Table I. Properties of Artificially

| | Strength | |
| | Tensile (%) | Tear (%) |
Fabric		
Original	100	100
Hydrolyzed 16 hr in 40% H_2SO_4	18.7	14.8
Heated 117 hr at 168°C	8.1	4.8
Irradiated, 50-Mrad dose	26.5	19.7
Irradiated, 100-Mrad dose	16.2	9.3

assigned to carboxyl absorption alone (13) and can be used to estimate the relative carboxyl content of the sample from the change in optical density between the base line and the peak maximum. The reliability of this simple calculation depends on one's assuming a constant concentration of ground fibers in the KBr pellet and a constant pellet thickness.

The carboxyl and aldehlde absorption bands which occur near 1667 cm^{-1} could not be used to assess oxidation because of interference from the H—O—H stretching peak at 1630 cm^{-1} arising from absorbed water (14). This interference occurred even though strenuous efforts were made to remove and to exclude moisture from the samples.

INFRARED CRYSTALLINITY INDEX. A measure of the relative degree of crystallinity was determined from the infrared spectra obtained in the preceding section by reporting the ratio of the optical density of the band at 1372^{-1} (7.29 μm) to that at 2900 cm^{-1} (3.45 μm). According to Nelson and O'Connor (15), the crystallinity index measured in this way compares well with data from x-ray diffraction, density measurements, and accessibility measured by moisture sorption.

MOLECULAR WEIGHT. Molecular weights were determined from viscosity measurements made on cadmium ethylenediamine hydroxide (Cadoxen) solutions. Three dilutions were used at concentration ranges which depended on the molecular weight of the sample. The intrinsic viscosity, $[\eta]$ in ml/g, was calculated by fitting a regression line to the three observed viscosity measurements. Molecular weights were calculated using the Mark-Houwink equation (16):

$$[\eta] = 38.5 \times 10^{-3} M_v^{0.76}$$

where M_v is the viscosity average molecular weight. Degree of polymerization (DP) was calculated using 162 as the molecular weight of the repeating unit.

Artificial Aging Experiments. RADIATION. Two types of degradation can be caused by radiation: photolysis produced by electromagnetic radiation and radiolysis produced by ionizing radiation. Ultraviolet light, a constant source of concern for the textile curator, is an example of electromagnetic radiation. While the intermediate processes differ, the two types of radiation produce much the same effects of chain scission with some oxidation and cross-linking. In both cases the 1,4-β-glucosidic link is the point of chain scission (17, 18). The formation of carbonyl

Aged Contemporary Print Cloth

	COOH Content		
DP	Turnbull's Blue Test (Arb. Units)	Infrared (ΔOD)	Infrared Crystallinity Index
2606	1	0.0	0.55
206	1.95	0.0	0.87
214	4.24	0.043	0.84
57	3.38	—	—
14	4.28	0.066	0.88

and carboxyl groups accompanies radiation attack. The rate of formation of the former is approximately 20 times greater than the roughly equal formation rate of carboxyl groups and of chain scissions.

The degrading effects of both ultraviolet light and ionizing radiation on textile materials are well documented. Although one might expect natural radiation damage to result mainly from ultraviolet exposure, it is the total amount of radiation energy absorbed that affects the extent of overall damage to cellulose rather than the source of the radiation (*18*, *19*). Therefore, a model degradation system using ionizing radiation should work as well as an ultraviolet system. Since a source of high energy ionizing radiation was available which could handle the relatively large amounts of fabric required, this type of radiation was chosen for the initial studies.

Radiation doses greater than 1 Mrad begin to degrade cellulose materials (*18*). To produce model degraded fabrics having strength losses of 75% or more, cotton fabrics were exposed to radiation doses of 50 and 100 Mrad in an electron accelerator manufactured by High Voltage Engineering Corp. operating at 550 kV. A dose of 100 Mrad could be obtained in less than one minute.

HYDROLYSIS. Cellulose can be hydrolyzed by acids and by enzymes derived from bacteria and other microorganisms. Enzymatic hydrolysis cleaves the 1,4-β-glucosidic link, decreasing the molecular weight, and produces an alkali soluble residue (*20*). Rapid strength loss occurs. In extreme cases of hydrolysis, the cellulose becomes water soluble. Crystallinity is initially increased during hydrolysis as severed chains in the disordered regions separate and reform into more crystalline patterns (*21*). Although the attack of some enzymes might be highly localized, in general, the amorphous regions of cellulose yield most readily to enzyme attack. The more crystalline areas must be penetrated from fringe areas; thus, chain scission gradually progresses inward (*22*).

In general, acid hydrolysis produces similar degradation. Since acids usually involve a much smaller molecule as the attacking agent, however, acids penetrate the amorphous area of cellulose more easily than enzymes and produce a faster drop in DP. Diffusion into the crystalline areas proceeds more slowly. Because acid hydrolysis is more easily controlled and is faster than enzymatic attack, acid hydrolysis was selected as the second aging system to be examined.

Two sets of hydrolysis experiments were carried out. In the first, fabric was exposed in a solution of 40% sulfuric acid at room temperature with a liquor-to-fabric weight ratio of 100:1. Samples were removed after 0.25-, 0.50-, 1-, 2-, 6-, and 16-hr exposures. For the second set, fabric was exposed for 30 min at room temperature in solutions containing 5, 10, 20, 30, and 40% H_2SO_4 also at a bath ratio of 100:1. After the samples were removed from the acid solution, they were washed thoroughly with tap water and rinsed in distilled water. The pH of the rinse water was then tested for neutrality by adding 2 drops of bromocresol purple and one drop of $0.1N$ NaOH. If the solution did not change from yellow to purple, rinsing was repeated. The neutralized samples were then air dried, equilibrated, and tested.

THERMAL DEGRADATION. Thermal degradation follows different paths depending upon whether moisture and oxygen are present. Above 140°C, however, moisture does not influence degradation. Continuous exposure to heat below the pyrolysis temperature can produce chain scission and autoxidation within the cellulose chains (23, 24). To produce thermally degraded samples for evaluation, cotton fabrics were exposed in a forced convection oven at 168° ± 4°C. Fabric was removed at intervals ranging from 24–211 hr for examination.

Comparison of Model Fabrics with Archaeological Specimens. To characterize the artificially degraded fabrics and to compare them with the naturally aged archaeological samples, the molecular weight, crystallinity, extent of oxidation, tensile strength, tear strength, and flexural rigidity of these materials were measured whenever possible using procedures described earlier.

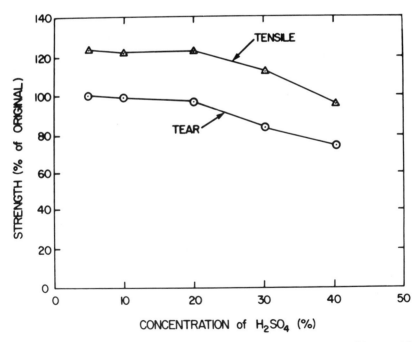

Figure 2. Strength of cotton print cloth after immersion in sulfuric acid for 30 min at room temperature as a function of acid concentration

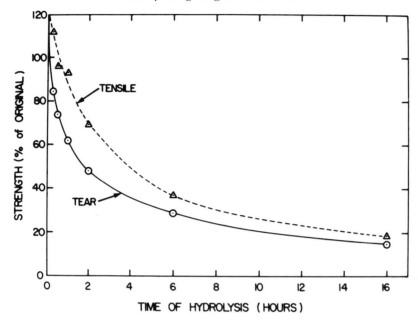

Figure 3. Strength of cotton print cloth after immersion in 40% sulfuric acid at room temperature for various times

Only limited and somewhat superficial comparisons can be made between the artificially aged fabrics and the naturally degraded samples because of our ignorance of the original conditions of the fibers and fabric of the now antique specimens. The cultivation of modern "wild" varieties from the same archaeological sites might provide a greater insight into comparative strength losses, but this type of testing has not been done. Therefore, the ancient samples can only be compared with modern commercial fiber and fabrics.

STRENGTH. The changes in strength of the artificially aged fabrics are shown in Figures 2, 3, and 4. The results for the fabrics exposed in varying concentrations of sulfuric acid for 30 min are shown in Figure 2. Somewhat surprisingly, the tensile strengths are all increased up to 25% except for the fabric exposed in 40% H_2SO_4, which had a loss of about 4%. Note that even in the 40% H_2SO_4 tensile strength after a 15-min exposure increased 12%. Immersion in 40% H_2SO_4 for longer times, as shown in Figure 3, drastically lowered both the tensile and tear strengths. After 16 hr, the tensile and tear strengths were reduced to 19% and 15% of that of the original fabric, respectively.

Strength losses produced by thermal degradation are shown in Figure 4. A rapid loss of strength during the first 70 hr of heating in air at 168°C is followed by a gradual decrease in the rate of strength loss at longer heating times. Strength losses measured on the irradiated samples and of the most severely degraded hydrolyzed fabric are also indicated on Figure 4.

Kulshreshtha and Dweltz report a similar initial rise in the tenacity of acid-hydrolyzed cotton and attribute it to the plasticizing action of the

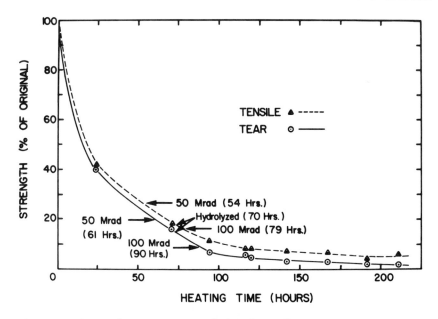

Figure 4. Strength of cotton print clothes thermally degraded by heating at 168°C for various times. The strength of fabrics degraded by hydrolyzing 16 hr in 40% sulfuric acid at room temperature and by high-voltage electron irradiation at doses of 50 and 100 Mrad are also indicated.

acid bath (25). The increase in crystallinity of acid-hydrolyzed cotton could also account for the initial tenacity gains. The severe strength losses of 73% and 84% resulting from 50- and 100-Mrad exposures indicated in Table I and Figure 4 are in line with those expected from earlier reports. For example, Teszler et al. (26) report a tensile strength loss of 45% for cotton yarn exposed to 26 Mrad of neutron radiation, while Gilfillan and Linden (27, 28) report a strength loss of 27% for cotton yarn exposed to 4.2 Mrad of electron radiation from a 2-MeV Van de Graaf accelerator.

Summaries of the properties measured on some of the artificially degraded fabrics and on the archaeological samples are given in Tables I and II, respectively. Strengths of the ancient samples range from the moderately weaker architectural and pit 9 samples having about 60% strength retention relative to modern cottons to the enormously fragile A.D. 1200 samples in which fibers could not even be separated from the yarns because of their extreme brittleness. The strength of the A.D. 1200 sample had to be measured by breaking the yarn at zero-gage length, which indicated a strength retention of only 2.5%. Deducing fiber strength from yarn strength at zero-gage lengths seems valid as shown by comparing the strength of fibers from the contemporary print cloth (2.08 gf/den) with the strength of yarn taken from the fabric and broken at zero gage (2.11 gf/den). The artificially degraded samples listed all had great strength losses, with strength retentions somewhat lower than the average of the naturally degraded samples. Unfortunately, the tear strengths could not be assessed on the archaeological samples since these measurements can only be made on fabrics. The degraded fabrics included in Table I were selected because their strength characteristics were similar to those of most of the ancient samples. Additional studies will of course have to be made on less severely degraded fabrics (~ 60% strength retention) for comparison with the pit 9 and architectural samples.

MOLECULAR WEIGHT. The DP of the thermally degraded and acid-hydrolyzed fabrics are 214 and 206, respectively, which approximate the leveling-off DP values of around 200 reported for hydrolyzed cotton (29). This level of hydrolysis is generally believed to represent the point at which all of the amorphous regions of the cellulose have been hydrolyzed, leaving the hard-to-penetrate crystalline areas relatively intact. Subsequent hydrolysis produces very little additional loss in the DP The DPs of the irradiated samples are much lower: 57 for 50-Mrad exposure and 14 for 100-Mrad exposure. These low DP values are remarkably close to those reported for similar exposures by Charlesby (17) to 800-kV electrons (43 and 22, respectively), and they strongly suggest that the radiation is severing bonds not only in the more easily attacked amorphous regions of the fiber but also in the more crystalline areas. Shafizadeh (30) has reported that cotton heated for 96 hr at 170°C in nitrogen reduces the DP to 800, while cotton heated in oxygen reduces the DP to 200. The latter value is similar to that measured here for cotton heated 117 hr in air at 168°C.

The molecular weights of two samples of the severely degraded A.D. 1200 fabric (DP = 184 and 192 for replicate measurements) were close

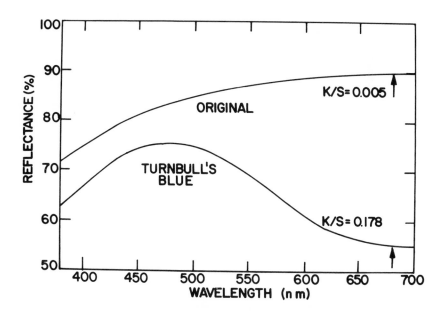

Figure 5. Reflectance as a function of wavelength of undegraded contemporary cotton print cloth before and after Turnbull's Blue test for carboxyl groups

to the leveling-off values for cotton. The architectural sample dating from 1000 B.C., which had the highest strength retention of all the naturally aged samples (61%), had a DP of 685, which compares with about 2600 for contemporary cotton. Yarns from pit 8, which had a strength retention of 22%, had a DP of 226. All the other 1000 B.C. samples, however, had DPs well below the leveling-off values. Note that the DP values of the unspun fibers from both pits 8 and 9 were well below the DPs of yarns taken from the same sites.

OXIDATION. Reflectance curves recorded before and after carrying out Turnbull's Blue reaction for the original contemporary fabric, the fabric degraded by 100-Mrad exposure, and the fabric degraded thermally by 211-hr heating at 168°C are shown in Figures 5, 6, and 7, respectively. In addition to using these curves to calculate the relative concentration of carboxyl groups in the cotton as described earlier, they can be used to assess the degree of yellowing by examining the reflectance in the blue end of the spectrum (380–400-nm region). Thus, the reflectance of those three fabrics before forming Turnbull's Blue pigment at 400 nm are 75%, 46%, and 11%, respectively, showing that irradiation has yellowed the fabric considerably while the thermally degraded fabric is even more discolored. In contrast, the sample hydrolyzed 16 hr in 40% H_2SO_4 is only slightly yellowed (reflectance 73%). The yellowing of the artificially aged fabrics does not interfere with the calculation of the

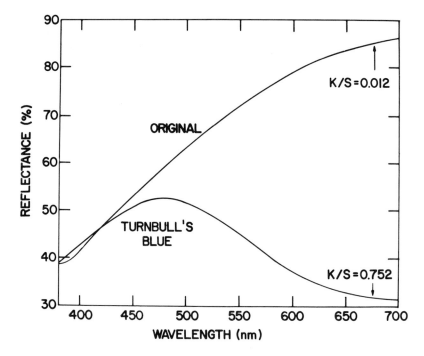

Figure 6. Reflectance as a function of wavelength of contemporary cotton print cloth degraded by a 100-Mrad dose of high-voltage electrons before and after Turnbull's Blue test for carboxyl groups

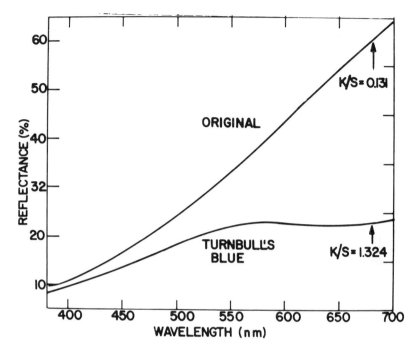

*Figure 7.   Reflectance as a function of wavelength of contemporary
cotton print cloth degraded by heating for 211 hr at 168°C before and
after Turnbull's Blue test for carboxyl group*

concentration of the blue pigment from the curves since the blue absorption occurs at 680 nm at the other extreme of the visible region.

The concentration of blue pigment calculated from the reflectance curve as a function of heating time is shown in Figure 8. The fact that this dependence is nearly linear suggests rather strongly that the method developed is quantitatively capable of measuring the concentration of carboxyl groups in the fabric. The relationship will have to be confirmed, of course, using an accepted analytical method for determining carboxyl groups before the validity of the reflectance method can be established. Shafizadeh (30) has measured the concentration of carbonyl and carboxyl groups in thermally degraded cottons, but his results cannot be directly compared with those reported here.

Thus far, this method can be applied only to fabrics since reflectance measurements cannot be made on small quantities of yarns and fibers. All the naturally degraded yarns and fibers gave a qualitatively positive response to Turnbull's Blue test, however. The ubiquitous presence of dirt in the archaeological samples will complicate the use of quantitative chemical tests for determining the state of oxidation.

Infrared analysis was also used to determine the state of oxidation of the samples. Unlike the reflectance method, this procedure applies also to yarns and fibers. Signs of oxidation were found in the architectural and pit 8 samples by the appearance of an absorption peak at 1724

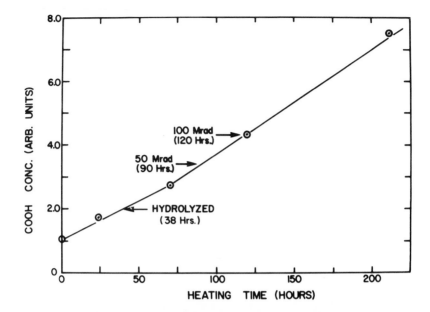

Figure 8.   Relative concentration of carboxyl groups measured by Turn-bull's Blue test in cotton print cloth degraded by heating at 168°C as a function of heating time. The concentrations of carboxyl groups in fabrics degraded by hydrolyzing 16 hr in 40% sulfuric acid at room temperature and by high-voltage electron irradiation at doses of 50 and 100 Mrad are also indicated.

cm^{-1}. An overriding H$_2$O peak centered at 1630 cm^{-1}, however, obscured the possible presence of carboxyl groups in the pit 9 sample.

Analysis of the modern degraded samples showed evidence of oxidation in both the thermally degraded samples and the 100-Mrad irradiated sample but not in the original or acid-hydrolyzed sample. Turnbull's Blue test of the hydrolyzed sample, however, did indicate a small degree

Table II.   Summary

Fiber	Tensile Strength	
	gf/den	% [a]
USDA calibration	1.80	92.8
From contemporary print cloth	2.08	107.2
A.D. 1200	2.11 [b]	108.8 [b]
1000 B.C.	0.048 [b]	2.5 [b]
Architectural	1.19	61.3
Pit 9	1.16	59.8
Pit 8	0.42	21.6

[a] Based on average of contemporary fibers as 100%.
[b] Yarn break at zero-gage length.

of oxidation. The infrared analysis considered together with the Turn-bull's Blue test indicate that a much greater degree of oxidation results from heat degradation and high-voltage electron irradiation than from acid hydrolysis. The relationship between the carboxyl concentration as measured by the reflectance test of the Turnbull's Blue fabric and the tensile strength retained by the artificially aged fabrics is shown in Figure 9. The results considered in this way suggest that all fabrics degraded to the same strength levels are not oxidized equally. Thus, at a given strength, electron irradiation results in greater oxidation, thermal, somewhat less, and hydrolysis, even less. As shown in Table II, the naturally aged samples also have different degrees of oxidation at given strength levels. For example, the A.D. 1200 sample having only 2.5% strength retention shows no sign of oxidation while the pit 8 sample with 22% strength retention has a carboxyl content somewhat greater than that of the fabric degraded by exposure to 100-Mrad electron irradi-ation (Tables I and II).

CRYSTALLINITY. The crystallinity index determined by infrared analysis suggests that while the naturally degraded samples are more crystalline than undegraded modern fabrics, their crystallinity is not nearly as high as any of the artificially degraded samples. Crystallinity increases during hydrolysis of cellulose (*31*) and may increase during heating and electron irradiation (*32*). Figure 10 shows the relationship between crystallinity index and strength retention. Most of the samples examined fall on a smooth curve except for the highly degraded A.D. 1200 fabric, which has a much lower crystallinity, and the hydrolyzed and 100-Mrad fabrics, which have higher crystallinities than the general curve. Thus, the evidence again suggests that not all aging mechanisms are alike and that several modes of degradation might be involved in natural aging.

FIBER FRACTOGRAPHY AND MORPHOLOGY. Fibers broken in tensile tests were examined in the scanning electron microscope to gain a better understanding of their failure mechanism. Such insight can be used to guide the development of consolidants that prevent such failures.

The length of the fracture surface or degree of taper of cotton fibers broken in tension is an index of their brittleness (*33*). For example, cotton fibers fractured in water or with standard moisture-regain produce

of Fiber Properties

DP		Infrared COOH Content (ΔOD)	Infrared Crystallinity Index
Yarn or Fabric	*Fiber*		
—	—	0.0	0.55
2606	—	0.0	0.55
184,192	—	0.0	0.64
685	—	0.130	0.62
120	23	[e]	0.60
226	37	0.073	0.71

[e] Overriding H_2O peak.

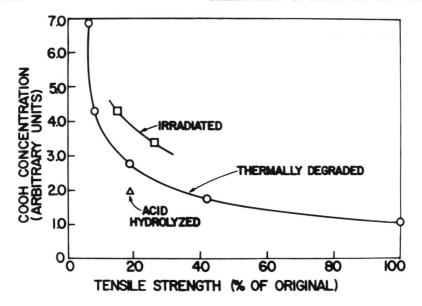

Figure 9. Relationship between relative concentrations of carboxyl groups as measured by Turnbull's Blue test and the tensile strength of degraded cotton print cloth

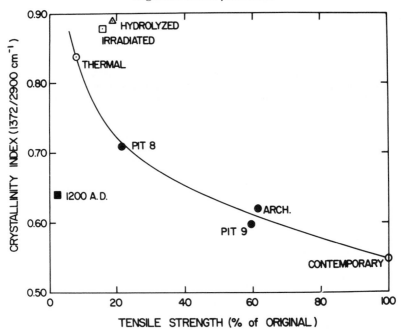

Figure 10. Relationship between crystallinity index and the tensile strength of degraded cotton print cloths and archaeological fibers

Figure 11. Fracture tip surface of a typical USDA calibration cotton fiber

long tapering breaks as shown in Figure 11 for a contemporary fiber. In contrast, dry fibers break over a shorter length with relatively blunt fracture extremities. Tensile breaks of brittle fibers such as those cross-linked with resins also occur over a very short length with blunt fracture tips. The fractured surface of a pit 8 fiber shown in Figure 12 has such a

Figure 12. Fracture tip surface of a typical Initial Period, ca. 1000 B.C., cotton fiber from test pit 8

Figure 13.   Fracture tip surface of a typical cotton fiber degraded by exposure to a 100-Mrad dose of high-voltage electrons

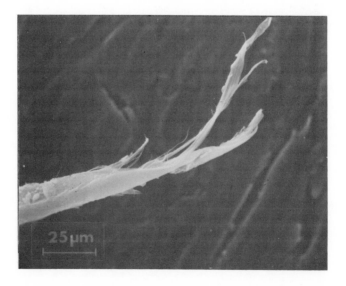

Figure 14.   Fracture tip surface of a typical Initial Period, ca. 1000 B.C., cotton fiber from an architectural site

Figure 15. Degraded surface of typical Peruvian cotton fibers, ca. A.D. 1200

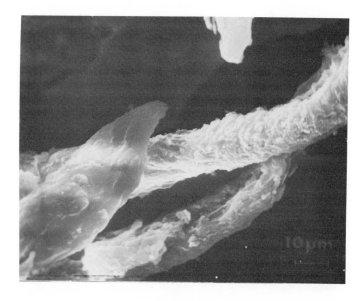

Figure 16. Degraded surface of typical cotton fiber from the Initial Period, ca. 1000 B.C., from test pit 8

characteristically brittle break. Artificially aged cotton also showed brittle fracture characteristics. The 100-Mrad irradiated fiber break shown in Figure 13 resembles the break of the test pit 8 fiber.

Age alone does not determine fracture morphology. The 1000 B.C. architectural fiber shown in Figure 14 has a fracture morphology similar to that of the undamaged contemporary fiber. Note that the architectural samples also performed well in other testing areas as shown in Table II.

All the fibers examined that were naturally degraded to a considerable extent (test pits 8 and 9 and the A.D. 1200 fragments) possess a granular surface as shown in Figures 15 and 16. The irradiated cottons examined show no signs of the granularity typical of some of the archaeological samples. The existence of this granular surface is not too surprising since the "dust" seen in containers of ancient fibers or fabrics undoubtedly results from the surface comminution and attrition of such fibers which have essentially no abrasion resistance. If lack of abrasion resistance must be considered as a second mode of failure in deteriorated textiles (taking tensile failure as the first), selection of an all-purpose consolidant will become even more difficult. It appears that as the molecular weight drastically decreases (as seen in Tables I and II), the microfibrils lose their integrity and the fiber fails by a brittle mechanism. A fundamental investigation into the degree and type of microfibrillar damage in these fibers should provide some insight into the exact nature of the failure. Such an investigation is underway.

Summary and Conclusions

Further characterization tests must be carried out on all these samples before an adequate understanding of their properties can be achieved. In particular, alternative methods of determining the degree of crystallinity and the extent of oxidation are needed even though an existing qualitative method for assessing the extent of oxidation of cellulose was used to obtain semiquantitative information. This method was based on measuring the reflectance of fabrics stained with a reagent that reacts with carboxyl groups. The use of solubility, moisture regain, and x-ray diffraction measurements will also provide much valuable information. A model system based on enzyme degradation and ultraviolet irradiation should also be considered.

As these results show, naturally degraded cellulose has not yet been fully characterized or duplicated. However, a sharp drop in DP and an accompanying strength loss are common to all the artificially and naturally degraded samples. Since it is the weakened condition of the textile that is being addressed in the consolidation study, any one of the model systems should serve as a useful substrate, at least in the initial studies, even if not all the properties of naturally degraded fabrics are matched.

As suggested in Figures 9 and 10 and Tables I and II, the DP, the degree of crystallinity, and the extent of oxidation as a function of strength loss can differ with different modes of degradation. Archaeological samples can also differ in these interrelationships. None of the aging techniques explored produced the severe granulation observed in some of the naturally degraded samples. Thus, much additional work remains before a start can be made in understanding the many aspects of natural degradation of cotton and how the process can be duplicated or mimicked to provide a more realistic substrate for evaluating consolidants.

Acknowledgments

The authors acknowledge the contributions of Kim Ellington and Donna McElwain who carried out many of these experiments and Ernest Fleming for providing the scanning electron photo-micrographs; all of these contributors are students of the School of Textiles at North Carolina State University. We also thank Joe Gratzl of the School of Forest Resources, North Carolina State University, for making the molecular weight measurements. We are especially grateful to Shelia Pozorski of the University of Texas' Department of Anthropology and to Nobuko Kajitani of the Metropolitan Museum of Art for providing the archaeological cotton samples.

Literature Cited

1. Leene, J. E., "Textile Conservation," Butterworths, London, 1972.
2. "The Conservation of Cultural Property," UNESCO, Paris, 1968.
3. Berger, G. A., "Testing Adhesives for the Consolidation of Paintings," *Stud. Conserv.* (1972) **17**, 173–194.
4. Fiske, P. L., "Archaeological Textiles," The Textile Museum, Washington, D. C., 1975.
5. Johnson, M., *AIC Prepr. 4th*, Dearborn, Mich., May, 1976, pp. 66–75.
6. Greathouse, G. A., Wessel, C. J., "Deterioration of Materials," Reinhold, New York, 1954.
7. Leene, J. E., Demeny, L., Elema, R. J., de Graaf, A. J., Surtel, J. J., "Artificial Ageing of Yarns in Presence as Well as in Absence of Light and under Different Atmospheric Conditions," *ICOM*, 4th Triannual Meeting, Venice, 1975.
8. "1975 Annual Book of ASTM Standards, Part 32," American Society for Testing and Materials, Philadelphia, Pa., 1975.
9. Grover, E. B., Hamby, D. S., "Handbook of Textile Testing and Quality Control," Interscience, New York, 1960.
10. Sundaram, W., Iyengar, R. L. N., "Handbook of Methods of Tests for Cotton Fibers, Yarns and Fabrics," Examiner Press, Bombay, 1968.
11. Judd, D. B., Wyszecki, G., "Color in Business, Science and Industry," Wiley, New York, 1975
12. O'Connor, R. T., DuPré, E. F., McCall, E. R., "Infrared Spectrophotometric Procedure for Analysis of Cellulose and Modified Cellulose," *Anal. Chem.* (1957) **29**, 7, 998–1005.

13. O'Connor, R. T., "Analytical Methods for a Textile Laboratory," J. W. Weaver, Ed., pp. 295–381, AATCC Monograph No. 3, 1968.
14. O'Connor, R. T., "Instrumental Analysis of Cotton Cellulose and Modified Cotton Cellulose," Dekker, New York, 1972.
15. Nelson, M. L., O'Connor, R. T., "Relation of Certain Infrared Bands to Cellulose Crystallinity and Crystal Lattice Type, Part II," J. Appl. Polym. Sci. (1964) 8, 1325–1341.
16. Brown, W., Wikstrom, R., "A Viscosity–Molecular Weight Relationship for Cellulose in Cadoxen and a Hydrodynamic Interpretation," Eur. Polym. J. (1965) 1, 1–10.
17. Charlesby, A., "Atomic Radiation and Polymers," Pergamon, New York, 1960.
18. Rutherford, H.A., "Radiation Effects on Organic Materials," R. O. Bolt, J. G. Carroll, Eds., pp. 431–437, Academic, New York, 1963.
19. Reich, L., Stivala, S. S., "Elements of Polymer Degradation," McGraw-Hill, New York, 1971.
20. Reese, E. T., "Advances in Enzymic Hydrolysis of Cellulose and Related Materials," Pergamon, New York, 1963.
21. Scallon, A. M., "A Quantitative Picture of the Fringed Micellar Model of Cellulose," Text. Res. J. (1971) 41, 647–653.
22. Nevell, T. P., "Recent Advances in the Chemistry of Cellulose and Starch," J. Honeyman, Ed., pp. 75–105, Interscience, New York, 1959.
23. Heuser, E., "The Chemistry of Cellulose," Wiley, New York, 1944.
24. Madorsky, S. L., "Thermal Degradation of Organic Polymers," Interscience, New York, 1964.
25. Kulshreshtha, A. K., Dweltz, N. E., "Modification of Cellulose and Other Polysaccharides," P. C. Mehta, H. C. Srivastava, N. E. Dweltz, S. N. Harshe, G. L. Madan, A. K. Kulshreshtha, H. U. Mehta, Eds., ATIRA, Ahmédabad, India, 1974.
26. Teszler, O., Kiser, L. Y., Campbell, P. W., Rutherford, H. A., "The Effect of Nuclear Radiation on Fibrous Materials, Part III," Text. Res. J. (1958) 28, 456–462.
27. Gilfillan, E. S., Linden, L., "Effects of Nuclear Radiation on the Strength of Yarns," Text. Res. J. (1955) 25, 773–777.
28. Gilfillan, E. S., Linden, L., "Some Effects of Nuclear Irradiation on Cotton Yarn," Text. Res. J. (1957) 27, 87–92.
29. Battista, O. A., Coppick, S., Housman, S. A., Morehead, F. F., Sisson, W. A., "Level-off Degree of Polymerization," Ind. Eng. Chem. (1956) 48, 333–335.
30. Shafizadeh, F., "Advances in Carbohydrate Chemistry and Biochemistry, Vol. 23," M. L. Wolfrom, R. S. Typson, Eds., pp. 419–474, Academic, New York, 1968.
31. Mann, J., "Methods in Carbohydrate Chemistry, Vol. III," pp. 114–119, Roy L. Whistler, Ed., Academic, New York, 1963.
32. Ranby, B., Rabek, J. F., "Photodegradation, Photo-oxidation and Photostabilization of Polymers," Wiley, London, 1975.
33. Hearle, J., Sparrow, J., "The Fractography of Cotton Fibers," Text. Res. J. (1971) 41, 736–749.

RECEIVED February 21, 1977.

Addendum

The values of infrared crystallinity reported in Tables I and II and Figure 10 are being reevaluated because of contamination. Corrected values will be reported later.

Reinforcing Degraded Textiles

Part II: Properties of Resin-Treated, Artificially Aged Cotton Textiles

G. M. BERRY, S. P. HERSH, P. A. TUCKER, and W. K. WALSH

School of Textiles, North Carolina State University, Raleigh, N.C. 27607

Various polymeric materials and grafting monomers were applied to artificially aged cotton fabrics to evaluate their potential as consolidants and reinforcing agents for protecting fragile textiles. The resins tested included finishes currently used by the textile industry as well as materials found in art conservation laboratories. Since the ideal conservation treatment should increase the strength and flexibility of the object without altering its appearance or hand, these criteria were the main ones considered in judging the value of the treatment. Of the 23 applications examined, the best enhanced the tearing strength of the model aged fabric by approximately 50% while maintaining tensile strength and flexibility. The long-term stability and ultimate consequences of the treatment must be determined, however, before these treatments can be recommended as satisfactory for application on valuable artifacts.

Part I of this series of papers (*1*) described attempts to prepare artificially degraded cotton fabrics which would serve as suitable substrates for evaluating materials intended for use in the textile conservation workshop. While no one system completely reproduced the characteristics of naturally degraded samples, fabrics aged by irradiation were judged adequate for the consolidation study.

This chapter describes the applications of a series of resins and monomers to the artificially degraded substrate and the effectiveness of the treatments as fabric consolidants. To be considered as useful, a treatment must enhance the strength and flexibility of the substrate without altering its appearance or hand. Aesthetic and historic considerations alike demand that the two factors—unchanged appearance and hand—be as closely met as possible.

Once these conditions are met, further testing is needed to determine the long-term effects of the treatment. Short-term improvements are not acceptable at the cost of accelerated degradation later. Thus, any material that satisfies the initial criteria must receive more stringent evaluation before it can be recommended for use in the conservation laboratory.

Experimental

In evaluating materials as consolidants, several classes of resins were examined. In all cases, an attempt was made to apply 5% of the material to each of three fabrics. These fabrics were the scoured, undegraded print cloth plus this fabric degraded by exposure to 50 Mrad and 100 Mrad of high-voltage electrons as described in Part I of this series (*1*). These degraded model fabrics were selected because their properties adequately mimicked the archaeological samples and because they could be prepared easily in large reproducible quantities.

The general method of resin application was to immerse the sample in an aqueous solution of the resin in a laboratory padder, pass it through squeeze rolls to give approximately 100% wet pickup, and then air dry. About 0.05% Triton X-100 was added to each water bath as a wetting agent. The bath also contained the required catalysts and polyethylene softeners when desired. Any variations in application procedures are cited when describing the individual treatments. Note that the padding method of applying the resins cannot be readily transferred to the conservation workshop. Once promising materials have been identified, however, it should be possible to develop suitable application methods.

The tensile and tear strengths of the fabrics were measured using the tests procedures described in Part I (*1*). Fabric flexural rigidity was measured using the cantilever test (ASTM test method D1388-64, Option A) (*2*). Normally, four replicates were measured on each test fabric. Only measurements made in the filling direction are reported. The materials applied can be grouped into four categories: I: acrylic latex emulsions; II: grafting monomers; III: fiber cross-linking resins; and IV: miscellaneous materials.

Series I: Acrylic Latex Emulsions. A series of four acrylic latex emulsions varying in glass transition temperature (T_g) (*3*) were applied first. T_g is the temperature at which the resin changes from a relatively flexible to a relatively stiff material. The acrylic latexes are made from water-insoluble monomers such as acrylates and alkyl acrylates polymerized in emulsion form to produce an aqueous dispersion or latex of the polymer. Upon drying, the emulsion is irreversibly broken so that the applied material becomes wash-fast. The application requires no catalyst or high temperature heating.

These resins were padded from 5% solutions and then oven dried at 105°–106°C for 20 min. The four acrylic latexes used were obtained from the Rohm and Haas Co. and are identified by the codes in Table I.

**Table I. Coded Acrylic Latexes and Glass
Transition Temperatures**

Code	Material	T_g
A-1	Acrylic latex Rhoplex K-3	−32°C
A-2	Acrylic latex Rhoplex Ha-8	−14°C
A-3	Acrylic latex Rhoplex Ha-12	17°C
A-4	Acrylic latex Rhoplex Ha-16	33°C

Rhoplex K-3 was also applied in combination with 1.2% polyethylene (Moropol 700, supplied by Mortex Chemical Products), a material that lubricates the surfaces of the yarns, gives the fabric more flexibility, and increases the tearing strength of resin-treated wash and wear fabrics (4). A second sample of Rhoplex K-3 with 1.2% polyethylene added was air dried instead of oven dried to assess the influence of different drying methods.

The results of this set of experiments are summarized in Table II and illustrated in Figures 1–6. As indicated in Figure 1, the 50-Mrad degraded but untreated fabric has 26.6% tensile strength retention. Application of the resins A-1, A-2, A-3, and A-4 increases the tensile strength. When applied to fabric degraded with 100 Mrad of irradiation, only latex A-4 increased the strength as illustrated in Figure 3. The

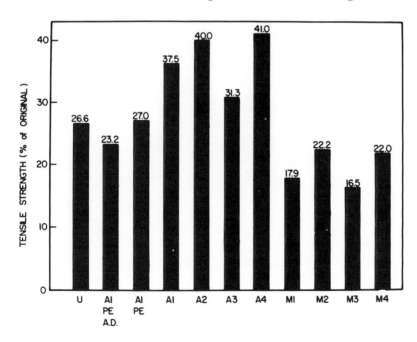

Figure 1.   The tensile strength of degraded cotton print cloth (50-Mrad dose) after application of various acrylic resins (A1–A4) and grafted monomers (M1–M4); U = untreated fabric, PE = polyethylene, AD = air dried. See text for identification of resins and monomers.

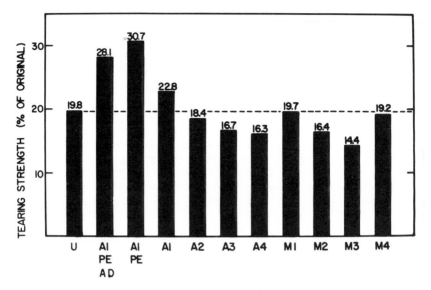

Figure 2. The tearing strength of degraded cotton print cloth (50-Mrad dose) after application of various acrylic resins (A1–A4) and grafted mono-mers (M1–M4); U = untreated fabric, PE = polyethylene, AD = air dried. See text for identification of resins and monomers.

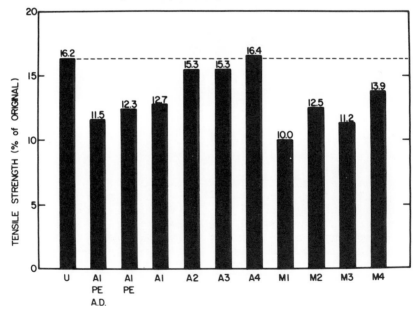

Figure 3. The tensile strength of degraded cotton print cloth (100-Mrad dose) after application of various acrylic resins (A1–A4) and grafted mono-mers (M1–M4); U = untreated fabric, PE = polyethylene, AD = air dried. See text for identification of resins and monomers.

only improvement in tearing strength obtained by applying an acrylic latex alone was with Rhoplex K-3 (A-1) on the 50-Mrad-irradiated fabric (Figure 2). When applied in combination with 1.2% polyethylene, however, this latex increased the tearing strengths of both degraded fabrics. The Rhoplex K-3/polyethylene mixture when oven dried gave the greatest improvement in tear strength. This treatment increases the tearing strength of the fabric degraded by 50 Mrad of irradiation from 19.8% of that of the undegraded fabric to 30.7%, an increase in strength of 55%. For the fabric degraded by 100 Mrad, the change is from 9.3% to 14.2%, an increase of 53% (Figure 4).

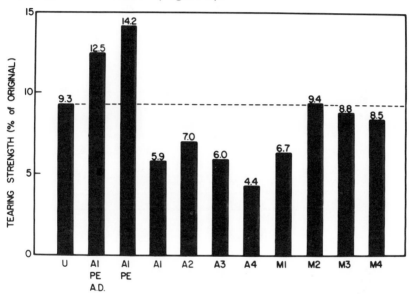

Figure 4. The tearing strength of degraded cotton print cloth (100-Mrad dose) after application of various acrylic resins (A1–A4) and grafted monomers (M1–M4); U = untreated fabric, PE = polyethylene, AD = air dried. See text for identification of resins and monomers.

The flexural rigidity of the treated fabrics is shown in Figures 5 and 6. Since T_g increases from A-1 to A-4, it is evident that the fabric stiffness increases dramatically as the T_g of the acrylic latex increases. A similar examination of Figures 1–4 indicates that the tensile strength also increases with increasing T_g but that the tearing strength decreases. All these T_g trends are expected since the higher the T_g, the stiffer the fabric should be. In fabric tearing, stiff fabrics would lead to lower strengths since the yarns would not have the flexibility and mobility required to respond to the applied stresses. Siakolah (5) also found that these mechanical properties depended on the T_g of applied acrylic resins.

Series II: Grafting Monomers. The second series of experiments involved padding the fabric with various monomers, followed by polymerization of the monomer inside the fabric to create a graft copolymer that might partially cross-link the fiber (6). It was hoped that cross-

Table II. Physical Properties of Chemically Treated

		Add-On	
		50 Mrad	100 Mrad
Code	Treatment	(%)	(%)
	Original	—	—
	Irradiated	—	—
A-1	K-3	4.0	1.8
A-1	K-3 with 1.2% PE[a]	5.9	4.7
A-1	K-3 with 1.2% PE, air dried	6.6	6.0
A-2	Ha-8	2.8	2.0
A-3	Ha-12	5.9	3.8
A-4	Ha-16	3.4	1.0
M-1	Acrylamide	5.4	0.8
M-2	N-Methylol acrylamide	9.8	4.2
M-3	Carbowax acrylate	5.2	0.9
M-4	50% Acrylamide/50%		
	Carbowax acrylate	3.9	0.9
C-1	Formaldehyde	3.4	5.8
C-2	Formaldehyde with 1.7% PE	3.1	4.4
C-3	Rhonite R-2 with 0.9% PE	5.6	3.2
C-4	Rhonite R-2 with 2.6% PE	6.4	3.7
C-5	Aerotex 23	8.3	5.7
C-6	Aerotex 23 with 2.9% PE	7.1	4.8
1	Moropol 700	4.8	4.1
2	Mowolith DCM 2	5.3	4.9
3	Alfabond M4	6.9	6.9
4	Butvar B-73	7.1	10.5
5	Gum arabic	6.5	5.6
6	Elvanol T-25	6.5	6.3
7	Carboxymethylcellulose	7.5	7.3
Usual no. of samples averaged		5	5
Pooled standard deviation		—	—
Pooled coefficient of variation (%)		—	—

[a] Polyethylene.

linking the grafted copolymer inside the fiber structure would increase the fabric strength. The padding solutions contained 20% monomer, 0.5% $K_2S_2O_8$ catalyst on the weight of monomer, and 0.5% Triton X-100. The fabrics were padded with this solution, air dried, cured in an oven at 120°C for 2 min, thoroughly rinsed, and air dried. Control grafting experiments using only a water bath resulted in weight losses of 1.2% and 2.8% on the 50-Mrad- and 100-Mrad-irradiated fabrics, respectively. Such weight losses are expected since Teszler and Hefti have previously reported that radiation degradation partially solubilizes cellulose (7). The add-ons reported in Table II for any fabrics washed after treatment were adjusted for these weight losses. The four monomer applications and their identifying codes are shown in Table III.

Cotton Print Cloth Degraded by Electron Irradiation

Tensile Strength		Tearing Strength		Flexural Rigidity/Unit Width	
50 Mrad (%)	*100 Mrad (%)*	*50 Mrad (%)*	*100 Mrad (%)*	*50 Mrad (mg-cm)*	*100 Mrad (mg-cm)*
100	100	100	100	36.7	36.7
26.6	16.2	19.8	9.3	30.3	31.8
37.5	12.7	22.8	5.9	9.3	24.3
27.0	12.3	30.7	14.5	55.8	36.7
23.2	11.5	28.1	12.5	35.9	36.8
40.0	15.3	18.4	7.0	50.0	36.1
31.3	15.3	16.7	6.0	111.3	69.6
41.0	16.4	16.3	4.4	404.7	310.3
17.9	10.0	19.7	6.7	35.5	30.3
22.2	12.5	16.4	9.4	35.4	39.4
16.5	11.2	14.4	8.8	37.9	27.0
22.0	13.9	19.2	8.5	33.1	26.8
21.5	23.5	17.7	10.4	21.5	23.5
23.3	27.3	24.8	12.5	23.3	27.3
20.5	12.5	22.2	14.1	25.5	27.9
19.3	12.9	27.6	13.4	28.2	26.2
23.7	12.9	22.3	10.8	50.7	44.4
20.5	12.7	25.0	12.4	24.3	24.4
29.4	15.2	23.0	10.5	63.1	54.3
30.2	13.4	19.8	11.3	87.8	90.9
36.6	20.9	16.7	6.6	391	320
33.2	17.1	18.3	7.0	555	434
32.9	12.4	21.9	8.2	396	386
31.0	18.7	16.8	6.2	831	661
33.1	17.9	18.5	7.0	1030	659
5	5	5	5	4	4
2.0	1.27	0.24	0.09	—	—
—	—	—	—	13.7	23.9

Table III.   Monomer Codes and Sources

Code	Material	Source
M-1	Acrylamide	Specification No. F1534 (American Cyanamid Co.)
M-2	*N*-Methylol acrylamide	(American Cyanamid Co.)
M-3	Carbowax acrylate	MPEG-550 acrylate (Union Carbide Corp.)
M-4	50% Acrylamide/50% Carbowax acrylate	

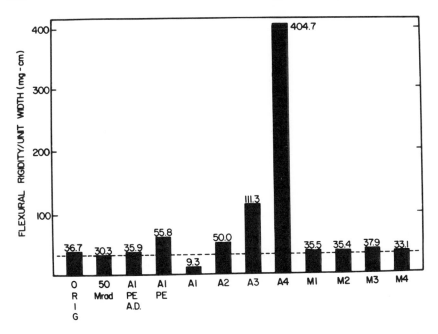

Figure 5. The flexural rigidity of degraded cotton print cloth (50-Mrad dose) after application of various acrylic resins (A1–A4) and grafted monomers (M1–M4); PE = polyethylene, AD = air dried. See text for identification of resins and monomers.

The results of the monomer applications are given in Table II and Figures 1–6. None of these treatments shows much promise since all tensile and tear strengths are below that of the untreated degraded fabrics. No significant change in fabric stiffness occurs.

Series III: Cross-Linking Resins. The third series of experiments attempted to create cross-links within the cellulose chains using resins traditionally used to impart crease-resistant properties to cotton and rayon fabrics (4, 8). Fabrics treated with the materials in Table IV were prepared.

The formaldehyde was first padded from a 5N HCL aqueous solution containing 18% HCHO. The padded fabrics were then reimmersed in the pad bath for 1 hr. The samples were next rinsed and soaked in water adjusted to a pH of 8.0 with NaHCO₃. After 3 hr, the samples were rinsed and air dried. The Aerotex resin 23 Special was applied from a 5% solution with 2% accelerator (Aerotex accelerator MX, American Cyanamid Co.) and 0.15% buffer (Aerotex buffer DCY, American Cyanamid Co.). The Rhonite R-2 samples were applied from a 5% solution with 0.1% catalyst (catalyst H-7, Rohm and Haas Co.). Aerotex 23 and Rhonite R-2 were applied by padding, followed by air drying and curing at 160°C for 3 min. The fabrics were then thoroughly rinsed and air dried.

The results of these six experiments, reported in Table II, show that all tensile strengths are decreased and that there is little change in fabric stiffness. The tearing strength increases slightly in all cases (except for

Table IV. Cross-Linking Resin Codes and Sources

Code	Material	Source
C-1	Formaldehyde	Fisher Scientific Co.
C-2	Formaldehyde plus 1.7% polyethylene	Moropol 700 (Moretex Chemical Products)
C-3	Partially polymerized urea formaldehyde plus 0.9% polyethylene	Rhonite R-2 (Rohm and Haas Co.); Mykon SF (Sun Chemical Corp.)
C-4	Partially polymerized urea formaldehyde plus 2.6% polyethylene	Rhonite R-2 plus 0.9% Mykon SF and 1.7% Moropol 700
C-5	Triazine–formaldehyde condensate	Aerotex resin 23 Special (American Cyanamid Co.)
C-6	Triazine–formaldehyde condensate plus 2.9% polyethylene	Aerotex resin 23 Special; Moropol 700

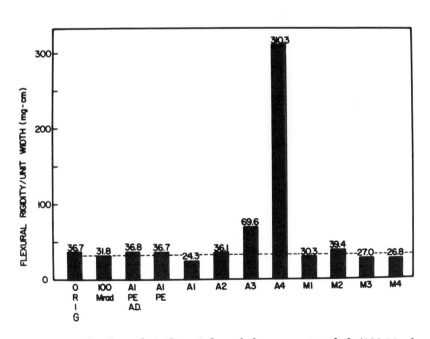

Figure 6. The flexural rigidity of degraded cotton print cloth (100-Mrad dose) after application of various acrylic resins (A1–A4) and grafted monomers (M1–M4); PE = polyethylene, AD = air dried. See text for identification of resins and monomers.

the formaldehyde treatment on the 50-Mrad-irradiated fabric). The increase in tearing strength observed is not so great as that reported for Rhoplex K-3 applied in combination with the polyethylene softener.

Series IV: Miscellaneous Materials. Various textile finishes were applied in this group of experiments. Many had been mentioned in the conservation literature as possible textile conservation aids (9, 10). These resins were padded from 5% aqueous solutions with the exception of Butvar, which was dissolved in 2-propanol. All samples were air dried (Table V).

Table V.   Textile Finishes with Codes and Sources

Code	Material	Source
1	Polyethylene	Moropol 700
2	Poly(vinyl acetate–vinyl dibutyl maleate) copolymer	Mowolith DCM 2 (Alfa Products, Ventron Corp.)
3	Poly(vinyl acetate) copolymer emulsion	Alfabond-M4 (Alfa Products, Ventron Corp.)
4	Poly(vinyl butryal)	Butvar B-73 (Monsanto Co.)
5	Gum arabic	Gum arabic U. S. P. (Cardinal Products)
6	Poly(vinyl alcohol)	Elvanol grade T-25 (E. I. Du Pont de Nemours & Co.)
7	Carboxymethylcellulose	CMC warp size (Hercules)

As shown in Table II, the finishes applied in this group produced only small increases or decreases in tensile and tear strengths. None of the increases, however, is as large as those noted for Rhoplex K-3 with polyethylene. Dramatic increases are observed in flexural rigidity, however, ranging from 71% to 3300%. The average increase is 1300%! Two highly recommended and much used consolidants, poly(vinyl alcohol) and poly(vinyl butyral), gave the stiffest fabrics produced (except for the carboxymethylcellulose sample on the 50-Mrad-irradiated fabric which was slightly higher). If fabric flexibility is a major requirement of a satisfactory consolidant, these two materials are not suitable candidates.

Summary and Conclusions

Additional research on textile aging and degradation and on the development of chemical systems for the preservation of such degraded textiles is required before an adequate understanding of the system is attained. Hence, the major findings and conclusions summarized below are speculative and require further confirmation.

1. The mechanical, physical, and chemical properties of degraded ancient cotton textiles were partially characterized in Part I (1). An

understanding of the nature and mechanisms of natural degradation is necessary to guide the intelligent development of conservation techniques and the preparation of artificially aged, model textiles.

2. Although some progress has been made in developing model degraded fabrics to serve as substrates for evaluating conservation treatments, the fabrics prepared thus far have not completely mimicked the degraded ancient cottons. Indeed, the prior results indicate that several modes of natural degradation might occur (*1*). For example, some of the naturally degraded cottons have low molecular weights but high crystallinities; some are not oxidized very much but are very weak. Thus, there may not be a single, unique degraded historic cotton that must be examined but several, depending on the exact mode or modes of degradation which have occurred.

3. Some modern resins have enhanced the tearing strength of artificially degraded fabrics by approximately 50% while at the same time maintaining flexibility.

4. The glass transition temperature (T_g) of a series of acrylic resins applied as consolidants to degraded fabrics had a significant effect on the resulting strength and bending stiffness. Tensile strength increased slightly, flexural rigidity increased dramatically, and tearing strength decreased moderately as the T_g increased. Thus, the most desirable combination of properties is obtained with resins having the lowest T_g.

Some suggestions for additional work in the model aging study were made in Part I (*1*). In the search for a better textile consolidant, the following areas still need to be examined:

• Screening of resins should continue in the search for the most suitable ones for consolidation of textiles.

• Once promising resins have been identified, application procedures must be optimized. Such factors as add-on, composition of any mixtures method of application, drying and curing procedure, and the placement of the resin on the appropriate sites in the object must be arranged to give the best possible combination of textile properties.

• Extensive literature exists on the application of resins to cellulosic fabrics to impart wash and wear or permanent press properties. Treatments of this type seriously degrade the tensile and tear strengths of the fabrics, and much effort has been devoted to improving the resiliency characteristics of the fabrics while at the same time minimizing strength losses. Some of the procedures developed might also prove beneficial for consolidation. Therefore, techniques which control the location of resins in the fiber or migration of resin in the fabric should be examined. These include such methods as vapor deposition of monomer; application of resins to swollen fabrics; application of resins to mercerized fabrics, either slack, or tensioned, or slack and restretched; radiation grafting of monomers; curing by fixation-cure processes using core cross-linking methods; and microwave drying (*11*).

• Before any procedures developed can receive an unqualified recommendation, the long-term stability and consequences of the treatment must be examined and considered.

Acknowledgments

The authors wish to thank Kim Ellington who carried out many of the experiments reported. We also wish to acknowledge the advice, many valuable suggestions, and encouragement offered by Nobuko Kajitani of the Metropolitan Museum of Art.

Literature Cited

1. Berry, G. M., Hersh, S. P., Tucker, P. A., Walsh, W. K., *Adv. Chem.* (1977) **164**, 228.
2. "1975 Annual Book of ASTM Standards, Part 32," American Society for Testing and Materials, Philadelphia, Pa., 1975.
3. Horn, M. B., "Acrylic Resins," Reinhold, New York, 1960.
4. Lynn, J. E., Press, J. J., "Advances in Textile Processing," Vol. I, Textile Book Publishers, New York, 1961.
5. Siahkolah, M. A., "The Effect of Glass Transition Temperature of Polymeric Additives on the Physical Properties of Cotton Fabrics," M.S. thesis, North Carolina State University, Raleigh, 1968.
6. Mehta, P. C., "Modifications of Cellulose and Other Polysaccharides," P. C. Mehta, H. C. Srivastava, N. E. Dweltz, S. N. Harshe, G. L. Madan, A. K. Kulshreshtha, H. U. Mehta, Eds., ATIRA, Ahmedabad, India, 1974.
7. Teszler, O., Hefti, H., "A Method for the Determination of Cotton Degradation after Radioactive Irradiation," *Text. Rundsch.* (1958) **13**, 61–66.
8. Marsh, J. T., "An Introduction to Textile Finishing," Chapman and Hall, London, 1966.
9. Leene, J. E., "Textile Conservation," Butterworths, London, 1972.
10. "The Conservation of Cultural Property," UNESCO, Paris, 1968.
11. Rowland, S. P., Nelson, M. L., Welch, C. M., Hebert, J. J., "Cotton Fiber Morphology and Textile Performance Properties," *Text. Res. J.* (1976) **46**, 194–214.

RECEIVED February 21, 1977.

Chemical Investigations on Pre-Columbian Archaeological Textile Specimens

N. S. BAER

Conservation Center, Institute of Fine Arts, New York University,
1 East 78th St., New York, N.Y. 10021

M. DELACORTE

The American Museum of Natural History, New York, N.Y. 10024

N. INDICTOR

Chemistry Department, Brooklyn College, City University of New York,
Brooklyn, N.Y. 11210

Nineteen archaeological pre-Columbian textile specimens from the collections of the American Museum of Natural History and the Metropolitan Museum of Art were examined. The textiles (Huari/Tiahuanaco, Ica, Paracas-Cavernas, and Paracas-Necropolis) are described. Elemental analyses for archaeological textile and modern wool samples (C, H, N, S, and ash) are reported. Elemental analyses for samples treated with distilled H_2O and CCl_4 are compared with analyses of modern wool samples similarly treated. An unambiguous direct correlation between loss of sulfur and embrittlement could not be made. The possibilities of dating and provenance determination by technical means are discussed.

Archaeological excavations at pre-Columbian sites have yielded especially rich collections of textile artifacts. These materials often reveal information of considerable anthropological and art historical significance. The difficulties of restoration, maintenance, and exhibition for archaeological textiles are well known to conservators and art historians (1). These materials are frequently recovered in a severe state of deterioration ranging from dangerous embrittlement to extreme friability. The

Table I.   Locations of Archaeological Sites and Period
Attributions of Specimens Examined

Culture or Site	Period of Specimen	Description
Huari/Tiahuanaco	8th–11th century A.D.	Bolivia
Ica		Peru, south coast
Paracas-Cavernas	Somewhat before 2nd–3rd century B.C.	Peru
Paracas-Necropolis	2nd–3rd century B.C.	Peru

many pathways to the deterioration of textiles make the condition of a textile an unreliable indicator of age. Deterioration can arise from thermal, light, chemical, mechanical, or biological sources and may affect the proteinaceous substrate as well as the naturally associated oleagenous materials (2). Prolonged exposure to heat or light generally lowers the molecular weight, reduces sulfur content, and causes marked alteration in physical properties. Textiles are also constantly subject to hydrolytic and oxidative deterioration (3, 4). Handling, storage, washing, cleaning, colorants, light, moisture, insects, fungi, and general environmental conditions can all play a part in the breakdown of the artifact.

Radiocarbon analysis is possible for dating ancient textiles only where sufficient sample is available. Unfortunately, the uncertainty in dating becomes unacceptably large with small sample size, contamination, and specimens of lesser antiquity (5). Chemical methods of dating are mainly limited to the observation that reducing the sulfur content of wool textiles appears to coincide, in some cases, with embrittlement and/or age (6). The presence of certain kinds of dyes and the manner in which they fade are sometimes used as the evidence of provenance (7).

The moderate success achieved in describing some Ancient Near Eastern ivories by examining their elemental analyses and observing a characteristically diminishing proteinaceous content (8) has suggested the examination of archaeological wool textiles in a similar manner. In the present study, elemental analyses and ash content are reported for 19 pre-Columbian textile specimens. The sites at which the textiles were excavated are given in Table I, and the individual specimens examined, including collection and accession number where available, are described in Table II. The results of the analyses for the archaeological specimens are compared with those of modern wool specimens.

Experimental

Specimen Selection. Specimens supplied by the American Museum of Natural History and the Metropolitan Museum of Art were chosen for well documented archaeological excavations. Most of the specimens

Table II.   Descriptions and Designations of Textile Specimens

Specimen	Description	Source
T-1976-01	Vermont sheep wool. Sheared and hand spun in 1975 by Shelburne Spinners, Vermont. Supplied by M. Ballard (MB-1), Institute of Fine Arts.	—
T-1976-08	Mexican sheep wool. Spun 1973. Supplied by N. Kajitani, Metropolitan Museum of Art.	—
T-1975-01	Single twisted red-brown strand. Mummy bundle B. J. Tello find. Paracas.	AMNH [a]
T-1975-02	Single twisted black strand. Mummy bundle B.	AMNH
T-1975-03	Single twisted dark green strand. #41.0/1543. Paracas.	AMNH
T-1975-04	Single twisted red strand. Paracas.	AMNH
T-1975-05	Single twisted red strand. Mummy bundle B. Shirt Epaulet. J. Tello find (1929). Paracas Necropolis.	AMNH
T-1975-06	Single twisted red-brown strand. Mummy bundle B. J. Tello find. Paracas.	AMNH
T-1975-07	Single twisted ochre strand. #41.0/1543. Paracas.	AMNH
T-1975-08	Single twisted black strand. Mummy bundle B. Shirt Epaulet. J. Tello find. Paracas Necropolis.	AMNH
T-1975-09	Two twisted light yellow-ochre strands. Department of Ica. Myron I. Granger expedition, Roland L. Olsen, Collector (1930–1934). #41.0/5296–5699.	AMNH
T-1975-10	Two twisted ochre strands. Supplied by J. B. Bird (JB-1B). #41.2/954.	AMNH
T-1975-11	Single twisted ochre strand. Fringe from mantle. Paracas Necropolis. ca 300–200 B.C. [c]	MMA [b]
T-1975-12	Single twisted red strand. Fringe from mantle. Paracas Necropolis. ca 300–200 B.C. [c]	MMA
T-1975-16	Padding from inside trophy head. Associated with pottery, gold, and textiles. Supplied by J. B. Bird (JB-8). #41.2/6039b. Paracas Cavernas. [d]	AMNH
T-1975-17	S-twisted strands of red, brown, and shades of gold. Interlocking tapestry weave. Supplied by J. B. Bird (JB-6). #41.0/5426. Tiahuanacan? Valley of Nasca.	AMNH

Table II. Continued

Specimen	Description	Source
T-1975-18	Strands (Z-twist) and cotton padding from false head from mummy. Supplied by J. B. Bird (JB-7). #41.0/5525. Paracas.	AMNH
T-1975-19	Single S-twisted stand. Cloth from outside trophy head. Supplied by J. B. Bird (JB-9). #41.2/6051.[d]	AMNH
T-1975-20	Three light brown strands woven with black strands. Light brown appear to be S-twist warp, and black appear to be weft. Also black dyed border. Supplied by J. B. Bird (JB-5). #41.0/5425. Tiahuanacan, Valley of Nasca.	AMNH
T-1975-21	Single S-twisted strand. Central seam area. Supplied by J. B. Bird (JB-2). #41.2/780. Coast Tiahauanacan.	AMNH
T-1975-23	S-twisted white warp and slight Z-twisted gold weft. Cotton warp, wool weft. Supplied by J. B. Bird (JB-1). #41.2/954. Tihuanacan.	AMNH

[a] AMNH denotes the American Museum of Natural History.
[b] MMA denotes the Metropolitan Museum of Art.
[c] Single strands taken from the same mantle.
[d] Samples from same trophy head.

Figure 1.   Vermont sheep wool sheared and hand spun in 1975 by Shelburne Spinners, Vermont. Specimen No. T-1976-01.

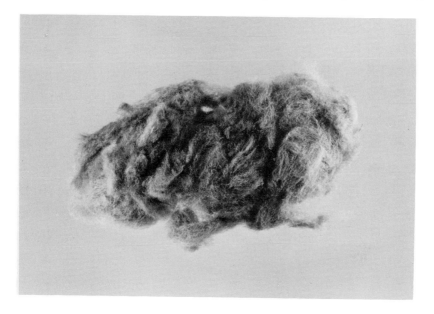

Figure 2.   Cotton padding from inside trophy head.   Paracas-Cavernas, Peru, ca. 2nd–3rd century B.C. *Specimen No. T-1975-16.*

were colored wool though several of them were cotton or mixed warp and weft (*see* Table II). Figures 1–4 illustrate typical specimens.

Analyses. Analyses of ash, carbon, and hydrogen by combustion; nitrogen by Dumas and micro-Kjeldahl methods; and sulfur by EDTA colorimetry were obtained from Schwarzkopf Microanalytical Laboratory, Woodside, N.Y. 11377.

Analytical Errors. Errors associated with these data arise from uncertainties in the analytical methods and from impurities introduced into or present in the textile. These added materials include inorganic salts from groundwaters, dye materials, and organic materials introduced in the conservation laboratory to soften friable artifacts (9).

The uncertainties for the analytical methods are as follows: ash by combustion residue, ±0.3% absolute; C, ±0.05 mg C; H, ±0.3% absolute; and N, by Dumas, ±μL or by micro-Kjeldahl, ±μg (10). In general, sample sizes were: C, H, and ash, 4–8 mg; N, 5–9 mg; and S, 7–14 mg. The large uncertainties in the measurements of carbon and hydrogen limit the usefulness of data for these elements for very small samples. Methods for lubricating brittle textiles artifacts (9) lead to high carbon and high hydrogen values generally. The treatment history of the specimens examined suggests that they were stored without further conservation.

Washing. Weighed samples of textile were immersed in 25–50 mL of distilled water or reagent grade CCl_4 in a stoppered iodine flask at ambient temperature without agitation. After 24 hr, the samples were removed from the wash liquid and dried to constant weight in a constant temperature humidity room (23°C; 50% r.h.). Dyed samples washed in

Figure 3. Twisted red-brown wool strand from mummy bundle, Paracas,
Peru, ca. 2nd–3rd century B.C. Specimen No. T-1975-01.

Figure 4. Three light brown strands woven with black strands. Huari/
Tiahuanaco, Valley of Nasca, Bolivia. 8th–11th century A.D. Specimen No.
T-1975-20.

water lost approximately 10% of their original dry weight, and the wash
water developed color. Identical samples washed in CCl_4 lost negligible
weight, and colors appeared to be fast.

Results

Modern Wool. Table III gives the animal sources and Latin names
of types of wool commonly encountered. Table IV presents literature
values of the elemental analyses reported for wool together with several

analyses of modern samples from various sources. In general, the C analyses are just under 50%, N is ≈14–16%, S is 3–3.7%, and ash was 0–2.3% for modern samples, depending on source and processing.

Archaeological Specimens. Table V presents data for the elemental analyses of untreated textile samples together with elemental analysis of modern samples for comparison. The archaeological samples all have lower C and H values than the modern samples. Nitrogen analysis is generally lower although one sample actually gave a significantly higher value than the modern samples. Sulfur content was about as frequently higher in archaeological samples as lower. An earlier study (Table VI) linked the embrittlement of ancient textiles with a depletion of sulfur and/or nitrogen (6). The extensive data of Table V clearly suggest the inadequacy of this generalization.

The ash content of archaeological samples, though quite variable, is appreciable (2.4–9.4%) in all samples thus far examined. The sources of ash may be accretion from the burial or residue from the dying processes.

Table III. Animal Sources of Common Wool and Related Materials

Material	Source	Latin Name
Alpaca[a]	Alpaca	*Lama pacos pacos*
Camel's hair	Bactrian camel	*Camelus bactrianus*
Cashmere wool	Cashmere goat	*Capra hircus laniger*
Llama	Llama	*Lama glama glama*
Mohair	Angora goat	*Capra hircus aegagrus*
Vicuña	Llama vicuña	*Lama vicugna*
Wool (common)	Sheep	genus *Ovis*

[a] Guanaco, vicuña, llama, and alpaca are four species of the camel family found in South America.

Table IV. Analyses of Modern Wool Specimens

Analysis No.	C(%)	H(%)	N(%)	S(%)	O[a]	Ash(%)	Ref.
1	49.2	6.6	15.8	3.7	24.7	—	*11*
2	—	—	16.69	3.5	—	—	*2*
3	—	—	16.5	3.34	—	—	*12*
4	—	—	—	2.8–5.8	—	—	*13*
5	—	—	14.7	3.0	—	—	*6*
6[b]	49.97	7.23	13.69	3.02	26.09	0	this work
7[c]	46.05	7.21	14.68	3.06	26.7	2.3	this work
8[d]	—	—	15.4	3.7	—	—	*6*

[a] Oxygen by difference in percentage from 100.
[b] Sample T-1976-01.
[c] Sample T-1976-08.
[d] Alpaca wool.

Table V. Analyses of Untreated Archaeological Textile Samples

Sample[a]	C(%)	H(%)	N(%)	S(%)	Ash(%)	Material
T-1976-01	47.97	7.23	13.69	3.02	0.0	wool (modern)
T-1976-08	46.05	7.21	14.68	3.06	2.3	wool (modern)
T-1975-01	42.21	6.36	12.38	3.78	3.0	wool
T-1975-02	42.98	6.20	13.81	3.99	—	wool
T-1975-03	40.73	5.92	11.35	3.14	—	wool
T-1975-04	39.67	6.05	11.87	3.41	—	wool
T-1975-05	42.56	6.17	13.15	3.48	—	wool
T-1975-06	43.37	6.75	13.28	3.79	—	wool
T-1975-07	40.07	5.90	12.56	3.41	—	wool
T-1975-08	41.02	5.70	13.05	3.80	—	wool
T-1975-09	44.52	6.32	14.18	4.08	—	wool
T-1975-10	43.60	6.35	17.22	3.91	—	wool
T-1975-11	42.40	6.03	12:46	2.94	2.4	⌈wool[b]
T-1975-12	42.20	6.52	12.08	3.46	3.3	⌊wool
T-1975-16	41.55	6.57	0.57	< 0.1	0.9	⌈cotton[b]
T-1975-19	39.62	6.79	0.46	< 0.1	2.7	⌊cotton
T-1975-17	42.77	6.66	13.18	3.34	3.0	wool
T-1975-18	41.37	6.20	0.43	< 0.1	3.3	cotton
T-1975-20	39.19	6.14	7.96	1.57	9.4	wool
T-1975-21	38.89	5.91	5.32	0.71	6.6	wool/cotton
T-1975-23	39.74	6.40	9.45	3.01	8.0	wool/cotton

[a] See Table II for description of specimens.
[b] Connecting lines indicate samples taken from same specimen.

Three of the specimens were cotton, and two contained both wool and cotton. As expected, the pure cotton specimens contained neither nitrogen nor sulfur, and the cotton/wool specimens had reduced nitrogen and sulfur contents.

Noteworthy is the absence of significant amounts of sulfur in the cotton specimens (T-1975-16, -18, -19) although the ash content ranges from 0.9–3.3%. This suggests the ash is generally free of sulfur salts and that the presence of sulfur in the elemental analyses may be ascribed to an organic source.

Table VI. Analyses of Archaeological Wool Specimens[a]

Specimen	Date	Condition	N(%)	S(%)
Sheep wool	modern	whole	14.7	3.0
Alpaca wool	modern	whole	15.4	3.7
Inca saddle strap	14–15th century A.D.	whole	13.6	3.3
Coptic textile	4–5th century A.D.	whole	13.5	2.2
Coptic textile	4–5th century A.D.	powder	11.6	0.9
Paracas fringe	2nd century B.C.	whole	13.0	2.4
Paracas fringe	2nd century B.C.	powder	12.7	1.1

[a] After Sheridan and Delacorte (Ref. 6).

Washing of Archaeological Specimens. The washing of modern wool samples (Table VII) demonstrates the general lack of soluble materials. The elemental analyses remain substantially unchanged with washing in CCl_4 or distilled H_2O. The archaeological wool sample T-1975-20 (JB-5) demonstrated a significant reduction in inorganic matter on washing with solvents. The removal of these contaminants was reflected in an increase in carbon and nitrogen content. The lack of generality for these washing effects is demonstrated by the behavior of sample T-1975-17 (JB-6). Less significant change could be detected in the elemental analytical data for washed samples when compared with the untreated sample. The presence of sulfur compounds removable by washing cannot be excluded in this case. Archaeological samples may require exhaustive treatment to remove colorants, accretions, and/or degradation products to assay the contents of the proteinaceous substrates.

Table VII. Analyses of Treated Archaeological Wool Samples

Specimen[a]	Treatment	C(%)	H(%)	N(%)	S(%)	Ash (%)
		Modern Mexican Sheep Wool				
T-1976-08	None	46.05	7.21	14.68	3.06	2.3
T-1976-09	H_2O	46.33	7.32	14.35	3.12	1.8
T-1976-10	CCl_4	46.21	7.21	14.72	3.09	2.1
		Wool Sample JB-5				
T-1975-20	None	39.19	6.14	7.96	1.57	9.4
T-1976-04	H_2O	41.75	6.40	9.09	1.41	6.31
T-1976-05	CCl_4	41.34	6.14	11.10	1.54	6.82
		Wool Sample JB-6				
T-1975-17	None	42.77	6.66	13.18	3.34	3.0
T-1976-06	H_2O	45.06	6.96	13.99	2.57	2.30
T-1976-07	CCl_4	43.76	6.51	12.81	2.70	3.70

[a]*See* Table II for descriptions.

Conclusions

Elemental Analyses. The data for textiles obtained from a variety of pre-Columbian sites display a nonuniform behavior specific to the conditions of treatment and burial for the individual artifact. It is suggested that extreme caution be observed in the interpretation of elemental analytical data for archaeological textile artifacts since the presence of dyes, colorants, and accretions can give analytical data which are misleading.

Additional Methods of Analysis. The use of radiocarbon dating where sufficient sample is available to permit adequate confidence in the date obtained is not precluded by the caution above. It is essential, however, that radiocarbon dates be obtained only for the proteinaceous or cellulosic substrate with care taken to exclude contaminants and coloring materials. Note should be made of the possibility of the introduction of lubrication materials in the conservation of brittle textiles.

The study of the dyes, mordants, and other coloring materials used in pre-Columbian textile artifacts remains an inadequately explored area of analytical endeavor. Thin layer chromatography and related techniques should prove productive in the identification of vegetable dyes (7). Inorganic materials can be readily identified by x-ray diffraction methods.

Perhaps the most promising method for understanding the degradation mechanism for woolen archaeological textiles is the systematic examination of specimens by amino acid analysis. The study of the changes in concentration and composition of the amino acids present in the wool substrate for archaeological and modern specimens is currently under investigation.

Acknowledgments

The authors are greatly indebted to M. Ballard, J. Bird, N. Kajitani, and R. Sonin for the samples used in this study. This project was sponsored by the National Museum Act (administered by the Smithsonian Institution).

Literature Cited

1. Leene, J. E., "Textiles," "Textile Conservation," Chapter 2, Butterworths, London, 1972.
2. Peters, R. H., "Textile Chemistry," p. 275, Elsevier, New York, 1963.
3. Greathouse, G. A., Wessel, C. J., "Deterioration of Materials," Reinhold, New York, 1954.
4. Leene, J. E., Demeny, L., Elema, R. J., de Graaf, A. J., Surtel, J. J., "Artificial Aging of Yarns in the Presence as Well as in Absence of Light and under Different Atmospheric Conditions," *ICOM Committee for Conservation, 4th Triennial Meeting, Venice, 1975, Preprints.* Paper No. 75/10/2, offprint, 11 pp.
5. Michels, J. W., "Dating Methods in Archaeology," pp. 163–164, Seminar Press, New York, 1973.
6. Sheridan, J., Delacorte, M., "A Comparison of the Chemical Characteristics of a Paracas and a Coptic Woolen Textile with Modern Sheeps Wool Fibers," IIC-AG Annual Meeting, 1964.
7. Hofenk-de-Graaf, J. H., Roelofs, W. G. Th., "On the Occurrence of Red Dyestuffs in Textile Materials from the Period 1450–1600," *ICOM Committee for Conservation, 3rd Triennial Meeting, Madrid, 1972. Preprints,* offprint, 35 pp.

8. Baer, N. S., Indictor, N., "Chemical Investigations of Ancient Near Eastern Archaeological Ivory Artifacts," *Adv. Chem. Ser.* (1975) **138,** Chapter 13.
9. Delacorte, M., Sayre, E. V., Indictor, N., "Lubrication of Deteriorated Wool," *Stud. Conserv.* (1971) **16** (1) 9–17.
10. Schwarzkopf, F., private communication.
11. Bell, J. W., "Practical Textile Chemistry," p. 27, Chemical Publishing, New York, 1956.
12. Moncrieff, R. W., "Wool Shrinkage and Its Prevention," Chapter 2, Chemical Publishing, New York, 1954.
13. Onions, W. J., "Wool: An Introduction to Its Properties, Varieties, Uses and Production," p. 30, Interscience, New York, 1962.

RECEIVED April 3, 1977.

Estimation of
Permanence

The Application of Chemical and Physical Tests in Estimating the Potential Permanence of Paper and Papermaking Materials

B. L. BROWNING

The Institute of Paper Chemistry, Appleton, Wis. 54911

Many factors which influence the permanence of paper and papermaking materials can be tested and analyzed. Permanent paper must incorporate fibers of high quality, be near neutral or slightly alkaline, and be free of materials which promote deterioration. However, the complex composition of paper and the probability that numerous chemical reactions may take place preclude successful application of one or a few tests in estimating probable permanence. Recourse has been made to procedures based on accelerated aging or response to heating in which deteriorative conditions are integrated and reactions rates are increased. Possible uncertainties still remain because of the influence of moisture content during aging or heating and because the effect of temperature on reaction rates of the many components is essentially unknown.

The permanence of paper is important in applications which require the retention of significant use properties over an extended period. Legal and administrative records, historical documents, books of permanent value, art works, and archival materials must retain their integrity and utility for many decades or centuries. The extent of permanence sought is variously stated to be from 100 to 500 years although numerical values of this kind are very imprecise.

Concern with the permanence of papers has existed for many years. Numerous contributions over the period have established a general background; a number of reviews and bibliographies have been prepared (1, 2). Although many aspects of the permanence problem remain to be clarified, it has been well established that poor permanence can result both from the quality of the paper as manufactured and from the conditions existing during subsequent storage and use.

The potential permanence is built into paper at the time of manufacture; it is determined by the materials used and the processes of manufacture. Three important factors are recognized: (1) deterioration of the cellulose fibers prior to manufacture into paper and the presence of noncellulose components; (2) the introduction of additives (sizing, loading, etc.) to the papermaking stock; and (3) the presence of deleterious impurities originating from the fiber furnish, additives, process water, and mill equipment.

Conditions which affect deterioration after manufacture include temperature, relative humidity, radiation, atmospheric contamination, and attack by microorganisms, insects, and rodents. These are the responsibility of those purchasing and using or storing the paper. Although they may profoundly influence the permanence of paper in use, they are beyond the scope of the present discussion.

The assurance of requisite potential permanence requires the attention of both the paper manufacturer and the user. When prior agreement is possible, it is the objective of both the manufacturer and the purchaser of a paper designed for application in which permanence is important to choose those materials and processes which meet the requirements. If the previous detailed history of the paper is unknown to the purchaser, reliance must be placed on tests of the finished product in judging its suitability for an intended use.

The question of paper permanence is concerned primarily with the stability of cellulose fibers. Pure cellulose in its native state is a very stable material. Cellulose textile fibers have been preserved under favorable conditions for long periods without loss of integrity. It has been observed that many papers manufactured 100 to 200 years ago from cotton or linen fibers have retained their essential usefulness.

When increasing demands for papermaking fibers in the 19th century led to introduction of cellulose fibers from wood as a more abundant source, it became evident that the wood fibers did not possess all the qualities of cotton fibers. For many years, cotton was considered the first choice for fibers in the manufacture of permanent papers, whereas wood fibers were considered less suitable. It was observed that many papers (particularly book papers) of relatively recent manufacture deteriorated so rapidly as to be useless after no more than a few decades.

The constitution and molecular weight of native cellulose in cotton or linen and in wood are essentially identical. Cotton and linen have a higher degree of crystallinity (lower accessibility) than isolated wood celluloses and therefore are less available to degradative chemical reactions. The poorer stability of wood cellulose fibers that is frequently observed is thought to result also from the rigorous procedures required for removing the major part of noncellulose components in wood—lignin, hemicelluloses, and extractives. The pulping and bleaching processes used in manufacture of wood pulp include high temperatures, strongly acid or alkaline solutions, oxidizing treatments, and mechanical effects of cutting, compression, and shear.

Studies over a number of years have now shown that papers of adequate permanence can be made from wood pulps if the wood is delignified without undue degradation and is carefully bleached and purified. Wood pulp papers sometimes do not have the initial high physical test values, particularly folding endurance, that can be achieved with sheets of cotton fibers, but the relative rates of loss on aging often approach those exhibited by cotton papers.

Sulfate (kraft) pulps are generally the choice of wood pulps; acid sulfite pulps are subjected to hydrolysis during pulping in the acid medium, and the cellulose has a lower molecular weight (viscosity). In addition, sulfite pulps have a higher percentage of hemicelluloses which are deleterious to stability. Sulfate pulps tend to have a lower content of reducing end groups because of their destruction during contact with highly alkaline pulping liquor. Additional purification of bleached wood pulps by extraction with strongly alkaline solutions, as in the preparation of "alpha" pulps, results in removal of carbohydrate polymers of low molecular weight and enhances the stability of the fibers.

Although it is generally recognized that paper of high stability and excellent permanence can be made from cotton, cotton linters, and cotton rags, the use of these fibers does not ensure permanence in paper made from them. Improper cooking and bleaching procedures used in preparation of the fibers for papermaking can result in a sheet of poor permanence. In addition, cotton is subject no less than wood fibers to degradation by hydrolysis if excess acidity is present in the paper.

If the question of fiber composition is recognized by both the manufacturer and the user, the choice of a fiber furnish which has the necessary qualities is achieved by agreement. When the fiber source is unknown to the purchaser, a fiber analysis is a necessary requirement. Procedures for fiber analysis are well standardized and reliable—e.g., TAPPI standard T401 (3) and ASTM D1030 (4).

The usual chemical evaluation of cellulose fibers, in their original state and following operations of purification and preparation for papermaking, includes several "quality" methods. The more important are: (1) determination of solubility in alkaline solutions; (2) the content of functional groups (carboxyl groups, carbonyl and other reducing groups); and (3) molecular weight.

Conventional methods of alkaline solubility tests are primarily determination of α-, β-, and γ-cellulose (TAPPI T203). Purified cellulose preparations of high molecular weight resist solution in strong (e.g., 17.5%) sodium hydroxide solutions. Degradation causing chain scission with a decrease in molecular weight and the introduction of functional groups results in a progressive decrease in α-cellulose content, an increase in β-, and ultimately an increase in γ-cellulose. Hemicelluloses remaining in wood pulps are mostly soluble in the alkaline solutions and appear in the β- and γ-cellulose fractions. Note that the α-cellulose test (more precisely, solubility in 18% sodium hydroxide) was devised originally for evaluation of cellulose preparations used in manufacture of regenerated cellulose by the viscose process.

The content of reducing groups in native cellulose is minimal and is essentially limited to the reducing end group of the polymer. The content of reducing or acidic groups resulting from hydrolysis or oxidation can be considered a measure of the degradative effects to which the cellulose has been subjected. Any hemicelluloses not removed in purification of wood pulps contribute to reducing group content because of their low average molecular weight and to carboxyl group content from acidic hemicelluloses. Lignin residues, if present, contribute added reducing power. The reducing groups are commonly determined by reduction of copper from the cupric to the cuprous state by the procedure given in TAPPI standard T215. A number of alternative methods are available, including those which measure aldehydic and ketonic groups separately.

The average molecular weight of a cellulose preparation may be found by a number of techniques, but it is most conveniently evaluated by determination of the viscosity in a suitable solvent. Detailed procedures are given in TAPPI standards T206 and T230 and in ASTM standard D1795, "Intrinsic Viscosity of Cellulose." The distribution of molecular weights can be determined for additional evaluation of the material, but the fractionation procedures required prohibit use of the necessary operations as a routine characterization.

These chemical tests on papermaking pulps can serve as general indicators of fiber quality. It has been well established that permanence of papers is enhanced if the solubility in alkaline solutions and the content of functional groups are low and the molecular weight or degree of polymerization (DP) is high. The relationships, however, cannot be stated except in general terms; it is not possible at the present time to establish specifications for these properties which will ensure permanence or to relate them except in an approximate way to the permanence that may be expected in actual use.

The quality tests are of greater value in evaluation of fibrous raw materials for manufacture of cellulose derivatives. The tests do, in a general way, serve to show the presence of grossly hydrolyzed, over oxidized, or otherwise seriously degraded materials. Products of such poor quality, however, are not normally to be expected from modern manufacturing practices; the resulting deficiency in the necessary strength properties would preclude use in most paper products.

The same considerations are equally valid in application of these methods to finished papers. Standard methods for copper number (TAPPI T430 and ASTM D919) and for α-cellulose (TAPPI T429 and ASTM D588) in paper have been established. The methods have been applied in a number of instances for the purpose of evaluating the extent and nature of chemical changes resulting from natural and artificial aging and from exposure to other degradative influences. In such applications the results may be of diagnostic value, but they are of more limited utility in estimating probable permanence. The viscosity test has been used to study the effects on molecular weight of cellulose during papermaking and drying operations. If the cellulose has a high original molecular weight, viscosity at high levels of DP is a more sensitive indicator of initial degradation than are the alkaline solubility and reducing value tests.

It has been observed that many papers containing groundwood exhibit poor permanence. The reason for this behavior is not clear because wood is a very stable material and, in the absence of decay, is known to endure as a structural material for many centuries. Some modification is possible in preparation of groundwood because the wood is subjected to instantaneous high pressure and shearing action and, possibly, localized high temperature in the grinder or disk refiner. Access of gases or liquids into wood is possible because it is a porous material and has a large internal surface area. The area available for reaction would be expected to increase only moderately during the grinding operation. In any case, workers in the field generally agree that the presence of groundwood in paper is deleterious to permanence. The presence of groundwood is shown readily by spotting the paper with acidic phloroglucinol solution or any other of the many stains that are specific for lignin.

It has been realized for many years that excessive acidity is the single most serious cause of degradative effects on paper (*1, 2, 5, 6*). Although acids may be present from many sources (carboxyl groups in cellulose resulting from oxidation and the presence of acidic hemicelluloses, bleach residues, some wet-strength resins, etc.), the most important source of acidity is the introduction of papermaker's alum, alone or in conjunction with rosin size. Hydrolysis of the alum produces sulfuric acid, which promotes rapid hydrolysis of cellulose and other polysaccharides.

The effect of acidity caused by alum-rosin size has been obviated by the substitution of sizing agents which are effective slightly on the alkaline side of neutrality. It has been established that papers of satisfactory permanence can be manufactured with such sizes. It is possible to use rosin as a size and to avoid the conjunction with alum by a number of processes. There are insufficient data on the aging characteristics of paper sized with the available modified rosin sizes to judge the effect on permanence. Possible reactions of the rosin, such as oxidation and formation of peroxides, must be considered.

The initial acidity or alkalinity of paper is measured conventionally by the pH of the water extract or by the total titratable acidity or alkalinity of the water extract (TAPPI T428 and ASTM D548). The extract for measurement of pH may be prepared as the cold water extract (TAPPI T509) or as the hot water extract (TAPPI T435 and ASTM D778). In the absence of hydrolyzable salts, it may be expected that hot and cold extraction methods will give approximately the same results. If hydrolyzable acid salts (particularly alum) are present, the hot extraction method yields a lower pH because of hydrolysis promoted at the higher temperature to yield free acids.

The measurement of surface pH of paper has been applied extensively for quick determination of acidity or alkalinity or for screening purposes when a large number of tests must be made. The surface pH test methods may be required when the integrity of the paper must be retained. The surface pH can be measured by application of appropriate indicators or by use of a glass electrode of the required shape—i.e., a "flat-head" electrode. A number of detailed procedures have been described (6).

Measurement of surface pH sometimes yields values close to those obtained by the water extraction methods, but frequently rather large differences are observed. Interpretation of test results must be qualified because the pH may not be uniform throughout the thickness of the sheet; particularly in coated papers, significant differences have been observed between the pH of the coating and that of the base stock.

It is not possible to specify an exact limit of pH below which undue acidic deterioration may take place. Many investigators consider that paper designed for permanence should not have a pH below 5.8 to 6.0 although it is likely that there is an intermediate range of pH values in which the contribution of acidity becomes progressively less important relative to other degradative influences.

The observation that acid hydrolysis is avoided by fabrication of paper which is neutral or slightly alkaline has led to the incorporation of an alkaline filler such as calcium carbonate. Some very old papers which contained calcium carbonate as a loading material or as residues from processing of the fiber stock have shown excellent stability.

Papers which are acidic as manufactured can be stabilized by a deacidification procedure. Several processes have been developed for this purpose, the most successful of which provide neutralization of the acid present and leave a residue such as calcium carbonate or magnesium carbonate as reserve alkalinity in the paper. This alkalinity serves to protect the paper as acidity develops from paper components during aging or is introduced by atmospheric contamination. The amount of reserve alkalinity can be determined by adding a measured volume of standard acid solution in excess to a weighed specimen of the paper and back-titrating the excess to neutrality with standard base solution.

Many common metallic impurities in paper, particularly compounds of some of the transition metals, contribute to degradation of cellulose by hydrolytic or oxidative reactions. The more important in commercial papers are iron and copper compounds, whereas some others such as magnesium compounds have been observed to exert protective effects (7). It is clearly desirable that the content of undesired metallic ions be kept low in permanent papers. Titanium dioxide, commonly used as a filler, has been observed to promote degradation by photochemical reactions. The predictive potential of metallic content in relation to permanence, however, does not allow the setting of permissible limits at the present time.

The content of acid-soluble iron in paper is determined by TAPPI standard T434 (iron combined in clay and other complex compounds is presumed to be nonreactive). The presence of iron can be shown by the color produced upon wetting the paper briefly with warm $6N$ hydrochloric acid and then adding a solution of potassium ferrocyanide or thiocyanate; localized specks of iron or rust are indicated by the more intense color formation. Complete analysis of paper for metallic elements has been accomplished by chemical procedures, emission spectrography, scanning electron microscopy/x-ray, and neutron activation.

Most commercial papers contain a variety of components which modify the basic sheet of fibers. Sizing materials, fillers, and dyes are commonly present. Many papers (including book papers) are coated; the composition of a coating formulation is complex and usually includes a number of supplementary substances. Many other additives are introduced into paper for specific purposes. When the presence of the many additives in paper is considered, and it is realized that most papermaking raw materials are commercial products containing by-products and impurities, it is evident that a very large number of substances may be present although often in minor or trace amounts. The contribution of these to permanence may frequently be unimportant, but it cannot be dismissed without consideration.

The mechanical properties of paper are determined primarily by the physical properties of the fibers and the manner in which they enter into the sheet structure. The properties contributed by fibers are modified by the presence of many common additives (sizing, loading, coating, and other materials) and to some extent by many other substances normally present in small or trace amounts. The manner of sheet forming, pressing, drying, calendering, and other operations incident to the papermaking process contribute to the measurable properties of the finished paper.

The individual fiber properties which contribute to the tensile properties of paper include the following (8): fiber tensile strength; mean fiber length; fiber cross-sectional area; perimeter of the average fiber cross section; density of the fibrous material; fraction of the fiber area bonded in the sheet; and the shear strength per unit area of fiber-to-fiber bonds.

Detailed examination of these properties is essential in fundamental studies of paper behavior, but they are too tedious and time-consuming for practical use and are of limited value in estimating probable permanence. Nevertheless, some of the properties, particularly fiber tensile strength and fiber-to-fiber bonding, change during aging and become significant in aging tests.

Although the physical and strength properties of paper are established by the properties of both the individual fibers and fiber bonds, the bonds are especially sensitive to degradative influences because they are readily accessible to hydrolysis and other reactions. They are not protected by elements of physical structure, and crystallinity at the cellulose surface is minimal so that it cannot exert a protective influence. The bonding between fibers is attributed principally to the strength of fiber–fiber bonds resulting from hydrogen bonding at the fiber surfaces (the contribution of fiber entanglement is small). Because of the high accessibility of the fiber surfaces and fibrils, adsorption of moisture in the bonding areas strongly influences the nature and extent of the bonding forces between fibers. Swelling and shrinkage in the bonded areas can lead to shifts of the hydrogen bonds with consequent effects on the strength of the bonds.

The important physical tests applied to paper are: (1) tensile properties of strength and extensibility; (2) folding endurance; and (3) tearing strength, commonly determined as internal tearing resistance (ASTM D689, TAPPI T414) or as tearing energy as measured by the in-plane mode of testing. The average fiber tensile strength can be found to a reasonable approximation by the zero-span tensile test on the paper sheet.

It is accepted that the strength properties of paper must be at a satisfactory level in the paper as manufactured in order to meet the necessary use requirements. Moreover, a paper of higher initial quality according to these tests may be expected to have a longer useful life than one of lower quality as progressive deterioration takes place if aging rates are similar under any established conditions.

The folding endurance deserves special attention because it is the most widely used test in investigations of the physical properties of paper during aging. It has found favor because the folding endurance decreases more rapidly than strength measured by other tests or changes in chemical properties during initial periods of either natural or accelerated aging.

Despite the sensitivity of the folding endurance to small initial changes in the character of the paper, the individual tests exhibit poor precision and an undesirably large scatter of data. The folding endurance is by its nature a kind of fatigue test. Averaging of results from a large number of test values permits only a moderate gain in confidence of the mean. The low precision of data obtained in testing of paper results in part from the considerable inhomogeneity of most papers from point to point over a small distance (a scale of micrometers to millimeters). The effects of slight differences in structure are magnified because of the large influence of localized stress concentrations which occur from point to point in the paper during folding.

Several instruments and methods of measuring folding endurance are in use. They differ in the manner in which the paper is folded during the test and in the amount of tension applied to the specimen which determines when the test is terminated. The tension applied sometimes represents a considerable fraction of the tensile strength before the sheet is subjected to the folding test. Because of the effect of tension and the mechanics of folding, interpretation of folding endurance tests and the decrease observed as the paper is aged under any specified conditions may be affected significantly by the details of the instruments and the procedure.

The folding endurance is primarily a measure of the response of fiber–fiber bonds and, to a lesser extent, that of the fibers to alternate compression and tension during the folding. The strength, flexibility, and other physical characteristics of these bonds are profoundly affected by any of the factors associated with aging. As noted above, this may be attributed to the more poorly organized structure and lower crystallinity and, consequently, greater accessibility of the bonds in the paper structure.

The moisture content of the paper has a strong effect on the folding endurance test. The swelling and shrinkage which accompany adsorption and desorption of water vapor cause shifting and rearrangement of the hydrogen bonds and the structure of the bonded surface. Humidity cycling during storage or prior to the test which promotes changes of this kind at the molecular level leads to a partially stabilized condition at intermediate moisture contents.

Another factor which may contribute to the nature of the bonding surfaces is the presence of impurities which can catalyze deleterious reactions; these impurities tend to be concentrated at the fiber surfaces during processing and so appear in the area of bonding. The presence of fiber fines has been considered deleterious to sheet permanence (9), but the effect may be caused as much by the greater content of impurities in the fines as by their physical characteristics. It is not to be expected that decrease in average fiber length produced by stock refining will result in a significant decrease in permanence of the paper. The relative bonding strength, bonded area, and flexibility of the bonds contributed by the fines may be important in the behavior of the sheet.

It is necessary to conclude that the predictive utility of initial chemical and physical tests on papermaking pulps and on fabricated papers has not proved great enough to furnish reliable estimates of permanence. Such tests have indeed proved useful in studying the nature and extent of deterioration and the ways in which the constituents of paper behave under certain established degradative influences.

Greater reliance has come to be placed on some kind of artificial or accelerated aging or heating test, which in a sense is capable of integrating many of the factors affecting potential paper deterioration into a single estimate. Any evaluation based on accelerated aging necessarily reflects the temperature dependence of rates at which changes take place; many reactions with different rate constants may be and probably are operative simultaneously. The effect of temperature and application of the Arrhenius relationship to interpretation of results obtained by accelerated aging are discussed by other contributors to this volume.

There is an obvious and profound interplay between the composition and properties of the components in a paper sheet, and the observable and measurable properties of the paper. Interaction of the many complex factors has presented much uncertainty in interpreting the behavior of paper from information about its component parts. The prediction of permanence on the basis of chemical and physical properties of paper and its constituents has likewise encountered considerable difficulty.

Literature Cited

1. Kantrowitz, M. S., Spencer, E. W., Simmons, R. H., "Permanence and Durability of Paper: An Annotated Bibliography from 1885 A.D. to 1939 A.D.," *U.S. GPO Tech. Bull.*, No. 22, Government Printing Office, Washington, D.C., 1940.

2. Byrne, J., Weiner, J., "Permanence," The Institute of Paper Chemistry, Bibliographic Series No. 213, 1964; Weiner, J., Pollock, V., Suppl. I, 1970.
3. "Standard Methods," Technical Association of the Pulp and Paper Industry, Atlanta, Ga., revised periodically.
4. "Annual Book of ASTM Standards," Parts 20 and 21, American Society for Testing and Materials, Philadelphia, 1976.
5. "Permanence/Durability of the Book," *W. J. Barrow Res. Lab. Publ.* (1963–1974) I–VII, Richmond, Va.
6. Browning, B. L., "Analysis of Paper," 2nd ed., Marcel Dekker, New York, 1977.
7. Williams, J. C., Fowler, C. S., Lyon, M. S., Merrill, L. C., *Adv. Chem. Ser.* (1977) **164**, 37.
8. Page, D. H., *Tappi* (1969) **52** (4) 674–691.
9. Wilson, W. K., *U.S.N.T.I.S. Rep. COM-75-10131*, May, 1974; Wilson, W. K., Parks, E. J., *U.S.N.T.I.S. Rep. COM-74-11378*, April, 1974, National Technical Information Service, U.S. Department of Commerce.

RECEIVED January 17, 1977.

20

Determination and Significance of Activation Energy in Permanence Tests

GLEN G. GRAY

Paper Service Division, Eastman Kodak Co., Rochester, N. Y. 14650

The Arrhenius equation is reviewed, and procedures required to determine activation energy are described. Activation energy values for a variety of papers are listed for several physical properties. Room temperature rates of change estimated with the Arrhenius equation are compared with other permanence test results using rank correlation coefficients. Data and references suggest that acidity is not a reliable singular factor on which to judge potential permanence of paper. Single-temperature aging tests are shown to yield misleading information on papers with different activation energies, while multitemperature studies will detect differences in temperature-dependent rate constants. Accelerated-aging ovens that control temperature, humidity, and continuous replenishment of air are described.

Permanence characteristics of various paper products are of interest to many consumers and producers alike, and the subject has received much attention. In 1964 Byrne and Weiner (1) listed 479 references on this subject, and a 1970 update by Byrne et al. (2) lists an additional 124 references on paper permanence. Although several accelerated-aging procedures or chemical specifications have been proposed, carefully controlled experiments and many years of natural aging would be required to verify predictions. Unfortunately, published literature has not provided adequate proof supporting any of the relatively simple accelerated-aging methods that have been proposed.

When significant developments occur in papermaking and related fields, detailed accelerated-aging studies using rate studies at several temperatures are made to supply more convincing evidence for important decisions that are to be based on these developments. This account reviews procedures involved, describes equipment options, and makes comparisons among rankings of papers based upon various methods of predicting paper permanence. The well-known Arrhenius equations (3, 4) can be used in many cases to express the relationship between the rate (k) of chemical reactions and the absolute temperature (T). This empirical equation is:

$$\frac{d\ln k}{dT} = \frac{A}{RT^2} \tag{1}$$

where R is the gas law constant and A represents the energy required per mole of reactants for a reaction to occur—i.e., activation energy. If A is independent of temperature in the range of interest, Equation 1 can be integrated to the following form:

$$\ln k = \frac{-A}{RT} + C \tag{2}$$

where C is an integration constant. For convenience, Equation 2 can be converted to a form using logarithms to the base 10 as follows:

$$\log k = \frac{C}{2.303} - \left(\frac{A}{2.303R}\right) \times \frac{1}{T} \tag{3}$$

Equation 3 is expressed in a form recognizable as that of a straight line, namely,

$$y = b - ax \tag{4}$$

where a is the slope of the line. In this case:

$$\text{slope} = -\frac{A}{2.303R} \tag{5}$$

The slope of an Arrhenius graph can also be expressed in the form:

$$\text{slope} = \frac{\log k_1/k_2}{1/T_1 - 1/T_2} \tag{6}$$

where k_1 and k_2 are rate constants at temperatures T_1 and T_2. Since Equations 5 and 6 are equal to the slope of an Arrhenius graph, they can be equated as follows:

$$-\frac{A}{2.303R} = \frac{\log k_1/k_2}{1/T_1 - 1/T_2} \tag{7}$$

Using the value 1.9872 cal $°K^{-1}$ g^{-1} mol^{-1} for R, the universal gas constant (5), Equation 7 can be rearranged as shown:

$$A = \frac{-2.303\,(1.9872)\,(\log k_1/k_2)}{1/T_1 - 1/T_2} \tag{8}$$

Numerical values for activation energy can be calculated from Equation 8 using the experimentally determined rates k_1 and k_2 at absolute temperatures T_1 and T_2.

It is well known that long-term degradation of paper results from hydrolysis, from oxidation, and unless shielded from radiant energy from photochemical reactions (6, 7, 8). Since changes in physical properties of paper occur as a result of chemical changes, there is a theoretical basis for evaluating an application of the Arrhenius equation to changes in physical properties. However, it is important to recognize that during degradation of paper:

(1) Several chemical reactions can occur simultaneously.

(2) Individual reactions can proceed at different rates.

(3) Reactions might not proceed independently of each other.

(4) Additional reactions may occur as the result of intermediates formed.

(5) Rate constants can vary with temperature.

(6) All physical properties of paper do not respond in the same fashion to chemical changes that might occur within the paper.

When accelerated-aging methods are used to predict long-term performance of products, the predictions are difficult to verify with natural-aging results. It is therefore desirable to ensure that the following criteria are met to generate reasonable confidence in accelerated-aging results:

A. Linear rates of change must be obtained at all temperatures used in the study by a consistent mathematical treatment of the data. This can be verified by measurements at multiple withdrawal times from accelerated-aging ovens.

B. It is also necessary that activation energy be independent of temperature. This can be assessed by using several temperatures in the study, including an accelerated-aging temperature only slightly greater than room temperature.

Reflective brightness (9) of paper enhances the legibility of photographs and print by providing image contrast and is therefore an important parameter in assessing papers for long-term performance. Many of the papers evaluated have yielded reasonably linear relationships when reflective brightness was plotted vs. incubation time.

Retention of "strength" is also an important consideration in assessing suitability of papers for historical purposes, but strength of paper can be measured by a variety of techniques. Folding endurance of paper (10) is very sensitive to degradation with age (*11*) and in many instances follows reasonably linear relationships when expressed as the logarithm of folding endurance vs. aging time; however, there are few, if any, practical situations where paper is folded while under tension. It is also common knowledge in the paper industry that tensile properties (*12*) and resistance to continuation of a tear (*13*) are appreciably less sensitive than folding endurance to degradation with age (*11*). With some papers tensile energy absorption and Elmendorf tear strength follow reasonably linear arithmetic degradation rates at elevated temperatures and are thus suitable for study with the Arrhenius equation.

Although linear relationships with each oven temperature have not been obtained with all papers tested, the following procedures have overcome nonlinear responses with some papers.

• Adequate sampling and replication are required to account for paper variability; this is particularly true with commercial papers containing sheets from more than one roll within a ream.

• With some papers the internal sizing and/or wet-strength agents have not been completely polymerized during passage down the paper machine, and strength factors can increase during initial phases of the incubation cycle if the papers are not completely "cured" before starting the accelerated-aging tests.

• Before they are placed in the ovens, specimens should be conditioned at room temperature to equilibrium with the moisture content that they will contain within the ovens.

Accelerated-aging equipment used in these studies is similar to that described by Ennis and Hulswit (*6*). A stainless steel chamber is fitted inside each commercially available air-circulating oven, and fresh air is continuously forced through the inner chamber that houses the test specimens. The air stream passes through a series of coils surrounding the inner chamber to attain the desired temperature before entering the inner shell. Air enters the inner chamber through a distributing baffle at the top and exits at the bottom of each oven. Test specimens well spaced from each other are suspended vertically and parallel with the air stream. This system of continuous air flow at rates which completely replenish the air at least every 90 minutes minimizes the effect of low diffusion rates on rates of degradation and avoids contamination among specimens.

To illustrate that diffusion rates influence the degradation rate of paper, stacks of paper were interleaved with smaller glass plates as shown in Figure 1. These interleaved arrays of paper were then placed in accelerated-aging ovens along with individually spaced replicates. Results of one such test after 14 days at 90°C and 53% relative humidity (r.h.) are shown in Figure 2. Discoloration was greater where the pressure of the glass plates inhibited diffusion. To ensure that contamination

Figure 1. Stacks of paper sheets interleaved with glass plates to increase intimacy of contact in the center of the sheets were incubated in ovens along with single sheets to note the effect of diffusion rates on degradation

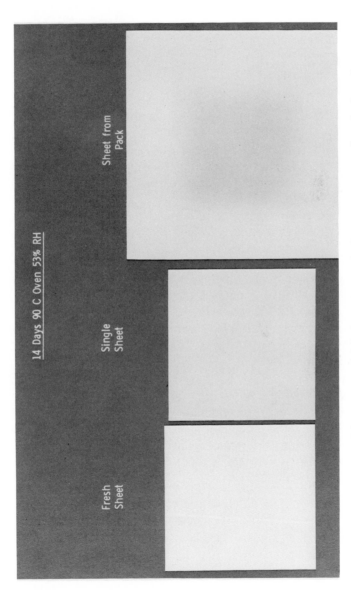

Figure 2. Sheets viewed by transmitted light. The fresh sheet was not incubated; the others were incubated 14 days in a 90°C, 53% r.h. oven. Single sheets are hung individually in oven. The sheet from pack came from Figure 1.

Table I.   Arid Ovens

Oven Temp. (°C)	Calculated (% r.h.)
110	1.04
105	1.23
100	1.47
90	2.12
80	3.14
75	3.87
70	4.78
60	7.45

among unlike samples in the same oven was avoided with this air-flow system, rates of change in physical and sensitometric properties of unlike, sensitized photographic papers were compared when incubated separately and together.

For special studies with arid ovens the air stream originates as laboratory air controlled at 23.9°C and 50% r.h. (14). The approximate humidity within each oven is shown in Table I. However, for most of the accelerated-aging studies conducted with this equipment the air stream is saturated at a selected lower temperature by bubbling it through water-filled jars in a constant temperature bath. The saturated air stream is preheated between each constant temperature bath and its associated oven to avoid condensation. The temperature of each saturating bath is adjusted to yield a humidity within its associated oven that results in a constant moisture content of the paper within each temperature series. Although the Arrhenius equation does not account for moisture levels in determining degradation rates, the effect of moisture can be determined by generating several sets of multi-temperature rate data with each set at a different level of paper moisture. Saturating-bath temperatures required to attain approximately 5% moisture in the papers studied at various oven temperatures are shown in Table II.

Table II.   Paper Moisture—5%

Oven Temp. (°C)	Bath (°C)	Approx. Oven r.h.
90	75	53
80	65	51
70	56	48
60	46	45
50	37	43
45	31.5	40
40	27.5	38

Study No. I

This study was part of a more extensive investigation conducted in 1967 and previously published (*15*). Since the object was to compare rankings of papers by multitemperature estimates of room temperature degradation rates with rankings by the Technical Association of the Pulp and Paper Industry (TAPPI) method of assessing retention of folding endurance (*16*), ovens at all temperatures were operated under arid conditions. Physical and chemical properties of the papers discussed are listed in Table III.

Table III. Properties of Papers in Study No. I

Property	E^a	F^a	G^b	H^b	J^b
Weight (lb/3000 ft²)	112.2	113.3	63.1	62.3	63.0
Caliper (mils)	5.80	5.98	3.95	4.23	4.07
Fold, MD[c]	168	847	5476	5442	2581
Fold, MD[d]	451	1300	5257	6352	2195
Reflectance (%)[e]	86.4	86.4	90.4	88.5	88.5
Pulp, cellulose %[f]	90.7	90.7	95.4	88.6	88.6
Pulp, pentosans %[g]	3.5	3.5	2.7	4.2	4.2
Pulp, copper no.[h]	1.4	1.4	0.5	1.7	1.7
Paper, pH (hot)[i]	5.0	5.2	5.0	4.9	5.7
Paper, pH (cold)[i]	5.2	5.6	5.2	5.3	6.0
Paper, acidity[j]	98	76	113	108	26

[a] Contained 65% virgin fibers and 35% recycled fibers.
[b] 100% virgin-fiber furnish.
[c] Machine direction.
[d] Cross direction.
[e] Reference 9.
[f] Reference 17.
[g] Reference 18.
[h] Reference 19.
[i] Reference 20.
[j] Similar to TAPPI Standard Method T-428su-67 except (a) four 1-hr extractions with boiling water on specimens in equilibrium with 50% r.h. and (b) report mL 0.01N acid/100 g paper.

Reasonably linear relationships were found on these papers when logarithms of the average MD (machine direction) and CD (cross direction) folding endurance values were plotted vs. incubation time. Statistical calculations for these data are listed in Table IV, and the Arrhenius graph is shown in Figure 3.

Values for activation energies and the rate of change at room temperature calculated for these data and the values for retention of folding endurance obtained from the single-temperature (105°C), single-withdrawal time (72 hr) TAPPI method (*16*) are listed in Table V.

Temp. (°C)	Intercept	(—) Slope × 10^{-3}	(—) Coef. Corr.	Standard Error

Table IV.   Log Folding Endurance

Roll E

Temp. (°C)	Intercept	(—) Slope × 10^{-3}	(—) Coef. Corr.	Standard Error
110	2.461	2.962	0.773	0.042
105	2.478	4.152	0.917	0.056
100	2.466	2.466	0.959	0.037
90	2.476	1.016	0.995	0.017
80	2.456	0.6069	0.969	0.031
75	2.416	0.3068	0.900	0.060
70	2.456	0.2044	0.985	0.028
60	2.396	0.0739	0.854	0.082

Roll G

Temp. (°C)	Intercept	(—) Slope × 10^{-3}	(—) Coef. Corr.	Standard Error
110	3.7430	11.06	0.985	0.034
105	3.7500	5.994	0.994	0.020
100	3.7560	3.427	0.993	0.021
90	3.7440	1.315	0.995	0.021
80	3.7240	0.4470	0.963	0.025
75	3.7212	0.2720	0.987	0.018
70	3.7270	0.1338	0.980	0.022
60	3.7180	0.0612	0.990	0.016

Roll J

Temp. (°C)	Intercept	(—) Slope × 10^{-3}	(—) Coef. Corr.	Standard Error
110	3.4670	1.833	0.804	0.055
105	3.4580	0.7760	0.943	0.023
100	3.4600	0.3127	0.912	0.023
90	3.4800	0.4429	0.994	0.012
80	3.4340	0.0816	0.798	0.035
75	3.4720	0.0526	0.967	0.018
70	3.4540	0.0294	0.915	0.028
60	3.3996	0.0158	0.840	0.024

The coefficient of correlation by rank for the two estimates of rates of change is only 0.20.

$$\text{rank coefficient correlation} = 1 - \frac{6\,(\Sigma d^2)}{N\,(N^2 - 1)}$$

d = difference between pairs
N = number of pairs

Data in Tables III and V show good correlation between paper acidity and retention of folding endurance as measured by the TAPPI

vs. Incubation Hours (Dry) (15)

Intercept	(—) Slope × 10⁻³	(—) Coef. Corr.	Standard Error

		Roll F	
3.0300	3.001	0.817	0.037
3.0420	2.854	0.972	0.022
3.0670	2.279	0.952	0.037
3.0260	0.8182	0.978	0.029
3.0260	0.3299	0.965	0.0179
3.0153	0.1457	0.963	0.0163
3.0481	0.1447	0.983	0.1219
3.0110	0.0475	0.863	0.0507

		Roll H	
3.812	7.797	0.948	0.045
3.818	4.947	0.969	0.039
3.810	2.925	0.979	0.031
3.804	1.184	0.986	0.033
3.793	0.3888	0.967	0.021
3.793	0.2271	0.965	0.025
3.775	0.1311	0.976	0.024
3.764	0.0460	0.975	0.019

Technical Association of the Pulp and Paper Industry

procedure (16). This relationship is well known in the paper industry but, as discussed later, does not establish either method as a good, singular predictor of paper permanence.

Although activation energy in degradation of paper is undoubtedly affected by a number of variables, it is interesting to arrange values from Tables III and V in the form shown in Table VI. From this relationship it appears that activation energy is influenced by the starting

Table V.   Activation Energies, Estimated Fold Loss, and Folding Endurance Retention at 105°C and a 72-hr Withdrawal Time

Roll	Activation Energy (kcal/mol)	Est. Loss Folds/hr × 10⁻⁶ (23.9°C)	Rank	% Ret. Folds[a]	Rank
G	26.8	0.3393	3	39.6	5
H	26.3	0.3189	2	47.5	4
J	23.2	0.1722	1	96.6	1
F	22.4	0.7351	4	63.7	2
E	20.1	2.0360	5	58.1	3

[a] Reference 16.

Table VI.   Influence of Initial Paper Strength on Activation Energies

Roll	Activation Energy (kcal/mol)	Initial Fold Strength	
		MD	CD
G	26.8	5476	5257
H	26.3	5442	6352
J	23.2	2581	2195
F	22.4	847	1300
E	20.1	168	451

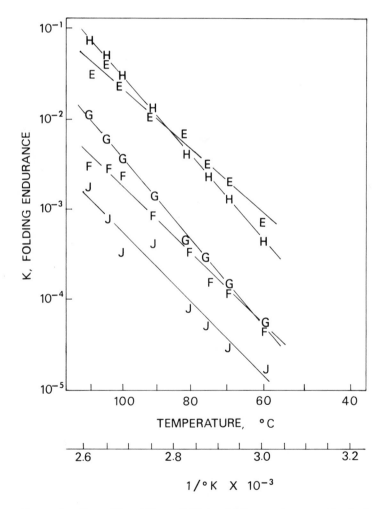

Figure 3.   Logarithm of k *vs.* 1/T *for folding endurance. Study I samples with dry-oven procedure. For samples E and H,* k × 10.

levels of paper strength. This concept is ignored in the TAPPI method (*16*) by calculating "percent retention of folding endurance" without regard for the possibility that an exceedingly strong paper with a reasonable degradation rate could outlast a weaker paper with a lower degradation rate.

When the estimated room temperature degradation rates from Table V and the acidity and α-cellulose data of Table III are arranged as shown in Table VII, the data tend to show that both variables influence permanence. A fairly high α-cellulose content paper with low acidity (roll G) has the lowest estimated degradation rate; rolls F and E with fairly high acidity and low α-cellulose content (35% recycled fiber) have high estimated degradation rates; and rolls H and G with high levels of α-cellulose but high levels of acidity have intermediate estimated room temperature degradation rates. Unfortunately, other variables thought to influence degradation rates (iron, copper, sizing level, etc.) were not measured on these papers.

During this 1967 study (*15*), a comparison was made between arid ovens (Table I) and humidity-controlled ovens designed to maintain approximately 5% moisture in the paper (Table II). Physical tests included the following:

(1) Average MD and CD folding endurance at 500-g tension.

(2) Average MD and CD residual tensile strength after 25 double folds under a pressure of 2 kg on 15-mm wide strips but under no tension, performed in a device similar to that described by Brecht and Wesp (*21*).

(3) Extensibility in the CD using 15-mm wide samples, a jaw span of 56.2 mm (same lengths as available from (2) above), and an initial elongation rate of 0.05%/sec.

(4) Reflective brightness (*9*).

The rolls of paper used (E^1 and F^1) were similar to rolls E and F listed in Table III. Although reaction rates are lower in arid ovens than in "moist" ovens at the same temperature, the activation energy values in

Table VII.   Influence on Permanence by Degradation
Rates, Acidity, and α-Cellulose Pulp

Roll	Est. Loss, Folds/hr $\times 10^{-6}$ (23.9°C)	Acidity	Pulp α-Cellulose	Recycled Fiber
J	0.1722	26	88.5	None
H	0.3189	108	88.5	None
G	0.3393	113	90.4	None
F	0.7351	76	86.4	35%
E	2.0360	98	86.4	35%

Table VIII indicate that the temperature dependency of the rate constants (slope) (a) is greater in arid ovens than in ovens maintaining 5% moisture within the test specimens and (b) is different for various physical properties since these are probably affected in different ways by chemical changes occurring within the paper.

Table VIII. Activation Energy (kcal/mol) for Various Physical Properties at Two Levels of Sample Moisture

Roll	Folding Endurance		Residual Fold Tensile		CD Extensibility		Reflective Brightness	
	Arid	5% H_2O	Arid	5% H_2O	Arid	5% H_2O	Arid	5% H_2O
E[1]	19.9	19.0	20.6	17.2	23.0	22.4	27.1	25.0
F[1]	21.3	18.7	21.0	15.1	22.4	19.9	25.9	23.8

Study No. II

The object of this study in 1971 was to assess the potential permanence characteristics of selected commercially available copy papers. Physical tests included folding endurance at 500-g tension (10) and reflective brightness (9). Sixty replicate measurements of folding endurance and 10 replicate measurements of reflective brightness were made on each paper in the fresh state and after each withdrawal time from each oven. Only three oven temperatures (60°, 70°, and 80°C) were used in this rate study with humidities adjusted as in Table II for moisture control. Comparison tests were also made using the TAPPI method (16), and the values obtained at 96 hr in the 80°C oven were used as a "single-temperature," "single-withdrawal" "moist oven" comparison.

Initial levels of folding endurance, paper acidity, retention of folding endurance in the arid 105°C oven and after 96 hr in the "moist" 80°C oven, levels of activation energy, estimated rates of loss in fold strength at room temperature, and ranking orders are listed in Table IX. Coefficients of correlation by rank are listed in Table X. Arrhenius graphs for folding endurance are shown in Figure 4.

It is apparent from these data that the three accelerated-aging methods do not correlate well. The arid conditions of the TAPPI method (16) yield negative coefficients with the moist oven data, and the 96-hr, moist 80°C values at best correlate only fairly with estimated room temperature rates. The copy papers in this study have a significant range in activation energy, and since a single-temperature test inherently assumes that all papers being compared have the same activation energy, results with the single-temperature test cannot be expected to correlate well with Arrhenius projections. It is also evident that paper acidity does not correlate well with room temperature estimates.

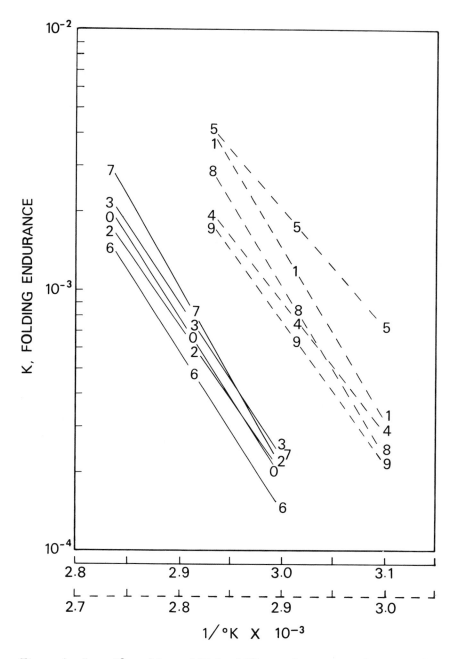

Figure 4. *Logarithm of* k *vs.* 1/T *for folding endurance. Study II samples controlled to 5% moisture in each oven.*

Table IX. Folding Strength Results and Paper Acidity for Papers in Study No. II

				% Retention			Est.[c]
				72 hr	96 hr	Activation	Room
	Fresh	Hot[a] Ext.		105°C[d]	80°C	Energy	Temp.
Paper	Folds	pH	Acidity[b]	Arid	Moist	(kcal/mol)	Rate
1	217	4.2	102	22.1	49.1	30.6	1.013
2	125	4.8	139	48.0	56.8	25.1	1.750
3	98	4.9	100	50.0	56.8	26.7	1.550
4	46	5.1	48	50.0	57.6	21.5	4.417
5	60	4.2	157	23.3	50.0	20.8	14.583
6	119	6.0	48	46.2	67.2	27.1	0.813
7	130	4.8	84	21.5	62.6	32.9	0.367
8	129	4.6	150	32.6	55.4	28.8	0.975
9	28	4.3	176	46.4	60.4	24.6	2.146
10	159	5.0	83	35.2	67.3	27.9	0.908

Ranking Order

1	1	9	5.5	9	10	2	5
2	5	5	7	3	6.5	7	7
3	7	3.5	5.5	1.5	6.5	6	6
4	8	2	1.5	1.5	5	9	9
5	9	10	9	8	9	10	10
6	6	1	1.5	4.5	1.5	5	2
7	3.5	6	3.5	10	3	1	1
8	3.5	7	8	7	8	3	4
9	10	8	10	4.5	4	8	8
10	2	3.5	3.5	6	1.5	4	3

[a] Reference 20.
[b] Similar to TAPPI Standard Method 428—exceptions noted in Table III.
[c] Estimated rate of change of log fold $\times 10^{-6}$/hr at 23.9°C.
[d] Reference 16.

When assessing changes in reflective brightness with accelerated aging, degradation is sometimes experssed as a post color number (PC#) from relationships described by Casey (22). From the Kubelka and Munk theory, two optical constants, S (scattering coefficient) and K (absorption coeffiicent), are characteristic of a diffusing material such as paper. The ratio K/S can be expressed as follows:

$$K/S = (1 - R\infty)^2 / 2R\infty \qquad (9)$$

where $R\infty$ is the reflectance of a pad sufficiently thick to be opaque.
The post color number is then calculated as follows:

$$PC\# = 100(\text{reverted } K/S - \text{initial } K/S) \qquad (10)$$

Initial levels of brightness, post color numbers, activation energy levels, estimated rates of change at room temperature, ranking orders, and coefficients of correlation by rank are listed in Table XI. Arrhenius graphs for reflective brightness data are shown in Figure 5.

Since changes in reflective brightness are not as dramatic as changes in folding endurance and since activation energy values for brightness changes in the various papers in the study are more nearly the same level, the coefficients of correlation are better for this property than for folding endurance. The difference between the arid and moist incubation conditions, however, is still apparent. Results also indicate that paper acidity, measured by either method, is a very poor singular predictor of reflective brightness retention as judged by any of the three accelerated-aging methods.

Study No. III

During the 1974–75 shortage of high-grade market pulps, new sources for fiber had to be developed; this study was therefore designed to compare 10 rolls of paper made with a variety of new and conventional fibers on the same machine. Variations in refining were made to meet formation and surface smoothness specifications. Two of the rolls (parts A and B) were made to weight specifications different from the others, but papermaking chemistry was the same for all, and all 10 rolls had approximately the same extractable (hot) pH as listed in Table XII. Two

Table X.   Coefficients of Correlation by Rank for Folding Endurance (Papers in Study No. II)

Comparison of Tests	Coef. of Corr. by Rank
TAPPI 453[a] vs. 96 hr (moist) 80°C	−.206
TAPPI 453[a] vs. room temperature estimates	−.039
Room temperature estimates vs. 96 hr (moist) 80°C	.510
TAPPI 453[a] vs. hot extractable pH[b]	.642
TAPPI 453[a] vs. paper acidity (*see* Table III)	.188
96 hr at 80°C vs. hot extractable pH	.682
96 hr at 80°C vs. paper acidity	.552
Room temperature estimates vs. hot extractable pH	.330
Room temperature estimates vs. paper acidity	.488
Hot extractable pH vs. paper acidity	.800

[a] Reference 16.
[b] Reference 20.

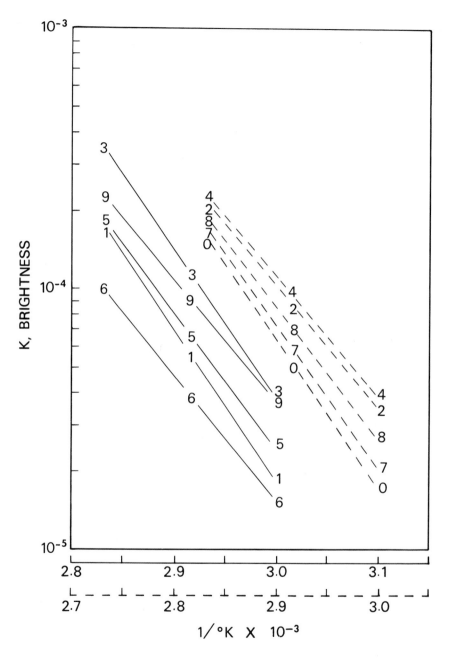

Figure 5.   *Logarithm of k vs. 1/T for reflective brightness. Study II samples controlled to 5% moisture in each oven.*

Table XI.   Reflective Brightness Data for Study No. II

Paper	% Reflective Brightness Initial	72 hr, 105°C[a] PC#	Rank	96 hr, 80°C[b] PC#	Rank	A[c] (kcal/mol)	Est.[d] Rate Room Temp.	Rank
1	88.0	2.43	7	0.92	2	26.4	0.113	1.5
2	85.0	2.15	5	2.11	7.5	21.5	0.583	7
3	83.2	2.71	10	2.82	10	21.2	0.675	10
4	81.7	2.56	9	2.47	9	21.2	0.663	9
5	87.0	1.36	2	1.25	3	23.9	0.256	5
6	84.3	1.09	1	0.87	1	22.4	0.210	4
7	81.9	2.49	8	1.44	5	25.4	0.157	3
8	84.2	1.92	3	1.65	6	23.4	0.290	6
9	86.7	2.33	6	2.11	7.5	21.5	0.596	8
10	79.9	2.12	4	1.29	4	26.2	0.114	1.5

Coefficients of Correlation by Rank for Reflective Brightness

Comparison of Tests	Coef. Corr. by Rank
TAPPI 453[e] vs. 96 hr (moist) 80°C	0.682
TAPPI 453[e] vs. room temperature estimates	0.855
Room temperature estimates vs. 96 hr (moist) 80°C	0.842
TAPPI 453[e] vs. hot extractable pH[f]	−.088
TAPPI 453[e] vs. paper acidity (*see* Table III)	−.173
96 hr at 80°C vs. hot extractable pH	−.200
96 hr at 80°C vs. paper acidity	−.164
Room temperature estimates vs. hot extractable pH	−.209
Room temperature estimates vs. paper acidity	−.230

[a] TAPPI method, Reference 16.
[b] One withdrawal only (96 hr), 80°C "moist" oven.
[c] Activation energy.
[d] Estimated rate of change of % reflective brightness/hr × 10^{-5} at 23.9°C.
[e] Reference 16.
[f] Reference 20.

additional rolls containing an experimental chemical added in the size tub were included in the study, but since they did not respond linearly with time at any of the accelerated-aging temperatures used, data from these rolls (parts C and D) are not included in this account. The lack of linear response on rolls C and D highlights one advantage of multi-temperature rate studies—i.e., a single-temperature, single-withdrawal aging test would not have indicated this different response. (The letter I is not used for sample identification because of its identity with Roman numeral I.)

Table XII. Physical Properties of Papers in Study No. III

Paper	Basis Weight (lb/3000 ft²)	Caliper (mils)	Extractable pH (Hot Method)[a]
A	95.3	6.28	6.2
B	95.1	6.61	5.9
E	105.8	7.72	6.5
F	108.6	7.66	6.7
G	108.4	7.66	6.2
H	107.1	6.09	6.4
J	108.0	6.12	6.7
K	106.2	7.76	6.7
L	109.8	6.45	6.3
M	109.0	6.85	6.1

[a] Reference 20.

Table XIII. Folding Strength Results for Study No. III

		% Retention			
Roll	Fresh Folds[a]	72 hr, 105°C Arid	384 hr, 80°C Moist	Activation Energy (kcal/mol)	Est. Rate[b] (23.9°C)
A	1309	61.3	37.3	21.1	6.304
B	1255	100.0	43.6	22.5	5.662
E	445	80.4	42.3	20.6	8.272
F	399	95.5	44.7	24.1	3.004
G	479	70.4	37.5	23.9	3.529
H	1831	71.7	58.3	26.3	1.161
J	299	100.0	64.2	25.5	1.363
K	332	100.0	62.9	26.2	1.662
L	723	51.7	37.0	18.9	10.777
M	3772	26.9	43.9	23.2	3.926
		Ranking Order			
A	3	8	8–9	8	8
B	4	1–2–3	5–6	7	7
E	7	5	7	9	9
F	8	4	4	4–5	4
G	6	7	8–9	4–5	5
H	2	6	3	1–2	1
J	10	1–2–3	1	3	2
K	9	1–2–3	2	1–2	3
L	5	9	10	10	10
M	1	10	5–6	6	6

[a] At 300-g tension/15-mm width, MD only.
[b] Estimated rate of change of log folds/hr $\times$ 10^{-6} at 23.9°C.

Twenty replicate specimens for MD folding endurance and five for reflective brightness, all cut from adjacent areas of handrolls, were used for fresh tests and for tests after each oven withdrawal time. Oven temperatures were 60°, 70°, 80°, and 90°C, and the humidity in each oven was maintained as listed in Table II. Five withdrawal times were used with each oven to establish rates of change.

The maximum time in each oven was 1344 hr at 60°C, 864 hr at 70°C, 528 hr at 80°C, and 336 hr at 90°C. Comparison tests were also run using the 72-hr, 105°C TAPPI method (*16*). Data at the 384-hr withdrawal time at 80°C were also used as a "single-temperature, single-withdrawal time moist-oven" comparison.

Initial folding endurance results are listed in Table XIII together with percent retention values from the two single-temperature, single-withdrawal time procedures; also listed are activation energy values and estimated room temperature degradation rates. On the 72-hr, 105°C test, incubated values for three of the paper averaged slightly higher than the fresh values but not greater than the variance of each set. Retention values for rolls B, J, and K are therefore listed as 100%.

From the ranking order assigned in Table XIII, coefficients of correlation by rank are listed in Table XIV for the pertinent relationships. As previously indicated, the arid TAPPI method (*16*) would not be expected to correlate very well with results of a procedure that maintained reasonable levels of moisture in the samples during incubation. Of particular concern is the very low retention values on roll M with the TAPPI test; roll M is an exceedingly well-formed, high-folding strength sheet that performed well in the other two accelerated-aging tests. Comments on the high correlation coefficient between 80°C data and Arrhenius estimates are made after the next section on retention of reflective brightness.

Initial brightness values for the papers in Study No. III are listed in Table XV; also listed are the post color numbers, activation energy values, and estimated rates of change at room temperature. In this instance, loss of reflective brightness for the two single-withdrawal pro-

Table XIV.   Coefficients of Correlation by Rank for Folding Endurance (Papers in Study No. III) (*15*)

Comparison of Tests	Coef. of Corr. by Rank
TAPPI method[a] vs. 384 hr (moist) 80°C	.697
Estimated room temperature rate vs. TAPPI method	.467
Estimated room temperature vs. 384 hr (moist) 80°C	.848

[a] Reference 16.   Technical Association of the Pulp and Paper Industry

Table XV. Reflective Brightness Data for Study No. III

Roll	% Reflective Brightness Initial	72 hr, 105°C		384 hr, 80°C		Activation Energy, kcal/mol	Est. Rate[a] (23.9°C)
		PC#	% Loss	PC#	% Loss		
A	87.4	0.83	4.4	1.10	5.5	28.1	0.652
B	87.4	0.77	4.1	1.30	6.1	26.8	1.010
E	85.6	1.02	4.6	1.31	5.7	29.6	0.440
F	84.4	1.31	5.3	1.39	5.5	27.5	0.667
G	85.1	1.34	5.6	1.40	5.8	25.4	1.375
H	86.4	0.98	4.7	1.41	5.8	26.6	0.912
J	83.0	1.46	5.3	1.67	5.9	29.0	0.428
K	83.9	1.25	4.9	1.44	5.5	28.1	0.542
L	87.9	1.26	6.4	1.66	7.8	27.8	0.830
M	87.8	0.87	4.7	1.58	7.6	28.9	0.631

[a] Estimated rate of change of % reflective brightness/hr $\times$ 10^{-5} at 23.9°C.

Table XVI. Reflective Brightness Ranking Order (Papers in Study No. III)

Roll	72 hr, 105°C		384 hr, 80°C		Est. Rate (23.9°C)
	PC#	% Loss	PC#	% Loss	
A	2	2	1	2	5
B	1	1	2.5	8	9
E	5	4	2.5	5.5	2
F	8–9	7.5	5	2	6
G	8–9	9	5	5.5	10
H	4	4	5	5.5	8
J	10	7.5	9.5	5.5	1
K	6–7	6	7	2	3
L	6–7	10	9.5	9.5	7
M	3	4	8	9.5	4

Table XVII. Coefficients of Correlation by Rank for Reflective Brightness (Papers in Study No. III)

Comparison of Tests	Coef. of Corr. by Rank
Estimated room temperature rate vs. 105°C PC#	−.218
Estimated room temperature rate vs. 105°C % loss	+.052
Estimated room temperature rate vs. 80°C PC#	−.236
Estimated room temperature rate vs. 80°C % loss	+.258

cedures are also listed. Although the reduction in reflective brightness is numerically similar for the 10 papers, small differences in brightness are visually detectable, and to illustrate the significance and limitations of activation energy and room temperature estimates, the data are ranked in Table XVI and the coefficients are listed in Table XVII.

Note that coefficients for single-withdrawal tests ranked with room temperature estimates are improved when loss of brightness values are used rather than post color numbers. Secondly, it is of interest to explain why a range in activation energy of 7.4 kcal/mol for folding endurance is accompanied by a coeffiicent of 0.848 between the 384-hr, 80°C test and room temperature estimates, while an activation energy range of only 4.2 for brightness loss on these papers has a coefficient of only 0.258. Data in Table XVIII show that the coefficient of correlation by rank between 384-hr, 80°C is 0.767; this suggests that the major reason for the low 0.258 coefficient is probably not a result of inaccuracies in determining k values.

Table XVIII.   Comparison of Data for 80°C Oven

Roll	k^a (80°C Oven)	Rank	80°C, 384 hr Rank % Loss	Coef. of Corr. by Rank
A	.01404	7	2	
B	.01572	8	8	.767
E	.01284	4	5.5	
F	.01233	2.5	2	
G	.01313	5	5.5	
H	.01485	6	5.5	
J	.01236	2.5	5.5	
K	.01162	1	2	
L	.01857	10	9.5	
M	.01839	9	9.5	

[a] Change in % brightness/hr in 80°C moist oven.

Figure 6 is an Arrhenius graph of folding endurance data for the highest and lowest activation energy papers in Study III projected to 23.9°C. Note that the lines cross at temperatures higher than 80°C; the ranking of these two papers is therefore unchanged at the 80°C and 23.9°C level. Arrhenius graphs in Figure 7 for the papers with highest and lowest reflective brightness activation energy values cross near 80°C, and therefore, correlations of rankings for papers in this set at 80°C and 23.9°C are seriously affected. These data illustrate a basic fact that is ignored when using single-temperature accelerated-aging tests—i.e., when rates of change and activation energy values for two materials being compared are at levels such that Arrhenius graphs cross at a temperature

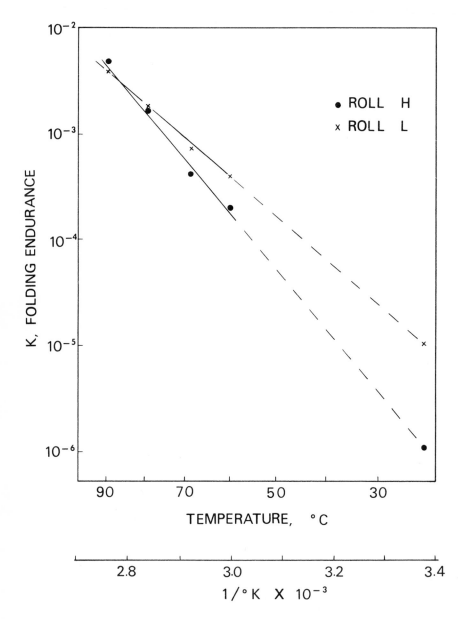

Figure 6.   Logarithm of k *vs.* 1/T *for folding endurance.   Study III samples with the highest and lowest level of activation energy.*

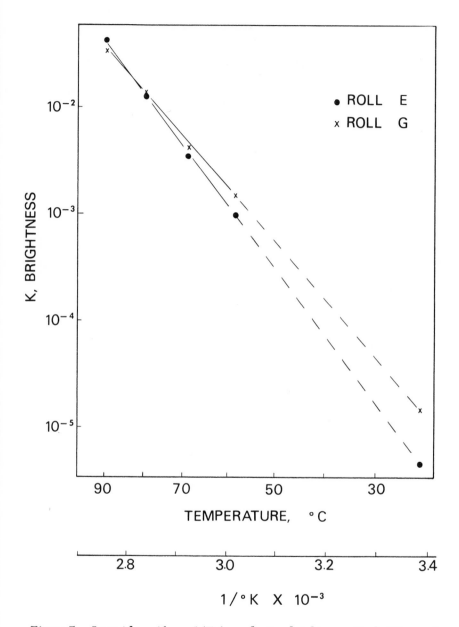

Figure 7. Logarithm of k *vs.* 1/T *for reflective brightness. Study III samples with the highest and lowest level of activation energy.*

lower than the accelerated-aging temperature, ranking indicated by the test will be reversed from room temperature.

Also, compare coefficients of correlation by rank for reflective brightness losses and post color numbers on the papers in Study No. II using the 96-hr, 80°C and estimated 23.9°C data. The coefficient increases from 0.842 to 0.952 when brightness data are used without converting to post color numbers. This advantage might be expected since accelerated-aging data and room temperature estimates are thereby expressed in the same units (loss of brightness). This high level of correlation results from three factors:

(1) There are significant differences in k values for the copy papers in the study.

(2) Differences in activation energy between papers are relatively minor.

(3) Some of the rate-of-change lines that cross do so above 80°C; rankings at 80°C and room temperature are therefore unchanged.

This high level of correlation, however, tends to demonstrate that, not withstanding (a) potential inaccuracies in establishing linear rates of change at each of several accelerated-aging temperatures, (b) potential inaccuracies in establishing an Arrhenius equation from several k values, and (c) magnified differences among papers caused by projecting results to room temperature, reproducibility of estimates using the Arrhenius equation can be comparable with single-temperature procedures. Obviously, great care must be exercised in replicate sampling, in controlling temperature and humidity of multiple ovens, and in measuring the properties of interest.

Discussion

Certain physical properties of some papers such as reflective brightness, tensile energy absorption, CD extensibility, and residual fold tensile follow reasonably linear relationships with dwell time when degrading at elevated temperatures, but linear responses for folding endurance are obtained as a logarithmetic function of folding endurance vs. dwell time. Many papers that show linear functions with dwell time also show linear functions with plots of rates vs. absolute temperature, such as with the Arrhenius equation. Room temperature degradation rates can be estimated for papers that follow these relationships. During these studies it has been found that papers have different levels of activation energy; this might be expected considering the wide range of variables in the pulping, bleaching, refining, sizing, and coating phases of the paper industry. By comparison, accelerated-aging tests for paper based upon a single-dwell time at a single temperature cannot indicate whether degradation rates are linear with dwell time, nor can they indicate differences in the temperature dependency of degradation rates (activation energy). The fundamental facts hold whether the single-dwell time, single-temperature procedure uses arid or humidity-controlled ovens, and they explain why a poor correlation was found between retention of folding endurance after 72 hr at 100°C and 36 yr of natural aging on papers made in the National Bureau of Standards (NBS) mill (25). In a second study at NBS (23) a good correlation was found between retention of folding endurance after 72 hr at 100°C and after 10 yr of natural aging on eight NSSC (neutral sulfite semi-chemical) papers, but the correlation was poor for the entire group of 20 papers in the study. Single-temperature, single-dwell-time accelerated-aging tests will probably become even more misleading in the future with the rapid changes occurring in the paper industry as new chemical additives are introduced.

It has been known for many years that acidity of paper is one of the variables adversely affecting permanence. However, publications such as the ASTM Specification D-3290-74 imply that paper acidity is the controlling factor in permanence and overrides all other variables such as pulp purity, chemical additives, iron and copper contamination, initial levels of strength, etc. A few practical examples are available to demonstrate the danger of such sweeping allegations:

A. The following are quotes from the NBS reports on a 36-yr, natural-aging study:

"Within a given group of papers, pH is related to permanence, but other variables in composition generally override the effect of pH" (23).

"Three alkaline papers performed well after 36 years of natural aging, but retention of properties was not as great as expected" (24).

"The data show that pH is not the only indicator of stability of paper, and that folding endurance is not a universal method of measuring degradation. For example, one would have expected the three alkaline papers to have retained a much higher percentage of their initial folding endurance" (26).

B. The extractable pH of many well-washed photographic prints has been in the range of 5.5 to 6.0 (only a medium permanence level by ASTM Specification D-3290-74), but well-washed photographic prints have endured for many years. Estimates of paper permanence based upon rates of change at several elevated temperatures assess the overall effect of degradative reactions and resistance to those reactions, including the effects of acidity.

Folding endurance under tension (10) is a favorite physical property for research on paper permanence and is the basis for the TAPPI method (16). Application of the mechanism involved in this test procedure, however, is unknown in practical uses for paper. Comparisons among product choices and estimates of their useful life should be based upon tests that assess physical properties of practical interest. Retention of reflective brightness, tear strength, tensile energy absorption, and residual tensile strength after folding under no tension are less sensitive to aging than folding endurance (*10*) but are of more practical significance in judging the useful life of paper products. Knowing the initial level of the property of interest and having estimates of the rate of change at room temperature from multitemperature rate data, estimates can be made (a) of the time to reach a limiting level or (b) of the level after selected time periods. Using a factor such as "percent retention of the initial level" as in the TAPPI heat method (*16*) does not consider significant differences in initial levels of product properties in comparing estimates of useful life. Since differences among rates of change are magnified by projection to room temperature through multitemperature rate studies and the Arrhenius equation, errors are also magnified. Statistical methods are available to assess significance of differences indicated by these projections (*27*).

Conclusions

• Single-temperature accelerated-aging tests for paper can be in serious error in ranking papers for permanence when the papers have different activation energies. Estimates of room temperature degradation rates cannot realistically be made from single-temperature accelerated-aging tests but can be made using multitemperature rate data.

• Specifications based upon extractable pH levels only cannot properly rank papers for permanence nor can useful life be estimated since several other factors are involved.

• An obvious disadvantage to multitemperature rate studies and estimates based upon use of the Arrhenius equation is the greater cost compared with single-temperature, single-dwell time tests. However, when decisions to be made are sufficiently important, the extra cost can be warranted.

Acknowledgments

The assistance of several members of the Paper Service Division staff is gratefully acknowledged; in particular a special note of thanks is due William J. Doran for supervising operation of the ovens and for much of the physical testing and to Thomas A. Weber who handled most of the statistical calculations. The author is also indebted to the Paper Manufacturing and Eastman Kodak Co. management for permission to publish the results of these permanence studies.

Literature Cited

1. Byrne, J., Weiner, J., "Permanence," Bibliographic Series No. 213, Institute of Paper Chemistry, Appleton, Wisc., 1964.

2. Byrne, J., Weiner, J., Pallock, V., "Permanence," Bibliographic Series No. 213 (Supplement 1), Institute of Paper Chemistry, Appleton, Wisc., 1970.
3. Arrhenius, S. Z., *Phys. Chem.* **4**, 226, 1889.
4. Perry, J. H., "Chemical Engineers Handbook," Third Ed., pp. 323–324., 1950.
5. *Ibid.*, p. 290.
6. Ennis, J. L., Hulswit, F. T., *Photogr. Sci. Eng.* (1963) **7**, No. 3.
7. Browning, B. L., Wink, W. A., *Tappi* (1968) **51** (4) 156.
8. Smith, D. R., *Libr. Q.* (1969) **39**, No. 2.
9. TAPPI Standard Method A-452m-58, "Brightness of Paper and Paperboard."
10. TAPPI Suggested Method T-511su-69, "Folding Endurance of Paper (MIT Tester)."
11. Casey, J. P., "Pulp and Paper," Second Ed., Vol. III, p. 1457, Interscience, New York, 1961.
12. TAPPI Suggested Method T-494su-64, "Tensile Energy Absorption of Paper."
13. TAPPI Standard Method T-414ts-65, "Internal Tearing Resistance of Paper."
14. TAPPI Standard Method T-402m-49, "Conditioning Paper and Paperboard for Testing."
15. Gray, G. G., *Tappi* (1969) **52** (2) 325.
16. TAPPI Standard Method T-453ts-63, "Relative Stability of Paper (by Effect of Heat on Folding Endurance)."
17. TAPPI Standard Method T-203os-61, currently T-203os-74, α-, β-, and γ-Cellulose in Pulp."
18. TAPPI Standard Method T-223ts-63, currently T-223os-71, "Pentosans in Wood and Pulp."
19. TAPPI Standard Method T-215m-50, currently T-430os-75, "Copper Number of Pulp, Paper, and Paperboard."
20. TAPPI Suggested Method T-435m-52, currently T-435su-68, "Hydrogen Ion Concentration (pH) of Paper Extracts—Hot Extractable Method."
21. Brecht, W., Wesp, A., *Papier (Darmstadt)* (1952) **(21/22)**: 443; **(23/24)**: 496.
22. Casey, "Pulp and Paper," pp. 1420–1425.
23. Wilson, W. K., Parks, E. J., *Nat. Bur. Stand. Rep., NBSIR* **73–249**, p. 8, July 30, 1973.
24. Wilson, W. K., *Nat. Bur. Stand. Rep., NBSIR* **74-501**, p. 6, May 23, 1974.
25. Wilson, Parks, *Nat. Bur. Stand. Rep., NBSIR* **74-632**, Fig. 5, Dec. 18, 1974.
26. Wilson, Parks, *Nat. Bur. Stand. Rep., NBSIR* **74-632**, p. 10.
27. Li, J. C. R., "Introduction to Statistical Inference," p. 328, Science Press, 1959.

RECEIVED March 9, 1977.

21

Stages in the Deterioration of Organic Materials

R. L. FELLER

Carnegie-Mellon Institute of Research, 4400 5th Ave., Pittsburgh, Pa. 15213

The action of oxygen that leads to the ultimate deterioration of organic materials tends to occur in a sequence of stages. Four successive stages are described: inception, induction, maximum rate or steady state, and declining rate. Examples of possible chemical processes that could be taking place in each of these proposed stages are cited. For example, an attack on weak links in a polymer might occur in the inception stage. The consumption of inhibitors frequently accounts for an induction stage, whereas a maximum rate or steady state stage should occur when the concentration of a major reactant reaches a maximum or constant level. Finally, a declining rate stage can be expected when the concentration of the principal reactant decreases.

The causes of the physical deterioration of organic materials owing to their reactivity with atmospheric oxygen are generally considered to be the result of chemical processes. The precise analysis of the kinetics of deterioration must, therefore, be firmly founded upon an understanding of the chemical reactions taking place. Investigators inquiring into practical problems in the aging of paints, varnishes, textiles, and paper have frequently neglected this fundamental rule, attempting instead to develop simple kinetic laws on the basis of changes in physical properties although these are nearly always the net result of a multiplicity of chemical reactions. It is true that a certain amount of information about the processes of deterioration has been learned by following a change in physical property such as the tensile strength of textiles or the folding endurance of paper. Moreover, individual workers have gone to the trouble to show the relationship of these properties to chemical constitution. Nevertheless, it has been the work of investigators such

314

as Bateman, Gee, and Bolland (*1*), Tobolsky (*2*), Mayo (*3*), and Guillet
(*4*) that has kept the study of oxidative deterioration focused on fundamentals. This has been achieved through their insistence that the proper
study of the kinetics of deterioration is the study of the chemical reactions
taking place as a function of time.

The pioneering investigations of autoxidation by Bolland provide a
prime example of the complexity of reactions that must be considered
in determining the mechanism of deterioration. Bolland, Gee, and their
associates proposed the involvement of six to eight chemical reaction
steps and were not satisfied until techniques had been developed for
measuring the rates and energies of activation for each individual reaction (*1*). This landmark series of investigations has served for more
than a decade as a model example of a search for an answer to the question, "What is the cause of the physical deterioration of an organic substance in terms of the chemical reactions that are ultimately responsible
for the changes observed?"

The conservation scientist responsible for the preservation of the
world's cultural patrimony—its art objects, artifacts, archival materials,
historic buildings and monuments—is concerned with developing methods and materials that can be used to impede the progress of deterioration in a wide range of organic, inorganic, and metallic materials. Broad
as the problems confronting the conservation scientist may be, unless he,
too, intends to come to grips with the basic chemical reactions involved,
efforts to preserve materials will be spent largely in the superficial treatment of symptoms, not in the discovery and alleviation of causes.

Admittedly, it is not a simple matter to isolate the individual chemical reactions responsible for the observed changes in physical properties.
However, it is the author's firm conviction that the observed changes in
the rate of oxidative aging of organic materials tend to take place in a
well-ordered sequence and that, moreover, the general types of chemical
reactions responsible for this behavior can be reasonably accounted for.
In this paper, four different stages in the overall rate of deterioration are
described. In addition, some of the chemical processes that may be
responsible for each stage are discussed, using examples both from the
literature and from the author's own work. It is hoped that this synthesis
of much of the information that we already know about oxidatively
induced changes in organic materials will facilitate a more systematic
analysis of the basic problems of deterioration and preservation that
confront museums and archives.

Four Stages in the Overall Process of Deterioration

To speak of a "rate of deterioration" is a convenient generalization.
However, if one thinks for a moment about the subject, one soon realizes

that changes in properties rarely occur at a fixed rate over the entire history of the physical usefulness of materials, from fabrication to the point of complete failure. The ordinary materials that we encounter—textiles, leather, paper—are usually extensive combinations of substances, and the physical properties of these composites, if we may call them that, tend to exhibit different rates of change at various stages in their life histories. Surely this is the consequence of the considerable number of individual chemical processes that take place concurrently each at a different rate relative to the others.

In 1966 Kelleher proposed a set of four curves to represent the rate of oxygen uptake observed in the thermal oxidation of thermoplastics. These are illustrated in Figure 1 (5). In the curve labelled "a," the amount of oxygen uptake is linear with time and the rate of oxygen gain is constant; "b" illustrates the autocatalytic condition in which both the amount and the rate of oxygen uptake increase with time. Curve "c" refers to the circumstance in which oxygen consumption proceeds at a decreasing rate, designated by Kelleher as the autoretardant case. A

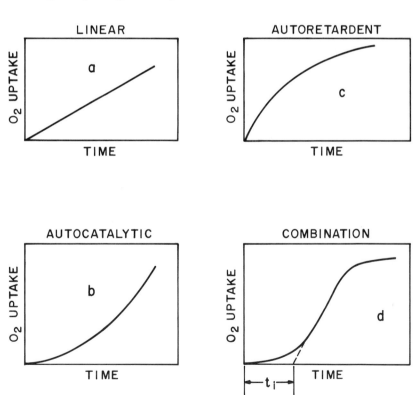

Figure 1.   Plots of oxygen uptake vs. time after Kelleher

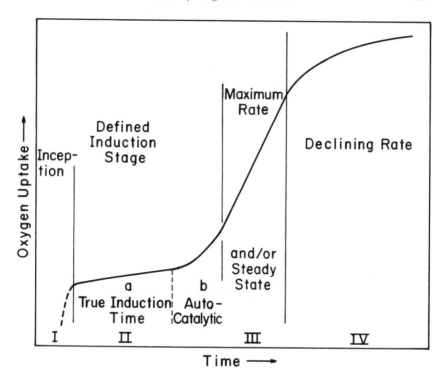

Figure 2.   *Possible stages of oxidative history (after Grassie (32))*

combination curve, "d," displays an S-shape with the portion "t_i" labelled as the induction time. These four are typical of the types of curves encountered in deterioration studies not only when chemical changes are followed but often when physical changes are observed as well.

Investigations of the deterioration and degradation of many kinds of organic materials in our laboratory have reinforced the author's conviction that the progress of deterioration resulting from reactions with atmospheric oxygen tends to occur in stages, very much as seen in Kelleher's combination curve, "d." The proposed stages, shown in Figure 2, are designated as follows:

    I. Inception stage
   II. Induction stage for III
  III. Rise and achievement of maximum rate and possible steady state
        stage
  IV. Declining-rate stage

In any particular experiment, one or more of these stages may not be apparent from the measured evidence. For example, the events of inception, Stage I, may occur so rapidly that they escape detection and attention. On the other hand, the experiment may be terminated before

Stage IV is reached. Nevertheless, as a conceptual guide for the study of deterioration processes, the possibility of observing all four stages should be kept in mind. A search for the reasons for failing to observe one or more of the stages will frequently prove enlightening. One can postulate, for example, that curves such as Kelleher's "a," "b," and "c" more than likely represent segments of the combined curve, "d," or of the proposed four-stage curve in Figure 2. In the following section, each stage is defined, the kinds of chemical reactions that may be responsible for each are discussed, and a number of specific examples are cited.

Definition, Discussion, and Examples of the Four Stages of Deterioration

Stage I: Inception. DEFINITION. The limited, generally rapid change that frequently occurs when samples are first placed under test, is designated—for want of a better term at the moment—as the inception stage. The experimenter often is tempted to ignore the first data points when plotting rate of reaction curves, attributing the deviation to the effects of small amounts of impurities (transition metal ions, residual catalyst, traces of monomer), lack of temperature equilibrium, and other experimental problems. The extent of any such initial event should be carefully observed and the possible reasons for it considered. Chemical reactions in this stage may prove to be the key to the ultimate stability of a particular material.

DISCUSSION. While a search for possible causes for the events in this initial stage should be profitable, there are a number of sound reasons for the initial rate to be rapid without its representing an experimental error or problem. The following are two of the better understood explanations for rapid initial reactivity that should not be overlooked. An initially high rate of oxygen consumption was predicted by Tobolsky, Metz, and Mesrobian in their analysis of the kinetics of autoxidation for the case in which the concentration of hydroperoxide at the beginning, $[ROOH]_0$, is much higher than the concentration under the steady state conditions, that is, the case in which $[ROOH]_\infty/[ROOH]_0 < 1.0$ (2). Such a situation may occur when a susbtance has accumulated a high concentration of peroxides during storage in the dark and is then suddenly exposed to heat or light.

Another instance of predictably rapid initial rate is the presence of "weak links" in the polymer chain, bonds that degrade more rapidly than the intended primary bonds in the polymer backbone. An example of such links would be the incorporation of traces of oxygen in the main sequence of polyethylene. Although much discussion, pro and con, has taken place in the past concerning whether weak links actually exist, there is little question at present that sites in polymers do occur that tend to be more susceptible to chain breaking than others. Cameron and Grazzie's study of the degradation of polystyrene provides a particularly convincing case (6).

EXAMPLES. Our investigation of the photochemical stability of polyvinylacetate (PVA) and of the Rohm and Haas methylmethacrylate–ethylacrylate copolymer, Acryloid B-72, revealed that these highly stable resins tend more to chain break rather than to cross-link upon exposure to visible and near ultraviolet radiation (7). This is indicated by the decrease in intrinsic viscosity shown in Figures 3 and 4. To guard against unexpected effects that might be caused by slight differences in spectral distribution, this conclusion was verified by using two different sources of radiation, a General Electric RS-type sunlamp and an ordinary "daylight" fluorescent lamp. (Compare Figures 3 and 4.)

Bryce and Greenwood as well as others before them have pointed out that the presence of weak links cannot be demonstrated simply by considering the fall in the average degree of polymerization or in the intrinsic viscosity as shown in Figures 3 and 4 (8). The degradation rate constant in the initial stages is not proportional to the average degree of polymerization ($\overline{DP}$) but to ($1/\overline{DP}$), and it is a plot of ($1/\overline{DP}$) vs. time that should be linear, at least in the initial stages. Thus, degradation may be conveniently followed by use of Equation 1:

$$[1/\overline{DP}_t - 1/\overline{DP}_0] = [\eta]_t^{-1/\alpha} - [\eta]_0^{-1/\alpha} = kt \tag{1}$$

where DP = average degree of polymerization; $[\eta]$ = intrinsic viscosity; t = time of exposure; 0 = time zero; α = the exponent in the equation, $[\eta] = K\overline{DP}^\alpha$; and k = kinetic rate constant divided by K from $[\eta] = K\overline{DP}^\alpha$. When data are plotted according to this equation, the presence of a fraction of rapidly degraded weak linkages is shown by an intercept on the ordinate, the curve not passing through the origin.

Our principal objective in the above experiment was to demonstrate that these two polymers tended more to chain break than cross-link upon exposure to light. Having confirmed this behavior, we further decided to plot the data of Figures 3b and 4b according to Equation 1, using Moore and Murphy's value of 0.5 for α, both for poly(vinyl acetate), and for convenience, Acryloid B-72 (9). As seen in Figure 5, the data for poly(vinyl acetate) indicate no weak links. An apparent intercept at 10–15 days even suggests that there may be an induction time before chain breaking sets in. The data for Acryloid B-72 may be interpreted in several ways, but it seems fair to say that they indicate the presence of a limited number of links that rapidly break after which the rate of degradation becomes negligible. This initial effort to analyze the behavior of these

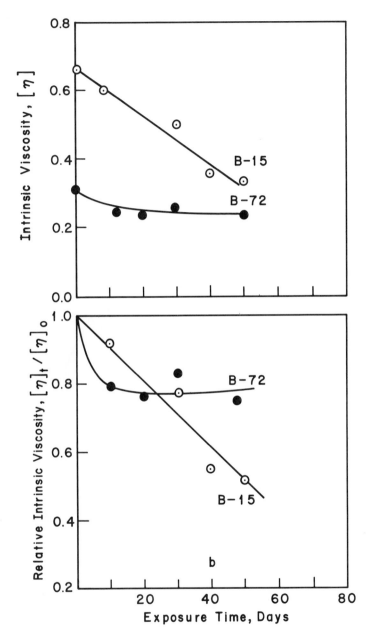

*Figure 3.   Fall of intrinsic viscosity of Acryloid B-72 and Vinac
B-15 (PVA) upon exposure to RS-type sunlamp*

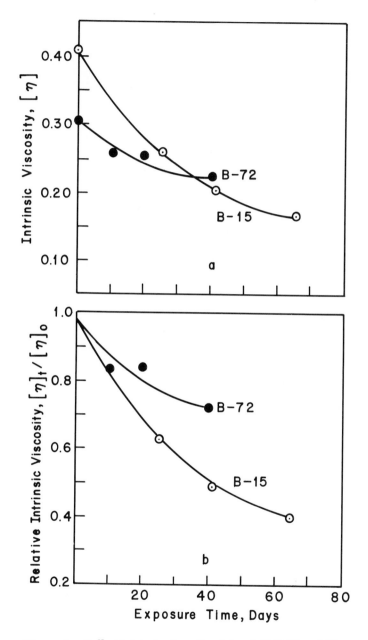

Figure 4. Fall of intrinsic viscosity of Acryloid B-72 and Vinac B-15 (PVA) upon exposure to fluorescent lamps

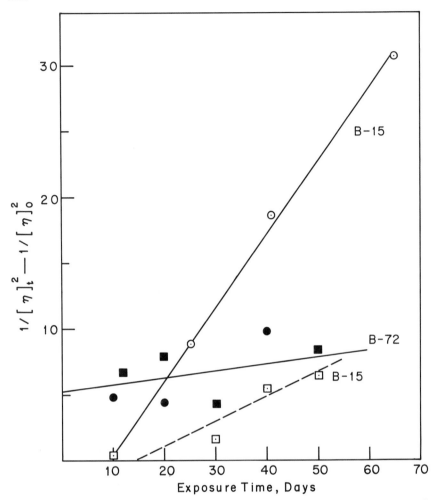

Figure 5.   Plot of data on relative intrinsic viscosity vs. time from Figures 3b and 4b according to Equation 1. ⊙ Vinac B-15 and ● Acryloid B-72: exposure under CW fluorescent lamp; ⊡ Vinac B-15 and ■ Acryloid B-72: exposure under RS-type sunlamp

polymers in terms of Equation 1 has thus suggested new facets concerning their degradation that will stimulate further investigation.

The intrinsic viscosity fell greatest in the case of the polyvinylacetate to about 45% of the initial value. An estimate of the number of scissions per molecule can serve to indicate whether this represents severe degradation or not. If we use Equation 2 to calculate the average number of scissions at the end of the experiment, as recommended by Shultz and Leahy (10), we find that the reaction had proceeded to the extent of about 4 scissions in the initial PVA molecule.

$$\text{scissions per chain} = ([\eta]_0/[\eta]_t)^{1/\alpha} - 1 \simeq ([\eta]_0/[\eta]_t)^2 - 1 \quad (2)$$

Members of the present conference are primarily interested in the stability of cellulose. When the data of Demeny on the photochemical deterioration of cotton yarns are plotted according to Equation 1, (essentially as he has done in plotting the number of scissions per 10,000 glucose units), there is an indication of a rapid initial reaction followed by a slower rate (*11*). The data of Daruwalla, D'Silva, and Mehta on the exposure of cotton in a carbon-arc fadeometer also indicate a more rapid initial reaction (*12*).

Investigators have been cautioned that the weak links can be broken at the time the cellulose is put into solution in preparation for the measurement of intrinsic viscosity rather than at the time of its exposure to ultraviolet radiation (*8, 13*). Nevertheless, regardless of the immediate cause of rupture, the existence of links weaker than normal bond strength can be detected through the use of Equation 1.

Stage II: Induction. DEFINITION. The concept of an induction stage has proved useful in many studies of reaction kinetics. There are a number of ways that the induction period may be defined, but the following conforms to the proposed scheme in Figure 2: it is the stage, following any inception stage that may be detected, that occurs before the maximum reaction rate is achieved.

This definition is intended to apply to the study of chemical reaction kinetics. The concept of induction time has also been used, and will continue to be used, to describe the period before a marked and relatively rapid change in a physical property occurs, but the author has suggested that the designation "apparent induction time" should be used for all situations other than those that fit the precise definition presented above (*14*). Thus, when the chemical processes that are occurring are not being specifically monitored, the adjectival modifier "apparent" should be used to indicate the lack of precise measure of a specific chemical reaction.

In reality, the induction period is ended when the autocatalytic stage "II-b" begins (Figure 2), but the moment of this event is not easily determined. For the sake of a convenient operational definition, the induction stage of a particular reaction is defined as occurring before its maximum rate is attained.

DISCUSSION. The apparent induction period frequently appears to be a time when almost nothing is happening. For example, if one is measuring the change in gloss or loss of weight of paints exposed to sunlight, there frequently will be a period of time during which the properties remain practically unchanged (the apparent induction time) following which a marked and generally abrupt change is observed. A bit of thought concerning this behavior leads to the conclusion that some of the chemical reactions responsible for the rapid change that ultimately occurs must have been in progress during this induction stage, albeit at a very slow rate, and that the reactions taking place in Stages I and II are the very ones that we should be concerned with in deterioration studies (*14*).

To preserve paper, textiles, and coatings, it would be necessary to treat them *before* the apparent induction stage is over to extend as long as possible the chemical processes that predominate during this period (essentially these are inhibition reactions). After the apparent induction period is passed—after paint has lost its gloss or after leather and paper have become brittle—it is likely to be too late to preserve the material effectively.

EXAMPLES. There are many reasons why a real or an apparent induction stage will occur in a sequence of chemical reactions. Tobolsky, Metz, and Mesrobian developed equations to show that the induction time in the autoxidation of hydrocarbons is related to the ratio of the steady state concentration of hydroperoxide to the initial concentration, $[ROOH]_x/[ROOH]_0$ or expressed another way, to the chain length of the propagation steps Equations (3) and (4) below (*2*).

$$R \cdot + O_2 \rightarrow ROO \cdot \tag{3}$$

$$ROO \cdot + RH \rightarrow R \cdot + ROOH \tag{4}$$

During the induction stage there is a fast reaction that competes with the particular reaction that the experimenter is attempting to monitor. For example, an inhibitor that is a free-radical scavenger tends to delay the dominance of Reactions (3) and (4) in the overall consumption of oxygen until the inhibitor is essentially used up (*see* Equations (5) and (6) below (*15*).

One must speak of an induction time with respect to a particular reaction or effect because it is to be expected that the rate of change in one particular component will show an induction time while that of another will not be apparent on the same time scale. Thus, peroxides in a polymer such as polyethylene may form almost immediately, whereas the formation of carbonyl groups and carbon dioxide may be delayed; the fall in molecular weight of a polymeric coating may begin almost at once, whereas cracking, chalking or brittleness—changes in physical properties—may be delayed. In the general sequence of reactions in which compound A yields B, which in turn yields C, one is much more likely to observe an induction time as a result of attaining a particular concentration of C than to observe an appreciable induction time for the disappearance of A.

If there is an appreciable initial rate of reaction and if the investigator doesn't carry the experiment far enough, he may miss the second stage, not recognizing the first, relatively modest rate of reaction as an induction stage. The inhibitor itself or its free-radical product frequently may react with oxygen sufficiently to give rise to a measurable rate of oxygen uptake even during the period before the maximum rate sets in (Reactions (5) and (6), where HA is the inhibitor). The data of Wilson and Forshee on the change in intrinsic fluidity of plasticized cellulose

$$R \cdot + HA \rightarrow RH + A \cdot \tag{5}$$

$$A \cdot + O_2 \rightarrow AO_2 \cdot \tag{6}$$

acetate provide a particularly good example of an appreciable rate during an induction stage (Figure 6) (*16, 17*). Other examples are the subtle change in rate of oxygen uptake in the studies of the inhibited rate of oxidation of polyisoprene by Shelton and Vincent (*18*) and the initial rate of increase in peroxide values in cottonseed and linseed oils reported by Lea (*19*). All of these investigations involved an appreciable reaction

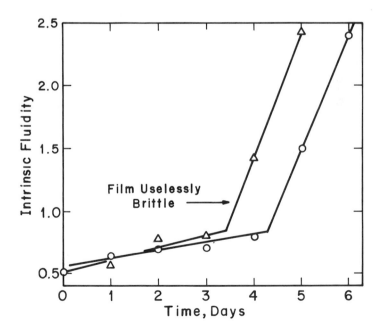

Society of Plastics Engineers Journal

Figure 6. Degradation of plasticized cellulose acetate at 110°C
(16)

at an early stage which could have caused an advanced stage such as III to have gone undetected if the studies had not been carried sufficiently far.

In contrast, induction times may be so short or the early data points so erratic that investigators will simply draw their curves through the origin, overlooking an induction stage that may be present. An example of this can be seen in the data of Harris and Jessup on the deterioration of silk, previously cited (*20, 21*). Even though the authors chose to draw the curve through the origin, an induction time seems apparent from their data for the samples treated with 0.1*N* NaOH.

An example of the manner in which the scheme in Figure 2 can stimulate investigation may be illustrated by our recent search for evidence of an induction stage which we believed should be present in the oxygen uptake of paper. Shortly before preparing this manuscript, we had initiated experiments intended both to measure the steady state rate of oxidation of paper and to obtain evidence of an induction stage. We did not succeed initially in achieving the latter objective, but immediately before presenting these remarks, our attention was drawn to a publication by Hernandi on the oxygen uptake of cellulose (*22*). Using an instrument that permits the rate of oxygen consumption to be observed within minutes of starting the experiment, Hernandi reported several curves that can be divided into three zones clearly corresponding to the proposed stages I, II, and III. The data display an induction time of about 1–1½ hr for the uptake of oxygen by cellulose at 190°C and one of about 2 hr at 160°C. At 130°C an induction time of about 9 hr is noted before the evolution of CO_2 becomes appreciable (*23*). These times are shorter than we had originally been seeking. Particularly intriguing is Hernandi's observation of a zone in the curves for oxygen uptake that corresponds to Stage I. The evidence thus seems to be that cellulosic materials tend to oxidize very much as proposed in the scheme in Figure 2.

Stage III: Maximum Rate and Steady State. DEFINITION. To express the overall rate of a sequence of reactions, a special mathematical treatment is often used, known as the steady state treatment. This is based on the assumption that the concentration of certain intermediate compounds or complexes is never large, that their concentration rises at the beginning of the reaction and soon reaches a constant (or steady) value, and that, at this point, the rate of change in the concentration, dc/dt, can be assumed to be zero. If the overall rate of reaction depends on the concentration of this intermediate, then the rate will have reached its maximum at this time.

DISCUSSION. In the autoxidation of organic compounds that takes place through the mechanism of hydroperoxide formation, one finds that following the induction stage steady state mathematics can be applied to account for the observed dependence of the rate of oxidation upon the concentration of the principal compound undergoing oxidation and upon temperature (2). If the concentration of the principal component is sufficiently great that it remains practically constant, one may expect to observe an appreciable steady state stage. This is a commonly encountered situation. If, on the other hand, the concentration of the principal reactant is low, the system will tend to pass into Stage IV rapidly, and the investigator will be confronted with an S-shaped curve, that is, with an *inflection point of maximum rate* rather than an appreciable period of time during which the rate is constant.

EXAMPLES. In the accepted theory of autoxidation, through the formation of organic hydroperoxides, the rate-controlling step in the maximum-rate stage is Equation (4). For this case, the observed rate of oxidation in Stage III is that of the key compound in question, RH. Thus, Tobolsky, Metz, and Mesrobian expressed the equation for maximum rate of oxygen uptake as Equation (7), where K stands for their $k_3^2 k_6^{-1}$ (2).

$$-\left[\frac{d[O_2]}{dt}\right]_{max} = K[RH]^2 \tag{7}$$

If Equation (7) is indeed the generally expected explanation for the rate of oxidation in the steady state stage, then it is very much in keeping with the objective of this volume to point out that the rates in Stages I or II do *not* represent the "characteristic rate of oxidation" of the key substance under consideration (RH in Equation (7)).

In practice one seldom encounters protective coatings, adhesives, and plastics in a condition in which Stage III is very far advanced (24). The reason for this is simply that, by the time the maximum-rate stage is reached, most materials will have lost so much strength and tenacity that they are no longer in a useful condition. A good example can be found in the work of Shelton and Winn on the oxidation of GRS-type rubber (25). When the reactivity of this material is considered over a range of temperatures, their data show all four stages. At one point the authors state that, before the final upswing in oxygen uptake is reached, that is, before the maximum rate is attained, the physical properties of the stock are degraded "to such an extent as to be of little practical value."

The findings of Hutson and Scott on embrittlement of inhibited polyethylene shown in Figure 7 also illustrate this point; their presentation is unusual in that the point of embrittlement is indicated on the curve (26). As can be seen, this occurred before Stage III was well advanced. A similar situation can be found in the data of Wilson and Forshee; the intrinsic fluidity of polymer that had degraded to a highly brittle state is indicated in Figure 6 (16).

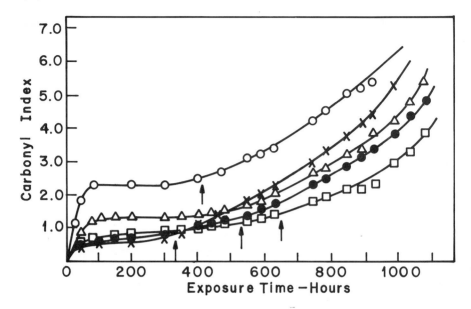

Journal of Polymer Science, Polymer Symposium

Figure 7. Effect on carbonyl index during uv exposure of HDPE with 1% inhibitor processed at various temperatures (26). ✕, control—no additive; ○, 100°C, 5 min; △, 200°C, 30 min; ☐, 200°C, 60 min; ●, 200°C, 90 min; ↑, embrittlement time.

Stage IV: Declining Rate. Definition. The declining rate stage is defined as a period of decreasing rate of reaction which tends to approach a limit in the amount of reactant consumed, or product produced (zero rate), under the prevailing conditions of temperautre, irradiance, partial pressure of oxygen, concentration of reactants, etc.

Discussion. There are a number of obvious reasons why a limit in the extent of reaction should be reached. The most compelling reason is simply that under given experimental conditions the most readily attacked sites in the molecules become used up. In many cases, the experiment cannot be carried to this advanced stage, and one may fail to observe the period of declining rate. Nonetheless, such a stage should be anticipated, especially under mild conditions.

While it may be true that many materials will become severely embrittled or discolored before Stage III is far advanced, some special situations exist in which a polymeric system can be regarded as being in Stage IV. For example, in the life history of polymers that tend to cross-link when exposed to near ultraviolet radiation, the conservator may have to remove them or at least have a sound understanding of their swelling properties in solvents under conditions in which the films are in Stage IV with respect to the formation of insoluble matter (27). In a similar sense, a film of highly cross-linked linseed-oil paint can be considered to be in Stage IV with respect to the formation of the intended paint film properties.

EXAMPLES. Data from an early experiment in which the gain in weight of dammar resin was observed, illustrated in Figure 8, indicate that a limit had been reached after one month (20). One may assume that the tertiary alcohol groups or the double bond in the vinyl groups, known to be present in this natural resin, were readily oxidized and that thereafter, one would need to increase the temperature or the energy of

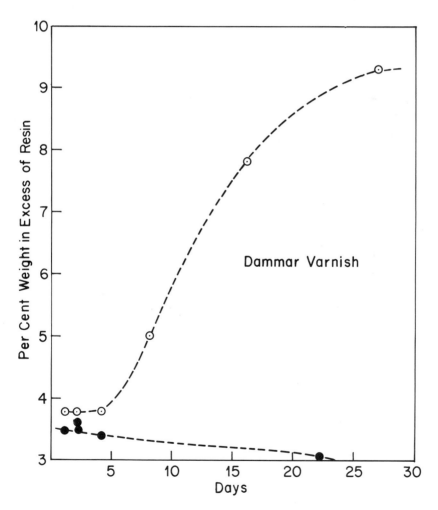

Figure 8.   Oxidative gain in weight of film of dammar varnish prepared from xylene solution. ⊙, under "daylight" fluorescent lamps at ~ 240 ft-c intensity and 90°F, 20% r.h.; ●, partially protected from the light in dust-free box.

the photons in order to cause further reaction with oxygen (28). If we assume that the average molecular weight of many of the triterpenes present is about 442, then the addition of two oxygen atoms and a loss of four hydrogen atoms would represent an increase in weight of 6.3%. This is close to the gain of 5.5% attained in the as yet incompleted process illustrated in Figure 8, suggesting that a stoichiometric gain of only one or two atoms of oxygen can readily account for the limited uptake of oxygen.

Another reason for an apparent, but not a true, limit to the amount of a particular product formed would be the existence of competing reactions such as chain breaking and cross-linking. Charlesby has developed equations to permit calculation of the ratio of chain breaking to cross-linking in thermoplastic polymers exposed to high energy radiation (29). These have been applied to analyze the effect of exposure of Acrylan, Mylar, nylon and polyethylene to 2537 Å ultraviolet radiation (30).

We have used Charlesby's principles in investigating the exposure of certain acrylic resins to near ultraviolet radiation to account for the limited build-up of insoluble matter in cases where the chain-breaking reaction is significant (31). Thus, when exposed in the carbon-arc fadeometer (Corex D filter) at 32.2°C, the poly(isobutyl methacrylate) polymer in Figure 9 seems to be tending towards a limit in the total amount of insoluble matter; in contrast, at 62°C, the polymer rapidly approaches a condition of near complete insolubility. (The isobutyl methacrylate polymer was prepared in refluxing toluene solution with benzoyl peroxide as a catalyst.) Charlesby, in plots of the log of the soluble matter against the log of elapsed time/gel time (or, what is similar, r/r_{gel}, the total irradiance relative to the radiation dose necessary to produce the first detectable insoluble matter), calculated a series of curves for the rate of decrease in the soluble matter as a function of the ratio of chain breaks to cross-links taking place, β/α. When the data of Figure 9 are superimposed on Charlesby's family of curves as shown in Figure 10, it can be seen that at the lower temperature the isobutyl-methacrylate polymer was experiencing a ratio of about seven chain breaks for every 10 cross-links formed ($\beta/\alpha = 0.7$), whereas at the higher temperature, the polymer tended to cross-link almost exclusively ($\beta/\alpha = 0.0$).

Analysis of the data in Figure 9 permits the investigator to reach a number of conclusions: (a) because the formation of insoluble matter begins at about the same time in Figure 9 despite the difference in temperature, the initiation step must largely be photochemical in character. (b) In contrast, because the ratio of chain breaks to cross-links is markedly influenced by temperature, the propagation and termination

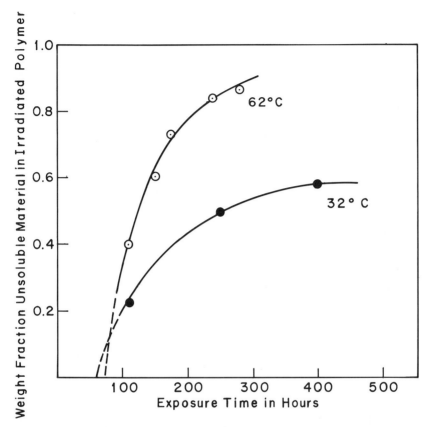

Figure 9.   Loss of solubility of poly(i-butyl methacrylate) exposed on aluminum foil in single carbon-arc fadeometer, Corex D-filter

steps are evidently thermally activated. (c) At 62°C the polymer undergoes cross-linking almost exclusively. (d) At the lower temperature of 32.2°C ,the relative rates of the propagation and termination steps are sufficiently altered so that there is an opportunity for appreciable chain breaking to occur.

The latter observation has important implications in accelerated-aging tests for the experiment has clearly demonstrated that raising the temperature can alter the relative importance of competing reactions and thereby alter the practical consequences of exposure. Thus, in Figure 10 one sees that at the temperature usually attained in the single-carbon-arc fadeometer, about 62°C, cross-linking was observed almost exclusively, whereas at the lower temperature considerable chain breaking occurred. The implication is that exposure of poly(isobutyl methacrylate) to near ultraviolet radiation at room temperature will result in a greater ratio of chain breaking to cross-linking than would be expected from the results of the usual accelerated-aging exposure in the older fadeometers without temperature control or even from our special test in which the sample was cooled to 32.2°C.

In investigations carried out in our laboratory some years ago, but as yet unpublished, neither poly(isoamyl methacrylate) or the more commonly encountered poly(n-butyl methacrylate) were found to exhibit a similar tendency to chain break at lower temperatures. Analysis of the data by Charlesby's method indicated that these two polymers still tended to undergo cross-linking almost exclusively even when exposed to visible and near ultraviolet radiation at temperatures as low as 25°–35°C.

Kelleher called curve "b" in Figure 1 the autoretardant case (5). Indeed, a third possible cause for a declining rate stage would be the generation of chemical entities that could interfere and retard the reaction of principal interest.

Conclusion

I had three purposes in presenting these remarks. The first was to call attention to the fact that in the course of thermally and photochemically activated deterioration, organic materials such as paper, paints and varnishes, textiles, and adhesives tend to react with oxygen in a reasonably well defined series of stages. This concept provides a guide for analyzing and investigating deterioration problems further (32).

The second point stressed was that the explanation of the rate of deterioration at any given stage must be based on an understanding of the *chemical* reactions taking place. If deterioration studies continue to rely heavily upon measurements of physical properties rather than upon attempts to elucidate the chemistry behind these effects, our understanding of the problems must by necessity remain limited.

As a corollary to this point, the potential advantages in applying kinetic analysis to chemical reaction rates can be emphasized. The investigator is often confronted with a rate of change that resembles Figures 1b, 3, 4, and 9. When these empirical results are analyzed according to the principles of chemical kinetics, as in Figures 5 and 10, order can frequently be achieved and valuable insights can be gained concerning the possible transition from Stages I and II (Figure 5) or from III and IV (Figure 10). Hope for elucidating the complex overall process of deterioration comes from just such kinetic analyses of the rate processes that occur in individual stages and in the transitions between them.

The third purpose was to discuss some of the types of chemical reactions that may occur and in a sense may be responsible for the rate of oxidation in each of the four proposed stages. More than a dozen general and specific examples have been cited.

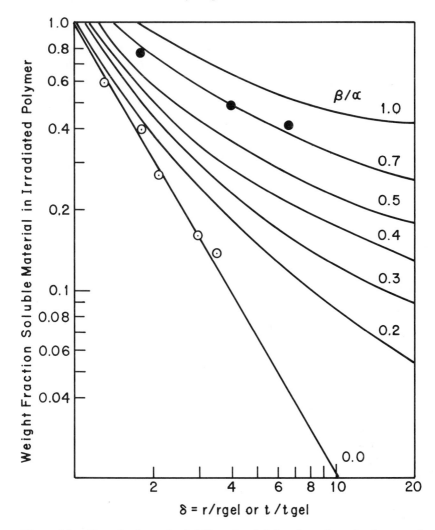

Figure 10. Data for loss of solubility of poly(i-butyl methacrylate) exposed in carbon-arc fadeometer, Corex D-filter superimposed on Charlesby's calculated curves. ⊙, data at 62°C; ●, data at 32.2°C.

In general, problems are most amenable to solution if they can be analyzed into their components. I hope that the concept of stages in oxidative deterioration will increase the effectiveness with which problems in preserving organic materials can be attacked and with which improved methods and materials for conservation can be developed. At the moment, many more questions are raised than answered. Nonetheless, the ideas presented here promise to stimulate and give direction to our research for some years to come.

Acknowledgment

The experiments represented in Figure 9 were conducted a number of years ago by Catherine Westervelt Bailie. The data in Figures 3 and 4 were obtained by Mary Curran, to whom I also gratefully acknowledge editorial assistance in preparing the manuscript.

Literature Cited

1. Uri, N., "Physico-Chemical Aspects of Autoxidation," Mesrobian, R. B., Tobolsky, A. V., "Autoxidation of Hydrocarbons Accelerated by Metals, Light and Other Agencies," Uri, N., "Mechanism of Autoxidation," "Autoxidation and Autoxidants," Vol. 1, Lundberg, W. D., Ed., pp. 55–168, Interscience, New York, 1961.
2. Tobolsky, A. V., Metz, D. J., Mesrobian, R. B., "Low Temperature Autoxidation of Hydrocarbons: The Phenomenon of Maximum Rates," *J. Am. Chem. Soc.* (1950) **72**, 1942–1952.
3. Mayo, F. R., Irwin, K. C., "Some Physical Organic Chemistry of Aging Processes," *Polym. Eng. Sci.* (1969) **9**, 282–285.
4. Somersall, A. C., Guillet, J. E., "Photochemistry of Ketone Polymers VIII," *Macromolecules* (1972) **5**, 410–415.
5. Kelleher, P. G., "Thermal Oxidation of Thermoplastics," *J. Appl. Polym. Sci.* (1966) **10**, 843–857.
6. Cameron, G. G., Grassie, N., "The Thermal Depolymerization of Polystyrene IV: Depolymerization in Naphthalene and Tetralin Solutions," *Polymer* (1961) **2**, 367–373.
7. Feller, R. L., "Studies on the Photochemical Stability of Thermoplastic Resins," paper 75/22/4, ICOM Committee for Conservation Fourth Triennial Meeting, Venice, 1975.
8. Bryce, W. A. J., Greenwood, C. T., "The Degradation of High Polymers," *J. Polym. Sci.* (1957) **25**, 480–483.
9. Moore, W. R., Murphy, M., "Viscosities of Dilute Solutions of Polyvinyl Acetate," *J. Polym. Sci.* (1962) **56**, 519–532. Intrinsic viscosities were determined in toluene at 30°C except for the data for PVA under the RS-type sunlamp, an early experiment in which ethyl acetate was used. For Figures 3b and 4b, practically the same curves are obtained and the same conclusions reached if the values of α is taken as 1 instead of 0.5.
10. Shultz, A. R., Leahy, S. M., "Random Chain Scission of Polyethylene Terephthalate by Light, Determination of Active Wavelength," *J. Appl. Polym. Sci.* (1961) **5**, 64–66.
11. Demeny, L., "Degradation of Cotton Yarns by Light from Fluorescent Lamps," *1967 London Conference on Museum Climatology*, p. 53–64, International Institute for Conservation, London, 1968.
12. Daruwalla, E. N., D'Silva, A. P., Mehta, A. C., "Photochemistry of Cotton and Chemically Modified Cotton, Part I: Behaviour During Exposure to Carbon-Arc and Solar Radiations," *Text. Res. J.* (1967) **37** (3) 147–172.
13. Sharples, A., "The Hydrolysis of Cellulose Part II Acid Sensitive Linkages in Egyptian Cotton," *J. Polym. Sci.* (1954) **14**, 95–104.
14. Feller, R. L., "Fundamentals of Conservation Science: Induction Time and the Autoxidation of Organic Compounds," *Bull. Am. Inst. Conserv.* (1974) **14** (2) 142–151.
15. Vink, P., "Changes in the Concentration of Some Stabilizers during the Photooxidation of Polypropylene Films," *J. Polym. Sci., Symp. No. 40* (1973) 169–173.

16. Wilson, W. K., Forshee, B. W., "Degradation of Cellulose Acetate Films," *Soc. Plast. Eng. J.* (1959) **15** (2) 146–156.
17. Wilson, W. K., "Deterioration and Preservation of Library Materials," Winger, H. W., Smith, R. D., Eds., p. 174, Figure 1, University of Chicago Press, 1970.
18. Shelton, J. R., Vincent, D. N., "Retarded Autoxidation and the Chain-Stopping Action of Inhibitors," *J. Am. Chem. Soc.* (1963) **85**, 2433-2439.
19. Lea, C. H., "Antioxidants in Dry Fat Systems: Influence of the Fatty Acid Composition of the Substrate," *J. Sci. Food Agric.* (1960) **11**, 143–150.
20. Feller, R. L., "The Deterioration of Organic Substances and the Analysis of Paints and Varnishes," "Preservation and Conservation: Principles and Practices," pp. 287–299, Smithsonian Press, Washington, D.C., 1976.
21. Harris, M., Jessup, D. A., "The Effect of pH on the Photochemical Decomposition of Silk," *J. Res. Nat. Bur. Stand.* (1931) **7** (6) 1179–1184.
22. Hernadi, S., "Thermal Ageing in Oxygen of Paper Made from Cellulose at Different Degrees of Beating," *Sven. Papperstidn.* (1976) **79** (13) 418–423.
23. Waller, R. C., Bass, K. C., Roseveare, W. E., "Degradation of Rayon Tire Yarns on Elevated Temperatures," *Ind. Eng. Chem.* (1948) **40**, 138–143; report on induction time of about 4 hr for the loss of strength of the rayon yarn in air at 135°C in the presence of 0.12 g water/g cellulose.
24. Hawkins, W. L., Bell Laboratories, Murray Hill, N.J., private communication.
25. Shelton, J. R., Winn, H., "Oxidation of GR-S Vulcanizates," *Ind. Eng. Chem.* (1946) **38**, 71–76.
26. Hutson, G. V., Scott, G., "Mechanisms of Phosphite Stabilizers in Polyolefins Subjected to Ultraviolet Irradiation," *in* "Mechanism of Inhibition Processing Polymers: Oxidation and Photodegradation," Sedacek, B., Ed., *J. Polym. Sci., Polym. Symp. No. 40* (1973) 67–71, Wiley, New York.
27. Feller, R. L., Stolow, N., Jones, E. B., "On Picture Varnishes and Their Solvents," pp. 202–210, Press of Case-Western Reserve, Cleveland, 1971.
28. Mills, J., Werner, A. E. A., "The Chemistry of Dammar Resin," *J. Chem. Soc.* (1955) (9) 3132–3140.
29. Charlesby, A., "Atomic Radiation and Polymers," Pergamon Press, London, 1960.
30. Stephenson, C. V., Moses, B. C., Burks, Jr., R. E., Coburn, W. C., Wilcox, W. S., "Ultraviolet Irradiation of Plastics II, Cross-linking and Scission," *J. Polym. Sci.* (1961) **55**, 465–475.
31. Feller, R. L., Bailie, C. W., "Studies of the Effect of Light on Protective Coatings Using Aluminum Foil as a Support: Determination of Ratio of Chain Breaking to Cross-linking," *Bull. Am. Group-IIC* (1966) **6** (1) 10–12.
32. Since the preparation of this manuscript, the author has found that the scheme illustrated in Figure 2 was described more than 20 years ago by N. Grassie ("Chemistry of High Polymer Degradation Processes," Fig. 61, p. 201, Interscience, New York, 1956). It is curious that Grassie's concept of four stages should have attracted so little interest among subsequent authors.

RECEIVED April 18, 1977.

22

Use of the Arrhenius Equation in Multicomponent Systems

N. S. BAER

Conservation Center, Institute of Fine Arts, New York University,
1 East 78th Street, New York, N.Y. 10021

N. INDICTOR

Chemistry Department, Brooklyn College, City University of New York,
Brooklyn, N.Y. 11210

*The literature contains a number of examples of the suc-
cesful application of the Arrhenius equation to multicom-
ponent systems where the principal component is paper.
In these studies, the logarithms of rate constants for
physical or chemical properties are plotted vs. 1/T to give
straight lines. This approach has been applied to systems
as diverse as rosin sized papers and clay filled papers.
However, for some systems, physical strength measurements
—e.g., folding endurance (TAPPI T-511su-69) and breaking
strength (TAPPI T-404ts-66)—demonstrate the independent
aging of the components leading to complex, nonlinear
Arrhenius plots. Examples from studies of various adhesive-
paper model systems are discussed.*

Synthetic polymers, often possessing uniquely desirable working properties and physical appearance, are finding ever wider use by artists and
conservators. For example, poly(vinyl acetate) emulsions have been
used for collages ($4, 5$), the production and conservation of books ($6, 7$),
and the conservation of textiles and paintings ($8, 9$). It has become
essential to study the behavior of new materials and to evaluate their
long-term behavior as individual materials and as components in the
complex systems which make up artistic and historic artifacts. Our
experience with a wide range of natural and synthetic polymers—e.g.,

methylcellulose (*10*), poly(vinyl acetate) (*3, 11*), poly(vinyl alcohol) (*1*), soluble nylon (*1*), glues (*2*), and starches (*10*)—as part of paper–polymer systems has demonstrated that the test procedures, well defined for papers, are generally difficult to apply to these more complex systems.

In the absence of sample banks of naturally aged materials (*12*), the need for data on the long-term behavior of such materials suggests the use of accelerated-aging techniques. Any reasonable testing procedure must demonstrate that no new chemical reactions are introduced under the conditions obtained in the test. The appropriate criteria for such procedures are embodied in the Arrhenius equation. Note that the goal of an evaluation program is often the evaluation of a series of related materials and is not necessarily the direct prediction of specific regression times for physical properties.

The Arrhenius equation and its use in paper permanence testing is reviewed elsewhere (*13*) in this monograph. It is, however, important to examine the problems which arise when Arrhenius plots are extended to complex systems. Since concentrations are not measured directly for paper/adhesive systems, rate constants must be obtained from analogs—e.g., folding endurance, tensile strength, brightness, etc. The most useful test measurement for untreated paper has been varying fold endurance with time of aging for elevated temperatures. Unfortunately, with polymer systems, changing fold strength arises from a multiplicity of mechanisms—e.g., solvent evaporation, oxidation, degradation, and chemical set—some of which tend to weaken and others to strengthen the system. In the current study of adhesive/paper systems we seek to identify those circumstances appropriate for the application of an Arrhenius equation and to identify those factors which preclude that simple application.

Tensile Stress

In Figure 1 the generalized behavior of adhesive/paper systems of varying physical properties is illustrated. Elongation and breaking strength under stress are generally relevant measurements for adhesive/paper systems although the limited elongations obtained for paper have led to a neglect of this significant variable. As shown in Figure 1, one may experience independent rupture of the paper and adhesive or simultaneous breaking, depending on the degree of penetration of the applied polymer into the paper substrate and depending on the brittleness of the polymer. It is important to observe and to record the physical appearance of specimens under tensile stress throughout the measurement rather than merely to record the stress–strain behavior.

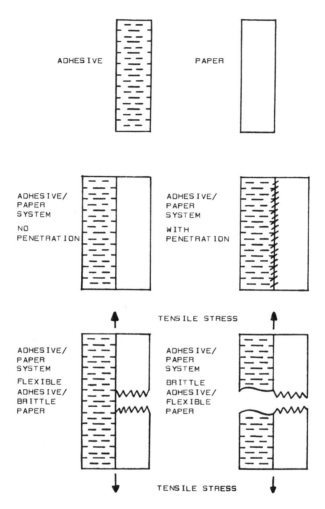

*Figure 1.   Behavior of adhesive–paper systems under
tensile stress*

Folding Endurance

Most frequently, studies of permanence have assumed or implied
first-order kinetics for folding endurance measurements on papers which
have undergone accelerated aging at elevated temperatures (*13–16*). The
general experimental arrangement for such measurements is presented in
Figure 2. It is obvious that the folding endurance measurement is a
function of many variables. The increasing stress at the edges as sheet
thickness increases has received only limited attention although thickness
appears in some proposed equations relating folding endurance to tension

(*17*). Also neglected is the role of elongation. As the folding progresses and elongation occurs, new surface is exposed during folding, and in spring-loaded folding endurance instruments, the tensile strength decreases. This continuous alteration of the system increases in importance for paper/polymer systems where the polymer may undergo significant elongation. It is therefore recommended that elongation for both paper and polymer be recorded and that an instrument with dead weight for tension be used in folding endurance measurements where elongations become appreciable.

Though all of the variables in the folding endurance measurement have not been identified, it is clear that abrasion resistance is one of the properties being measured. This combined with the increased stress on the edges complicates the data for composite systems. For a brittle adhesive only partially penetrating a paper substance, the embrittlement of the adhesive may substantially reduce the folding endurance of the system; if such an adhesive is removed mechanically from the substrate, the paper alone suffers little reduction in folding endurance. Similarly, in a study of papers laminated with Ultraphan HK (*18*), the laminated

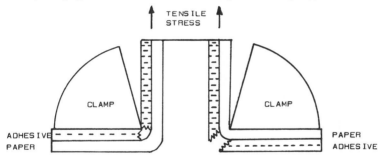

FOLDING ENDURANCE BRITTLE ADHESIVE FLEXIBLE PAPER

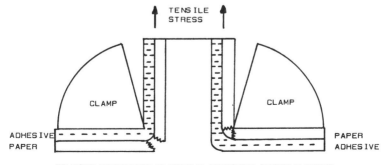

FOLDING ENDURANCE FLEXIBLE ADHESIVE BRITTLE PAPER

Figure 2. Folding endurance behavior of adhesive–paper systems

system demonstrated reduced folding endurance when compared with the unlaminated paper. This behavior persisted under conditions of accelerated aging. It was noted that the original laminating sheet was 40 μ thick and increased the thickness of the paper substrate by 20 μ to 150–170 μ. The combined effects of penetration and increased thickness led to a system with reduced folding endurance though an examination of the individual components predicted the opposite effect.

In the examples presented below, polymer–paper systems are examined for cases where there is complete impregnation of the substrate to form what behaves as a single component (poly(vinyl alcohol), soluble nylon, and Regnal); for cases where penetration is limited and the polymer and substrate behave in a generally separate manner (glues); and for cases where a range of behaviors—from apparent interactive to apparent independent—is observed although penetration is limited (poly-(vinyl acetates)).

Table I. Designations and Suppliers of Materials

Designation	Supplier	Form Applied
Impregnating Agents		
Poly(vinyl alcohol) U228	J. T. Baker	5% in water[a]
Regnal Copolymer	World Patent	5% stock solution[b, c]
Zytel 61 Nylon[d]	Development	5% in 90/10
	E. I. DuPont	methanol/water
Glues		
Ganes Flexible Glue	Gane Bros. & Lane	24%, 35% and 47%
849 Sta-flat	S. Schweitzer	in water
Yes Stikflat	Gane Bros. & Lane	34%, 67% in water
		36%, 71% in water
Poly(vinyl acetate) Emulsions		
Airflex 400	Air Products	as supplied
Booksaver	Delkote	as supplied
Elmer's Glue All	Borden	as supplied
Elvace 1874	E. I. DuPont	as supplied
Everflex A[e]	W. R. Grace	as supplied
Everflex G	W. R. Grace	as supplied
Flexbond 800	Air Products	as supplied
Jade 403	Jade Adhesives	as supplied

[a] All solute percentages given by weight.
[b] The major solvent component is ethanol.
[c] The product is also supplied with a 5% $Mg(C_2H_3O_2)_2$ buffer.
[d] Currently available as Elvamide 8061.
[e] Also available as Daratak A.

Experimental

Materials and Methods of Application. All paper substrates for the impregnating agent/paper system studies were a buffered wood sulfite, Gracie & Sons Acid-Free Lining Paper, Lot 3 (supplied by Charles R. Gracie & Sons, Inc., New York, N.Y. 10022). Samples were all cut in 0.5 × 6-in. strips with the long direction parallel to the machine direction.

All paper samples for the poly(vinyl acetate)/paper and glue/paper studies were Whatman chromatography paper #1, basis weight 87 g/m², thickness 0.16 mm, medium flow rate, supplied in 0.5-in. × 300-ft rolls, cut in 6-in. lengths. The materials used to prepare the polymer–paper composite systems are listed in Table I. Complete descriptions including suppliers' comments are provided in earlier studies (*1, 2, 3*).

The procedure for applying the polymer material to the paper consisted of brushing the material on a single side of the test paper and permitting solvent evaporation in a controlled atmosphere (23 ± 1°C, 50% r.h.) for 24 hr. A loaded ¾-in. brush was brought back and forth over the paper sample for a total of five strokes. For measurement of breaking strength and elongation of poly(vinyl acetate)/paper "sandwiches," two strips of Whatman chromatography paper held together by a layer of adhesive were prepared and aged. The samples were prepared by brushing a ¾-in. brush loaded with adhesive back and forth over one strip of paper for a total of five strokes. A second strip was immediately placed on top and pressed lightly. The samples prepared in this manner were placed between 12-in. square Teflon sheets under a 10-lb weight for 3 days. After this period, the samples were equilibrated in an environmentally controlled room (23 ± 1°C, 50% r.h.) for one day and then aged at 95°C for varying periods.

Aging of Samples. The treated and untreated samples were placed in ovens at various temperatures (21°C, 50% r.h.; 60°C, 10% r.h.; 80°C, < 10% r.h.; 95°C, < 10% r.h.; and 100°C, < 10% r.h.) for periods of 1, 5, 9, 16, and 50 days. On completion of each aging period, six replicate samples were removed and equilibrated at 23 ± 1°C, 50% r.h. for 72 hr.

Folding Endurance Tests. Measurements were performed on a Tinius-Olsen model no. 2 instrument (also known as a "folding endurance tester" (MIT)) according to ASTM method D-2176-63T on samples cut in the same machine direction.

The large standard deviation observed (compared with untreated papers) reflects nonuniformity in sample thickness produced by the above methods of adhesive application. Generally, it was observed that the treated paper ruptured before the adhesive. The double folds to rupture the paper and the double folds to complete rupture of the system are reported.

Breaking Strength and Elongation. The test specimens were then examined under tensile stress on an Instron model TM-M 1101 Universal Tester equipped with 100-kg tension load cell (2-, 5-, 10-, 20-, 50-, 100-kg ranges) and pneumatic grips. The data were recorded as stress vs. time under a uniform increase in extension. The initial jaw separation was 38.1 mm and the initial elongation rate was 0.02 mm/sec. The breaking strength (kg) and elongation (mm) were read from this stress–elongation curve.

Results and Discussion

Impregnating Agents. The materials studied, poly(vinyl alcohol), soluble nylon, and Regnal, are described in Table I. All materials impregnated the paper substrate completely, leading to a system which behaved as a single component in folding endurance tests (Table II). This result was not unexpected since many papers evaluated in paper permanence studies were sized with similar polymeric materials. A way to interpret these data is to attribute the entire deterioration of fold endurance to the polymer. One set of data defies this interpretation—i.e., Regnal to which magnesium acetate was added. There the alkaline reserve of the buffered paper was inadequate to overcome the detrimental effects of the hydrolysis of the magnesium acetate, leading to a reduction in folding endurance to a value below that of the untreated paper aged for a comparable period.

Glues. Three glue preparations, Yes, Sta-flat, and Ganes Flexible Glue, are described in Table I. Folding endurance was obtained for samples of paper coated with varying thicknesses of glue and then aged as a system at temperatures of 21°C, 50% r.h.; 60°C, 10% r.h.; 80°C, < 10% r.h.; and 100°C, < 10% r.h. for periods of up to 50 days (Tables III–VI). The Ganes light-coat data are also presented graphically in Figure 3. The heavily coated specimens behaved erratically, suggesting nonuniform sample composition. In general, the paper and adhesive ruptured simultaneously. As expected, the rate of diminution of folding endurance increased with increasing temperature. At long aging times a marked fold strength weakening was observed whereas at shorter aging times (one and five days) increased strength was usually observed, corresponding to chemical set or solvent evaporation. Such increases in fold strength were most noticeable at lower temperatures.

To consider the applicability of the Arrhenius equation, these data were used to produce a plot of the log folding endurance as a function

Table II. Double Folds to Rupture [a] **for Artificially Aged (100°C, < 10% r.h.) Papers Treated with Impregnating Agents**

	Aging Time				
	0 Days	1 Day	5 Days	9 Days	16 Days
Untreated	13 ± 2	15 ± 1	16 ± 3	17 ± 5	13 ± 2
Poly(vinyl alcohol) U228	77 ± 14	66 ± 11	64 ± 19	58 ± 15	35 ± 10
5% Regnal (unbuffered)	67 ± 18	72 ± 10	48 ± 6	34 ± 10	14 ± 2
5% Regnal (5% buffer)	70 ± 17	68 ± 8	32 ± 6	19 ± 4	8 ± 1
Zytel 61 Nylon	171 ± 23	147 ± 55	142 ± 42	89 ± 22	47 ± 11

[a] Refers to the paper–adhesive system, 1.5-lb tension.

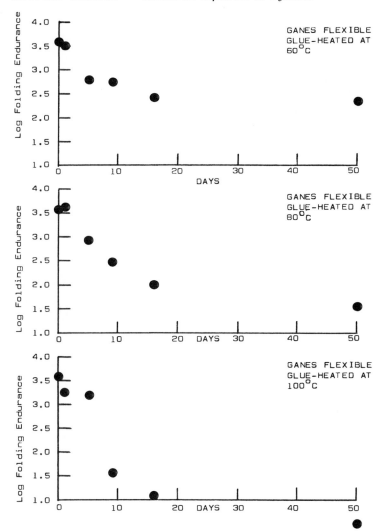

Figure 3.   Log folding endurance vs. time of heating at 60°, 80°, and 100°C for Ganes Flexible Glue

of days of aging to obtain a rate. By omitting the data for 50 days and using the best straight line, Figure 4, the data suggest that the behavior of a glue/paper system can roughly be characterized as first order. This result is not entirely unexpected since glues have a long history as sizing material (*19*) and in thin surface coats have been considered as a part of papers evaluated for permanence. The difficulties experienced in applying Arrhenius plots to thick coats of these materials may be attributed to

Table III. Double Folds to Rupture[a] for Artificially

	Aging Time	
Adhesive	0 Days	1 Day
Untreated	60 ± 15	60 ± 15
Yes (L) [b]	180 ± 43	68 ± 11
Yes (H)	302 ± 137	99 ± 45
Sta-flat (L)	2388 ± 1624	318 ± 176
Sta-flat (H)	232 ± 93	5 ± 5
Ganes (L)	4147 ± 895	3243 ± 1066
Ganes (M)	5174 ± 1646	1455 ± 564
Ganes (H)	3466 ± 1225	2096 ± 587

[a] Refers to the paper–adhesive system, ½-kg tension.

Table IV. Double Folds to Rupture[a] for Artificially

	Aging Time	
Adhesive	0 Days	1 Day
Untreated	60 ± 15	58 ± 20
Yes (L) [b]	180 ± 43	52 ± 20
Yes (H)	302 ± 137	218 ± 120
Sta-flat (L)	2388 ± 1624	254 ± 89
Sta-flat (H)	232 ± 93	80 ± 64
Ganes (L)	4147 ± 895	3263 ± 643
Ganes (M)	5174 ± 1646	4414 ± 2499
Ganes (H)	3446 ± 1225	1763 ± 838

[a] Refers to the paper–adhesive system, ½-kg tension.

Table V. Double Folds to Rupture[a] for Artificially

	Aging Time	
Adhesive	0 Days	1 Day
Untreated	60 ± 15	60 ± 11
Yes (L) [b]	180 ± 43	44 ± 8
Yes (H)	302 ± 137	152 ± 15
Sta-flat (L)	2388 ± 1624	116 ± 55
Sta-flat (H)	232 ± 93	27 ± 21
Ganes (L)	4147 ± 895	4431 ± 1042
Ganes (M)	5174 ± 1646	6173 ± 1414
Ganes (H)	3446 ± 1225	2407 ± 1315

[a] Refers to the paper–adhesive system, ½-kg tension.

Aged (21°C, 50% r.h.) Papers Treated with Glues

Aging Time

5 Days	9 Days	16 Days	50 Days
60 ± 15	60 ± 15	60 ± 15	60 ± 15
138 ± 46	29 ± 6	28 ± 7	28 ± 5
268 ± 136	74 ± 38	167 ± 175	199 ± 103
722 ± 305	27 ± 12	18 ± 12	36 ± 11
85 ± 99	12 ± 10	11 ± 5	36 ± 14
706 ± 250	666 ± 248	338 ± 188	232 ± 66
703 ± 199	705 ± 428	187 ± 73	88 ± 32
1474 ± 491	914 ± 420	2565 ± 870	2131 ± 385

[b] L, M, H denote light, medium, heavy coats, respectively.

Aged (60°C, 10% r.h.) Papers Treated with Glues

Aging Time

5 Days	9 Days	16 Days	50 Days
61 ± 15	61 ± 16	51 ± 6	60 ± 15
160 ± 22	26 ± 5	23 ± 6	29 ± 7
444 ± 96	260 ± 126	153 ± 49	210 ± 121
391 ± 346	7 ± 3	4 ± 3	4 ± 2
129 ± 72	21 ± 8	54 ± 19	35 ± 36
632 ± 196	584 ± 252	271 ± 162	233 ± 99
848 ± 182	1412 ± 160	484 ± 176	255 ± 203
3596 ± 777	1911 ± 1003	1286 ± 460	1893 ± 476

[b] L, M, H denote light, medium, heavy coats, respectively.

Aged (80°C, < 10% r.h.) Papers Treated with Glues

Aging Time

5 Days	9 Days	16 Days	50 Days
70 ± 24	56 ± 19	57 ± 14	21 ± 3
132 ± 32	17 ± 5	13 ± 3	11 ± 2
280 ± 55	56 ± 35	53 ± 49	17 ± 9
222 ± 155	1 ± 1	1 ± 1	1 ± 1
23 ± 14	0	8 ± 4	3 ± 2
780 ± 217	265 ± 122	107 ± 73	36 ± 33
1037 ± 193	861 ± 374	67 ± 51	212 ± 158
2131 ± 428	2144 ± 1560	5587 ± 311	1711 ± 441

[b] L, M, H denote light, medium, heavy coats, respectively.

Table VI. Double Folds to Rupture[a] for Artificially

| Adhesive | Aging Time | |
	0 Days	1 Day
Untreated	60 ± 15	55 ± 10
Yes (L)[b]	180 ± 43	25 ± 7
Yes (H)	302 ± 137	81 ± 61
Sta-flat (L)	2388 ± 1624	17 ± 11
Sta-flat (H)	232 ± 93	2 ± 1
Ganes (L)	4147 ± 895	1900 ± 832
Ganes (M)	5174 ± 1646	3533 ± 976
Ganes (H)	3446 ± 1225	1183 ± 578

[a] Refers to the paper–adhesive system, ½-kg tension.

the unevenness in film coating, nonuniform solvent evaporation, and chemical set.

The extended data points (50 days) at elevated temperatures all lie above the extrapolated rate line. As the glue deteriorates, the paper may play a greater role in the fold endurance of the system.

Poly(vinyl acetate) Emulsions. Table I lists the poly(vinyl acetate) emulsions examined. Folding endurance (Table VII) and break strength and elongation (Table VIII) were measured for coated samples and "sandwiches" of adhesive between two strips of paper substrate before and after aging at 95°C. The wide ranges of folding endurance behavior made Arrhenius plots inappropriate. In two of the systems, Booksaver and Elmer's Glue All, the only homopolymers in the group, the paper and adhesive ruptured simultaneously with substantial reduction in fold-

Table VII. Double Folds to Rupture[a] for Artificially Aged (95°C,

| Aging Time (Days) | Adhesive | | | |
	Airflex 400	Booksaver	Elmer's Glue All	Elvace 1874
0	817 ± 97 (744 ± 97)	235 ± 25	12 ± 4	435 ± 20 (340 ± 40)
1	618 ± 76 (600 ± 76)	9 ± 1	1	768 ± 82 (194 ± 58)
5	511 ± 45 (448 ± 49)	8 ± 1	2	556 ± 50 (165 ± 28)
9	376 ± 29 (304 ± 30)	4 ± 1	1	592 ± 119 (114 ± 24)
16	453 ± 38 (409 ± 36)	3 ± 1	2	853 ± 81 (105 ± 16)

[a] Rupture of the paper–adhesive system. Where the paper ruptured first, result is

Aged (100°C, <10% r.h.) Papers Treated with Glues

Aging Time

5 Days	9 Days	16 Days	50 Days
68 ± 22	56 ± 16	48 ± 18	34 ± 4
56 ± 12	5 ± 2	4 ± 1	3 ± 1
71 ± 80	3 ± 3	1 ± 1	1 ± 1
31 ± 22	1 ± 0	1 ± 1	1 ± 1
3 ± 1	0 ± 1	2 ± 1	2 ± 1
1698 ± 1006	36 ± 26	12 ± 5	1 ± 1
250 ± 194	111 ± 94	17 ± 10	1 ± 0
1802 ± 773	168 ± 115	52 ± 49	2 ± 2

[b] L, M, H denote light, medium, heavy coats, respectively.

ing endurance for the system when compared with untreated paper. The small differences between the breaking points of the paper and adhesive for Airflex 400, a vinyl acetate–ethylene copolymer, suggest that these samples behaved as a single interdependent system. The three systems, Everflex A, Everflex G, and Flexbond 800, behaved similarly enough to the untreated paper to suggest that the paper and adhesive behaved independently. Both Elvace 1874 and Jade 403 show more complex aging behavior, suggesting that the effects of setting or curing are different from the other systems.

In all cases the breaking strength and elongation for the system was greater than that of untreated paper. As anticipated, the two homopolymer emulsion-treated systems (Elmer's Glue All and Booksaver) which rapidly embrittled, leading to greatly reduced fold strength, showed the

<10% r.h.) Papers Treated with Poly(vinyl acetate) Emulsions

Adhesive

Everflex A	Everflex G	Flexbond 800	Jade 403	Untreated Paper
165 ± 91	213 ± 26	128 ± 7	956 ± 200	83 ± 9
(75 ± 4)	(197 ± 28)	(108 ± 10)	(423 ± 76)	
806 ± 33	102 ± 11	94 ± 8	799 ± 90	69 ± 14
(95 ± 5)	(99 ± 12)	(78 ± 8)	(476 ± 213)	
507 ± 130	263 ± 128	104 ± 8	1839 ± 595	77 ± 16
(110 ± 9)	(90 ± 10)	(92 ± 8)	(266 ± 49)	
724 ± 90	91 ± 7	130 ± 23	1188 ± 393	83 ± 12
(82 ± 11)	(87 ± 4)	(85 ± 8)	(250 ± 52)	
755 ± 74	129 ± 22	118 ± 7	854 ± 7	82 ± 11
(88 ± 5)	(105 ± 16)	(92 ± 7)	(404 ± 78)	

given in parentheses. Average of six samples.

Table VIII. Breaking Strength (kg) and Elongation (mm)

Aging Time (Days)	Adhesive			
	Airflex 400[b]	Booksaver	Elmer's Glue All	Elvace 1874
0	7.2 ± 0.2	7.2 ± 0.1	10.7 ± 0.5	8.7 ± 0.2
	(2.9 ± 0.1)	(3.2 ± 0.1)	(4.0 ± 0.4)	(3.2 ± 0.1)
1	8.2 ± 0.1	10.7 ± 0.2	13.7 ± 0.6	8.9 ± 0.2
	(2.4 ± 0.2)	(2.3 ± 0.1)	(2.2 ± 0.2)	(3.0 ± 0.1)
5	8.5 ± 0.2	11.0 ± 0.2	12.8 ± 0.2	8.6 ± 0.2
	(2.5 ± 0.1)	(2.3 ± 0.1)	(2.4 ± 0.2)	(2.8 ± 0.2)
9	7.9 ± 0.3	10.7 ± 0.3	12.9 ± 0.1	8.5 ± 0.1
	(2.2 ± 0.1)	(1.9 ± 0.1)	(2.1 ± 0.2)	(2.4 ± 0.1)
16	8.3 ± 0.3	11.0 ± 0.2	13.0 ± 0.2	9.1 ± 0.2
	(2.2 ± 0.1)	(2.0 ± 0.1)	(1.8 ± 0.1)	(2.7 ± 0.2)

[a] System of two paper strips held together by a layer of adhesive.
[b] All measurements are given as the average for six specimens together with "Studentized" standard deviation of the mean. The first number given is the breaking

greatest break strength and lowest elongation under tensile stress. Also observed was a general increase in break strength and decrease in elongation as samples were aged.

The differences among the breaking strengths of the several adhesives may be attributed, in part, to the variation in amount of adhesive present in the sample. The loading factors, the mass of dried adhesive per unit area of paper support, however, reveal no such correlation. For example,

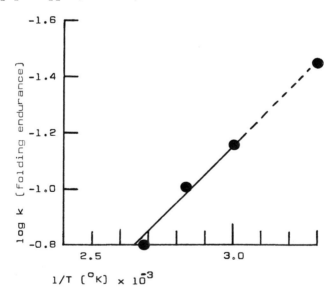

Figure 4.   Arhenius plot for Ganes Flexible Glue

for Paper–Adhesive Systems [a] **Aged at 95°C and $<$ 10% r.h.**

Adhesive

Everflex A	Everflex G	Flexbond 800	Jade 403	Untreated [e] Paper
9.1 ± 0.3	7.3 ± 0.2	6.6 ± 0.1	8.3 ± 0.2	6.4 ± 0.1
(3.3 ± 0.3)	(3.2 ± 0.1)	(2.6 ± 0.1)	(2.9 ± 0.2)	(1.4 ± 0.1)
9.5 ± 0.2	9.4 ± 0.1	7.2 ± 0.1	9.3 ± 0.5	6.9 ± 0.1
(3.0 ± 0.1)	(3.1 ± 0.1)	(2.6 ± 0.1)	(2.4 ± 0.1)	(1.3 ± 0.1)
9.5 ± 0.3	8.6 ± 0.6	7.0 ± 0.1	9.2 ± 0.2	6.8 ± 0.1
(3.0 ± 0.2)	(3.0 ± 0.1)	(2.6 ± 0.2)	(2.4 ± 0.1)	(1.3 ± 0.1)
10.3 ± 0.2	9.2 ± 0.1	7.2 ± 0.1	8.5 ± 0.3	6.8 ± 0.1
(2.9 ± 0.1)	(3.1 ± 0.2)	(2.6 ± 0.2)	(2.2 ± 0.1)	(1.1 ± 0.1)
10.4 ± 0.3	9.2 ± 0.2	7.5 ± 0.1	8.9 ± 0.2	7.1 ± 0.1
(3.0 ± 0.1)	(2.9 ± 0.2)	(2.3 ± 0.1)	(2.1 ± 0.1)	(1.2 ± 0.1)

strength (kg) and the second, given in parentheses, is the elongation (mm).
 [e] System consists of two strips of paper with no adhesive.

Everflex A and Airflex 400 have virtually identical loading factors yet the breaking strength of Everflex A is 25% greater than that of Airflex 400 (3). The differences in breaking strength appear to derive from differences in the mechanical properties of the base copolymers.

The absence of correspondence between the results of folding endurance tests and tensile properties demonstrates the need for both measurements in the evaluation of adhesives.

Conclusions

The examination of fold endurance and tensile strength of a series of polymer–paper systems under thermal accelerated aging indicates that only in the most favorable of circumstances is it possible to apply the Arrhenius equation to the system. It also seems unlikely that a sample addition relationship exists between the behavior of the individual components and their behavior as a system. A straight line plot of log folding endurance vs. aging time may reflect a fortuitous composite of several experimental variables leading to pseudo-first-order deterioration.

Attempts in this laboratory to characterize real or artificial aging with other kinds of analytical observations (color, reflectance, pH, etc.) and to subject these data in turn to Arrhenius plots has been even less successful. In general, the magnitude of the observed change and the inherent analytical errors do not allow Arrhenius plots. Among the test methods used, folding endurance is unusually sensitive compared with other test methods with respect to aging and component composition.

The lack of an unambiguous method for demonstrating predictive validity of thermal accelerated-aging methods warrants extreme caution in extrapolating to long-term behavior for polymer–adhesive systems. The usefulness of such studies is often best applied to a ranking of preferred behavior under evaluative criteria.

Acknowledgment

This project is sponsored by the National Museum Act (administered by the Smithsonian Institution).

Literature Cited

1. Baer, N. S., Indictor, N., Joel, A., "The Aging Behavior of Impregnating Agent—Paper Systems as Used in Paper Conservation," *Restaurator* (1972) **2**, No. 1, 5–23.
2. Baer, N. S., Indictor, N., Joel, A., "An Evaluation of Glues for Use in Paper Conservation," "Conservation and Restoration of Pictoral Art," Chapter 25, Butterworths, London, 1976.
3. Baer, N. S., Indictor, N., Schwartzman, T., Rosenberg, I. L., "Chemical and Physical Properties of Poly(vinyl acetate) Copolymer Emulsions," *ICOM Prepr.*, Committee for Conservation, 4th Triennial Meeting, Venice, 1975, 75/22/5–1, 75/22/5–20, ICOM, Paris, 1975.
4. Chaet, B., "Collage Transformed: Interview with Corrado Marca-Relli," *Arts*, June 1958, pp. 64–65.
5. Majewski, L. J., private communication.
6. "Permanence/Durability of the Book IV: Polyvinyl Acetate (PVA) Adhesives for Use in Library Bookbinding," W. J. Barrow Research Laboratories, Richmond, Va., 1965.
7. Horton, C., "Cleaning and Preserving Bindings and Related Materials," 2nd Ed., Appendix 2, Library Technology Program, American Library Association, Chicago, 1969.
8. Scott, K., "Conservation of a Third Century Fayum Portrait on Linen," *IIC-AG Technical Papers from 1968–1970*, pp. 145–149, IIC-AG, New York, 1970.
9. Landi, S., "Notes on the Use of a Vacuum Hot-Table for Textiles," *Stud. Conserv.* (1973) **18**, No. 4, 167–171.
10. Indictor, N., Baer, N. S., Phelan, W. H., "An Evaluation of Pastes for Use in Paper Conservation," *Restaurator* (1975) **2**, No. 2, 139–150.
11. Baer, N. S., Indictor, N., Phelan, W. H., "An Evaluation of Poly(vinyl acetate) Emulsions for Use in Paper Conservation," *Restaurator* (1975) **2**, No. 2, 121–137.
12. Baer, N. S., Indicator, N., "Proposal for a Repository for the Materials of Book and Paper Conservation," *ICOM Prepr.*, Committee for Conservation, 4th Triennial Meeting, Venice, 1975, 75/9/3–1, 75/9/3–6, ICOM, Paris, 1975.
13. Gray, G. G., "Determination and Significance of Activation Energy in Permanence Tests," *Adv. Chem. Ser.* (1977) **164**, 286.
14. Barrow, W. J., "Permanence/Durability of the Book II: Test Data of Naturally Aged Papers," W. J. Barrow Research Laboratories, Richmond, Va., 1964.
15. Smith, R. D., "New Approaches to Preservation," *Libr. Q.* (1970) **40**, No. 1, 139–171.

16. Smith, R. D., "A Comparison of Paper in Identical Copies of Books," *Restaurator* (Supplement No. 2) (1972) pp. 14–25, 37–46.
17. Williams, J. C., Krasnow, M. R., "Folding Endurance and Tensile Strength of Paper," *Bull. Am. Inst. Conserv.* (1973) **14**, No. 1, 25–41.
18. Santucci, L., "Report on Paper Strength and Stability," Joint Meeting of the ICOM Commitee for Scientific Museum Laboratories and the ICOM Subcommittee for the Care of Paintings, 1965, 16 pp., mimeographed.
19. Browning, B. L., "Analysis of Paper," Chapter 9, Marcel Dekker, New York, 1969.

RECEIVED May 25, 1977.

23

Thermal Analysis Study of Paper Permanence

ALLEN A. DUSWALT

Hercules, Inc., Research Center, Wilmington, Del. 19899

The oxidative degradations of three types of paper were studied by differential thermal analysis (DTA). For each case, an activation energy of about 34 kcal/mol was found for the first oxidation exotherm. The DTA kinetic values were able to predict the degree of reaction of experimentally aged samples with good accuracy. The observed oxidative stability of the papers agreed with their ranking by Library of Congress oven aging/folding endurance tests. The Arrhenius kinetic values for a paper were easily determined within a day with a precision of ±2% standard deviation for the activation energy.

Accelerated tests of paper permanence are usually carried out by aging samples for several days at temperatures near 100°C. Changes are then often observed with respect to color, folding, or tearing strength. Frequently, tests are carried out at one temperature for varying lengths of time to rank different paper compositions. More complex studies have involved tests at more than one temperature and the use of the Arrhenius equation to predict lifetime stabilities under ambient conditions (1). These tests have presented a number of difficulties, including nonlinear Arrhenius plots, poor precision, and lengthy aging times.

A number of articles have been published describing the application of DTA to paper degradation (2–5). However, the papers studied in these works were pyrolyzed in an inert atmosphere, and measurements were consequently made on an endothermic reaction peak. The relationship between pyrolysis results and resistance to normal aging of paper can be questioned. The present study concerns a different DTA approach which enables the degradation reaction to be examined in air or oxygen. Reaction measurements are made on resulting exothermic oxidation peaks.

Over the past few years several papers have been published describing the application of differential thermal methods to the determination of Arrhenius reaction parameters (6–9). These are generally short-term, high temperature procedures which greatly accelerate the reaction. An isothermal aging technique for observing reactions at lower temperatures has also been described (6). A technique which has proved to be broadly applicable and experimentally simple is based on determining the reaction peak temperature as a function of the programmed heating rate of the sample. Doyle (10) has described a good approximation for the relationship as

$$E \simeq 4.35[\Delta \log \beta / \Delta (1/T_m)] \tag{1}$$

where E is the activation energy, β the linear programmed heating rate, and T_m the reaction peak maximum temperature in degrees Kelvin. The "constant" 4.35 is an approximation which depends on the value of E. For reactions with an E/RT value between 20 and 60, the error in the "constant" is less than 3%. A more accurate relationship is

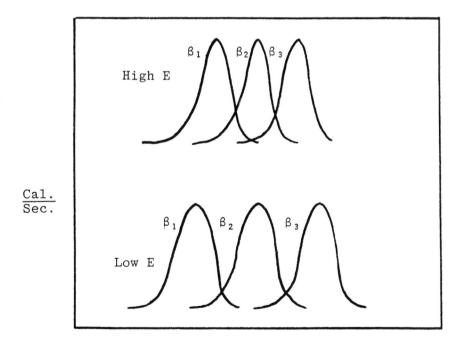

Figure 1.   *Effect of activation energy, E, on reaction curves for different heating rates: β_1, β_2, β_3 °C/min*

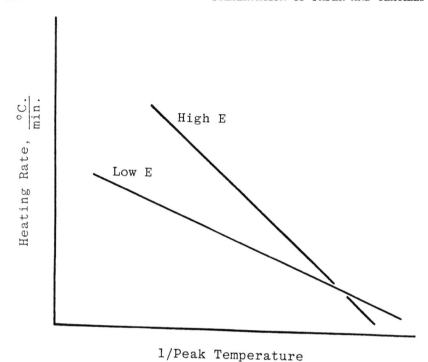

Figure 2.   Data plot for determining activation energy. Slope $\simeq$ E/4.35.

$$E = \frac{R[\Delta(\ln \beta)/\Delta(1/T_m)]}{\dfrac{1}{(X+3)} - \dfrac{1}{X} - \dfrac{1}{(X+2)} - \dfrac{1}{(X+4)} - 1} \tag{2}$$

where $X = E/RT$ and R is the gas constant (*11*). Figure 1 is an idealized illustration of the relationship between the programmed heating rate and the peak maximum temperature for the reactions with different activation energies. Figure 2 shows a data plot for two such reactions.

After E is calculated from Equation 1 or 2, an Arrhenius frequency factor (*6*) can be calculated from the same thermal data.

$$Z = \frac{\beta E}{R T_m{}^2} e^{E/RT} \tag{3}$$

This is the first-order form of the expression derived by Murray and White (*12*) and used to calculate pre-exponential factors by Rogers and Smith (*13*).

Paper Samples

The paper formulations studied in this work were characterized by a series of oven aging–folding endurance tests. The test results and samples of the formulations were received from Williams (*14*). The identities of the sheets and their corresponding folding endurance test results are given in Table I.

A plot of the fold test data is shown in Figure 3. The plotted fold data include the range covered by the standard deviation. The scatter is sufficient to hide possible nonlinear behavior. However, aging clearly

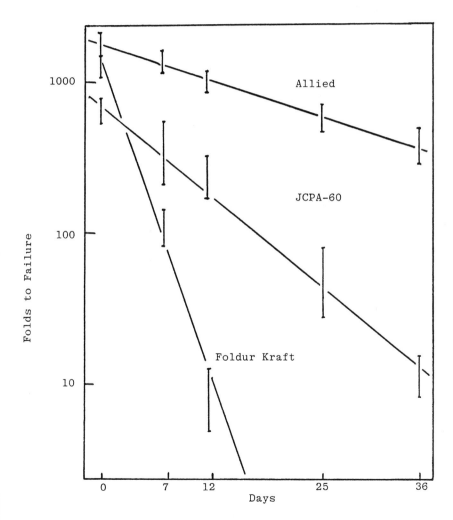

Figure 3.   Folding endurance vs. aging time at 100°C

Table I.   Folds to Failure

Paper	Number of Days Aged	
	0	7
Allied Superior Offset	1904 ± 285 [b]	1470 ± 256
Gov't. Printing Office JCPA-60	687 ± 134	395 ± 172
Champion Foldur Kraft	1367 ± 220	117 ± 31

[a] Aging temperature 100°C, 0.5-kg test load.

affects the Allied paper least and the Foldur Kraft most severely with respect to folding endurance.

Differential Thermal Study

Discs of paper, ⅛-in diameter, were punched from sheets. The discs were placed in ¼-in diameter aluminum foil pans and covered with 80-mesh stainless steel screen to prevent coiling. The samples were then linearly temperature programmed at various rates in a DuPont 990 differential thermal analyzer under a 50-cc/min flow of air or oxygen. The paper reaction peaks were recorded, and the peak maximum temperatures were measured and corrected for thermal resistance, thermo-

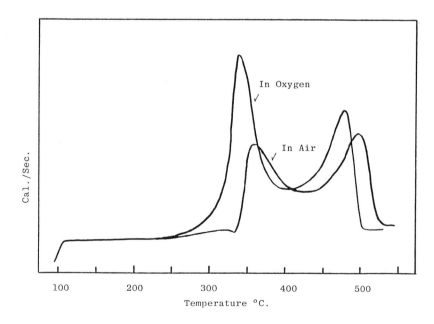

Figure 4.   Oxidation curves for JCPA-60 at temperature programming rate of 15°C/min

of Oven Aged Paper[a]

	Number of Days Aged		Est. Days for
12	*25*	*26*	*Fold Drop to 1*
1081 ± 179	628 ± 123	415 ± 117	176
257 ± 84	57 ± 28	12.4 ± 3.7	60
9 ± 4	0	0	18

[b] Standard deviation.

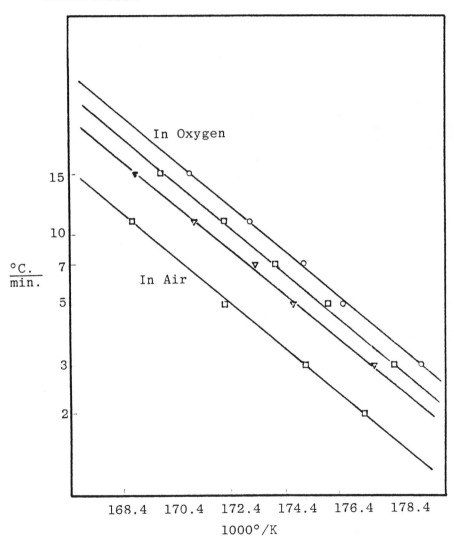

Figure 5. *Plot for heating rate vs. reaction peak temperature for paper oxida-tion reactions.* ○, *Foldur Kraft;* □, *JCPA-60;* ▽, *Allied Superior.*

couple nonlinearity, and heating rate lag. The peaks are plotted as cal/sec of reaction energy vs. temperature.

Reaction thermograms for JCPA-60 paper run in air and oxygen are shown in Figure 4. The first peaks represent, among other reactions, a carbonizing of the paper. This is evidenced by a gradual blackening of the paper as the recorder traces the first peak. The residual black mass completely oxidizes during the tracing of the second peak, leaving a small amount of white ash residue. Reaction thermograms of JCPA-60 in air resulted in a linear temperature-vs.-heating-rate plot and a calculated activation energy of 33,700 cal/mol from Equation 2. However, the initial part of the air-oxidation curve shows evidence of endothermic activity—possibly a result of oxygen starvation. The lower peak temperatures and the lack of obvious complexity for the corresponding oxygen oxidation peak support this theory. Kinetic studies were carried out in oxygen to minimize oxygen insufficiency and to enable treating of the data on a pseudo first-order basis.

Plots of the corrected data for the paper reactions in oxygen are shown in Figure 5. The linear, essentially parallel lines obtained for the three papers indicate very similar or identical activation energies. The air oxidation plot is parallel to the others, showing a similar activation energy and suggesting that the reaction mechanism may be the same. The slopes of the lines were calculated from a linear regression analysis of the plotted points. The data and calculated activation energies are given in Table II.

The above results agree with those of the folding endurance test carried out at 100°C—i.e., the Allied paper is most stable, the Foldur Kraft least stable, and the JCPA-60 is intermediate.

Table II.   Data and Results for Paper Reaction

	Corrected Peak Maximum Temps. (°C)			
Heating Rate (°C/min)	*Allied*	*In Oxygen JCPA-60*	*Kraft*	*In Air JCPA-60*
20				351.0
15	334.7	331.6	327.7	
10	327.1	323.2	319.8	335.5
7	319.0	316.5	312.7	
5	314.0	309.5	307.7	323.0
3	303.8	301.4	298.1	312.5
2				305.0
	Calculated E			
(kcal/mol)	34.0 ± 0.7[a]	34.1 ± 0.8	35.0 ± 0.7	33.7 ± 0.5

[a] Standard deviation.

Isothermal Test of Calculated Activation Energies

The accuracy of the activation energies can be tested by predicting the degree of reaction for a sample held isothermally for a specific time and temperature and observing if experimental aging results agree with the prediction.

For extrapolation purposes, a value of 34.0 ± 0.7 kcal/mol was used as the activation energy for the oxidation reaction. Corresponding preexponential factors were calculated from peak temperature data and Equation 3. The degree of reaction for an aged sample can be predicted from the Arrhenius equation

$$k = Ze^{-E/RT_a} \tag{4}$$

and the first order rate expression

$$(1 - C) = e^{-kt_a} \tag{5}$$

where $(1 - C)$ is the residual unreacted fraction, k the specific rate constant, and T_a and t_a the aging temperature and time, respectively. Calculations were made for the percent reaction of the paper samples held 63 hr at 195°C. A calculation was also made for JCPA-60 paper held 19 hr at 212°C. These predictions and an "error range" including the standard deviation and a ±1°C variation in aging temperature are given in Table III.

Paper samples were then aged in the DTA instrument for oxygen for the times and temperatures described above. Subsequent programmed reaction curves for an aged and unaged sample are shown in Figure 6. The rate of heat evolution at the peak maximum is proportional to the amount of reacting material present and therefore, relative peak heights can be used as a measure of conversion. Table III lists the percent reaction found for the aged paper samples, calculated from peak height measurements as in Figure 6.

Table III. Calculated vs. Experimental Conversion

Sample	Calculated[a] Z, ($\times 10^{12}$)	Calc. % Conversion	Error[b] Range (%)	Found % Reaction	Aging (°C)	Aging Conditions (hr)
Allied	1.13	44	37–50	52	195	63
JCPA-60	1.35	50	43–56	50	195	63
JCPA-60	1.35	48	42–54	45	212	19
Kraft	1.61	56	49–63	58	195	63

[a] Z = preexponential factor in reciprocal minutes.
[b] Error range for ± one standard deviation of E and ±1°C aging temperature.

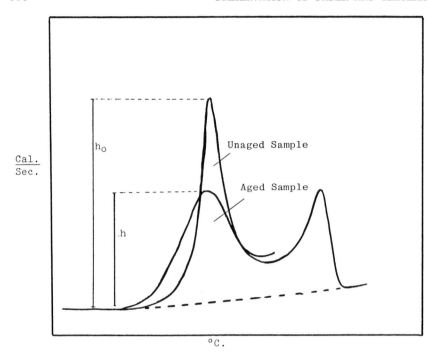

Figure 6. Isothermal test for JCPA-60 aged sample held 19 hr at 212°C. Peak heights are h *and* h*₀ for aged and unaged samples, respectively.* % *reaction* = h × 100/h*₀.*

Conclusions

Results from the high temperature study of the oxidation reaction of the paper products appear to correlate well with those of folding endurance tests carried out on dry paper after aging at 100°C. If the correlation is general, the DTA technique offers advantages in analysis time and precision over conventional paper testing methods. A single point for ranking purposes can be obtained easily in 15 minutes.

Calculations from the thermal data indicate an activation energy near 34 kcal/mol for the oxidation reaction of the papers studied. Calculations using this value were able to predict isothermal reaction rates for samples aged approximately 100°C below the programmed peak temperatures. The observed conversions were within, or close to, an error range bounded by a ±2% relative standard deviation of the activation energy and a ±1°C variance in the isothermal aging temperature.

If the oxidation rates observed by DTA are assumed to be a valid measure of paper permanence, the technique can be very useful. The relative effects of trace metals, pH, antioxidants, and other nonvolatile additives can be assessed rapidly and precisely by temperature programming samples in an oxidative atmosphere. The effects of volatile components—e.g., water—can be examined by preliminary aging in sealed cells at relatively high temperatures. Subsequent programmed runs of the aged samples will show rate effects, which can be extrapolated to ambient temperatures.

Literature Cited

1. Browning, B. L., Wink, W. A., *Tappi* (1968) **51** (4), 156.
2. Herbert, R. L., Tryon, M., Wilson, W. K., "Differential Thermal Analysis of Some Papers and Carbohydrate Materials," *Tappi* (1969) **52**, 1183.
3. Parks, E. J., "Thermal Analysis of Modified Cellulose," *Tappi* (1971) **54**, 537.
4. Wilson, W. K., Herbert, R. L., "Evaluation of the Stability of Manifold Papers," *Tappi* (1972) **55**, 1103.
5. Parks, E. J., Herbert, R. L., "Thermal Analysis of Ion Exchange Reaction Products of Wood Pulp with Calcium and Aluminum Cations," *Tappi* (1972) **55**, 1510.
6. Duswalt, A. A., *Thermochim. Acta* (1974) **8**, 57.
7. Ozawa, T., *J. Therm. Anal.* (1970) **2**, 301.
8. Freeman, E. S., Carrol, B., *J. Phys. Chem.* (1958) **62**, 394.
9. Coats, A. W., Redfern, J. P., *Nature* (1964) **201**, 68.
10. Doyle, C. D., *J. Appl. Polym. Sci.* (1961) **5**, 285.
11. McCarty, J. D., Green, C. E., presentation at *Third Middle Atlantic Regional Meeting, Div. Anal. Chem.*, Philadelphia, 1968.
12. Murray, P., White, J., *Trans. Br. Ceram. Soc.* (1955) **54**, 204.
13. Rogers, R. N., Smith, L. C., *Anal. Chem.* (1967) **39**, 1024.
14. Williams, J. C., Library of Congress, Wash., D. C., private communication.

RECEIVED April 7, 1977.

24

Thermogravimetric Analysis of Pulps

III: TGA Profiles

R. D. CARDWELL

New Zealand Forest Products, Ltd., Private Bag, Auckland, New Zealand

P. LUNER

Department of Paper Science and Engineering, SUNY College of
Environmental Science and Forestry, Syracuse, N.Y. 13210

*Thermogram profiles of a number of papermaking pulps are
examined. Differences between the profiles are attributed to
variations in hemicellulose content and in apparent crystallinity. Differential rate of weight loss vs. weight fraction
plots indicate reaction orders between 0 and 1. Changes in
the thermogram with changes in the rate of heating show
evidence of competitive reactions which may be more clearly
differentiated by using more extreme heating rates. The
apparent crystallinity of some aged pulps increased over
that of unaged controls, indicating a preferential decomposition of the amorphous regions.*

Studies of the pyrolysis of wood and paper samples have shown that the
thermogram profiles of these materials are partial composites of the
profiles of the individual components. Figure 1 shows integral and differential curves for ponderosa pine, cellulose powder, and sulfuric acid
lignin as determined by Tang (1). This figure illustrates the clear
differences between the lignin and cellulose components and the composite character of the shape of the wood thermogram. The breakdown
temperatures, and hence the position of the thermogram on the temperature scale, for the main components of paper—namely, hemicellulose,
cellulose, and lignin—have been found to increase in the order listed
and fall in the ranges 200°–260°C, 240°–350°C, and 280°–500°C, respectively. These temperature ranges, however, considerably depend on the
experimental details of the pyrolysis technique used. Since the major

component of all paper pulps is cellulose, it could be expected that the main influence on the thermogram would be attributable to this component, and a substantial number of investigators have studied the thermal degradation of cellulose and the effect of modifications by various chemical treatments, substitutions, or cross-linking reactions (2, 3, 4, 5). Hemicellulose and lignin have only been studied to a limited extent with much of the reported work confined to differential thermal analysis or included as a minor consideration in survey studies of cellulosic materials (6).

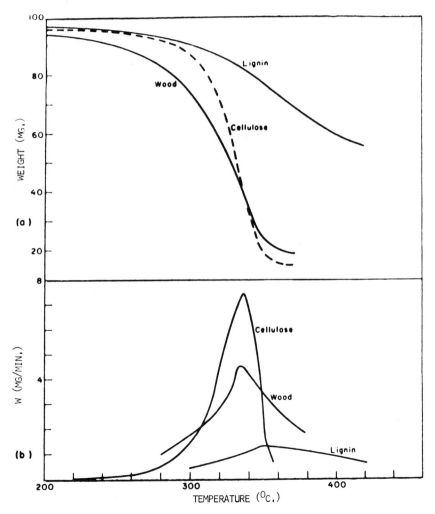

U.S. Forest Service, Research Paper FPL 71

Figure 1.   Integral and differential thermograms of wood components (1)

The physical structure of a papermaking pulp, either at the fiber or at the supramolecular level, as well as the chemical characteristics of its components will affect the characteristic shape or profile of its thermogram. While the primary bond energies contribute the greatest to the heat stability of a compound, additional strength and stability can be contributed by secondary or van der Waals' bonding forces or by hydrogen bonding. It could be expected then that the crystalline or amorphous nature of pulp fibers would contribute to the pulp's relative stability and that this in turn would be reflected in the thermogravimetric profile. Irregularities in the structure such as chain ends, weak links, or chain folding may be sites for the initiation of reactions with lower energy than for a more regular structure. In addition to these physical structural effects, submicroscopic features such as pore size, shape, and distribution may also influence the pyrolysis reaction. To the extent then that different papermaking pulps differ in chemical and physical characteristics, their thermogram profiles may be expected to reflect such differences.

Natural or artificially accelerated aging of papermaking pulps is characterized by two important reactions, scission of the polymeric cellulose chains and some cross-linking reaction (7, 8, 9), the exact nature of which remains unknown. Since the mechanical properties of aged paper are modified by these two simultaneous reactions, it was of interest to determine whether these chemical effects influence the thermograms of artificially aged papers.

In this paper, the thermogram profiles of a number of papermaking pulps are examined. Different methods of presenting such curves are discussed, and the effects of changes in the rate of heating on the curves are examined. Where possible, the effects of such aspects as wood species, fiber preparation, crystallinity, or artificial aging on the thermograms are also discussed.

Experimental

Materials. A number of papermaking pulp samples, including bleached and unbleached, sulfite and sulfate, hardwood and softwood, and semichemical varieties, were analyzed thermogravimetrically. Some of these pulps, artificially aged at elevated temperatures and humidity, were also included. A list of the pulps and the codes assigned to them for easier reference are given in Table I.

Methods. A Perkin-Elmer model TGS/thermobalance was used according to the manufacturer's instructions. These details are incorporated elsewhere (10). One set of pulp samples was run at a fixed, programmed heating rate of 40°C/min (Figures 2–5) in a nitrogen atmosphere, and in these cases, at least two replicates of each pulp were evaluated for each of the thermogravimetric and differential thermogravimetric modes. After modifying the apparatus by adding a Cahn derivative

Table I. Pulps and Code Identification

Pulp Type	Identifying Code
Cotton linters	cotton
Rayon fibers	rayon
Scandinavian bleached birch kraft	BBC
As above, aged 12 days at 90°C, 73.5% r.h.	BBC aged
Scandinavian bleached pine kraft	BPC
As above, aged 12 days at 90°C, 73.5% r.h.	BPC aged
Scandinavian bleached pine sulfite	BPS
New Zealand bleached pine kraft	BRK
Scandinavian bleached spruce sulfite	BSS
As above, aged 24 days at 80°C, 57% r.h.	BSS aged
Bleached mixed hardwood neutral sulfite semichem.	FB
As above, aged 12 days at 90°C, 73.5% r.h.	FB aged
Unbleached mixed hardwood sulfite	HS
Scandinavian unbleached semichem. birch sulfite	SBS
As above, aged 12 days at 90°C, 73.5% r.h.	SBS aged
Scandinavian bleached pine kraft	SKA
As above, aged 12 days at 90°C, 73.5% r.h.	SKA aged
Unbleached mixed softwood sulfite	USS
As above, aged 12 days at 90°C, 73.5% r.h.	USS aged

computer, which enabled both thermogravimetric and differential thermo-gravimetric modes to be recorded using one sample, a second set of pulps was run at a number of heating rates varying from 5°–80°C/min (Figures 6 and 7). Since a complete recalibration of the apparatus was necessary after this modification, the two sets of samples are not strictly comparable and so are used to demonstrate different thermal characteristics. In all cases, replicates were made whenever anomalies in a particular pyrolysis or set of pyrolyses were apparent, which was infrequent.

Results and Discussion

Integral Plots. Figures 2A–D show the integral thermal degradation curves obtained from eleven different pulp samples. In some cases, specific curves have been repeated in more than one figure to give a reference curve or a specific grouping of pulps. The curves have been corrected for temperature calibration of the apparatus within the signifi-cant temperature range and normalized with reference to the oven-dry sample weight by expressing the weight loss as a weight fraction.

The general profile of the integral plots is a sigmoidal shape showing a slow loss of weight at the lower temperatures, starting at about 275°C and continuing to about 350°C, a much more precipitous loss of weight between about 350°–410°C, followed finally by a very gradual loss of weight above about 425°C. Since the temperature zones indicated above are greatly influenced by the programmed heating rate, being shifted

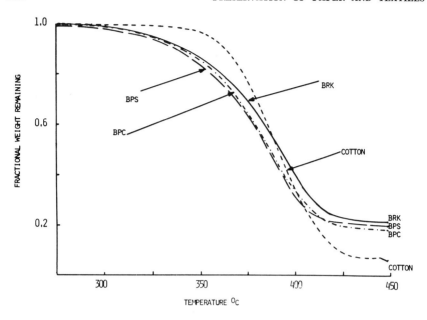

Figure 2A. Integral thermograms of cotton, sulfite, and kraft pulps. Rate of heating: 40°C/min.

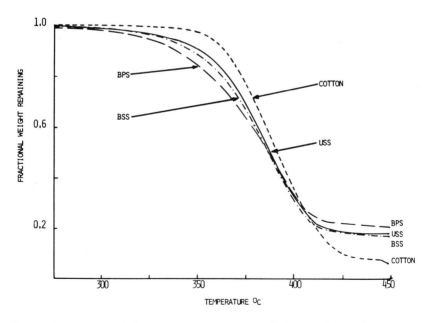

Figure 2B. Integral thermograms of cotton and three sulfite pulps. Rate of heating: 40°C/min.

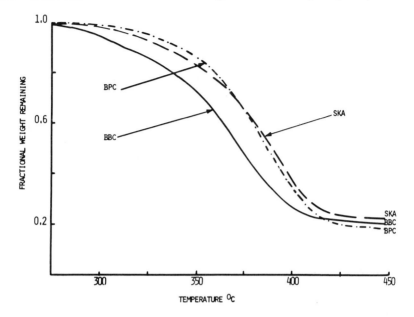

Figure 2C.   *Integral thermograms of three kraft pulps.   Rate of heating:*
40°C/min.

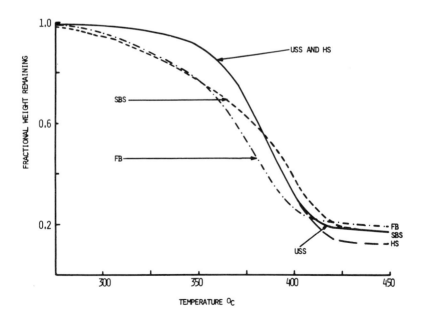

Figure 2D.   *Integral thermograms of sulfite and sulfite semichemical pulps.*
Rate of heating: 40°C/min.

upwards by using higher heating rates, these comparisons are made on curves produced at a constant heating rate of 40°C/min. The effect of changing the heating rate is discussed fully later.

Figure 2A compares a cotton linter pulp with a bleached pine sulfite pulp, BPS, and two different bleached pine kraft pulps, BPC and BRK. It is immediately apparent that the initial weight loss from the cotton linters pulp occurs at a higher temperature than for the three wood pulps, and in fact, this was true for all the other wood pulps as well. In addition, the residue at the conclusion of pyrolysis was lowest for the cotton linter pulp. Figure 2 also shows that although the early pyrolytic behavior of the three wood pulps is similar, the later behavior and the residues are differentiated. In fact, the two pine kraft pulps, BRK and BPC, are more dissimilar than are the BPS and BPC pulps, which are bleached pine sulfite and bleached pine kraft pulps, respectively. In the latter two pulps, the species of pine is the same whereas the pine kraft, BRK, is from a different pine species grown in the southern hemisphere.

Figure 2B shows a group of sulfite pulps with the cotton linters pulp shown again for comparison. The USS and BSS pulps, unbleached and bleached spruce sulfite, respectively, are quite similar and fall between the cotton linters pulp and the bleached pine sulfite pulp with respect to both initial decomposition and final residue.

Figure 2C compares three kraft pulps. Two bleached pine kraft pulps, SKA and BPC, show a relative crossover in their degradation curves; and a bleached birch kraft pulp, BBC, shows an initial loss of weight at a lower temperature but has about the same residue as the other two pulps.

Figure 2D compares a number of sulfite pulps. Two of them, an unbleached spruce sulfite, USS, and an unbleached mixed hardwood sulfite, HS, have remarkably similar degradation curves but show different final residues. A bleached neutral sulfite semichemical pulp, FB, and an unbleached semichemical birch sulfite, SBS, have similar and much steeper initial degradation curves than the other two pulps. The semichemical birch sulfite pulp, SBS, has a degradation curve which crosses over those of the other three pulps shown in Figure 2D.

Thus, each pulp has an integral weight loss profile characterized by three main features: the temperature at which significant degradative weight loss begins (threshold temperature), the slope of the central portion of the sigmoidal curve (which is usually almost linear), and the final residual fraction. The low initial rate of loss can be attributed to the dehydration of cellulose to "dehydrocellulose," the steep central portion of the curve mainly to volatilization of the tarry material, levoglucosan (1,6-anhydro-β-D-glucopyranose), and the residual char fraction to the breakdown of the "dehydrocellulose" formed early in the reaction. These three stages of cellulose degradation were proposed by Kilzer and Broido (*11*). Figures 2A–D show that those pulps having a higher threshold temperature usually also have a steeper central portion and a lower residual fraction. This indicates that in these cases the "dehydrocellulose" reaction is relatively minor and that although the material may be initially more thermally stable, the levoglucosan volatilization takes place very rapidly once initiated. These conditions might be expected to occur in highly crystalline materials as suggested by Golova and co-workers (*12*).

Differential Plots. The differential plots shown in Figures 3 and 4 are of two types. Figures 3A–D show rate of weight loss vs. temperature whereas Figures 4A–D show the rate of weight loss vs. weight fraction lost. The pulps shown in these figures are the same as those shown in the integral plots of Figures 2A–D.

RATE OF WEIGHT LOSS VS. TEMPERATURE. Figures 3A–D clearly show the point of maximum rate of weight loss for each pulp which, with the three exceptions of pulps BBC, FB, and SBS (Figures 3C and 3D), falls just under 400°C for this heating rate of 40°C/min. Of these exceptions, the temperature of maximum rate of weight loss falls lower than the average for pulps BBC and FB and higher than the average for pulp SBS. These three pulps also show evidence of an earlier small peak which is most clearly differentiated in the case of pulp BBC and appears near 310°C. Of the other pulps, the bleached pine kraft pulp, BRK, also shows indications of an earlier peak near 330°C (Figure 3A). This early peak may be attributed to reactions in the hemicellulose components known to be less thermally stable, possibly as a result of their greater accessibility (*13*). The semichemical pulps, FB and SBS, and the birch kraft pulp, BBC, are likely to have higher hemicellulose contents than the other soft-wood chemical pulps (*14*), but whether the pulp BRK also contains a higher-than-average hemicellulose content is not known. Figures 3A and 3B also show the higher rate of weight loss for the cotton linters pulp, probably attributable to its highly crystalline structure.

RATE OF WEIGHT LOSS VS. WEIGHT FRACTION. Another method of presenting thermogravimetric data that has been used by Flynn, Wall, and others (*15, 16*) is shown in Figures 4A–D. In these figures, the rate of weight loss is plotted against the weight fraction lost. For dynamic thermogravimetry such plots ignore temperature differences between pulps but appear to differentiate more clearly between early weight loss behavior. The residues after pyrolysis are also clearly differentiated as in the integral plots. This type of plot has been found to be quite informative in isothermal studies where no temperature differences are involved (*17*). Flynn and Wall (*14*) have shown that it is possible to obtain a qualitative understanding of the early kinetics from the limiting characteristics of such plots. If the curve is initially concave with respect to

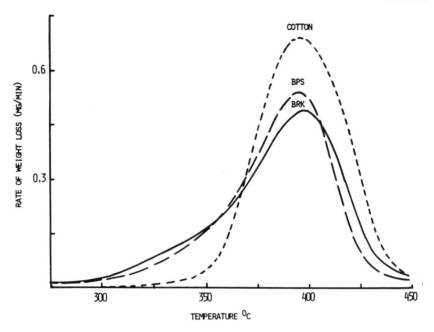

*Figure 3A. Differential thermograms of cotton, sulfite, and kraft pulps.
Rate of heating: 40°C/min.*

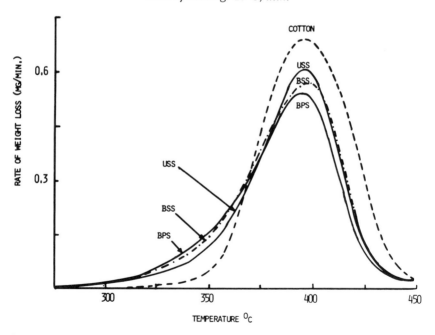

*Figure 3B. Differential thermograms of cotton and three sulfite pulps.
Rate of heating: 40°C/min.*

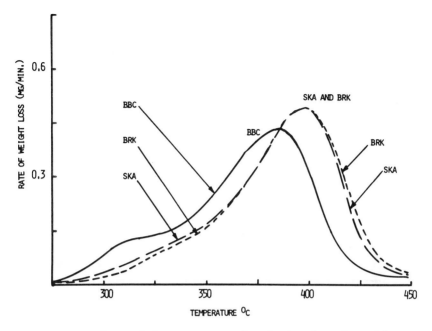

Figure 3C.   Differential thermograms of three kraft pulps.   Rate of heating: 40°C/min.

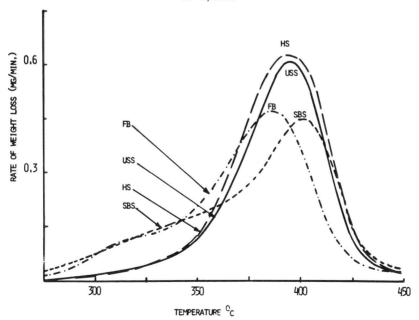

Figure 3D.   Differential thermograms of sulfite and sulfite semichemical pulps.   Rate of heating: 40°C/min.

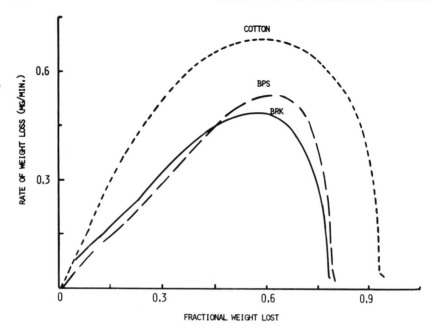

Figure 4A. *Rate of weight loss as a function of fractional weight loss for cotton, sulfite, and kraft pulps. Rate of heating: 40°C/min.*

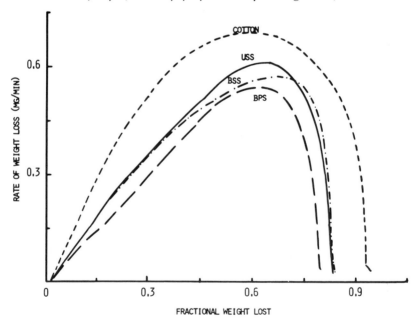

Figure 4B. *Rate of weight loss as a function of fractional weight loss for cotton and three sulfite pulps. Rate of heating: 40°C/min.*

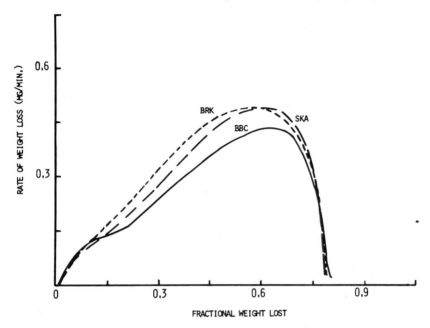

Figure 4C.   Rate of weight loss as a function of fractional weight loss for three kraft pulps. Rate of heating: 40°C/min.

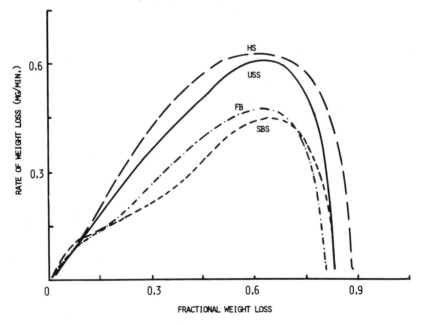

Figure 4D.   Rate of weight loss as a function of fractional weight loss for some sulfite and semichemical sulfite pulps. Rate of heating: 40°C/min.

the conversion axis, an initially increasing isothermal rate is indicated, characteristic of a negative order. Initial convexity suggests positive order while approximate linearity indicates initial kinetics not far removed from zero order. In all cases the initial slope, which is E/RT^2, gives an approximation of the initial energy of activation.

Figures 4A–D show that most of the pulps have initial kinetics approaching zero order. Pulps FB, SBS, BBC, and BRK all show two-component curves with a minor peak indicated between 0.05 and 0.1 conversion, possibly corresponding to the hemicellulose fraction as discussed earlier. The maximum rate of weight loss occurs for all pulps at about 60–65% loss of initial weight. This corresponds to plots of theoretical rate of weight loss vs. conversion plots of reaction order ½ to 1 (*14*).

It can be seen from these three types of plots that the most obvious differences between pulps are the early loss behavior with regard to temperature and rate of weight loss, the maximum rate of weight loss (or slope of the integral curve), and finally the amount of residue remaining. Although there are some exceptions to the following generalization, the later the initiation of weight loss occurs with respect to temperature, the higher the rate of weight loss is and the lower the final residue is. Reaction orders between 0 and 1, as indicated by the isothermal analysis (*18*), are also supported by these plots.

Artificially Aged Pulps. Figures 5A and 5B show differential plots of rate of weight loss vs. temperature for five different artificially aged pulps. Comparisons between these plots and those for the corresponding unaged pulps show an increased rate of weight loss after aging for the USS, SKA, and BSS pulps with a slight displacement toward lower temperatures. On the other hand, for the cases of FB and SBS pulps, only minor differences are apparent. Hence, no clear-cut interpretation of the changes in thermal stability for artificially aged pulps is possible at this time.

Effect of Heating Rate. Flynn and Wall (*15*) have shown that analyses of changes in thermogravimetric data brought about by varying the rate of heating are the basis for the most powerful methods for determining kinetic parameters. They also mathematically examined the effect of varying the heating rate by a factor of 1000:1, a ratio not readily achievable experimentally, on the behavior of theoretical cases of two independent first-order reactions and of two competitive first-order reactions. For the case of two independent first-order reactions of widely differing activation energies, lowering the heating rate β progressively leads to a separation of the differential plot of dy/dT vs. T into two distinct peaks. For a simple reaction, increasing β results in a decrease in $(dy/dT)_{max}$. In the case of two competitive first-order reactions,

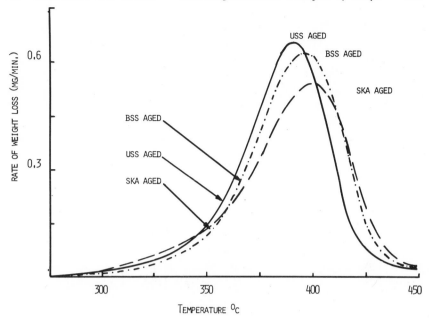

Figure 5A.   Differential thermograms of three artificially aged pulps. Rate of heating: 40°C/min.

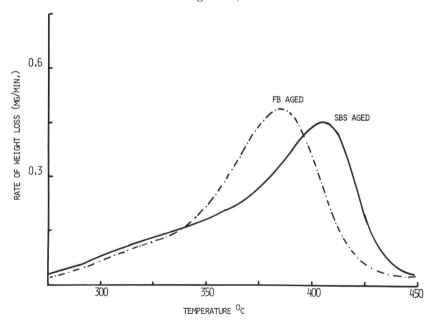

Figure 5B.   Differential thermograms of two artificially aged sulfite semichemical pulps. Rate of heating: 40°C/min.

however, increasing β results in a temporary increase in $(dy/dT)_{max}$ as a result of the inclusion of the high energy reaction.

A number of pulps selected from among the pulps analyzed at a 40°C/min heating rate were rerun, after modifying the apparatus, at several heating rates ranging from 5°C/min to 80°C/min. The effects of these differences in heating rate can be demonstrated in the thermogravimetric and differential thermogravimetric plots of pulp BBC. Figure 6A shows that an increase in the heating rate displaces the integral thermogravimetric curve towards higher temperatures and tends to leave less residual char. The curves obtained at different heating rates diverge as the extent of reaction increases, but similar features are exhibited at all the heating rates used. While the same trends are noticeable in the more shape-sensitive differential thermogravimetric plot, Figure 6B, two maxima are clearly distinguished. A displacement of the curve towards higher temperature results from an increased rate of heating, but a trend towards decreased rate of loss of weight/°C with increased heating rate is apparent as is a slight tendency to smooth out the initial peak. These features are consistent with the mathematically derived data of Flynn and Wall (15) and clearly demonstrate one of the features associated with competitive first-order reactions (the increase in maximum rate of weight

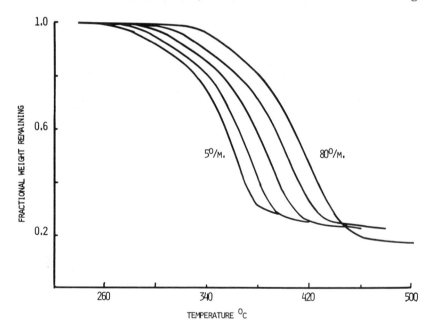

Figure 6A.   The effect of heating rate on the integral thermogram of a hardwood kraft pulp. All curves are for pulp BBC. Rate of heating from left to right: 5°, 10°, 20°, 40°, and 80°C/min.

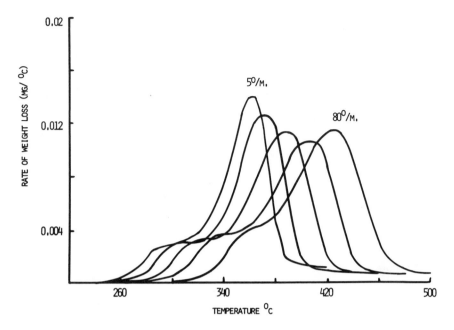

Figure 6B.   The effect of heating rate on the differential thermogram of a hardwood kraft pulp. All curves are for pulp BBC. Rate of heating from left to right: 5°, 10°, 20°, 40°, and 80°C/min.

loss at the highest heating rate) and also one of the features indicative of independent first-order reactions (the tendency for the two peaks to merge at higher heating rates).

Figures 7A and 7B show thermogravimetric and differential thermogravimetric plots, respectively, for another pulp, BPS. While features similar to Figure 6A (BBC) are observed in Figure 7A (BPS), the degradation curves of Figure 7A are noticeably smoother, especially in the early weight loss region. The differential thermogravimetric plots of pulp BPS, Figure 7B, are noticeably simpler than those of pulp BBC, Figure 6B, since they have a smoothly decreasing maximum rate of loss at increasing heating rates and only a barely perceptible hint of a first peak at about 330°C evident only in the lowest heating rate curve. It is possible that this peak could be more clearly differentiated at much lower heating rates. The other pulps tested exhibited behavior similar to one or the other of the two pulps described, which, however, were the clearest cases for discussion. The existence of an apparently lower energy reaction more obvious in a pulp with higher hemicellulose content tends to support the idea that early loss of stability is a result either of the hemicelluloses or of the entire amorphous content of the pulp which includes them.

Table II. Apparent Crystallinity of Some Different Pulps

Pulp	Apparent Crystallinity (%)	Crystallite Width (Å)
Cotton Linters	76.2	64
BBC control	60.6	45
BBC (3) [a]	64.7	45
BBC (6)	65.1	47
BBC (9)	65.8	47
BBC (12)	62.9	49
BPC control	66.2	46
BPC (3)	69.1	47
BPC (6)	70.0	47
BPC (9)	69.2	47
BPC (12)	69.3	52
BPS control	61.0	43
BPS (12)	66.9	43
HS control	61.9	45
HS (12)	66.4	41
SBS control	50.8	45
SBS (12)	56.9	40
USS control	65.3	43
USS (12)	69.5	43

[a] Numbers in brackets after pulp type indicate number of days aged at 90°C dry bulb/82.5°C wet bulb.

Apparent Crystallinity of Pulps. To further investigate the effects of crystallinity of pulps on thermal stability, a number of pulps, both unaged and artificially aged, were tested for apparent crystallinity using the x-ray diffractometer method of Weinstein and Broido (*19*). The results obtained are shown in Table II. The results of crystallite width calculations using the Sherrer formula (*20*) are also given in this table. The results show a definite trend for apparent crystallinity to increase as aging proceeds, followed by a decrease at longer aging times. This is most apparent in samples BBC and BPC for which more aging time values were available, but all samples showed an increase in crystallinity at some aging time. The crystallite width of all the wood pulps was similar, and a slight rise with aging time in some pulps was balanced by a decrease in other cases. No overall trend of change in crystallite width was obvious. The cotton linters pulp, included for comparison, had much higher crystallinity and crystallite width values than any of the wood pulps.

One possible explanation for the increase in apparent crystallinity exhibited by all the aged pulps is that the initial degradation of the pulps takes place in the amorphous regions, the reduction of amorphous material leading to an apparent increase in crystallinity. Murphy (*21*) has indicated that the lower and earlier of two activation energies he found for the thermal decomposition of cellulose may be regarded as attributable to some secondary aspect of the cellulose structure, possible the amorphous fraction. Another possible, and not necessarily mutually exclusive, explanation is that thermal cross-linking effectively expands the crystalline regions at the expense of the amorphous regions. Weinstein and Broido (19), heating samples at considerably higher temperatures up to 260°C rather than the 90°C used here to artificially age pulps, did not observe this phenomenon with pure cellulose samples, but when samples treated with trace quantities of inorganic salts were heated similarly, the apparent crystallinity increased. It is not unrealistic to expect similar results from papermaking pulps which must contain small amounts of inorganic salts. These results indicate preferentially catalyzed decomposition of the amorphous regions.

Summary and Conclusions

Much useful and interesting information can be obtained from a study of the features and profiles of integral and differential thermograms. Papermaking pulps have more or less unique thermograms show-

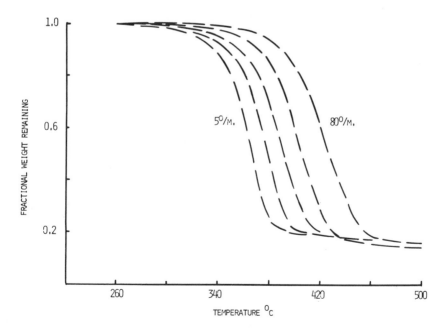

Figure 7A. *The effect of heating rate on the integral thermogram of a softwood sulfite pulp. All curves are for pulp BPS. Rate of heating from left to right: 5°, 10°, 20°, 40°, and 80°C/min.*

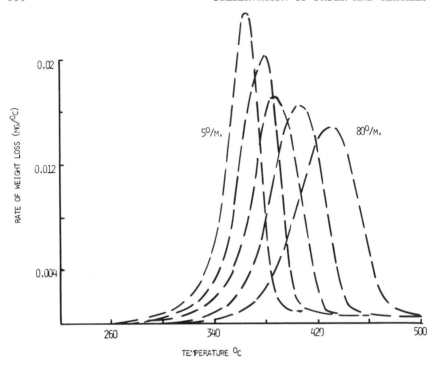

Figure 7B. The effect of heating rate on the differential thermogram of a softwood sulfite pulp. All curves are for pulp BPS. Rate of heating from left to right: 5°, 10°, 20°, 40°, and 80°C/min.

ing distinct differences between major categories such as the wood species and the cooking process used. Differential plots seem to reveal these differences more clearly. Such differences between the profiles may be attributed to variations in hemicellulose content and in apparent crystallinity.

Differential rate of weight loss vs. weight fraction plots indicate reaction orders between 0 and 1. Only minor differences between some artificially aged and control pulps were noted, whereas other pulp types showed an increased rate of weight loss with a slight displacement of the thermograms toward lower temperatures. No clear-cut interpretation of these differences is yet possible.

Changes in the thermogram with changes in the rate of heating have been shown to be consistent with the mathematically derived data of Flynn and Wall (15) and show evidence of competitive reactions which may be more clearly differentiated by a choice of more extreme heating rates. The apparent crystallinity of a number of aged pulps increased over that of unaged controls. This was interpreted as indicating a preferential decomposition of the amorphous regions.

Since the production of thermogram profiles is a relatively rapid operation now that suitable commercial equipment is available, it seems very likely that differences in papermaking pulps introduced by pulping and other chemical or physical treatments of pulps could be readily and rapidly followed with these techniques. It is even possible that further development and refinement, coupled with the use of well-defined standard pulp samples, may make such techniques applicable to process or quality control functions.

Literature Cited

1. Tang, W. K., *U.S. For. Serv. Res. Pap. FPL 71*, Forest Products Laboratory, Madison, Wis. (1967).
2. Parks, E. J., *Tappi* (1971) **54**, 537.
3. Hobart, S. R., Berni, R. J., Mack, C. H., *Text. Res. J.* (1970) **40**, 1079.
4. Hurduc, N., Schneider, I. A., Simionescu, C., *Cellulose Chem. Technol.* (1970) **4**, 3.
5. Vigo, T. L., Daigle, D. J., Mack, C. H., *J. App. Polym. Sci.* (1971) **15**, 2051.
6. Beall, F. C., Eickner, H. W., *U.S. For. Serv. Res. Pap. FPL 130*, Forest Products Laboratory, Madison, Wis. (1970).
7. Back, E. L., *Pulp Pap. Mag. Can.* (1967) **68**, T165.
8. Graminski, E. L., *Tappi* (1970) **53**, 406.
9. Desai, R. L., Shields, J. A., *Polym. Lett.* (1970) **8**, 839.
10. Cardwell, R. D., Ph.D. thesis, SUNY College of Environmental Science and Forestry, Syracuse, N.Y., 1972.
11. Kilzer, F. J., Broido, A., *Pyrodynamics* (1965) **2**, 151.
12. Golova, O. P., Pakhomov, A. M., Andrievskaya, E. A., Krylova, R. G., *Dokl. Akad. Nauk SSSR Ser. Khim.* (1957) **115**, 122; Chem. Abstr. (1958) **52**, 4165.
13. Domansky, R., Rendos, F., *Holz Roh-Werkst.* (1962) **20**, 473.
14. Rydholm, S. A., "Pulping Processes," Chapter 21, John Wiley & Sons, New York, 1965.
15. Flynn, J. H., Wall, L. A., *J. Res. Nat. Bur. Stds.* (1966) **70A**, 487.
16. Audebert, R., Aubineau, C., *J. Chemie Phys.* (1970) **67**, 617.
17. Wall, L. A., Flynn, J. H., *Rubber Chem. Technol.* (1962) **XXXV**, 5, 1157.
18. Cardwell, R. D., Luner, P., *Wood Sci. Technol.* (1976) **10**, 131.
19. Weinstein, M., Broido, A., *Combust. Sci. Tech.* (1970) **1**, 287.
20. Klug, H. P., Alexander, L. E., "X-ray Diffraction Procedures," pp. 491–538, John Wiley & Sons, New York, 1967.
21. Murphy, E. J., *J. Polym. Sci.* (1962) **58**, 649.

RECEIVED May 2, 1977. Contribution No. 109 from the Empire State Paper Research Institute, State University of New York, College of Environmental Science and Forestry, Syracuse, N.Y. 13210.

25

Thermogravimetric Analysis of Pulps

IV: Thermal Stability Indices

R. D. CARDWELL

New Zealand Forest Products, Ltd., Private Bag, Auckland, New Zealand

P. LUNER

Department of Paper Science and Engineering, SUNY College of
Environmental Science and Forestry, Syracuse, N.Y. 13210

*The thermal stability of papermaking pulps is considered
with particular reference to the criteria for establishing
thermal stability indices. The difference between several
indices are examined. The residual weight after pyrolysis
is shown to be a useful guide to low temperature thermal
stability. A new stability index is formulated and used to
rank papermaking pulps. An index independent of the
heating rate allows stabilities of materials to be compared
even though they were tested initially at different heating
rates. Thermal stability rankings according to activation
energies did not correlate well with rankings obtained by
empirical indices of stability or by the rate of loss of physical
properties with accelerated aging. A much closer relationship exists between rankings based on changes in physical
properties and empirical indices derived from the thermogravimetric profiles.*

In a previous study (*1*) a wide range of papermaking pulps was
subjected to elevated temperatures and the rate of loss in the mechanical properties measured. This rate of loss (or gain), when normalized
with respect to the original value, was used as an index of pulp stability.
A comparison of the rankings for individual tests with the overall ranking
based on all the tests showed that reasonable, consistent rankings were
obtained. The three most accurate predictive tests were breaking length,
tensile energy absorption, and load to give 300 folds. Folds at 1-kg load

and zero-span breaking length gave rankings less consistent with the overall rankings, while the wet breaking length is the least accurate indicator of the overall rankings.

In a subsequent study (2) the thermal stability of these pulps was analyzed directly by thermogravimetric analysis. The data were analyzed by both differential and integral methods. While activation energies for the pyrolysis reaction were the main parameter evaluated, other indices of stability can be developed which are based on either single or multiple features of the thermograms. This paper attempts to correlate the thermo-mechanical stabilities of pulps with several thermogravimetric stability indices, including activation energies, and to draw conclusions concerning the predictive performance of these pulps in terms of thermal stability.

Evaluation of Stability Indices

Significance of Weight Change Data. Thermal stability indices can be based on features of the thermogram profiles. Such features are influenced by a number of experimental variables, including the rate of heating, and also by the superficial criteria of decomposition chosen, such as the temperature at which a given percent weight loss occurs or the temperature of some peak in the thermogram. Thus, such indices, although useful, are limited by these dependencies, and Doyle and others refer to them as "procedural decomposition temperatures" (3).

In arriving at a stability index from weight loss experiments, it is essential that the weight loss be related to the degradation process and thus to the end-use properties of the material. Some polymers may be useless for their intended purpose after a small weight loss while others may retain substantially unchanged physical properties after much larger weight losses (4). Thus, empirical stability indices are best applied to a series of similar polymeric materials, as is the case in this study of a series of papermaking pulps. Similarly, unless the end-use characteristics for permanence are well defined, even stability indices based on changes in physical properties with time and temperature are subject to similar difficulties of interpretation. For example, if fold is the primary end-use characteristic, stabilities based on brightness may be misleading.

Single- and Multiple-Feature Criteria. Suitable criteria or indices of thermal stability should be uniquely and consistently available from the thermogram patterns for any of the materials to be analyzed. The values should not be unduly disturbed by features of the thermogram not related to thermal stability such as early moisture content loss. Criteria for stability may be conveniently divided into two groups, those in which a single feature is used and those in which cumulative data or multiple features are used. One of the difficulties of most single-feature

indices is that cases may arise in which the feature of interest either fails
to appear, occurs more than once, or cannot be accurately located.

Indices based on a single feature of the thermogram may be the
initial decomposition temperature, the knee or initial bend in an integral
thermogram, the peak temperature or maximum rate of weight loss of a
differential thermogram, or the final temperature of a weight change step.
The difficulties inherent in the use of single-feature criteria may sometimes be overcome by using cumulative or multiple-feature indices.
Examples of such indices are the temperature at which a given fractional
weight loss occurs and the integral procedural decomposition temperature
(*ipdt*) of Doyle (5). The temperature span during degradation studies—
i.e., the limits of temperature at which initial degradation occurs and at
which the reaction is essentially completed—has also been used as a
significant feature of pyrolysis curves. Such indices have their own
shortcomings, however. The choice of a given fractional weight is arbitrary, as is the ultimate temperature to establish total weight loss. The
idpt method, which makes use of the areas under thermogravimetric
curves, is somewhat cumbersome in calculation for a preliminary stability
index and tends to emphasize the stability of the residual material rather
than that of the original sample (6). The general concepts of stability
indices and the details of their calculations and shortcomings are considered in more detail by Doyle (3).

Criteria of Stability. Table I identifies the pulps used in this study.
Table II shows that for a heating rate of 10°C/min the temperature at
which 10% decomposition (10% DT) and 50% decomposition (50%
DT) occurred, together with the temperature of maximum rate of volatilization (MRT). The rate of loss at this temperature is also given
(MRV). Samples are ranked in terms of decreasing temperatures and
decreasing rates of decomposition since it has been shown that higher
rates of losses are usually associated with more thermally stable materials.

Table I. Pulps and Code Identification

Pulp	*Identifying Code*
Cotton linters	cotton
Rayon fibers	rayon
Scandinavian bleached birch kraft	BBC
As above, aged for 12 days at 90°C, 73.5% r.h.	BBC aged
Scandinavian bleached pine kraft	BPC
As above, aged for 12 days at 90°C, 73.5% r.h.	BPC aged
Scandinavian bleached pine sulfite	BPS
Unbleached mixed hardwood sulfite	HS
Scandinavian unbleached semichemical birch sulfite	SBS
Unbleached mixed softwood sulfite	USS

Table II. Decomposition Criteria for Some Papermaking Pulps[a]

Pulp	10% DT[b] (°C)	50% DT[c] (°C)	MRT[d] (°C)	MRV[e] (mg/°C × 10²)
Cotton linters	328.7(1)[f]	361.6(1)	365.8(2)	1.92(8)
Rayon	309.5(7)	345.0(8)	353.4(7)	2.38(3)
BBC	290.0(9)	342.7(9)	353.4(7)	1.72(9)
BBC aged	295.4(8)	341.9(10)	352.3(10)	1.99(7)
BPC	314.0(5)	349.5(7)	353.4(7)	2.07(6)
BPC aged	312.4(6)	355.7(4)	362.7(4)	2.24(5)
BPS	322.7(4)	354.7(5)	360.6(6)	2.57(2)
HS	325.1(3)	358.5(3)	363.7(3)	2.30(4)
SBS	284.4(10)	349.7(6)	372.2(1)	1.62(10)
USS	325.6(2)	358.6(2)	361.6(5)	2.64(1)

[a] Rate of heating = 10°C/min.
[b] 10% DT = temperature at 10% decomposition.
[c] 50% DT = temperature at 50% decomposition.
[d] MRT = temperature at maximum rate of decomposition.
[e] MRV = maximum rate of decomposition.
[f] Numbers in brackets indicate ranking order.

Inspection of the values contained in Table II and the relative rankings obtained show that, in general, rankings are similar but there are some notable differences. For example, pulp SBS, ranking 10th by two of the indices used (10% DT and MRV), ranks first by another index (MRT). Similarly, cotton linters, ranking first or second by three of the indices, ranks eighth by the fourth. The two conversion temperature methods, 10% DT and 50% DT, are related very closely, showing a major difference only in the case of pulp SBS. Since the percent degradation temperatures are cumulative, that is, multiple-feature criteria, they should give more reliable rankings than the other two indices which are both based on single features only. All these methods, however, will give different values but not necessarily different rankings if other heating rates are used.

A more complete use of the conversion temperature concept, which amounts to a simplified thermogravimetric plot similar to that used by Hurduc and co-workers (7) for one heating rate, can be obtained when the %DT values averaged over several heating rates are plotted as a function of conversion. Two such plots are shown in Figures 1 and 2. Figure 1 shows the relative degradation plots of eight pulps while Figure 2 compares unaged and artificially aged pulps of two types. Here it can easily be seen that, with one exception (SBS), the pulps tested follow approximately parallel degradation curves over most of the pyrolysis range and thus can be ranked in an overall way. The ranking is visual, however, and no empirical parameter is obtained as in the case of percent degradation temperature rankings. The behavior of pulp SBS is seen to be unlike the others in that its degradation curve crosses over many of the others.

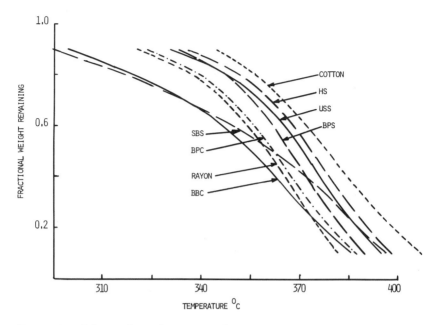

Figure 1.   Relative degradation of eight papermaking pulps as a function of temperature.   Rate of heating averaged over all heating rates.

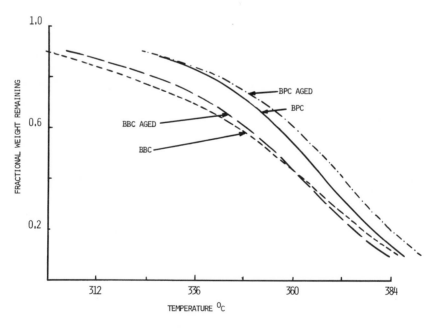

Figure 2.   Comparative degradation of two unaged and two artificially aged papermaking pulps.   Rate of heating averaged over all heating rates.

Figure 2 shows that over most of the conversion range, the two artificially aged pulps, BBC aged and BPC aged, are more resistant to further thermal degradation than their unaged counterparts.

A method of assigning a numerical value rather than a visual indication to represent the overall thermal stability of pulps would be to calculate the mean degradation temperature of all conversions from .1 to .9. The results of ranking pulps in terms of mean degradation temperature are shown in Table III. From this table it can be seen that cotton linters ranks highest, followed by sulfite pulps—both hardwood and softwood and bleached and unbleached. The pine kraft pulps are less stable according to this ranking method, especially in the case of hardwood kraft. Rayon and semichemical birch sulfite are also poor. The slightly greater thermal stability of pulps after artificial aging is also clear.

Table III.   Overall Degradation Temperature of Various Pulps

Pulp	*Mean Degradation Temp.* (°C)	Rank
Cotton linters	377.6	1
HS	371.4	2
USS	368.3	3
BPS	365.3	4
BPC aged	363.3	5
BPC	359.8	6
Rayon	357.0	7
SBS	354.8	8
BBC aged	351.5	9
BBC	350.1	10

[a] Mean degradation temperature is the average of fractional decomposition temperatures over 0.1, weight fraction increments from 0.1–0.9, and heating rates 5°, 10°, 20°, 40°, and 80°C/min.

RESIDUAL WEIGHT AFTER PYROLYSIS. The residual weight at the plateau of a thermogravimetric curve following the main pyrolysis reaction varies with the pulp and the heating rate. Table IV shows that the percent residue of all the pulps decreased with an increased heating rate except for the rayon sample which had anomalous residue values at the two highest heating rates.

Another trend was that the pulps having the lower residual weights at any given heating rate were generally ranked higher in mean degradation temperature than those having higher residual weights. When the anomalous rayon was ignored, the correlation coefficient value obtained for the mean degradation temperature and the mean residual weight was 0.81, which means that 65% of the variation in mean degradation temperature can be accounted for by the variation in residual weight. Thus, residual weights alone are a rough index of stability of papermaking

Table IV.   Residual Weight after Pyrolysis at Various Heating Rates[a]

| Pulp | Heating Rate (°C/min) | | | | | Rank |
	5°C %	10°C %	20°C %	40°C %	80°C %	
Cotton	13.4	15.3	11.5	10.1	9.3	1
Rayon	8.8	8.0	7.4	2.7	11.8	2
BBC	29.8	27.0	24.8	24.6	19.2	8
BBC aged	26.9	24.4	23.2	21.7	20.4	9
BPC	24.7	22.2	20.5	18.4	17.9	6
BPC aged	24.7	24.1	23.3	22.2	20.4	10
BPS	21.6	20.4	19.2	16.8	17.2	4
HS	14.5	14.6	14.2	14.4	13.5	3
SBS	23.8	19.7	18.6	18.1	17.6	4
USS	27.7	21.9	21.2	21.0	19.0	7

[a] Values in table are percentages of oven-dried sample weight.

pulps. In general, the lower the residual weight, the higher is the mean degradation temperature and so the more stable is the pulp. The residual weight has been associated with the early dehydrocellulose formation. Cellulose held at 250°C for a day had three times the residual weight after pyrolysis to 400°C than a control sample (8). Thus, the residual weight is related to low temperature reactions and could be a useful guide to low temperature thermal stability or permanence.

A New Index for Pulp Stability (SI). All of the indices of stability so far discussed suffer from the disadvantage that the values they give depend extremely on the heating rate used. Since multiple-feature criteria are superior to single-feature criteria, a method of combining several obvious and significant pyrolytic profile features into a stability index that is not drastically affected by changes in the heating rate was seen to be very desirable. Such an index, which can be further refined, is now considered.

Typical differential pyrolysis curves for a single heating rate have both a shape profile and a position relative to the temperature axis. This position could be defined in one way by specifying the temperature, a, at which the maximum rate of loss of weight occurs. In a simpler way, the shape can be defined by specifying its height, b, and width, c. It can be seen that b is the maximum rate of weight loss. The width, c, may be specified in a number of ways. The points of departure from the temperature axis could be used, but these are not well defined in many cases. Alternatively, the temperature difference between two given percentage weight losses could be used as a measure of curve width. Perhaps the simplest method, however, is the half-width concept—i.e., the width of the differential thermogravimetric peak at half the maximum height or rate of weight loss. This is shown schematically in Figure 3. Thus, the parameter a defines the position of the curve with reference to the temperature scale, whereas parameters b and c jointly define the curve shape. These three parameters can be combined by taking into account their relationships with thermal stability. With other features remaining the same, larger values of the parameter a indicate greater stability. Similarly, larger values of b/c generally indicate higher stability. More stable compounds appear to have a narrow degradation range of temperature but a high rate of loss within this range. Only division of the two parameters b and c still retains any information regarding shape. Their addition or subtraction would be meaningless. Multiplication gives an indication of the area under the curve, i.e., the weight loss, a known factor, but loses all information regarding shape. If a and c are measured in °K and b in terms of fractional weight loss/°K, we can combine them as an index ab/c with units of °K⁻¹. Alternatively, and purely empirically, we can define the stability index, SI $= a^2b/c$, which is now dimensionless. Such an index will give slightly more weight to the parameter a. The order of ranking of materials using the index involving the a^2 term will be the same as that involving a. However, the spread and values obtained will be greater. Table V shows the SI values obtained at various heating rates for the pulps tested.

The stability index, SI, was found to decrease as the heating rate increased such that plots of SI vs. $1/\log \beta$ were almost linear with high

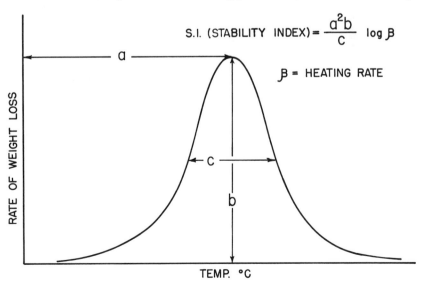

$$\text{S.I. (STABILITY INDEX)} = \frac{a^2b}{c} \log \beta$$

β = HEATING RATE

Figure 3.   Schematic of stability index. S.I. (stability index) $= a^2b/c \log \beta$

Table V.   Stability Index a^2b/c for Various Pulps and Heating Rates

Pulp	Stability Index a²b/c (Rate: °C/min)					r² (%) for SI vs. 1/ log β	Slope (m)
	5°C	10°C	20°C	40°C	80°C		
Cotton	207	150	117	115	98	98.2	119.1
Rayon	272	251	250	180	158	72.6	118.0
BBC	197	148	109	92	86	99.3	128.4
BBC aged	266	191	162	105	99	97.5	188.6
BPC	276	193	197	146	112	91.4	164.6
BPC aged	290	235	161	125	129	95.9	194.8
BPS	409	289	195	165	128	99.5	313.3
HS	354	233	195	167	109	97.8	250.6
SBS	197	167	128	103	90	96.1	121.0
USS	306	304	164	162	138	80.2	205.7

correlation coefficients (Table V). This indicated that if the SI were corrected by an appropriate factor, a value could be obtained for any heating rate used or even for heating rates not actually used, with the precaution that they were within or close to the limits of those studied.

The slopes of the SI vs. $1/\log \beta$ plots varied from pulp to pulp (Table V). This indicates that the effect of changing the heating rate is different for different pulps and demonstrates how the ranking of pulps for thermal stability can depend in some instances upon the heating rates chosen. The advantage of using several heating rates is that such effects become obvious and do not remain concealed as they may if only one heating rate is used.

The equation of the regression line is given by

$$SI = m/\log \beta + \text{constant} \tag{1}$$

where m is the slope. Application of this equation to two heating rates and subsequent subtraction gives the equation

$$SI_1 - SI_2 = m/\log \beta_1 - m/\log \beta_2 \tag{2}$$

If we consider β_1 to be a reference heating rate equal to 10°C/min, then Equation 2 simplifies to

$$SI_{ref} = SI + F \tag{3}$$

where F is the correction factor given by

$$F = m - m/\log \beta \tag{4}$$

Thus, the use of the correction factor F enables SI values determined at any heating rate β to be corrected to a reference heating rate of 10°C/min. The use of Equation 2 would allow SI values determined at one heating rate to be converted to any other.

By using the correction factor F, corrected SI values can be determined which are substantially independent of the actual heating rate used. Table VI lists corrected stability indices calculated according to the above definitions. It can be seen that in spite of some fluctuations in value there are no consistent trends with changing heating rate. As might be expected from the high correlation coefficients obtained, the corrected values are close enough to be averaged as if they were all obtained at the same heating rate. Since these mean values are based on five determinations, they must be more reliable than those based on one determination only.

Activation Energies. Activation energies have been calculated using both dynamic differential and integral methods. These are shown in Table VII (2). To determine if the ranking of the samples according to the activation energy of pyrolysis is related to that obtained from pyrolytic stability indices or thermomechanical performance tests, we have to consider what is meant by activation energy. The Arrhenius equation

$$k = A \cdot \exp(-E/RT) \tag{5}$$

indicates that molecules must acquire a certain critical energy E before they can react. The Boltzmann factor, $\exp(-E/RT)$, represents the

Table VI.   Corrected Stability Index for Various Pulps and Heating Rates

Pulp	Corrected Stability Index[a] $(a^2b/c + F)$ (Rate: °C/min)					Mean for All Rates (Rank)
	5°C	10°C	20°C	40°C	80°C	
Cotton	158	150	145	160	155	153.6(8)
Rayon	221	251	277	224	214	237.4(4)
BBC	142	148	139	140	147	143.2(10)
BBC aged	185	191	206	176	189	189.4(7)
BPC	205	193	235	208	190	206.2(6)
BPC aged	206	235	206	198	221	213.2(5)
BPS	274	289	268	283	277	278.2(1)
HS	246	233	253	261	228	244.2(2)
SBS	145	167	156	149	147	152.8(9)
USS	217	304	212	239	236	241.6(3)

[a] Corrected stabiltiy index $a^2b/c + F$ corrects values at each heating rate to the same basis as if tested at a reference heating rate of 10°C/min. F is the correction factor $m - m/\log \beta_1$ regression line and β_1 is the heating rate used in any given run.

Table VII.   Activation Energies for Pyrolysis of Various Pulps (2)

Pulp	Activation Energy (kcal/mol)[a]	Rank
Cotton	33.8	7
Rayon	32.5	9
BBC	41.9	2
BBC aged	37.7	6
BPC	42.9	1
BPC aged	39.6	4
BPS	40.1	3
HS	32.3	10
SBS	33.6	8
USS	37.9	5

[a] Based on the mean value of one differential and two integral methods.

fraction of molecules that manage to reach this necessary energy. The pre-exponential factor A is a measure of the number of collisions per second, so that the Arrhenius equation merely states that the speed of a reaction is equal to the number of collisions per second times the fraction of such collisions that are effective in producing chemical change. Since the Boltzmann factor $\exp(-E/RT)$ is large compared with the pre-exponential factor A, the rate is affected predominantly by E in such a way

Table VIII.   Comparative Stability Rankings of Papermaking Pulps[a]

Pulp	Method of Ranking[b]			
	Mechanical Properties[c]	Mean Degradation Temp.	Activation Energy	Stability Index
SBS	1	5	5	5
HS	2	1	6	2
USS	3	1	4	3
BPS	4	3	3	1
BPC	4	4	1	4
BBC	6	6	2	6
BPC aged	N/A	3½	3½	3½
BBC aged	N/A	5½	4½	4½

[a] Pulps were ranked according to decreasing thermal stability as indicated by the method chosen. When numerical values of the index chosen were identical, the same ranking is given and the following rank omitted. For the artificially aged pulp subgroup, fractional ratings are given to avoid disturbing the main group comparison. A ranking of 3½ indicates the pulp ranked between the third- and fourth-ranked members of the main group.

[b] Cotton and rayon were omitted from ranking since their mechanical properties cannot be compared with pulps.

[c] Based on the overall ranking of six physical and one optical property. The rank was determined on the basis of rate of loss or gain per day of artificial aging, expressed as a percentage of the initial unaged value (1).

that the larger the value of E, the slower is the reaction. In terms of thermal stability then, this would indicate that pulps having large activation energies should be more stable than those with lower activation energy.

Table VIII shows the relative ranking in terms of decreasing activation energy, of empirical indices of thermal stability, and of their rate of loss of strength with aging time. Ideally, if all the rankings related to the same type of stability, they should have approximately the same values. Slight inconsistencies of ranking would be caused solely by the inability to separate closely ranked pulps resulting from experimental scatter. Inspection of Table VIII, however, shows that the rankings according to activation energy cannot be considered to be closely related to any of the other methods of ranking. The other three ranking methods do show very similar trends with the exception that pulp SBS ranks high in the physical property ranking and low in the thermal rankings. As we have seen previously (9), pulp SBS showed different behavior to all the other pulps in that its thermogravimetric curve crossed over many of those of other pulps.

Table VII shows that the activation energies of artificially aged pulps BBC and BPC are consistently lower than for the control samples. The lower values indicate that the rate-determining reaction can proceed more readily after artificially aging. This may be a result of the introduction of carbonyl groups or of the introduction of chain ends as a result of hydrolysis of the hemicellulose and cellulose. Such modifications of the original pulp may act as weak links or sites at which further degradation is facilitated.

A measure of the closeness of the rankings according to two different methods can be obtained objectively by summing the absolute values of the differences between the ranks for each pulp. When this is done, it can be seen that the worst match in rankings is between the activation energy (AE) and the physical property (PP) methods, those between AE and Stability Index (SI) and between AE and Mean Degradation Temperature (MDT) also being poor. Good correlations are found between SI and PP and between MDT and PP. As could be expected from these latter relationships, the correlation between SI and MDT is also good.

The rankings and the relationships between them indicate that the activation energies obtained are mainly influenced by chemical reactions —e.g., levoglucosan formation and breakdown—which are not closely related to those chemical reactions involved in determining paper permanence. The earlier hydrolysis reaction which most likely is correlated with relative permanence characteristics does not sufficiently influence the value of activation energy obtained, even at the lowest extent of reaction used in this study. On the other hand, these early reactions do affect the thermogravimetric profiles, and empirical indices derived from these profiles thus have a better capability for predicting relative permanence rankings. The significance of this capability in terms of greatly reduced evaluation time is apparent. By suitable preliminary evaluation using thermal methods, the extremely time consuming process of permanence evaluation by aging studies could be restricted to those materials most likely to give satisfaction. Thus, thermal analytic methods are a useful ancillary tool in permanence evaluations.

The results obtained in this study by ranking according to activation energy (Table VII) can be compared with those of Chatterjee and Conrad (10) and with those of Hurduc, Schneider, and Simionescu (11). These authors also compared cotton with other celluloses although not with commercial papermaking pulps. Both determined initial and "propagation" or steady state activation energies. Chatterjee and Conrad (10) found that cotton had intermediate initiation and propagation activation energies when compared with other cellulosics, including mercerized and treated cotton, microcrystalline cellulose (Avicel PH), dewaxed cotton, and vibratory ball-milled cotton. Hurduc and co-workers (11) examined cotton, α-cellulose, viscose rayon, and cellulose and found that cotton had the lowest initiation and steady state activation energies. These results are apparently contradictory, especially since cotton has proved to be more stable than wood cellulosics in actual use at moderate temperatures. The true relationship between activation energy and thermal stability will only be realized if and when kinetic analyses that are based on a sufficiently detailed mechanism of pyrolysis can be carried out.

If the rankings obtained from activation energy values are compared not with rankings obtained from changes in physical properties during artificial aging but with the initial values of these physical properties, a different trend is seen. Table IX shows the relative rankings according to both activation energy and initial physical properties and includes two other empirical stability indices for comparison. The results given in this table show that the initial physical property rankings correlate well with activation energy rankings but not with those of the empirical indices. This indicates that the overall activation energy, like the initial physical properties, is also a measure of the strength—i.e., the degree of integrity of the cellulosic chains. However, at the moment the reason for this is far from clear since cotton has a low activation energy.

Summary

The thermal stability of papermaking pulps was considered with particular reference to the criteria for establishing thermal stability indices. Several such indices are presented, and differences between

Table IX.   Ranking of Stability Indices and Initial Physical Properties of Papermaking Pulps

| Pulp | Activation Energy | Physical Properties | | | | Mean Degradation Temp. | Stability Index (SI) |
		Zero-Span BL	Tensile Energy Absorption	Tensile BL	Folding Endurance		
BPC	1	1	1	1	1	4	4
BBC	2	2	2	3	4	6	6
BPS	3	5	3	5	3	3	1
USS	4	4	4	1	2	2	3
SBS	5	6	6	6	6	5	5
HS	6	3	5	4	5	1	2

them are examined. The residual weight after pyrolysis is shown to be a useful, simply obtained guide to low temperature thermal stability. A new stability index is formulated based on simple features of the thermogram profiles and used to rank papermaking pulps. This index can readily be made independent of the heating rate by utilization of a linear relationship between it and the inverse logarithm of the heating rate. This relationship allows stabilities of materials to be compared even though they were tested initially at different heating rates.

Ranking thermal stability according to activation energy did not correlate well with rankings obtained by empirical indices of stability or by the rate of loss of physical properties with accelerated aging. This was interpreted to mean that the rate-determining step governing pyrolysis of cellulosics is not identical with the rate-determining step corresponding to the loss of physical properties during accelerated aging. A much closer relationship exists between rankings based on changes in physical properties and empirical indices derived from the thermogravimetric profiles. This is interpreted to mean that these empirical indices may be useful for initial screening of pulps for permanence characteristics.

Literature Cited

1. Luner, P., Cardwell, R. D., "Fundamental Properties of Paper Related to Its Uses," Vol. 2, Technical Division, British Paper and Board Industry Federation, London, 1976.
2. Cardwell, R. D., Ph.D. thesis, SUNY College of Environmental Science and Forestry, 1971.
3. Doyle, C. D., "Techniques and Methods of Polymer Evaluation," Vol. I, Thermal Analysis 113, Marcel Dekker, 1966.
4. Reich, L., Levi, D. W., "Macromolecular Reviews I," p. 173, Interscience, New York, 1967.
5. Doyle, C. D., *Anal. Chem.* (1961) **33**, 77.
6. Reich, L., Levi, D. W., *Makromol. Chem.* (1963) **66**, 102.

7. Hurduc, N., Simionescu, C., Schneider, I. A., *Cellul. Chem. Technol.* (1971) **5**, 37.
8. Kilzer, F. J., Broido, A., *Pyrodynamics* (1965) **2**, 151.
9. Cardwell, R. D., Luner, P., *Adv. Chem. Ser.* (1977) **164**, 362.
10. Chatterjee, P. K., Conrad, C. M., *J. Polym. Sci.* (1968) **6**, 3217.
11. Hurduc, N., Schneider, I. A., Simionescu, C., *Cellul. Chem. Technol.* (1968) **2**, 569.

RECEIVED May 2, 1977. Contribution No. 110 from the Empire State Paper Research Institute, State University of New York, College of Environmental Science and Forestry, Syracuse, N.Y. 13210.

INDEX

INDEX

The text of this book is set in 10 point Caledonia with two points of leading. The chapter numerals are set in 30 point Garamond; the chapter titles are set in 18 point Garamond Bold.

The book is printed in offset on Text White Opaque, 50-pound. The cover is Joanna Book Binding blue linen.

Jacket design by Norman Favin.
Editing and production by Kevin Sullivan.

The book was composed by Service Composition Co., Baltimore, Md., printed and bound by The Maple Press Co., York, Pa.